Perspectives on
Financial Control

The Chapman & Hall Series in Accounting and Finance

Consulting editors
John Perrin, Emeritus Professor of the University of Warwick and Price Waterhouse Fellow in Public Sector Accounting at the University of Exeter; Richard M.S. Wilson, Professor of Management and Accounting at the University of Keele; and L.C.L. Skerratt, Professor of Financial Accounting at the University of Manchester.

H.M. Coombs and D.E. Jenkins
Public Sector Financial Management

J.C. Drury
Management and Cost Accounting (3rd edn)
(Also available: **Students' Manual, Teachers' Manual, Spreadsheet Applications Manual** and a set of **OHP Masters**)

C.R. Emmanuel, D.T. Otley and K. Merchant
Accounting for Management Control (2nd edn)
(Also available: **Teachers' Guide**)

C.R. Emmanuel, D.T. Otley and K. Merchant (editors)
Readings in Accounting for Management Control

D. Henley, A. Likierman, J. Perrin, M. Evans, I. Lapsley and J.E.H. Whiteoak
Public Sector Accounting and Financial Control (4th edn)

R.C. Laughlin and R.H. Gray
Financial Accounting: method and meaning
(Also available: **Teachers' Guide**)

G.A. Lee
Modern Financial Accounting (4th edn)

T.A. Lee
Income Value Measurement (3rd edn)

T.A. Lee
Company Financial Reporting (2nd edn)

T.A. Lee
Cash Flow Accounting

S.P. Lumby
Investment Appraisal and Financing Decisions (4th edn)
(Also available: **Students' Manual**)

A.G. Puxty and J.C. Dodds
Financial Management method and meaning (2nd edn)
(Also available: **Teachers' Guide**)

J.M. Samuels, F.M. Wilkes and R.E. Brayshaw
Management of Company Finance (5th edn)
(Also available: **Students' Manual**)

B.C. Williams and B.J. Spaul
IT and Accounting: The impact of information technology

R.M.S. Wilson and Wai Fong Chua
Managerial Accounting: method and meaning (2nd edn)
(Also available: Teachers' Guide)

Perspectives on
Financial Control

Essays in memory of Kenneth Hilton

Edited by

MAHMOUD EZZAMEL
Manchester School of Management
University of Manchester Institute of Science and Technology

and

DAVID HEATHFIELD
Department of Economics
University of Southampton

CHAPMAN & HALL
University and Professional Division

London · Glasgow · New York · Tokyo · Melbourne · Madras

Published by Chapman & Hall, 2–6 Boundary Row, London SE1 8HN

Chapman & Hall, 2–6 Boundary Row, London SE1 8HN, UK

Blackie Academic & Professional, Wester Cleddens Road, Bishopbriggs, Glasgow G64 2NZ, UK

Chapman & Hall, 29 West 35th Street, New York NY10001, USA

Chapman & Hall Japan, Thomson Publishing Japan, Hirakawacho Nemoto Building, 6F, 1–7–11 Hirakawa-cho, Chiyoda-ku, Tokyo 102, Japan

Chapman & Hall Australia, Thomas Nelson Australia, 102 Dodds Street, South Melbourne, Victoria 3205, Australia

Chapman & Hall India, R. Seshadri, 32 Second Main Road, CIT East, Madras 600 035, India

First edition 1992

© 1992 Chapman & Hall

Typeset in 10/12 pt Times by Pure Tech Corporation, India

Printed in Great Britain by TJ Press (Padstow) Ltd, Padstow, Cornwall

ISBN 0 412 40980 1

A catalogue record for this book is available from the British Library

Library of Congress Cataloging-in-Publication Data
Perspectives on financial control: essays in memory of Kenneth Hilton
/ edited by Mahmoud Ezzamel and David Heathfield.
    p. cm.
    Includes index.
    ISBN 0–412–40980–1
    1. Managerial accounting.   2. Controllership.   I. Hilton, Kenneth.
II. Ezzamel, Mahmoud.   III. Heathfield, David F.   IV. Title: Essays in memory of Kenneth Hilton.
HF5657.4.P47 1992
658.15′ 11—dc20   92–25127   CIP

The late Kenneth Hilton; to whom this title is dedicated.

Contents

Contributors

The late Kenneth Hilton
Professor of Financial Control
University of Southampton
1970–90

Michael Bourn
Department of Accounting and Management Science
University of Southampton

Chris Burke
School of Accounting, Banking and Economics
University of Wales, Bangor

John Cable
Department of Economics
University College of Wales, Aberystwyth

Chris Chapman
Department of Accounting and Management Science
University of Southampton

Ian Colville
The School of Management
University of Bath

John Cubbin
National Economic Research Associates

Christine Ennew
Institute of Financial Studies
University of Nottingham

Mahmoud Ezzamel
School of Management
University of Manchester Institute of Science and Technology

David Gwilliam
Department of Accounting
The University College of Wales
Aberystwyth

Alan Hamlin
Department of Economics
University of Southampton

David Heathfield
Department of Economics
University of Southampton

Trevor Hopper
Department of Accounting and Finance
University of Manchester

Keith Hoskin
Warwick Business School
University of Warwick

Hilary Ingham
School of Management
University of Manchester Institute of Science and Technology

Linda Kirkham
Department of Accounting and Finance
University of Manchester

Irvine Lapsley
Institute of Public Sector Accounting Research
University of Edinburgh

Richard Laughlin
School of Management and Economic Studies
University of Sheffield

Richard Macve
Department of Accounting
The University College of Wales
Aberystwyth

David Otley
Department of Accounting and Finance
University of Lancaster

Michael Page
Portsmouth Business School
Portsmouth Polytechnic

Robert Scapens
Department of Accounting and Finance
University of Manchester

Len Skerratt
Department of Accounting and Finance
University of Manchester

Ken Starkey
Institute of Financial Studies
University of Nottingham

Charles Sutcliffe
Department of Accounting and Management Science
University of Southampton

Steve Thompson
School of Management
University of Manchester Institute of Science and Technology

Cyril Tomkins
School of Management
University of Bath

Steve Ward
Department of Accounting and Management Science
University of Southampton

Mike Wright
Institute of Financial Studies
University of Nottingham

Preface

The purpose of this book is to offer a small token in memory of Ken Hilton, who died prematurely at the age of 52 in February 1990. The book contains contributions from a number of leading academics; some were close colleagues of Ken's at the University of Southampton, some have been at other universities but knew Ken fairly well, and still some who never met Ken but who knew of him through his work. The unifying motivation for all of them, however, was their immense sense of loss of an extremely proactive and excellent academic.

Having led the research group on the Southampton Econometric Model project for three years, Ken was appointed to the Chair of Financial Control at the University of Southampton in 1970; at that time this was one of only a handful of similar Chairs in the UK. Most of Ken's subsequent academic career was devoted to contributing to the study of financial control, initially in the private sector and subsequently in the public sector. The breadth of his interests was demonstrated by his enviable ability to contribute to the areas of industrial economics, accounting, and management science. We hope therefore that this volume which embraces contributions from leading academics in each of these three fields is a fitting tribute to Ken's work.

While the importance of financial control as an academic discipline was slowly gaining recognition in the UK in the late 1960s, developments in the 1970s and 1980s have resulted in unprecedented elevation of financial control in the worlds of both academics and practitioners. These developments included: (a) increased intensity of international competition propelled by weakening national economic protectionism and barriers to entry; (b) increased intensity of local competition in the UK markets stimulated, among other things, by the deregulation of major service industries (for example, gas, water, electricity, and telecommunications); (c) radical developments in manufacturing technology, and the invention of the 'factory of the future' with its emphasis on flexible manufacturing systems and the restructuring of work flow; and (d) the information technology revolution which has enabled the invention of powerful, yet compact and affordable computers which in turn have culminated in enormous economies in storing, arranging, processing and retrieving data.

The above factors in combination with the depressed economic climate of the 1980s, created the need for, and possibility of, sophisticated financial control systems for monitoring economic performance. Thus in the UK (and in other Western and American economies) we have recently been witnessing a significant increase in the demand for financial control systems. In the private sector, there is increasing use of tight financial control systems to improve the firm's competitive position. More importantly, financial control systems are now extending in areas where they had previously played only a minor role; these include the National Health Service (NHS), higher education, school education, central government, and local government. The contributions in this book should therefore be of immediate interest to a wide range of readers. It should be of relevance to academics interested in the intellectual development of the subject and those wishing to gain an informed view of the social and organizational contexts of these systems. This book also offers a stimulating set of technical, yet accessible, contributions which could form the basis of an advanced third year undergraduate, or postgraduate course on financial control. Finally, practitioners and policy makers would find within this volume numerous issues which are either of immediate relevance to their day-to-day activities or which deserve their careful medium- to long-term consideration.

The contributions to this volume span not only differing research emphases but also wide-ranging research methods. As the researchers come from different, but related, disciplines they have utilized different perspectives to examine various issues of financial control. The contributions are a combination of theoretical and empirical papers. The theoretical papers focus on the conceptual development and/or mathematical modelling of financial control. The empirical papers range in their research method from those seeking to report some preliminary findings (because of the novelty of the research topic), through those employing conventional econometric testing, to those utilizing case study-based naturalistic research (participant/non-participant observeration). Yet, despite this diversity the book addresses two main themes, hopefully in a coherent manner: first, financial control and the theory of the firm; and second, the social and organizational implications of financial control. The book is divided into three main parts.

Part One provides an introduction to financial control systems and contains two papers. The first, by Mahmoud Ezzamel, provides an overview of the literature on financial control, linking it to the broader corporate governance structures and locating it in its organizational context. The second paper, a version of an early work by Ken Hilton, examines the use and misuse of financial control systems in facilitating the attainment of organizational objectives, and draws some examples from the UK university sector.

Part Two contains both theoretical and empirical papers on financial control and the theory of the firm. Chris Chapman and Steve Ward develop a model, based on Pearce separability, which facilitates financial control of portfolio management decisions. Alan Hamlin and David Heathfield provide a model of working capital management in multiplant firms. John Cubbin details many of the insights, as well as the limitations, of using Data Envelopment Analysis in the banking sector. Hilary Ingham's paper models, and empirically tests, the costs of structural adjustments as firms change from centralized to multi-divisional structures. Steve Thompson provides empirical evidence on agency costs, incentives and management buyouts in the context of management failure to resolve corporate problems within some forms of divisionalized structures. Mike Wright, Christine Ennew and Ken Starkey provide new evidence on control, internal organization and divestment in the financial services sector.

Part Three deals with some of the social and organizational implications of financial control. In their paper David Gwilliam, Keith Hoskin, and Richard Macve examine financial control in Lloyd's of London and identify the limitations of accounting-based performance indicators used. Irvine Lapsley's papers charts the development of recent financial initiatives in the NHS with respect to management control, capital accounting and the operating environments, and examines some of the serious problems of imposing these controls on the NHS. Cyril Tomkins and Ian Colville address the issues relating to financial control and devolved management in central government in the context of organizational change, with special emphasis on HM Customs and Excise. Trevor Hopper, Linda Kirkham and Len Skerratt evaluate the policy recommendations, with respect to the brands debate, of critical theory and market-based research, and identify a number of significant commonalities.

Each of the papers is followed by a discussant's comments which aim to set the paper in a broader context and appraise it.

The completion of this book in such a relatively short period would not have been possible without the help of many colleagues and friends. We are grateful to Chris Chapman (University of Southampton), to John Perrin, Len Skerratt and Dick Wilson in their capacities as academic advisers to Chapman & Hall, and to Alan Nelson of Chapman & Hall, for their guidance and encouragement when the idea of editing this book was first conceived. Much of our gratitude also goes to the contributors to the book not only for expressing their willingness to contribute, but also for keeping to the tight timetable. Throughout the eighteen months during which the book was completed Alan Nelson was extremely supportive and understanding. We are also grateful to the Department of Accounting and Management Science, University of Southampton for providing financial support for holding a special conference in honour of Ken Hilton in Southampton, April 1991, at which the papers in Parts Two and Three were presented. Sue Westcott administered the conference smoothly and many of Ken's colleagues and friends were very supportive through their active participation in the debate. Paul Geroski kindly volunteered to circulate the conference details to industrial economics academics in the UK. Lizzie Burrows worked very patiently and cheerfully on word processing the editorial changes throughout the whole manuscript. Our gratitude goes to our families for their constant encouragement and support. Since giving her approval to this project, Dorothy Hilton has been a constant source of gentle encouragement. We had a small glimpse of the kind of support she gave Ken throughout his career.

Mahmoud Ezzamel (Manchester)
David Heathfield (Southampton)

Foreword

ALAN BUDD

It is a great privilege to have been invited to write a Foreword to this collection of papers in honour of Kenneth Hilton, following his tragic early death.

I first met Kenneth Hilton in 1966. The occasion was a staff meeting in the Economics Department at Southampton University which was arranging the allocation of the teaching and administrative duties for the coming year. This was shortly before I joined the Department. My impressions of Ken at that meeting rapidly established all the qualities for which I continue to remember him. First, there was the shrewd political flair which immediately saw the full implications of any proposal. Second, there was the firm insistence on applying rules impartially. Finally there was the willingness to press his case even if it meant opposing his superiors. All this was combined with a disarming sense of humour so that even those who found themselves outmanoeuvred could not bear a grudge against him.

During my years at Southampton Ken was always a source of sound and sensible advice, whether on university matters or on more mundane questions of where and how to find domestic bargains. Where academic work was concerned, he always had the ability to ask that one awkward question that discovered the weak point in one's argument.

I cannot speak from personal knowledge of his later career at Southampton University, though I greatly enjoyed the period that I spent as external examiner for his department. He recognized, from an early date, the considerable increase in the number of university applicants seeking to study commercial subjects and played a major part in increasing the resources available to meet their demands. A notable move was the establishment, in 1978, of the Department of Accounting and Management Science. In his inaugural lecture he described the history of the departments of Economics and of Commerce and

Accountancy. The two departments had merged at the time of Ken's appointment to the new Chair in Financial Control. The year 1978 saw yet another twist in that long tale.

In addition to his teaching and research work, Ken somehow found the time to act, at different periods, as Head of the Department of Economics, Dean of Social Sciences, President of the Senior Common Room, President of the Southampton Association of University Teachers and Senior Deputy Vice Chancellor. He was also, for a time, editor of *Banker's Magazine* and played his part in local matters. It represented an outstanding example of service to the University and to the local community.

It is interesting to look back at his inaugural lecture in which he set out to describe the content of Financial Control. He emphasized the need to analyse financial data within a proper framework and pointed out the dangers of misusing such information. He went on to describe three further arguments in support of his 'new' subject. First, he suggested that there was a real need for increased competence in the fields of management and finance. Second, he referred to the recognition, by at least some of his colleagues, of a need for their students to understand the financial framework within which they would be practising their skills. Finally he quoted the clear evidence from university applications of students' desire to study courses involving commerce or accountancy.

He concluded his lecture by suggesting that economic and social control systems were relevant in a wide range of disciplines. He found it difficult to find any discipline in which they were not relevant; at the same time he believed that the subject of financial control needed the active participation of other disciplines. The papers in this collection show the breadth of the content and application of financial control. They are a most worthy tribute to his memory.

On a personal note it was typical of Ken that he always retained traces of his northern accent. I can also recall an occasion on which, in the middle of an important meeting, he opened a briefcase to reveal a teddy bear sitting among his papers. He commented that he thought that Dorothy had probably placed it there to make sure that he did not become too self-important. In my experience, he never did.

Alan Budd

PART ONE
Financial control
systems

1

Corporate governance and financial control

MAHMOUD EZZAMEL

INTRODUCTION

The discipline of financial control has undergone major developments in recent years and this has rendered it more fluid and less susceptible to precise definition. These developments have in part been prompted by the increased intrusion of financial controls into arenas in which they had previously played only a minor role. For example, the last decade in the UK witnessed the emergence of numerous financial initiatives aimed at public sector organizations, such as the National Health Service, central government, local government, universities, schools, and military organizations. These initiatives seek to emulate the private sector achievements (i.e. economic efficiency) perceived to be associated with financial control regimes in the public sector. Moreover, the economic climate of the 1980s, characterized by increased levels of international competition, deregulation of major industries, and the demands posed by modern work and information technologies, has led to greater emphasis on the use of financial control in the private sector.

But financial control is intertwined with models of corporate governance. Hence, a sound understanding of financial control is facilitated by an informed appreciation of the roles of governance structures in modern organizations, be they in the private or public sector. Financial control can be meaningfully conceptualized when perceived as part of a much broader framework of gov-

Perspectives on Financial Control: Essays in memory of Kenneth Hilton.
Edited by Mahmoud Ezzamel and David Heathfield.
Published in 1992 by Chapman & Hall, London. ISBN 0 412 40980 1.

ernance structures, a framework which encompasses numerous other means of control and social order. When perceived within that broader perspective it becomes easier to understand how financial control relates to, and interacts with, other types of control, and to identify which conditions, if any, give rise to, and perpetuate specific modes of financial control compared with others.

The location of financial control within a broad theoretical framework of governance structures raises a number of important questions. These relate to the extent to which corporate governance structures, in seeking to mediate and regulate transactions in a particular manner, call upon measures of financial control to achieve specific ends; the extent to which such measures of financial control are interwoven with other, non-financial controls; the extent to which financial controls are mediated by and also impact upon the organizational context in which they operate; and finally the extent to which perceiving financial control within the governance structure framework poses serious limitations for the analysis.

This paper seeks to address these issues. Rather than aiming to provide a novel contribution to the literature, the main purpose of this paper is to offer a synthesis of previous research as a background for the remaining contributions in this volume. As a starting point in our exposition we explore the problem of corporate governance, and describe and evaluate a relevant model developed by Ouchi. This is followed by a discussion of the scope of financial control and of its roles under specific governance structures. The fourth section on p. 16 focuses on the interrelationship between financial control and the organizational setting. The fifth section (p. 19) explores the limitations of the previous analysis and alludes to some of the external critiques that have been levelled against it. The last section brings together the main conclusions of the paper. Overall, the paper suggests that the corporate governance literature is problematic in terms of: being biased towards the market discipline; overstating the case of technical rationality to the exclusion of substantive rationality; and being historically flawed. Despite these serious limitations, it is argued in this paper that the corporate governance literature offers a powerful means of understanding the economics of internal organization, with their attendant financial controls, in modern enterprises. The paper however warns that this type of research should always be reassessed in the light of social and political considerations.

THE PROBLEM OF CORPORATE GOVERNANCE

Many researchers have been preoccupied for decades with the problem of control and co-ordination of corporate activities, and with the development of alternative 'governance structures'. According to Williamson (1981, p. 1544) a 'governance structure' represents an 'explicit or implicit contractual frame-work within which a transaction is located (markets, firms, and mixed modes – e.g. franchizing-included)'. A governance structure aims to: (a) regulate relationships between multiple agents; (b) specify the extent of adjustments to be effected on negotiated items; and (c) promote co-operative behaviour by parties interested in transactions (see Spicer and Ballew, 1983).

Early economists have tended to perceive the organization not as a mode of governance structure but rather as a production function with a profit maximizing objective. Such a view treats the organization as a 'black box' and suppresses the importance of hierarchical arrangements as a viable form of governance. Coase (1937) was one of the first economists to allude to the limitations of that view. He argued that within firms market transactions are supplanted with internal arrangements as alternative means of co-ordinating production. As Johnson and Kaplan (1987, p. 88), paraphrasing Coase, have pointed out, 'a firm will grow until the marginal cost of discovering opportunities for gain within the firm exceeds the marginal cost of discovering opportunities for gain in the market'.

Ever since the pioneering work of Coase, several economists have been explicitly concerned with studying the factors which affect the extent of firm integration, be it backward, forward, or lateral. For these researchers, firms and markets are treated as alternative governance structures (see in particular Williamson, 1970; 1975; 1981). Subsequent research emphasis has centred primarily on drawing the boundary between markets and firms, by explicitly identifying situations in which each dominates as a governance structure as well as situations in which they both overlap (see for example Brown, 1984; Imai and Itami, 1984; Buckley, 1988). Further, this body of research has been extended to include other governance structures, and in particular what is now known as 'clan control' (Ouchi, 1977; 1979; 1980). Building on these contributions, Ouchi developed a useful framework for the analysis of various governance structures.

Ouchi's framework of corporate governance

Ouchi (1977) has classified governance structures along two dimensions, or what he calls 'antecedent conditions'. The first dimension is the extent of availability of output measures which ranges from low to high. The second dimension is the extent of knowledge of the transformation process, i.e. the means–ends relationship involved in the production or service activities, which ranges from imperfect to perfect. He has invoked a transaction-costs perspective, according to which the attributes of different control modes with respect to the above two dimensions determine their relative efficiency. Efficiency is measured in terms of minimization of transactions cost.

A transaction represents the transfer of a good or service across a technologically separable interface, such as processing and assembly stages. But transactions vary along various dimensions. They may reflect different degrees of standardization. They may be recurrent or may occur occasionally. They may necessitate different levels of investment in human and physical assets. They may relate to the very short term or extend over the long term. They may be performed under situations with varying levels of uncertainty (see, for example, Williamson, 1981). In summary, there exists a variety of clearly distinguishable transactions. Also, there exists a variety of viable governance structures. Ouchi's framework attempts to match alternative governance structures to the various transactions depending upon the specific attributes of such transactions, and with the objective of achieving economic efficiency by keeping transactions cost to a minimum.

In the transactions-cost approach, the organization is treated as a network of exchanges or transactions which should be regulated by control modes in the most economically efficient manner. Different control modes have different characteristics which are associated with costs arising from the structure of property rights in organizations. Attaining equity, or reciprocity, in the terms of exchange between the parties involved is a fundamental notion. Transactions cost is intertwined with reciprocity. This cost arises when the goods or services to be exchanged do not lend themselves to easy and precise valuation. To achieve equity in such cases, experts (third parties) tend to be called upon to value the services or goods subject to exchange. This leads to greater transactions cost.

Thus, it is held that transactions cost is incurred in pursuit of more information which are perceived to be relevant to a particular transaction. Such cost includes: (a) pre-contract search and information cost caused by desire to supplement imperfect information about trading opportunities; (b) bargaining and decision cost relating to investigating terms and conditions that are mutually acceptable to transaction parties, and (c) monitoring and enforcement cost required to prevent ex-post violation of contractual terms by transaction parties (see Dahlman, 1979).

Each governance structure is associated with distinctive costs of its own. The problem is then reduced to seeking to identify which governance structure minimizes transactions cost under some specific circumstances. 'Organizational failure' occurs when transactions cost associated with a particular governance structure, for example markets, can be minimized by co-ordinating and monitoring relevant transactions via an alternative governance structure, for example, hierarchies.

In developing his framework, Ouchi (1979), has distinguished between two types of control: behaviour control and output control. Behaviour control refers to monitoring the behaviour of people while output control refers to monitoring the outputs which result from human behaviour. With the two dimensions suggested above (knowledge of the transformation process and availability of output measures), and the two types of control (behaviour and output), Ouchi provides a typology of governance structures as depicted in Table 1.1.

When the ability to measure output is high but knowledge of the transformation process is imperfect, such as in a life insurance sales agency or an advertising agency, output control mechanisms are deemed most appropriate. This role can be performed by hierarchies, but quite likely markets will offer a more economical control mechanism. The reason is that, given clarity of output measurement, there will be little need for writing detailed, and thus costly, contracts, and there will also be little need for extensive internal monitoring and for the mediation of third parties.

When the ability to measure output is low but knowledge of the transformation process is high, Ouchi suggests that emphasis would need to shift from output measurement to behaviour measurement. In this case, control through markets becomes associated with high transactions cost, since third parties would need to be hired in order to offer assessments of output. They would face relatively high uncertainty in their assessments and in the guarantees which they may have to offer; hence, they will typically insure against such uncertainty by commanding high fees.

In such circumstances, hierarchies offer a more economical mode of organizational control. They rely on employment relations which represent incomplete contracts and are thus an economical means of regulating transactions. Employment relations give legitimate rights to the organization to direct, regulate and monitor employees' work activities. Moreover, compared with markets there is usually a higher commonality of purpose and trust (but see

Table 1.1 Modes of corporate governance

		Knowledge of the transformation process		
		High		Low
Ability to measure output	High	Output/behavioural measurement *Markets/hierarchies* 1	 2	Output control *Markets*
	Low	 3 Behavioural measurement *Hierarchies*	4 	Ritual and ceremony *Clans/culture*

Fox, 1974) and a greater sense of affiliation among exchange parties within a hierarchy. These feelings are fostered by a sense of belonging to the same organization, and by the emphasis of hierarchies on technical expertise which is promoted through skill training and socialization into professional standards. It is argued that these properties reduce the potential for opportunistic behaviour and minimize the need for elaborate and expensive monitoring systems. As Williamson (1970) has pointed out, whereas markets have a serious disadvantage in obtaining internal information, hierarchies can obtain it at a low cost, and while markets are typically restricted to non-managerial adjustments, hierarchies can engage in both fine tuning and discrete adjustments. In summary, a number of factors – uncertainty, small numbers of transacting agents, information impactedness, opportunism, etc. – limit the discipline of the market in minimizing transactions cost and render *hierarchy* an economically more efficient form of corporate governance.

When the ability to measure output is high and knowledge of the transformation process is sound, as in the case of the tin can plant or the car assembly plant, it would be possible to measure, relatively accurately, both behaviour and output. In this case, there is a choice of either behaviour control or of output control. These functions can be performed either by markets or hierarchies, the ultimate choice being dependent upon the cost of each alternative.

Finally, when the ability to measure output is low and knowledge of the transformation process is highly imperfect, as in the case of foreign services, neither markets nor hierarchies offer economically efficient means of corporate governance. Control through markets becomes inefficient because there will be a greater need for using detailed written contracts, extensive internal monitoring systems and experts or third parties. Control through hierarchies becomes inefficient because as tasks become unique or highly ambiguous it becomes difficult to monitor performance through formal hierarchical mechanisms. Ouchi (1981) has argued that, under these conditions, control through clans or corporate culture is the most economically efficient mode of control. Clans are 'intimate associations of people engaged in economic activity but tied together through a variety of bonds' (Ouchi, 1981, p. 83). Further, the clan 'functions by socializing each member completely so that each merges individual goals with the organizational ones, thus providing them with the motivation to serve the organization' (Ouchi and Price, 1978, p. 36). The essence of clan control is the high degree of employee discipline attained through the dedication of each individual to the interests of the whole. The overlap between individual and organizational interests is assumed to minimize the chances for opportunistic behaviour, and equity in exchange can be attained at relatively low transactions cost. The behaviour of clan members is regulated through mutual monitoring using symbols and norms not readily susceptible to precise translation into performance measures. Clan control promotes high discipline and aversion to opportunism because members recognize that given the impossibility of establishing unambiguous performance measures, opportunistic behaviour could have serious consequences for the clan as a whole. Moreover, employees tend to be selected carefully in order to guarantee that they exceed generally accepted standards of competence (Ouchi, 1977). Also, in this last cell, control may be expressed in the form of rituals. These rituals may serve to endow organizational activities with apparent rationality and legitimacy, even though actual practices may be based on arguments far removed from those associated with economic efficiency (Meyer and Rowan, 1977).

In summary, the above framework suggests that the extent of performance ambiguity and the extent of knowledge of the transformation process should both be carefully matched to the appropriate (most cost-efficient) mode of corporate control (markets versus hierarchies versus clans). The framework emphasizes the efficiency of economic exchange, through the minimization of transactions cost, as the ultimate objective of organizations. Ouchi (1980) developed the above framework further by discriminating between governance structures (markets, hierarchies and clans) along two dimensions: their underlying *normative* and *informational* requirements. These are summarized in Table 1.2.

In Table 1.2, 'normative requirements' refer to the basic social agreements shared by the exchange parties in order to minimize transactions cost. As has already been indicated, reciprocity engenders equity and fairness in exchange, and if widely held would result in minimizing transactions cost. Legitimate authority facilitates the use of hierarchical control not only in assigning tasks to employees but also in regulating and monitoring their performance. Common values and beliefs promote greater congruence between individual and organizational interests. Ouchi contends that reciprocity is a universal norm,

Table 1.2 The normative and informational requirements of modes of control

Normative and informational requirements		
Mode of control	*Normative requirements*	*Informational requirements*
Market	Reciprocity	Prices
Bureaucracy	Reciprocity Legitimate authority	Rules
Clan	Reciprocity Legitimate authority Common values and beliefs	Traditions

Reprinted with permission from *Administrative Science Quarterly*, Vol. 25, No. 1, William G. Ouchi 'Markets, Bureaucracies and Clans', © ASQ 1980.

and that legitimate authority is accepted by employees in formal organizations, albeit in varying degrees. In contrast, it is held that common values and beliefs are relatively rare in formal organizations (see Wilkins and Ouchi, 1983). As can be seen in Table 1.2, the repertoire of normative requirements expands as one moves from markets through hierarchies to clans.

Informational requirements are those postulated to match the normative requirements of the particular mode of control. Prices are a highly sophisticated form of information, but frequently it is difficult to derive correct prices particularly in situations of high task interdependence. By comparison with prices, rules are a less sophisticated form of information. Rules tend to be problem-specific and they also tend to be highly formalized for routine decisions. When exceptional situations are encountered by lower-level participants they are typically referred to policy makers at the top of the hierarchy who frequently have to invent new rules as required. Traditions are implicit, that is they are not formally specified rules, and are thus not readily accessible to new organizational members in particular. Compared to prices and rules, traditions are the crudest informational devices. They gain organization-wide acceptability through the process of organizational socialization, and if accorded sufficient acceptability could form the basis of an overall organizational philosophy (Ouchi, 1980).

Although Ouchi's framework of corporate governance is utilized here in order to place the subsequent analysis into perspective, it should be noted that the framework has a number of limitations emanating from its reliance on the transactions cost paradigm and from its adoption of the basic tenets of institutional economics. These limitations are discussed in detail in a latter section, but now we turn our attention to an examination of the interconnections between financial control and corporate governance.

FINANCIAL CONTROL AND GOVERNANCE MODES

In this section we seek to provide a definition, tentative though as it may be, of the term 'financial control', and then to explore the extent to which this whole field of inquiry contributes to each of the modes of corporate governance discussed earlier.

Towards a definition of financial control

Precisely, what does the term 'financial control' denote? In 1975 when Ken Hilton delivered his Inaugural Lecture as the holder of the newly established Chair of Financial Control at the University of Southampton, he found the term much too illusive and indicated that different individuals, and institutions, attach differing connotations to it. Seventeen years later, we are none the wiser, for the term remains highly fluid and ill-defined. Available definitions range from those that ascribe to financial control a rather narrow focus to those who conceptualize it in much broader terms. For example, Emmanuel and Otley (1985, p. 29) argue that 'financial control is concerned with the regulation of the flow of money through the enterprise and, in particular, with ensuring that cash is always available to pay debts when they fall due'. They go on to argue that financial control only deals with the finance function to the exclusion of other functions, for example production, marketing and industrial relations. Similarly, Ken Hilton (1975, and also in this volume) alluded to the use by others of quite specific definitions of the scope of financial control such as the protection of stewardship rights, or the prevention of fraud in an audit context.

In contrast, while not explicitly providing specific definitions, several researchers have extended the roles of financial control well beyond the mere regulation of the flow of money to encompass the regulation of human agents in organizations, segments of the organization, and the organizations themselves (e.g. Hopwood, 1980; Tomkins, 1980; see also Tomkins and Colville, this volume, pp. 255–280).

While wishing to avoid the temptation of prescribing a concise definition of financial control which, in common with many definitions in the social sciences, may turn out to be inherently problematic, it is nevertheless believed that it would be useful to readers to have, at the very least, a general statement describing financial control as used within the context of this book. Hence, with the intention of promoting healthy debate and constructive dialogue, but at the same time hoping to avoid becoming immersed in contentious arguments, a broadly conceived statement of the scope of financial control is advocated here. Financial control is perceived here as the function which, through the use of financially-based concepts, techniques, rules and procedures, seeks to promote the smooth functioning of organizations and the attainment of the organization's basic mission. Financial control is seen as multi-layered, permeating hierarchical levels, both vertically and laterally, and reaching the innermost of the organization. In this sense, financial control is closely aligned, but not identical, to organizational control, the latter having a very similar focus but utilizing a wider array of techniques, procedures, and rules which are both financial and non-financial, quantitative and qualitative (see Ezzamel and Hart, 1987).

Roles of financial control

At the expense of possible costly omissions, a list of some of the most important areas in which financial control is likely to play a crucial role is provided below:

- Performance measurement, monitoring, and evaluation schemes for individuals, groups, sub-units, and whole organizations. These could involve the use of budgets, standard costs, activity costing, profitability measures, inventory and production control models, internal audit, and other financial indicators.
- Reward schemes which link explicitly financial reward/sanction mechanisms, to performance, such as General Motors' well-known executive bonus scheme.
- Resource allocation systems seeking to secure the distribution and monitoring of the use of resources within the organization, for example allocation of funds among the departments of a university and major capital investment allocations. Examples include incremental and comprehensive (Zero-Base Budgeting, ZBB, and Planning, Programming and Budgeting systems, PPBS) allocation schemes.
- Portfolio investment activities seeking to attain the most risk-return efficient deployment of resources both internally and externally. Broadly interpreted, this would include mergers, acquisitions, buyouts, and divestment activities as well as product mix decisions.
- The financial management of assets and liabilities including liquidity management, both short-term and long-term, to ensure the financial viability of the organization.
- Organization-market interface, by soliciting and processing market-based information for transacting in markets.

While not intended to be an exhaustive list, the above should suffice to illustrate how broad the perspective of financial control advocated here is. The need for financial control is also perceived as being in part predicated upon the existence of specific antecedent conditions which give rise to, propagate, and sustain various forms of this control, but clearly there are many situations in which the emergence and prevalence of financial control cannot be sensibly explained in the context of a mechanistic response to prevailing conditions. Indeed, the existence of financial control in some organizations may pre-date, or at the very least shape and reshape, these so-called antecedent conditions. More problematic perhaps is the recognition that the precise direction of causation between antecedent conditions and modes of control may not be clear cut. However, we proceed to develop Ouchi's framework further in order to explore the roles of financial control in supporting various modes of governance; this is shown in Table 1.3.

When markets are deemed to be the appropriate mode of control, i.e. cells 1 and 2, financial control becomes market-based. In this setting, financial control would seek to ensure that the normative requirement of reciprocity (or equity) in exchange relationships is regularly observed and maintained. When

Table 1.3 Roles of financial control

	Knowledge of the transformation process	
Ability to measure output	**High**	**Low**
High	*Subject of control:* Output/behaviour *Mode of control:* Markets/hierarchies *Normative requirements:* Reciprocity and legitimate authority *Informational requirements:* Prices/rules *Financial controls:* Either as per cell 2 or cell 3 (cell 1)	*Subject of control:* Output *Mode of control:* Markets *Normative requirements:* Reciprocity *Informational requirements:* Prices *Financial controls:* Market-based; collecting and summarizing market prices; overseeing the implementation of market-based contracts. Assessment of market opportunities and threats and developing decision models based on market prices (cell 2)
Low	*Subject of control:* Behaviour *Mode of control:* Hierarchy *Normative requirements:* Reciprocity and legitimate authority *Informational requirements:* Rules *Financial controls:* Hierarchic-based: designing systems utilizing financial measures of performance for monitoring human behaviour (budgeting systems, ROI, standard cost systems, financial reward structures; inventory control models; administrative internal pricing systems, etc) (cell 3)	*Subject of control:* Ethical/social commitment *Mode of control:* Clan *Normative requirements:* Reciprocity, legitimate authority and common values and beliefs *Informational requirements:* Traditions *Financial controls:* Tradition-based: mechanisms aimed at promoting cost-consciousness; establishing the importance of financial considerations as part of tradition; promoting self-discipline and peer control (mutual financial monitoring) focusing on the decision process (cell 4)

reciprocity is violated, the financial implications of such violation for the contracting parties have to be fully assessed and disclosed, and the appropriate financial settlements have to be decided. Financial control would then involve the collection, processing and reporting of market prices, the overseeing of the effective implementation of contracts, the assessment of market opportunities and threats, and the development of decision-making models based on market prices.

When hierarchies are assumed to be the effective mode of control, i.e. cells 1 and 3, hierarchic-based financial control is likely to be more in evidence. The normative requirements in this setting are reciprocity of contractual arrangements and legitimate authority. In addition to contributing to the maintenance of reciprocity, financial control would promote and sustain the legitimate authority of the hierarchy. These objectives would be accomplished through the judicious design and use of information packages containing financial rules and procedures which guide the everyday activities of organizational actors. To be effective in regulating human behaviour, financial control would have to be rooted in the organizational setting in which it is deemed to operate. The array of controls and techniques used would include specifically designed financial measures of performance for monitoring human behaviour through hierarchical configurations. Examples of these controls are budgeting systems, profitability based measures of performance such as return on investment (ROI), standard costing systems, financial incentive packages, inventory control models, administrative internal pricing systems, and overhead allocation schemes. These, and similar, financial mechanisms establish, reinforce, and legitimize the organizational chain of command and lines of authority and responsibility. This in turn helps establish and reinforce the right of higher-level managers to direct, assess, and monitor the behaviour of lower-level organizational participants.

When neither markets nor hierarchies are deemed suitable as modes of corporate governance, they are supplanted by clans (cell 4) which have an extended set of normative requirements. In addition to promoting reciprocity and legitimate authority, financial control should contribute to the development and organization-wide acceptance of common values and beliefs. Rather than focusing on the monitoring of output, as in the case of market control, or the monitoring of behaviour through hierarchy, as in the case of bureaucratic control, the emphasis of financial control would be on constructing and reconstructing 'ethical values', manipulating the ethical conformity and social commitment of organizational actors, and mobilizing them towards the attainment of top management's (the organization's?) objectives. Financial control would then have to seek to establish and sustain, but also occasionally reconstruct, organizational tradition. In turn, tradition, through becoming ingrained in the immediate memories of organizational actors, provides guidelines for establishing priorities in the work place, defining appropriate decision parameters, and taking action. In this setting financial control would seek to evolve tradition-based mechanisms which would aim to promote cost-consciousness, establishing the importance of financial considerations as part of tradition, and promoting self-discipline and peer control through mutual financial monitoring. Many of the financial control mechanisms developed for hierarchical control will be utilized in this setting but with three major differences. First, the essence of control is likely to be hierarchical and more mutual/consensual. Second, extensive financial-based education (organizational socialization) of organizational members will be sought in order to establish and perpetuate a financial tradition in the organization even though this is likely to be subordinated to cultural values and traditions (see Bourn and Ezzamel, 1986; 1987; Ezzamel and Bourn, 1990). Third, the focus of financial control will be centred more on the socialization process, rather than on output or behaviour.

The extent of prevalence and influence of financial control is likely to vary depending upon which of the four cells in Table 1.3 one is concerned with. In general, financial control is likely to be much more in evidence, and hence much more influential, when hierarchical control is used. This is because, compared with hierarchies, markets and clans have access to a wider array of control mechanisms thereby reducing the need for internal financial control arrangements. Thus, in the case of markets: (a) valid external prices are, in the main, readily available at no or low cost and this reduces the need for the financial control system to simulate market-based prices and to generate additional information seeking to compensate for the imperfections associated with these simulated prices, (b) the ability to measure output lessens the need for monitoring-related information, and (c) explicit and detailed contracts, written guarantees, and the forbidding cost of litigation, make the regulation and monitoring of market-based transactions less dependent upon internal financial control arrangements. In the case of clan control there exists a large repertoire of norms of socialization and culture which create and sustain tradition and common values and beliefs, which are largely non-financial in nature, even though ultimately they may indirectly contribute to the financial performance of the organization.

In contrast, hierarchical control does not typically have ready access to many of these controls nor to external financial controls, except in the case of appointed third parties. Instead, financial control in hierarchies tends to be buttressed by structural, non-financial, controls such as the definition of employment relations detailing work duties and rewards, the various mechanisms seeking to monitor the decision making process (for example, authorizing decisions sequentially or through committees, and separation of decision management from decision control), and other co-ordination and integration mechanisms (e.g. Jensen and Meckling, 1976; Mintzberg, 1979; Fama and Jensen,

15

1983a; 1983b; Ezzamel and Hart, 1987). Despite the importance of such structural controls, the role of financial control in hierarchies is particularly prevalent since the philosophy of hierarchical control is rooted in financial terminology.

Quite how important financial control is to a particular organization depends to a large extent on the mix of modes of control in operation. As more hierarchic controls interpenetrate arenas previously governed by market-based and/or clan-based controls so increased internal financial control will be observed, as in the case of, for example, hospitals (see Lapsley, this volume) and schools in the UK at present. Further, this will also be affected by the extent to which the activities of the organization are suited to the apparatus of financial control; contrast for example a private, profit making organization and a voluntary charitable organization. What is more important to emphasize is that, to a greater or a lesser extent, in virtually all organizations financial control has several roles to play. The contributions contained in this book explore some, but by no means all, of these roles. In the following section, we examine briefly the organizational context of financial control.

FINANCIAL CONTROL AND THE ORGANIZATIONAL SETTING

The discussion in the preceding section demonstrates the importance of the organizational context in the choice of the most cost-effective governance mode; it assumes that a specific configuration of some antecedent conditions gives rise to an optimal governance mode, although the overall validity of this assumption is challenged in the following section. Despite this evident link the above analysis underscores the importance of the organizational linkages to control, and in our case to financial control. Evidently, financial control and the organizational setting are inextricably intertwined: as they both evolve they constrain each other and promote changes into each other. Hence, they are both the determinant and consequence of each other. Caught in these dynamics, financial control frequently becomes implicated, both intentionally and unintentionally, in political manoeuvres and power games which take place at both the intra-organizational and inter-organizational levels. Hopwood (1980, p. 238) makes a particularly telling comment in this respect:

> Although invariably introduced in the name of economic efficiency, their (financial control practices) origins and functioning have been seen to have as much to do with political and social, as with economic rationality. Whilst they can, and do, facilitate economic decision making, they can also be used to introduce a particular political order, reinforce patterns of organisational power and segmentation, and provide for the legitimacy and understanding of the organisational past as well as playing a role in

the organisational future. Once introduced into an organisation, the use which is made of financial practices, and thereby the consequences which they have, is shaped by the ways in which they interrelate with other complex organisational processes. Capable of being influenced by a wide variety of pressures, practices and beliefs, they can have a range of possible consequences, only some of which would be deemed to be compatible with the furtherance of economic performance.

Given the inevitability of the behavioural and political dimensions of financial control, it is imperative that they should be explored and understood, instead of being perceived as of secondary importance and as being subservient to the technical dimension. This is not intended to underplay the importance of the technical dimension of financial control, for without carefully designed and implemented financial techniques much of the potential that collectivities of individuals, or organizations, hold in promise may never materialize. Indeed, several contributors in this book bear witness to the importance of this dimension. But equally the importance of the behavioural and social dimensions of financial control has to be acknowledged. Not only are these dimensions worthy of exploration and understanding in their own right, but they do also interact with the technical dimension being influenced by it and also shaping its future developments, its use, and the meanings and rationales ascribed to its outcome, i.e. financial information. The political and behavioural dimensions can render technical financial controls legitimate or illegitimate, they can endow them with professional competence and power or incompetence and vulnerability, they can create and perpetuate new meanings and rationales for information or simply make them ambiguous and mystifying and they can also broaden or narrow the scope of their application (see Ezzamel and Bourn, 1990).

Having emphasized the importance of the organizational setting for understanding and developing the roles of financial control, we now seek to explore some of its characteristics. Given the illustrative examples of the potential uses of financial control provided earlier, it is quite evident that control is exercised both by external and internal agents. External agents include non-manager owners (investors), debt holders, tax agencies, regulatory bodies, and the public at large; but financial information is also used in the context of financial analysis, rather than control, by investment analysts and potential investors. Internal financial control is exercised by managers occupying various hierarchical levels within the organization ranging from the Board of Directors to workers on the shop floor.

The prerogative of internal financial control can be highly centralized or highly decentralized. In highly centralized systems, detailed financial rules and procedures are used extensively by top management to motivate, co-ordinate and monitor the everyday behaviour of lower-level managers. While implementation of decisions, and possibly initiation of decision proposals,

17

would be entrusted to lower-level managers, decision ratification and monitoring (decision control) for most decisions are vested in top management (Fama and Jensen, 1983a). In contrast, decentralized financial control involves the use of summary statistics by top management to monitor the behaviour of lower-level managers from a distance, as exemplified by the use of return on investment to monitor divisional activities (Johnson and Kaplan, 1987; Ezzamel, Hoskin and Macve, 1990). In the latter case, financial and operating details are left in the hands of local managers, with top management relying on the use of summary financial statistics and financial reward schemes to align local interests with corporate interests.

The scope and process of financial control are dependent upon where in the organization control is to be exercised; centrally or locally (Argyris, 1977; Jönsson and Gronlund, 1988). This stems from the fact that different tasks are faced at each of these two levels and hence control needs are different. Many of these differences are encapsulated in Table 1.4 below which contrasts the impact on individual behaviour of distant management information systems (MIS) against that of local MIS. Central control is goal driven, output orientated and fairly abstract. Because it emphasizes integration and co-ordination of disparate lower-level activities it tends to be based on comparison, and hence have established standards of performance which are then built into the formal structure. In contrast, local control is contemporaneous, processual, concrete and casual in orientation. Learning at local levels tends to be experiential and rooted in direct observation of processes (i.e. practical knowledge) and thus control focuses more on behaviour than on output. Financial information needs are therefore likely to be different; central control tends to depend more on 'hard' information in order to attend to the 'stewardship' function whereas local control tends to make more use of 'soft' information which may be less accurate but timely in order to promote learning, experimentation and building causal linkages. Such significant differences between central and local control illustrate why there is an inherent problem in translating abstract organizational goals into local objectives and in aligning local processual control and central output-orientated control.

To the extent that they are valid, these, and similar, matchings can contribute to a better understanding of observed differences in human behaviour triggered by specific attributes of financial control systems. They can also inform managerial attempts, leaving aside whether these are ethical or unethical, aimed at manipulating the behaviour of their subordinates in the desired direction by changing the attributes of the information systems. However, as indicated in the following section, these matchings should be interpreted with care for they imply a highly flawed notion of determinism, such as that which underlies the literature on governance structures. It is to these issues that we now turn.

Table 1.4 Impact of MIS on human behaviour

Distant MIS induces individuals	*Local MIS induces individuals*
To think abstractly and rationally.	To think concretely and intuitively.
To conceptualize stable variance and general overall conditions and trends.	To conceptualize variable processes and specific conditions.
To distance self from processes that produce results, and focus primarily on the results of the performance.	To become close to processes that produce results, and focus on them as much as on the results.
To identify errors that are exceptional.	To identify errors and correct them before they become exceptional.
To infer causality from information lacking specifity of causal processes or mechanics.	To infer causality from information rich with situational causality related to specific mechanisms.

Reprinted with permission from *Accounting, Organizations and Society*, Vol. 2, C. Argyris, Organizational learning and management information systems, © 1977, Pergamon Press PLC, Oxford, UK.

CORPORATE GOVERNANCE: AN EVALUATION

As indicated above, the literature on corporate governance underpins much of the literature on financial control. It is therefore imperative that the main criticisms levied against the literature on corporate governance be considered carefully in order to understand more fully the ramifications and repercussions arising from the use of financial control in modern organizations. There are three arguments worthy of investigation.

First, the historical underpinnings of the tenets of the transactions cost theory are flawed. Thus, Williamson and Ouchi (1981, p. 365) have suggested that transactions cost can be used to explain the motives underlying organizational and institutional change in both preindustrial and industrial societies:

> Applications of transactions cost economies will include product market organization and also changing labor and capital market forms of organization through time.

But as Robins (1987, p. 75) has pointed out, 'Although transaction-cost theory offers powerful tools for understanding the implications of specific social institutions for economic activity, it is incapable of explaining historical transformations in those social institutions'. Indeed, the transactions cost theory neither offers a comprehensive framework within which all known governance structures can be located, nor a non-problematic chronology of the emergence and evolution of governance structures through time.

An example of the first limitation relates to the emergence of medieval craft guilds in Britain. Flamholtz (1983) argues that these highly specialized craft guilds, which became well organized by 1300, were organized neither as

19

markets nor hierarchies but were instead federations of 'autonomous work-shops whose owners, the masters, normally made all decisions and established the requirements for promotion from the lower ranks' (p. 148). A guild typically sought to guarantee fair prices and high quality products, and to standardize the size, quality and price of its core products, as a payback to its customers for the privilege of monopoly power it enjoyed in a particular town. While some aspects of the clan form can be traced in the craft guilds, for example organizational socialization through apprenticeship, the output of the guild members, unlike that postulated by Ouchi for clan control, was susceptible to more precise measurement. Similarly, Flamholtz documents further historical evidence which indicates that the rise of specific governance structures, such as hierarchies, had little to do with the desire to minimize transactions cost but was driven by the state's desire to attain political and economic power. Among the examples Flamholtz provides is the organization of mercantilism in France under Louis XIV. These examples suggest that the transactions cost paradigm offers an incomplete explanation of the organization of production and labour, for:

(a) it fails to accommodate all types of governance structures, for example the craft guilds; and
(b) it is not the only force that drives alternative modes of governance, the impetus for the emergence of such structures in many cases frequently comes from outside the firm and has more to do with political and economic motives at the level of the state than with the desire for personal economic gains.

The second limitation, the problematic chronology of the emergence of alternative structures of corporate governance under transactions cost theory, has been explored by Robins (1987). Transactions cost theorists perceive the process of economic evolution as being dominated initially by the presence of markets: 'in the beginning there were markets' which were subsequently supplanted by hierarchies in order to cope with increased operational complexity which the market framework cannot deal with in a cost-efficient manner. But as suggested earlier, national economic and political motives had more to do with the rise of hierarchies in some instances (e.g. the use of a centralized system of tariffs and a united currency contributed to a flourishing mercantilism in early industrialized England) than did the desire to minimize transactions cost. Robins has also pointed out that Chandler's (1977; 1980) work, on which Williamson's thesis is based, while taking account of organizational change ignores some fundamental changes in the nature and level of economic activity in the USA. Robins relates the rise of hierarchies in the nineteenth-century to the growth in the level of commerce, that is the growth in the density and activity of the economy:

The history of nineteenth-century economic development is less a story of hierarchy displacing markets than a tale of social and political centralization creating the conditions for large-scale commerce and large-scale production of goods: (Robins, 1987, pp. 76–7).

Second, it is to be recalled that the literature on corporate governance is heavily rooted in the theories of property rights and institutional economics. It is based on the main assumption that minimizing transactions cost is the single most important criterion for determining optimal governance structures. Although the framework explicitly entertains the feasibility of three governance modes (markets, hierarchies, and clans) the choice among which is assumed to be dictated by associated levels of transactions cost, there is an inherent bias towards control mechanisms which are developed within the 'disciplined' context of the market place. So, even in situations where hierarchies are deemed more optimal than markets, the quest is for simulating market-like controls such as internal labour markets, internal capital-markets, and internal markets for goods (intra-company transfers). This bias is not simply restricted to private sector organizations which have profit motives and which interact with the market in several significant domains. More critically, such market-based controls are currently being extended to other, quite different organizational arenas such as non-profit making public sector organizations. For example, quite recently the UK government has been seeking to reorganize the National Health Service (NHS) along the lines of the market model by introducing 'market-disciplined' measures, including internal markets and financial control systems such as resource management and external sub-contracting (see Ezzamel and Willmott, 1991; Lapsley, this volume).

The absence of such market-based controls is assumed by some (e.g. the UK government, some academics, etc.) to encourage the pursuit of selfish interest at the expense of public interest (Tullock, 1976). Further, given the asymmetry of knowledge concerning the consequences of budgetary changes between bureaucrats (administrators) and tax-payers, hierarchical methods of monitoring expenditures are deemed too passive to be effective in unravelling and correcting inefficiency (Kristensen, 1980). The absence of the market, it is held, leads to inefficient operations: increased risk aversion, over-manning and non-optimal pricing and investment, and increased incidence of slack building in budgets (Downs, 1967; Buchanan *et al.*, 1978).

The transactions cost theory is therefore rooted in the assumption that markets are the natural form of corporate governance. Historical evidence indicates that this assumption is not tenable; there is nothing natural nor primeval about the market mechanism. As Robins (1987, p. 77) suggests:

Market organization was preceded by (among other things) feudalism, city states, and cave-dwelling tribes. Large-scale market activity is relatively recent and remains relatively rare as a means of coordinating exchange. Although economic forces may push society in the direction of efficient forms of exchange, they act within the bounds of social and political systems. As Weber (1958) argued, the balance of historical evidence probably tips in the direction of seeing ideological, religious, and cultural change as occurring exogenous to and often prior to economic change.

Further, as Ezzamel and Willmott (1991, p. 19) have pointed out, 'Little, and often no, account is taken of the costs – economic and otherwise – of introducing such market disciplines in terms of the quality of working life'.

Third, invoking the argument of economic efficiency, reflected in the minimization of transactions cost, as the sole criterion for explaining the choice of governance structures is problematic. As Boisot and Child (1988) have suggested, obsession with the minimization of transactions cost overlooks the extent to which the efficient operation of different governance structures is supported or inhibited by a country's social relations, which reflect 'the behavioural and structural expressions of its culture and development'. Ezzamel and Willmott (1991, p. 3) go even further by suggesting that, 'the identification of economic efficiency, and associated shifts in the form of governance structure, are mediated by (political) *discourses and practices*'.

However, despite these serious limitations, transactions cost theory maintains a firm hold on much of the literature in economics and, to a large degree, accounting as evidenced by existing literature and also by some of the contributions to this volume. In some ways this is not surprising, for the theory offers a powerful analytical framework which builds on the interplay between historical conditions and economic processes to yield apparently unambiguous, but as indicated above, problematic, statements concerning the most economically efficient means of organizing transactions. There is little doubt that research utilizing this particular paradigm has yielded very powerful insights into the internal operations of firms and markets, and into the impact of specific organizational forms on performance. There is also little doubt that future parallel research is likely to yield improved understanding of the economics of internal organization (see the relevant contributions in this volume). But what is particularly crucial is that transactions cost theory should not be taken as an over-riding, all-encompassing theory of governance structures. The findings of this approach should be located and interpreted within the wider social and political system.

The contributions in this volume which utilize transactions cost theory provide a good step in this direction. Rather than seek to establish the primacy of transactions cost theory over other theories, the authors merely demonstrate how the application of that theory can contribute to a better understanding of the attributes of internal governance structures within firms, and how incentive schemes can be designed and operated with the purpose of guiding corporate performance towards specific objectives. Further research along these lines will provide a much clearer, though by no means complete, understanding of the internal operations of modern organizations.

CONCLUSIONS

The main purposes of this paper were to provide an overview and a critical examination of the literature on corporate governance; examine the extent to which specific governance structures give rise to, or are more aligned to, specific types of financial controls; and briefly reflect on the extent to which financial control relates to the organizational setting in which it operates.

In examining the literature on corporate governance, rooted in transactions cost theory, it was stated that the theory posits that the emergence and prevalence of specific governance structures can be explained and rationalized in terms of their economic efficiency attributes; that is their ability to minimize transactions cost. Three specific modes of governance were discussed in some detail; markets, hierarchies (bureaucracies), and clans. Their economic performance attributes were analysed along two dimensions; knowledge of the transformation process and ability to measure output. Further, the normative and informational requirements of each governance mode were discussed. The normative requirements ranged from reciprocity through legitimate authority to common values and beliefs. The informational requirements included prices, rules, and traditions. The implication of that analysis is reflected in a mechanistic notion of 'fit', on the one hand between the normative requirements and modes of governance, and on the other hand between the informational requirements and the normative requirements.

In a later section, we examined the main arguments made against transactions cost theory (and by implication the literature on corporate governance). Three specific points were made.

1. The historically-flawed imputation of (a) the comprehensiveness and completeness of the modes of governance proposed, and (b) the primacy of market controls over all other controls.
2. The inherent preference for, and bias in favour of, the discipline of the market and the failure to account adequately for the costs, economic and otherwise, of market controls.
3. The exclusive focus on technical rationality (as manifest in economic efficiency) to the exclusion of substantive rationality.

It was stated that, in spite of these serious limitations, the transactions cost theory has provided, and continues to provide, extremely valuable contributions towards developing a better, but by no means complete, understanding of the economics of internal organization and incentive structures within modern organizations. The call was made, however, for the results of such research to be modified to take account of changes brought about by social and political systems.

We have also proposed a fairly broad definition of financial control, and explored the extent to which the use of specific types of financial controls is associated with specific forms of governance structures. It was stated that, in general, financial control is likely to be relatively more in evidence, and also more influential, under hierarchies than under either markets or clans. The main reason for this is that hierarchies lack the so-called 'market discipline', and they also lack the cultural discipline propagated by clans through organizational socialization. Increased measures of financial control are therefore brought into the organizational arena to make up for these deficiencies.

Finally, we briefly hinted at the importance of locating the design and study of financial control within its organizational setting. Financial control does not operate in an organizational vacuum; rather it is intertwined with the organizational setting; they are at the same time both the consequence and precondition of each other. We also provided, by means of illustration, a discussion of some of the attributes of distant financial control systems contrasted against those of local systems. Although the discussion there focused on demonstrating how each type influences the behaviour of organizational participants, it should be recognized that, in consistency with the arguments advanced above, the attributes of these systems are largely conditioned by the organizational context and they, in turn, moderate that context.

REFERENCES

Argyris, C. (1977) Organisational Learning and Management Information Systems, *Accounting, Organizations and Society*, **2** (2), 113–23.

Boisot, M. and Child, J. (1988) The Iron Law of Fiefs: Bureaucratic Failure and the Problem of Governance in the Chinese Economic Reforms, *Administrative Science Quarterly*, **33**, 507–27.

Bourn, M. and Ezzamel, M. (1986) Organisational Culture in Hospitals in the National Health Service, *Financial Accountability and Management*, **2** (3), Autumn, 203–25.

Bourn, M. and Ezzamel, M. (1987) Budgetary Devolution in the National Health Service and Universities in the United Kingdom, *Financial Accountability and Management*, **3** (1) Spring, 29–45.

Brown, W.B. (1984) Firm like behaviour in markets – the administered channel, *International Journal of industrial Organization*, **2**, 263–76.

References

Buchanan, J.M. *et al.* (1978) *The Economics of Politics*, Institute of Economic Affairs, London.

Buckley, P.J. (1988) Organisational firms and multinational companies, in *Internal Organisation, Efficiency and Profit*, (eds S. Thompson and M. Wright), Philip Allan, Oxford 127–44.

Coase, R.H. (1937) The Nature of the Firm,' *Economica*, **4**, 386–405.

Chandler, A.D. (1977) *The Visible Hand: The managerial revolution in American business*, Belknap Press, Cambridge, MA.

Chandler, A.D. (1980) The United States: Seedbed of Managerial Capitalism, in *Managerial Hierarchies* (eds A.D. Chandler and H. Daems), Harvard University press, 9–40.

Dahlman, C.J. (1979) The Problem of Externality, *Journal of Law and Economics*, April, 141–62.

Downs, A. (1967) *Inside Bureaucracy*, Little Brown, Boston.

Emmanuel, C.R. and Otley, D.T. (1985) *Accounting for Management Control*, Van Nostrand Reinhold, UK.

Ezzamel, M. and Bourn, M. (1990) The Roles of Accounting Information Systems in an Organization Experiencing Financial Crisis, *Accounting, Organizations and Society*, **15** (5), 399–424.

Ezzamel, M., Hoskin, K. and Macve, R. (1990) Managing it all by numbers: a review of Johnson and Kaplan's *Relevance Lost*, *Accounting and Business Research*, **20** (78), 153–66.

Ezzamel, M. and Hart, H. (1987) *Advanced Management Accounting: An organisational emphasis*, Cassell.

Ezzamel, M. and Willmott, H. (1991) *Corporate governance and financial accountability: the new public sector*, Paper presented at 'The New Public Sector?', workshop on Change Notions of Accountability in the UK Public Sector, The London School of Economics and Political Science, May.

Fama, E.F. and Jensen, M.C. (1983a) Separation of Ownership and Control, *Journal of Law and Economics*, June, 301–25.

Fama, E.F. and Jensen, M.C. (1983b) Agency Problems and Residual Claims, *Journal of Law and Economics*, June, 327–49.

Flamholtz, D.T. (1983) The markets and hierarchies framework: a critique of the model's applicability to accounting and economic development, *Accounting, Organizations and Society*, **8** (2/3), 147–51.

Fox, A. (1974) *Beyond Contract: Work, power and trust relations*, Faber and Faber, London.

Hilton, K. (1975) *Control Systems for Social and Economic Management*, An Inaugural Lecture, University of Southampton, (also in this volume, pp. 27–40).

Hopwood, A.G. (1980) The Organisational and Behavioural Aspects of Budgeting and Control, in *Topics in Management Accounting*, (eds J. Arnold, B. Carsberg and R. Scapens), Philip Allan, Oxford, 221–40.

Imai, K. and Itami, H. (1984) Interpenetration of organization and market: Japan's firm and market in comparison with the US, *International Journal of Industrial Organization*, **2**, 285–310.

Jensen, M.C. and Meckling, W.H. (1976) Theory of the firm: managerial behaviour, agency costs and ownership structure, *Journal of Financial Economics*, **3**, October, 305–60.

Johnson, H.T. and Kaplan, R.S. (1987) *Relevance Lost*, Harvard Business School Press.

Jönsson, S. and Grönlund, A. (1988) Life with a sub-contractor: new technology and management accounting, *Accounting, Organizations and Society*, **3** (5), 512–32.

Kristensen, O.P. (1980) The logic of political-bureaucratic decision making as a cause of government growth, *European Journal of Political Research*, **8**, 249–53.

Lapsley, I. (1992) Reforming Financial Control in the NHS – Or is the NHS a 'Deviant Organisation'?, this volume, pp. 233–50.

Meyer, J.W. and Rowan, B. (1977) Institutionalized organizations: formal structure as myth and ceremony, *American Journal of Sociology*, **83**, 340–63.

Mintzberg, H. (1979) *The Structuring of Organizations*, Prentice-Hall, Englewood Cliffs, NJ.

Ouchi, W.G. (1977) The relationship between organizational structure and organizational control, *Adiminstrative Science Quarterly*, **22**, March, 95–113.

Ouchi, W.G. (1979) A conceptual framework for the design of organizational control mechanisms, *Management Science*, **25**, September, 833–48.

Ouchi, W.G. (1980) Markets, bureaucracies and clans, *Administrative Science Quarterly*, **25**, 129–41.

Ouchi, W.G. (1981) *Theory Z*, Addison Wesley.

Ouchi, W.G. and Price, R.L. (1978) Hierarchies, clans and theory Z: a new perspective on organizational development, *Organisational Dynamics*, Autumn, 25–44.

Robins, J.A. (1987) Organizational economics: notes on the use of transaction–cost theory in the study of organizations, *Administrative Science Quarterly*, **32**, 62–86.

Spicer, B.W. and Ballew, V. (1983) Management accounting systems and the economics of internal organization, *Accounting, Organizations and Society*, **8** (1), 73–96.

Tomkins, C.R. (1980) Financial planning and control in large companies, in *Topics in Management Accounting* (eds J. Arnold, B. Carsberg and R. Scapens), Philip Allen, Oxford, pp. 241–61.

Tomkins, C.R. and Colville, I. (1992) Financial control and devolved management in central government, this volume, pp. 255–80.

Tullock, G. (1976) *The Vote Motive*, Institute of Economic Affairs, London.

Weber, M. (1958) *The Protestant Ethic and the Spirit of Capitalism*, Charles Scribner, New York.

Weber, M. (1978) *Economy and Society*, University of California, Berkeley.

Wilkins, A.L. and Ouchi, W.G. (1983) Efficient cultures: exploring the relationship between culture and organizational performance, *Administrative Science Quarterly*, **28**, 468–81.

Williamson, O.E. (1970) *Corporate Control and Business Behaviour*, Prentice-Hall, Englewood Cliffs, NJ.

Williamson, O.E. (1975) *Markets and Hierarchies: Analysis and antitrust implications*, Free Press, New York.

Williamson, O.E. (1981) The modern corporation: origins, evolution, attributes, *Journal of Economic Literature*, **XIX**, December, 1537–68.

Williamson, O.E. and Ouchi, W.G. (1981) The Markets and Hierarchies and Visible Hand Perspectives, in *Perspectives on Organization Design and Behaviour*, (eds A.H. Van de Ven and W.F. Joyce), John Wiley & Sons, 347–70.

2
*Control systems for social and economic management**

KENNETH HILTON

INTRODUCTION

What is my subject?[1] The Vice Chancellor has referred to me as Professor of Financial Control. What is financial control? It may seem rather odd to ask the holder of a chair 'What *is* your subject?' Does one ask a Professor of Physics, 'What is physics?', or a Professor of Music, 'What is music?' or even a Professor of Philosophy 'What is philosophy?'. No. For most subjects many of the members of an inaugural lecturer's audience have at least some idea of the nature of the subject: but perhaps there are reasons for expecting today's audience to be ignorant of what a Professor of Financial Control at Southampton University is intended to profess.

1. The term financial control is a specialist one sometimes used in the accounting profession to distinguish a particular area of accountancy: that relating to auditing or quasi-legal control. But even if you knew this: it is not the meaning that is intended for financial control here at Southampton.
2. There are, so far as I am aware, only two other established chairs of financial control in this country (and one of these was vacant at the time of writing). In both these institutions the term is used to describe a second or third chair in the financial field. Again this meaning in not intended!

* This paper is an abridged and slightly revised version of the late Professor Hilton's Inagural Lecture given at the University of Southampton in 1973, and published internally in 1975.

Perspectives on Financial Control: Essays in memory of Kenneth Hilton.
Edited by Mahmoud Ezzamel and David Heathfield.
Published in 1992 by Chapman & Hall, London. ISBN 0 412 40980 1.

3. The intention of the University appears to have been to use the term 'financial control' in a very special way: to describe the holder of a Chair whose responsibilities would include the areas of commerce, accountancy and financial control.

The title of Professor of Financial Control is thus rare and the particular meaning given to it as this University is unique. The Chair is, to repeat, a new one: can the establishment of this Chair indicate there is a 'new' subject being developed in the University? 'Newness' is a relative attribute, but on most definitions the subjects for which I am accountable, are not new to this University. For the past sixty years commerce, usually under that name, has been taught at this institution.

MANAGEMENT CONTROL SYSTEMS

Management and its study is as old as man; we could debate whether or not management is a phenomenon found in non-human animal kingdoms, and whether or not control systems are necessary for a man in isolation, but certainly, since man collaborated with other men, management became important.

Man found that there were benefits to be gained from collaboration and engaged in division of labour. As the breadth of activities continued to widen, and as the tasks of controlling groups became intricate, man found it more and more difficult to be omnipotent on his own, and so increasingly he relied on others. This implies division of work; and often this involves delegation.

Formal delegation is not a pre-requisite for a system of control. One informal control mechanism that has existed for thousands of years is known as the price or market mechanism. This system involves the provision of information and incentives via prices and markets, and it has been extensively studied by economists. The informality of the system does not mean it is the 'natural' or 'normal' control mechanism. The effectiveness of this control system must be judged in terms of its results in relation to the results we desire of the system. Some members of society have never been satisfied with this mechanism. More and more there is considered a need to modify this system by government action. The recent inflation experience, the unemployment of the 1930s and the doubt about the capacity of the market mechanism to deal adequately with the problems of natural resource depletion, are examples of events that have given rise to this concern. It appears that this control system has failed to satisfy the demands placed upon it; yet it still forms the basis on which the rest of the economic and social control systems in our society rely. The prices paid by hospitals and prisons are prices that result, in the main, from market forces; they are typically no different from prices paid by private institutions.

Hence even in non-market situations, account must be taken of this basic control system in our society.

Other control systems (within companies, public corporations, Universities etc.), like the price mechanism, can be evaluated only in terms of the objectives that are set for them. There are alternative possibilities for the evaluation of a control system: one may evaluate in terms of the objectives that society as a whole has in mind or one may evaluate in terms of the objectives of the particular institution or group of people concerned. So a control system that maximizes profits for a particular company may satisfy the requirements of that company but may not satisfy the objectives of society as a whole. In such a case as this, where companies may be regarded as having power delegated to them by the rest of society, it could be argued that the system of control between society as a whole and the individual company is at fault. But this is the kind of conflict that often causes confusion in the evaluation of management systems.

As I have said, the evaluation of control systems requires an objective, but one also requires an *information feedback*, both to operate a control system and to evaluate it. That is: one needs to know what has been achieved as well as what is wanted. A third requirement for the effective operation of a control system is that there should be *incentives*. Many of the incentives operated in our society are monetary ones but it would be a caricature of human existence to suggest that material wealth is their sole objective. A fourth requirement is that there should be a *mechanism of control* either implicit or explicit.

This discussion, and indeed the title of this lecture, may have led many of you to wonder why one needs the study of control systems independent of the study of control engineering, with which it appears superficially to have much in common. Many of the phrases I have used such as feedback, systems, control, etc. are those derived from a control engineering framework. Some of the techniques of control engineering can be adapted to suit social and economic systems but I would argue that they are designed to face different problems.

First, the objectives of a control engineering system are usually well specified, while the objectives of social and economic control systems are often multiple and a mixture of optimizing objectives, non-optimizing objectives and constraints. It is not unusual to find situations in which the objectives at particular points in time (and objectives vary over time) are not independent of the outcomes that are achieved by the system. The business organizations most concerned about profits are those that have made losses; and the trustees of widows and orphans funds vie with Receivers in Liquidation for being the people most concerned about the maximization of income or wealth. This is but one source of the variation in objectives: people change, and so do their positions of power in organization and the external environment changes.

29

Second, there is the information problem. The sheer deficiency of appropriate data makes it impossible to apply without modification many formal techniques. Associated with this is the complexity of the relationships to be either analysed or controlled. Recent attempts made by Bray to apply control engineering techniques devised by Professors Westcott, Box and Jenkins to the analysis of the UK economy have not been very successful. Part of this lack of success stems from the larger number of variables and relationships found in such economy wide systems.

Third, there is uncertainty about the effects of the control systems: there is uncertainty about what has already been achieved; there is uncertainty about the objectives of the system; there is uncertainty about the environment external to the control system, and the shocks that the environment may provide. It is not that such uncertainty cannot be incorporated in formal systems but the all pervasive nature of such uncertainty makes some of the problems very difficult to handle in a physical sciences framework.

Finally, there are the differences of approach necessitated by human intervention in the control system. This has benefits as well as costs for the system's examiner or controller. If we study physical or animal systems we cannot ask the objects involved in the systems what their feelings are nor why one subject is acting in one way rather than another. In the case of economic and social control systems we can sensibly ask such questions, and incorporate this information, or information gained from the controller's or investigator's own intuition, into the analysis of the system. In practice, there is a danger of taking too much account of what people say they are doing. For as well as having the propensity for speech they also have the propensity to provide misleading information either intentionally or unintentionally.

There is another corollary of the human element in social and economic control systems that I have considered implicitly in this lecture. Unlike physical systems one can not only analyse but also prescribe solutions to problems raised by the actors in the system. The use of a system to control human beings often leads to the failure to recognize that the aim of the overall system is human welfare in the main; the way the instruments of this system (i.e. human beings) are used is not independent of the objectives of the system, nor is it independent of the extent to which those objectives will directly be achieved.

FINANCIAL CONTROL SYSTEMS

The most frequently used control system in capitalist economies is a financial control system. This follows in part from the market mechanism but could exist without it. To talk of *financial* control systems merely denotes the use of a particular *numeraire*, money, which happens to serve as a medium of exchange. Like all control systems an information feedback is a necessary part of this control system: the provision of this information feedback lies at the base of the role accountants have played for more than six centuries. Until this century the primary function of the accountant's information was to expose fraud; it was an auditing task – hence the close inter-relation between the Department of Law and the teaching of Accountancy in this University before the Second World War. This very close relationship persists in some universities, particularly in Scotland, where Accounting is typically taught in a Faculty of Law. The need to comply with the Income Tax law in the provision of records to ensure the Revenue was not defrauded led to the income tax side of the accountant's work, which is still a major part of the small accounting practice today. To many, the accountant *is* an income tax consultant – a kind of lawyer's auxiliary help. Yet in principle it is but a minor part of his potential role.

Often the distinction is made between:

(a) accounting for stewardship – deciding how many spoils of the business there are to distribute and how they should be distributed;
(b) accounting for control – here control is used to denote control of people; and
(c) accounting for decision taking – which is often considered the central part of management accounting.

As an indication of historical development or as a teaching device, this may be a useful taxonomy, but why do we want accounting records if not for decision taking of one form or another? They should properly be regarded as part of the information feedback. Consider the accounts of limited liability companies. There are confusing documents for the layman. As one well-known expert in company law – an expert especially well-known in Southampton[2] – remarked:

> To the average investor or creditor – 'The man on the Clapham Omnibus' – company financial statements are cryptograms which he is incapable of solving.

It is partly because of this, that such records are viewed with suspicion. But more importantly is the fact that they so often appear useless or simply wrong. Rolls Royce, Pergamon Press, Vehicle and General are names associated with failure of published accounts to perform their task satisfactorily. The open disputes that arise in the accounting profession about particular problems – accounting for inflation is the current vogue – similarly do not inspire confidence in the layman.

The problem it seems to me is a fundamental one associated with all accounting information systems. It is their general purpose nature: financial statements are not usually designed to satisfy one objective but many. In attempting to satisfy the many they fail on all counts. It is precisely this that causes the confusion over company accounts. Why are they prepared? A possible list of answers may run:

1. To show that fraud has not taken place.
2. To show how much profit is available for distribution.
3. To show creditors of the company how secure their money is.
4. To show how well the management of the company has performed.
5. To provide information to assess the future prospects of the company.
6. To provide supporting evidence to beguile the Inland Revenue.
7. To provide a measure of the benefits to society at large.

The accounts suitable for one purpose will not be suitable for another. The current disputes over how to incorporate the existence of price level changes in company accounts arise largely from this very point. The Rolls Royce accounts were not devised to show the creditor how secure his funds are (although a tutored observer could have deduced that they were not safe: indeed some of our colleagues at Manchester used the accounts of Rolls Royce (anonymously) as a case study of a company likely to go into liquidation, some years before it did!).

If one asks a practising accountant for what purpose he is preparing accounts, the usual answer is, surprisingly, to permit an evaluation of the future prospects of the company. Yet this is precisely the legal obligation they do not have!

The general point remains: accounting information systems cannot satisfy all that is demanded of them from one set of published accounts. Information for different purposes should be specified, or at least information provided to permit this to be done. In the process ranges of 'error' ought to be shown for some of the estimates – how can one sensibly say that a piece of machinery has depreciated by exactly £5337 in one year? I have a certain sympathy with some of the arguments used to distinguish the recording function of the accountant from the measurement function of the accountant by the use of cash-flow accounting: but again this is only a means to an end.

Financial accounting is not the only area in which the 'multiple purpose' problems arise. Management accounts are similarly conceived as multi-purpose, and 'cost' is one of the most abused words in the English language. The answer to the question: 'What is the cost?' should always be 'Why do you want to know?'

Problems such as this are not confined to the business sector. As I have said, hospitals, prisons, charities, etc. all have their particular as well as general problems. One kind of institution that has particular problems in an acute form is a university. Here – I do not mean only Southampton University in this context! – there is a set of issues associated with objectives. On this occasion I have not the time to consider these issues, except to say that given the conflicts between objectives that exist within a university, a control system should be designed to take account of these conflicts; it should ensure that when a choice has to be made between one group and another it should not in the process provide by-products that are not wanted by any of the groups existing in the university. Perhaps more important – I am convinced of its importance – there should be relevant information provided so that proper evaluation of the costs and benefits of alternatives can be made. I do not wish to ride this particular hobby-horse of mine this evening; so let me provide an example of a current issue in universities, and the use or abuse of financial information to help in the solution of the problems raised.

FINANCIAL CONTROL: AN APPLICATION IN THE UNIVERSITY SECTOR

The problem[3] relates to contracts made to universities to enable them to engage in research on a particular subject. The charge the university should quote in these contracts has been the subject of certain debate. The department or faculty that wishes to take the contract will presumably ensure that the payments made are such as to cover their variable costs, e.g. hiring of additional staff, additional materials etc., or be willing to bear such costs. But there are costs imposed on the rest of the university; given the university already exists and it does not wish to recover any of the costs that would otherwise be incurred, then the only costs we need to be concerned about are the variable costs imposed on the rest of the university, i.e. those that arise outside the department concerned as a results of the contract. A direct assessment of such costs could be made but would be rather difficult and expensive, e.g. library and computer services, the finance office's overtimes etc. There are indeed considerable conceptual problems here; for unless the research contract is very large, many of the costs may appear only as increasing discomfort for library users, longer delays on the computer, harder work for the finance office, etc. ... For most contracts the sheer cost of finding out would be prohibitive. As a result of problems such as this arising, the University Grants Committee (the UGC)[4] offered 'guidelines' to universities, which universities are presumably intended to take seriously.

The UGC looked at different universities (all those in England excluding London). They tried to see how far variations in central expenditure (administration, library, computing, maintenance of building, lighting, heating, etc.) were associated with variations in size of the different universities. They came up with a diagram like Figure 2.1 which shows on the vertical axis, Central

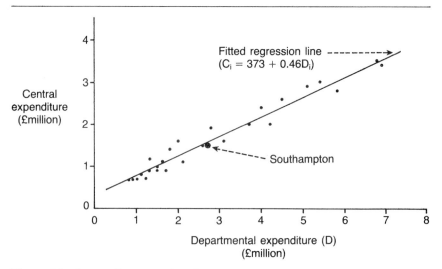

Figure 2.1 Scatter diagram: university central expenditure and departmental expenditure, England 1968–9.

Expenditure (including libraries, computers, etc), and on the horizontal axis, Departmental Expenditure (i.e. all expenditure on teaching and research directly attributable to departments, including academic salaries), both in 1969. For example, Southampton in 1969 had Teaching plus Research Expenditure of £2.7m, and Central Expenditure of £1.5m.

The UGC researchers then found that if one fits a regression line to this data, roughly to see what the average kind of relationship is between central expenditure and teaching plus research expenditure, that on average central expenditure (including rates etc.) was greater by about £46 for every £100. Teaching plus research expenditure was greater. They also found that teaching plus research 'explained' variations in central expenditure 'better' than either teaching or research alone. They concluded that the minimum a university should normally add for a research contract should be 45% (with a deduction for rates etc. this became 37%) unless there were good reasons for doing otherwise.

I would like to look at this example further to indicate that the problem is not so simple nor the solution so satisfactory as at first appears.

First let us see what this kind of analysis implies.

There is an extensive literature on the use of cross-section data to derive conclusions relating to changes at the individual unit level. The argument for any such approach is in simple terms: if A is now bigger than B, we can see what growth will mean to B by assuming that if it grows to the size of A it will have A's attributes. For this approach to be useful at least three conditions need to be satisfied:

1. A and B are reasonably homogeneous in the respects to be analysed (I exclude the ideal possibility of a complete model to explain the differences between the particular characteristics of A and B).
2. The existing characteristics of A and B must not be affected by transitional factors (i.e. both should be in the same state of equilibrium or disequilibrium).
3. There must be no possibility that the causation runs from B to A rather than A to B.

On (1), the exclusion of the very large and very small observations, London and the business schools, does help, but other universities do have characteristics that may in some cases dominate the explanations of overheads. For example, the determination of Maintenance of Premises, the major item of central overheads, is likely to be arbitrary across universities. Consider the component items:

Rates	excluded by the UGC 'because' grant is earmarked
Rent	determined largely by historical accident of purchase/ rent decision
Heating and lighting	
Repairs and maintenance	All these items will likely be dominated by the age of the buildings, their sites, etc.
Salaries of maintenance staff	(For example Sussex has half the expenditure on maintenance than Salford, a university that is roughly the same size)
Insurance	

Naturally, one may obtain good correlations even between 'maintenance of premises' and departmental expenditure, because both are correlated with the size of the university; and one may find better correlations with total department expenditure than with teaching expenditure for the same reason. But this does not mean that an increase in research expenditure (total departmental expenditure – teaching expenditure) has the same effect on maintenance of premises as an increase in teaching expenditure. If one wished to use the UGC approach on maintenance of premises, it would be sensible to make some attempt to allow for these factors, e.g. by considering implicit rents, allowing for age of buildings etc. These and other arbitrary variations in costs may not matter, providing that they do not dominate the relationship, and that they do not conceal or distort the underlying relationship between the variables. For example, *prima facie* Oxford and Cambridge would appear to be different

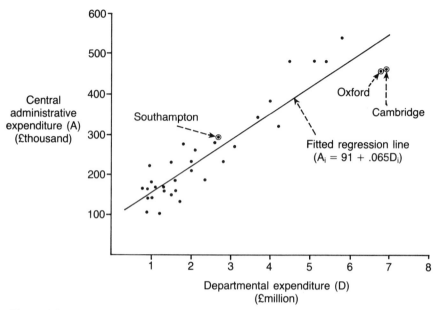

Figure 2.2   Scatter diagram: university central administrative expenditure and departmental expenditure, England 1968–9.

animals to other institutions. They have a smaller proportion of central expenditure going on maintenance of premises and administration and a large proportion going on academic services and directly on teaching and research. This is illustrated in Figure 2.2 which shows Oxford and Cambridge with lower central administration expenditure.

Let us, however, ignore this problem for the moment and examine the UGC's results. Implicitly, by treating teaching and research expenditure as a single mass, the UGC analysis *assumes* (one cannot derive this inference from their results as they suggest) that the effect of an increase in teaching expenditure is the same as that of research expenditure. It would seem appropriate to test this by seeing whether or not we can explain central expenditure better when we take separate account of teaching expenditure and research expenditure. This we have done for the aggregate and some of the components. This multivariate approach cannot be easily illustrated on a two dimensional scatter diagram; the results are summarized in Table 2.1.

The total equation implies that for a £100 difference in teaching expenditure there is on average a £56 difference in central overheads, but for a £100 difference in research expenditure (with a given teaching expenditure) there is on average a £9 difference in central overheads, i.e. using the UGC approach

36

Table 2.1 Cross section regression results on university expenditure 1968–9

	Const	(T + R)	Teaching	Research	R^2	(T − R)
Total overheads	373	0.46			0.956	
(central expenditure)	(55)	(0.02)				
	326		0.56	0.09	0.968	0.47
	(49)		(0.04)	(0.11)		(0.14)
Academic services	3	0.11			0.714	
	(38)	(0.01)				
			0.07	0.23	0.731	− 0.16
			(0.03)	(0.09)		(0.11)
Maintenance of	165	0.16			0.839	
premises (net of rates)	(40)	(0.01)				
	128		0.25	− 0.13	0.894	0.38
	(35)		(0.03)	(0.07)		(0.10)
Administration	91	0.07			0.874	
	(14)	(0.01)				
	86		0.08	0.02	0.883	0.06
	(14)		(0.01)	(0.03)		(0.04)
Other educational	− 13	0.06			0.844	
expenditure	(11)	(0.01)				
	− 15		0.05	0.03	0.847	0.02
	(11)		(0.01)	(0.02)		(0.03)
Other expenditure	93	0.07			0.824	
	(18)	(0.10)				
	78		0.10	− 0.05	0.877	0.15
	(16)		(0.01)	(0.04)		(0.05)

Notes:
1. $T + R$ is total expenditure on teaching and research ⎫ Table 44 *Statistics of Education*
   R is expenditure from research grants ⎭　　Vol. 6, 1968–69
2. Standard errors are shown in brackets
3. There are 33 observations: all English universities except London, LBS and MBS.
   Estimation was by ordinary least squares. The standard errors for $(T − R)$ are derived from
   equations of the form: $C_i = \alpha + \beta(T + R)_i + \gamma T_i + u_i$ when γ is the required coefficient.

the appropriate level of central on-cost would appear to be 9% (not 37%) for research contracts.

Let us turn to the disaggregated results.

The coefficients for administration seem reasonable enough: 8% teaching, 2% research. Similarly the negative but non-significant results for other expenditure (examinations, students' welfare, etc.) are reasonable for we would expect variations in research expenditure to have little effect on these items. But the results of (a) maintenance of premises and (b) academic services are totally implausible in the framework used.

For maintenance of premises the negative coefficient on research expenditure is difficult to explain except in the terms outlined above, i.e. other factors dominate the relationship. For academic services (library, computer facilities, etc.) this may also be the explanation for the very high coefficient on research: but also possible is the inversion of the relationship, i.e. high expenditure on computer and library may mean that more research grants are obtained because more industrial firms wish to use the services of the university. In this case the high overheads may cause the high research expenditure rather than the reverse.

It could be argued that the disaggregation is not relevant for it may be that high expenditure on one item is offset by low expenditure on another, and that there is some mechanism (implicit or explicit) that provides for this. But I do not find this convincing.

One further approach – that of seeing how far changes in central expenditure between 1964 and 1969 were correlated with changes in teaching and research expenditure – was tried. The conclusions one might derive from this possibly more valid approach are no more sensible. Similarly, looking at other years yields similar results.

In simple terms, the approach as it is used by the UGC is unsatisfactory and the conclusions that the UGC have chosen to draw cannot be derived from their study.

CONCLUSIONS

I emphasize that the above example is merely illustrative of the difficulties involved: it is a very simple method of analysis, and not in any way indicative of the kinds of tools that are available or used in this subject. But it does suggest two points.

1. Without a proper framework, the analysis of financial data may yield rather silly results.
2. A little knowledge in this field may yield positively the wrong results.

Here lies part – but only part – of the importance of the study of the subjects of commerce and accountancy. You would expect any Professor to emphasize the importance of his subject – I offer three further points of my position.

First, there is a real need for increased competence in the fields of management and finance. One can quote several business disasters as examples of the failure of accounting and management: I would see it more as an example of the need for greater competence – whether by accountants and managers or by engineers in the understanding of finance and accounting.

In more general terms one can point to the doubling of output possible without technical progress in some industries merely by raising the level of efficiency in all firms to the current best practice firm. This is not to decry the importance of technical progress – of course it has a valuable role to play (especially if it permits us to operate closer to our possibility frontiers without the increased usage of natural resources), but even here, management and financial systems have a valuable role to play.

This increased demand for competence in the field is reflected in the high level of demand for graduates in this area where there is no problem of graduate unemployment.

Second, the views of one's colleagues are interesting on the usefulness of one's subject. The Dean of Medicine commented at his inaugural lecture:

> One starting point from which to consider improvements in medical education is the shortcomings of present day doctors. High up on any list, I fancy, would be our ignorance of, and often our contempt for, management and its techniques, and our lack of understanding of the economic constraints within which we must operate. Whatever branch of medicine our students choose to enter they are certain to be confronted with problems of management and of a limited budget.... If we are to equip students to meet these problems we must give them due emphasis in the curriculum.

Perhaps it is unfair to quote this speaker after a lapse of three years especially as I cannot find management, economics or finance in the syllabus for the medical school!

Another inaugural lecturer remarked 'The argument that management is important and that everybody should therefore study it leaves us cold.' There are now proposals for the introduction of management into the syllabus of that inaugural lecturer's department.

Third, some account should be taken of students' preferences. My colleagues have heard me before on this topic on too many occasions. But it is of relevance in this context to point to the number of students who apply for admission for undergraduate courses; more than one in every twelve of all applications to the university in 1972 were for courses involving commerce or accountancy, and the teaching of commerce and accountancy represents only a minority part of the teaching programme of one of the thirty Departments in the University.[5]

Hence I would argue, in the eyes of students, colleagues and society at large, these subjects are important ones.

I hope I have shown that my subjects are not the narrow book-keeping or descriptive areas that are often ascribed to them. I see economic and social control systems as being of relevance in a wide range of disciplines: I have difficulty in finding one in which it is not of relevance. Similarly, I believe the subject needs the active participation of other disciplines. In terms of inputs and outputs it is, to use a hackneyed phrase, interdisciplinary.

Finally I confess I do not believe in the importance of finance and management – *except* as a means to the ends that mankind seeks. Too often in this world people are blinded by the veil of money and the mystique of management techniques. As well as developing improved systems for control in social, economic and business fields, we must seek to remove some at least of this mystique.

NOTES

[1] It behoves the first holder of a new Chair to explain to the University at large something of his subject, and its role in this institution. I confine myself to this task, rather than attempt to offer an original contribution to knowledge.

[2] L.C.B. Gower (1969) *The Principles of Modern Company Law*, Stevens, London, p. 454. Professor Gower was the then Vice-Chancellor of the University of Southampton (the editors).

[3] The discussion that follows is intended to illustrate possible abuses of financial data; it is not intended to provide a rigorous analysis of the problem, nor to offer solutions to this problem.

[4] Now the University Funding Council (the UFC) (the editors).

[5] At that time accountancy and commerce were taught within the Department of Economics at the University of Southampton (the editors).

PART TWO
Financial control and the theory of the firm: theory and empirical evidence

3
Financial control of portfolio management decisions

CHRIS CHAPMAN and STEVE WARD*

INTRODUCTION

'Portfolio' management is usually characterized by a limited quantity of resource to be allocated among a number of possible uses when various levels of resource could be allocated to each use and where significant uncertainty and associated risk is involved. The amount of resource available may be limited in a strict sense, but this need not be the case. A typical example would be the selection of a portfolio of securities. A less obvious example would be the allocation of crops to farm land. There is a large number of other important applications.

The Markowitz (1959) mean-variance model is the classic theoretical framework for portfolio management decisions. While it has its limitations (Joyce and Vogel, 1970), it is a very powerful theoretical basis. Efficient algorithms

* The initial development of the approach outlined in the fourth section was stimulated by High Lavis of IBM UK, for presentation at an IBM seminar in London. It was subsequently presented to the Operational Research Society Annual Conference, September 1989, Southampton University, and the IBM European Institute, Financial Mathematics and Computing, July 1990, Oberlech, Austria, at the invitation of Diem Ho, IBM France. This written version was the first prepared. Another version will be prepared for publication with other IBM European Institute papers in the *Journal of Applied Stochastic Models and Data Analysis*. The authors are grateful for the comments of a number of colleagues, in particular Chris Burke, Mahmoud Ezzamel, David Heathfield, Michael Page, Philip Powell and Charles Sutcliffe.

Perspectives on Financial Control: Essays in memory of Kenneth Hilton.
Edited by Mahmoud Ezzamel and David Heathfield.
Published in 1992 by Chapman & Hall, London. ISBN 0 412 40980 1.

for quadratic programming (QP) to solve such models soon followed Marko-witz (1959): for example, see Hadley (1964). A large number of simplifica-tions were also forthcoming, which make operational forms easier to use: for example, see Sharpe (1963) or Wallingford (1967).

Despite the wide range of important portfolio management problems, the theoretical power of the mean-variance model, the development of efficient quadratic programming algorithms to solve mean-variance models, and a range of operational simplifications, all available for some thirty years, few operational implementations of such models have been reported in the lit-erature. Recently there is evidence of increased interest and some success, but it is still less than one might expect. Why?

A number of explanations might be offered, including a wish to keep suc-cessful applications confidential. This paper suggests a wider perspective than that traditionally associated with decision modelling and which embraces a full set of objectives for a decision support system for financial control of portfolio management, and offers a way of pursuing those objectives.

The second section of this paper considers the role of management science models in relation to security selection decision support systems for brokerage firms, providing the perspective which underlies the suggested approach. The third section introduces a special form of nested pairwise separability central to the proposed approach. The fourth section outlines a suggested operational approach to security portfolio management by a brokerage firm. The fifth section discusses how some of the issues raised earlier relate to wider portfolio management situations and other aspects of financial control.

THE ROLE OF MANAGEMENT SCIENCE MODELS

The central role of a mean-variance model used to assist portfolio management is generally assumed to be prescriptive allocation identifications with respect to risk efficiency (the least risk for a given level of expected return) and risk-return balance (neither more risk and less return nor less risk and more return are appropriate, assuming risk efficiency).

In basic textbook terms, in a security selection context, where there are n available securities, $i = 1 \ldots n$, and

> E_i is the expected terminal value of £1 invested in security i,
> V_i^2 is the variance associated with E_i,
> V_{ij}^2 is the covariance associated with E_i and E_j,
> X_i is the amount to be invested in security i,

a quadratic expression for the variance associated with the terminal value of the portfolio at the end of a decision period,

$$V^2 = \sum_{i=1}^{n} V_i^2 X_i^2 + \sum_{i=1}^{n} \sum_{j \neq i=1}^{n} V_{ij}^2 X_i X_j,$$

is minimized subject to a given total investment in the portfolio,

$$X = \sum_{i=1}^{n} X_i,$$

and a given expected return on the portfolio,

$$E = \sum_{i=1}^{n} E_i X_i.$$

E is varied from a maximum through to a minimum risk efficient value in discrete steps to define in discrete terms the risk efficient boundary portfolios, from which investors choose a portfolio with an appropriate risk-return balance.

The authors suggest that attempting to achieve risk efficiency and risk-return balance in this sense is an appropriate underlying goal of a portfolio management decision support system, but a number of other objectives need to be tackled directly if this underlying goal is to be approached.

There are three basic reasons why this wider set of objectives needs explicit attention:

1. A number of people with different skills and responsibilities are typically involved in the decision process.
2. Decisions need to be made on a real-time basis, mostly by those with the least seniority or authority, (i.e. the 'traders'), with appropriate guidance from various levels of 'management';
3. While automated computer trading might be feasible and appropriate in some circumstances, in general this is not the case. The computer's role as the basis of a financial control information system is extremely complex in the main because of unavoidable human interactions.

Put more generally, we have a financial control situation which involves important information generation and communication issues. All the wider objectives are summarized by 'an efficient and effective basis for the generation, evaluation and communication of appropriate information'. Some particular examples are the provision of an efficent and effective means of:

1. capturing important corporate knowledge in a useful form;
2. initiating discussion when appropriate, on a management-by-exception or need-to-know basis;
3. distinguishing between good luck and good management, bad luck and bad management, as a basis for fair rewards and sanctions;

45

4. relating tactical issues to strategic issues;
5. relating quantitative analysis to issues which are less amenable to quantitative analysis and may resist formal qualitative analysis;
6. encouraging the grasping of opportunities, enhancing lateral thinking, and avoiding any apparent reduction in the 'fun' involved in the process; and
7. avoiding crises and promoting confidence, by using a transparent model which can be understood by those involved, and which permits careful analysis to be performed (for example testing the validity of the assumptions).

NESTED PAIR WISE SEPARABILITY

The basis of 'demand analysis' or 'consumer behaviour theory' as approached by economists (for example, see Brown and Deaton, 1972) is the notion of an ordinal utility function for a typical consumer,

$$U_t(Q_{1t}, Q_{2t}, \ldots, Q_{nt}),$$

where Q_{it}, $i = 1, \ldots n$, is the quantity of commodity i consumed over some decision period t. 'Rational' behaviour requires that the consumer maximize U subject to a budget constraint which limits total expenditure,

$$X_t = \sum_{i=1}^{n} P_{it} Q_{it},$$

where P_{it} are prices.

'Rational' behaviour on the part of the consumer also means U_t is well behaved and allows the derivation of a set of demand equations,

$$Q_{1t} = F_{1t}(X_t, P_{1t}, P_{2t}, \ldots, P_{nt}),$$

$$Q_{2t} = F_{1t}(X_t, P_{1t}, P_{2t}, \ldots, P_{nt}),$$

$$Q_{nt} = F_{nt}(X_t, P_{1t}, P_{2t}, \ldots, P_{nt}),$$

which have properties which constrain the parameters of the functions $F_{1t} \ldots F_{nt}$: for example, no 'money illusion' – a 5% increase in expenditure and a 5% increase in all prices will result in exactly the same commodity consumption pattern, because if it was previously optimal it must be optimal after such a change.

An obvious problem when fitting these demand equations with available data is that too many degrees of freedom are used as the number of goods (n) increases. Even if the system of equations is estimated simultaneously, making full use of all the constraints on the parameters suggested by the economic theory, the upper limit of n will range between 10 and 20, the actual limit depending upon the amount of data available and the number of explanatory variables in addition to X_t and P_{it} which in practice may also be of interest.

One method of economizing on data is by way of separability. This allows us to deal with small groups of commodities, and leads to a 'top down' budgetary process: allocating expenditure among broad categories such as cars, holidays, food, and clothing first with one system of demand equations. Allocations within these groups of commodities are considered next, with one system of demand equations for each commodity group.

This process may involve more than two stages, up to the limit of $n - 1$ stages – each involving only two commodities, and separability within each level is assumed: any of the U could be written

$$U_t(U_{1t}(Q_{1t}, U_{2t}(Q_{2t}), \ldots U_{nt}(Q_{nt})).$$

A key theoretical and operational difficulty with this separability approach is the choice of groupings. This requires that sensible allocations could be made at an aggregate level before knowing how allocations were made within those groups.

Pearce (1964) introduced a form of pair wise separability which he called 'neutral want association', but which has subsequently been referred to as 'Pearce separability'. Pearce separability is sometimes taken to mean strong separability; a form used by Pearce for some empirical work, equivalent to the complete separability illustrated by U_t above. Weaker separability forms, not requiring separability within each pair, is particularly powerful, because the restrictiveness of always using pairs is more than compensated for by the lack of separability within each pair and a number of special advantages associated with $n = 2$ which are lost for $n > 2$ (Chapman, 1975).

For example, to estimate a system of partial demand equations of the form

$$Q_{it} = F_{it} (X_{kt}, P_{it}, P_{jt}, \ldots, U_{it}),$$

$$Q_{jt} = F_{jt} (X_{kt}, P_{it}, P_{jt}, \ldots, U_{jt}),$$

where $\qquad X_{kt} = P_{it} Q_{it} + P_{jt} Q_{jt}$,

and U_{it} and U_{jt} are error terms, we can use a simple single equation estimation form (Chapman, 1975),

$$Q_{it}/Q_{jt} = a_k(P_{it}/X_{kt})^{b_i} (P_{it}/X_{kt})^{b_j} e^{u_{kt}}$$

where a_k, b_i and b_j are constants, e is the exponential number, and U_{kt} is a random error such that

$$U_{kt} = U_{it} - U_{jt}.$$

This simple single equation approach automatically imposes all the restrictions suggested by economic theory, and appropriate econometric restrictions on

47

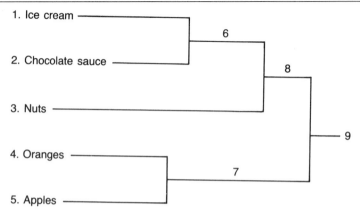

Figure 3.1 A five commodity example.

U_i, U_j and U_k. It can be derived from an indirect utility function which re-
solves the aggregation problem noted earlier: a 'bottom up' approach can be
considered such that Q_{kt} can be associated with a unique interpretation in
utility theory terms, facilitating and justifying related top down approaches
(see Chapman, 1975, for a discussion of the specifications of the utility function implied here).

Restricting ourselves to two commodities allows us to illustrate with simple
two dimensional pictures bottom up and top down decisions. Consider a simple
example. Assume $n = 5$, with a pairing structure indicated by Figure 3.1.

Figure 3.1 illustrates a separability structure of the form

$$U_{9t} (U_{8t} (U_{6t} (Q_{1t}, Q_{2t}), Q_{3t}), U_{7t}(Q_{4t}, Q_{5t})).$$

This in turn implies a simple diagram of the form of Figure 3.2 could be used
to optimize U_9 as follows.

Our 'consumer' could first associate Figure 3.2 with $i = 1$ and $j = 2$, ice
cream and chocolate sauce. For various values of X_{kt} illustrated by X_{kt}^i, X_{kt}^{ii}
and X_{kt}^{iii} on Figure 3.2, the consumer would select the preferred combination,
defining a locus of optimal combinations as indicated. Implicit in this diagram
are indifference curves tangential to the X_{kt} lines, but the consumer need
simply address the question would he or she wish to move to the left and up
or to the right and down on each X_{kt} line, with direct explicit implications for
Q_{it} and Q_{jt} tradeoffs.

Our consumer would next associate Figure 3.2 with $i = 6$ and $j = 3$, ice cream
+ chocolate sauce and nuts. The process would be the same, apart from the
need to define Q_{6t} via the combination of Q_{1t} and Q_{2t} fixed by the locus on the
first graph. Our consumer could next associate Figure 3.2 with $i = 4$ and

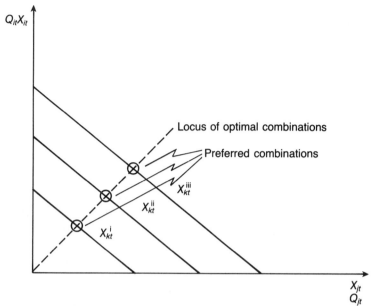

Figure 3.2 A graph for commodity selection.

$j = 5$, oranges and apples, as for $i = 1$ and $j = 2$. Finally, our consumer could associate Figure 3.2 with $i = 8$ and $j = 7$, ice cream + chocolate sauce + nuts and oranges + apples. In this last case a fixed budget, X_{9t}, would determine X_{7t} and X_{8t}, which would in turn determine X_{6t}, X_{5t}, X_{4t}, X_{3t}, X_{2t} and X_{1t}.

The process is akin to dynamic programming (DP), with a weaker form of separability than that used for DP, in a graphical form, with no need to formally define U_{9t}, the subfunctions of U_{9t}, or the associated indifference curves. The separability used for DP would not allow a lack of separability within each pair, being of the form

$$U_t(U_{1t}(Q_{1t}), U_{2t}(Q_{2t}), U_{3t}(Q_{3t}), U_{4t}(Q_{4t})\ U_{5t}(Q_{5t})).$$

This implies any ordering of the commodities would be appropriate – there is nothing special about the relationships implied by structure of Figure 3.1.

In what sense is the restrictive nature of the separability which allows this pair wise approach important?

Our consumer has to choose a preferred ice cream and chocolate sauce combination without explicit reference to how many nuts might be consumed, although he or she might have in their mind's eye a given combination for a 'sundae' (ice cream and chocolate sauce and nuts), only considering additional nuts to be eaten on their own when allocating X_{8t}. Further, the combination of oranges and apples chosen should not affect the combination of ice cream, chocolate and nuts, or visa-versa, which suggests oranges and apples are not eaten as part of the 'sundae', or with nuts. But the consumption pattern for all commodities in the previous period could be considered as a basis of decisions this period, making only the marginal changes assuming separability: F_{kt} may become functions of $Q_{1t-1} \ldots Q_{nt-1}$. Alternatively, the decision process could be repeated iteratively to eliminate the lag, each successive iteration reducing the marginal dependence on separability. Hence, these limitations are negligible. At a fairly nominal cost in terms of restrictions the consumer has an efficient solution procedure with very useful implications for associated demand equation systems.

How does this relate to selecting a portfolio of securities?

Say our consumer was interested in investing in five companies, each selling one of five commodities: ice cream, chocolate sauce, nuts, oranges or apples. Assume our consumer was prepared to consider only the expected value at the horizon of current investment and associated variance, via a basic Markowitz mean-variance model, apart from using the separability structure implied by the tree of Figure 3.1. In such a case the equivalent of Figure 3.2 is Figure 3.3, where i and j are ordered such that $E_{it} < E_{jt}$.

Figure 3.3 displays three special characteristics.

1. Investing the whole of X_{kt} in investment j will maximize expected return, since $E_{it} < E_{jt}$, defining a linear maximum expected return boundary along the X_{jt} axis.

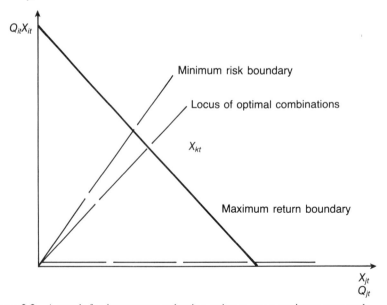

Figure 3.3 A graph for investment selection using a mean variance approach.

2. A linear minimum risk boundary exists as shown: any solution below this boundary is risk efficient, any solution above it is risk inefficient, in variance = risk terms; see Chapman (1974) for a formal derivation in slightly different form.
3. A linear locus of optimal combinations exists as shown, defined by the optimal V_{kt}^2 to E_{kt} tradeoff. The derivation in Chapman (1974) noted above is easily modified to give this result.

If the consumer had appropriate estimates for E_{it}, E_{jt}, V_{it}^2, V_{jt}^2, V_{ijt}^2 and the E_{kt} to V_{kt}^2 tradeoff, these loci could be solved for directly without recourse to bottom up or top down procedures, following Chapman (1974). Sufficient conditions (Chapman, 1974) for such an approach in terms of the restrictions imposed by the separability structure are

$$V_{63t}^2 = V_{13t}^2 = V_{23t}^2,$$

and

$$V_{87t}^2 = V_{14t}^2 = V_{24t}^2 = V_{34t}^2 = V_{15t}^2 = V_{25t}^2 = V_{35t}^2 :$$

there is nothing special about the covariance between the nut company and either the ice cream or the chocolate sauce company; and there is nothing special about the covariance between either of the fruit companies (oranges and apples) and any of the other three companies. However, note that these conditions imply some common covariances, and allow other covariances to be unique. This is very much weaker in the sense of being less restrictive than simplifications analogous to the separability used for DP or conventional Beta analysis which require all covariances to be zero.

If the consumer did not have estimates of E_{it}, E_{jt}, V_{it}^2, V_{jt}^2 V_{ijt}^2 and the V_{kt}^2 to E_{kt} tradeoff, the approach of Figure 3.2 could be used, which involves estimating these parameters. If the latter approach were adopted, less restrictive assumptions than those adopted for the mean-variance model could be used, including measures of risk which go beyond variance or any other single decision criteria, and beyond other additional criteria, like the stance of the organization on equal opportunity or environmental issues. Such criteria could be measurable and measured or not. If they were measured, tables indicating the tradeoffs associated with movement along X_{kt} lines could be provided to assist with the assessment of an appropriate combination of X_{it} and X_{jt}. The only essential requirement is the need to choose $X_{it} X_{jt}$ combinations on a few X_{kt} lines to define the loci within each pair.

SUGGESTED OPERATIONAL APPROACH

A suggested operational approach for a stock broking firm is outlined in the following steps:

1. Ask the management of the brokerage firm to draw up a pairing structure analogous to that of Figure 3.1 for the potential investments of interest for the firm's own portfolio. The basis could be purely intuitive. If there is no obvious basis for some subsets, the choice could be arbitrary. Senior management could start the definition at the top, and pass the task on to lower level managers in relation to their areas of responsibility.

2. Using a top down approach, starting with the most senior management, define a set of target ratios using the managers or management teams responsible, with associated bounds for each pair, for a week or some other relatively long time period, as indicated in Figure 3.4.

    Targets and bounds may be based on an intuitive view of what is appropriate given uncertainty about the coming week. Minimum return bounds and maximum risk bounds may differ in form: for example, parallel with the target line. No bounds may be appropriate at lower levels.

3. Define a set of linear constraints which represent all the minimum return and maximum risk bounds associated with step 2. Add to these constraints any other relevant constraints, in a linear form. For example, if the firm is a market-maker minimal holdings may be appropriate for most securities. Use all these constraints to construct a linear programming (LP) model, where the object function to maximize is

$$E_t = \sum_{i=1}^{n} E_{it} X_{it},$$

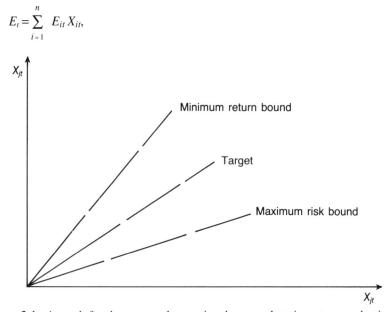

Figure 3.4 A graph for the proposed operational approach to investment selection.

where E_t and E_{it} are defined as for the QP model discussed in the second section, but i distinguishes between securities held and securities not held, and associated E_{it} include transaction costs. This implies a set of linear constraints reflecting current holdings.

4. Elicit estimates of E_{it}, $i = 1 \ldots n$, from the traders or managers responsible for actual buy and sell operation. Do so in an automated form appropriate to each decision maker. For example, one may deal with securities normally purchased for a period of months, another may deal in currency transactions with a planning horizon of minutes, and both may wish to relate a current price to a price at the appropriate horizon.

5. Use the LP model to identify desirable trades which are feasible with respect to the constraint set. Communicate these trades to the responsible dealer or manager, ordered by expected additional return if the trade is made, to assist prioritizing, as there may not be enough time to implement all desired trades before circumstances change. Store this advice, the E_{it} which gave rise to it, transactions actually made, and actual prices associated with the E_{it}. The LP model could be used in a partitioned manner. For example, each trader could have his own model running within his own work station optimizing within a nominal maximum investment for that trader, with higher level models considering redefinitions of these nominal budgets.

6. Use the LP solution discussed in step 5 to identify risk constraints with exceptionally large shadow prices. In an appropriate form, formulate a communication about these shadow prices to the manager or management team responsible for the constraint. For example, one manager may prefer this information in the form 'the LP model suggests a 10% relaxation of your maximum risk constraint on i and j should yield an x per cent increase in return over the next day – would you like to relax this constraint, or talk to Messrs X and Y whose estimates are critical?' Messrs X and Y might be warned, giving them an opportunity to reconsider their estimates, before sending the communication. Messages to managers of this kind could be ordered in terms of their expected contribution to return if the constraint revision is made to assist with prioritization. Store all such advice, and associated revised E_i.

7. Use the data acquired by this process to assist traders and managers at all levels to refine their judgements. For example: traders could be given feedback on their bias with respect to E_{it} estimates; associated variances and covariances could be used to test the assumptions associated with the pairing structure in terms of covariance patterns; managers could be given feedback on any apparent significant inconsistencies in the risk-return balance position for different aspects of their responsibilities.

8. Once the feedback in step 7 has allowed the process to stabilize, use the data acquired by this process to refine the intuitive basis of the model. For example, a QP model which used no constraints on the variance structure could be compared to a QP model using the constraints implicit in the pairing structure and both sets of results compared with decisions actually taken to assess relative predicted and actual performance. This could form the basis of a background research programme concerned with assessing the benefits of simplifying assumptions in relation to their costs, with a view to moving towards a better choice of simplifications, retaining complexity whenever doing so was worthwhile.

9. At this stage a 'what-if' service might be provided, to allow research into the likely effects of major events.

10. At this stage a tracking and prediction research function might be established, to provide feed-forward to all involved decision takers.

11. Once the process is stabilized and confidence is established via steps 7, 8, 9 and 10, the process might be used as a basis for performance assessment and related payments. For example, senior managers could be given feedback on significant discrepancies in the return and risk-return balance positions of lower level managers, who in turn could receive feed-back on traders' performance.

12. At this stage a related range of services for investors using the brokerage firm might be developed and marketed. Investors with no expertise might be sold an investment comparable to a unit trust. Investors who wish to estimate their own E_{it}, use their own V^2 and define their own constraints might buy services comparable to those provided to the brokerage firm's traders and management. There is a range of intermediate possibilities.

A wide range of additions or revisions to this approach is feasible. For example, debt might be considered. However, the steps just outlined should indicate the flavour of possibilities and the nature of the process. Partioned LP models specified in an intuitively acceptable transparent manner provide fast local decision guidance, the associated shadow prices are an important basis for communication, and the associated data gathering process provides a rich basis for feedback, feed-up, feed-down, feed-forward and performance assessment. Optimizing portfolio management is approached indirectly via a direct attempt to optimize the financial control process recognizing the importance of communication between people and the need for real-time decisions.

Not all the 'means' or features of financial control cited by Ezzamel (this volume) are embedded in the process just described. But most are. Certainly the focus is consistent with their broad definition of the concerns of financial control. In particular, it shares the concern for efficient forms of information transfer.

CONCLUSIONS AND IMPLICATIONS

The separability framework discussed in the third section was presented in relation to portfolio decisions in a slightly different form more than fifteen years ago (Chapman, 1974). Lack of implementation could be explained in a number of ways, but the authors believe a failure to associate it with the wider objectives of the second section is the key.

An appreciation of the importance of the wider objectives of the second section was developed by the authors primarily through experience with the management of risk related to large engineering projects' timetables, costs, performance, technical choices and associated contractual issues: for example, see Chapman (1990) and Ward, Curtis and Chapman (1989). In these areas the authors can claim a significant number of successful implementations.

Most people do not see project planning as portfolio management. Certainly the Markowitz mean-variance model has no direct operational role. However, project planning in a high risk environment is about the allocation of resources to a set of tasks which must be achieved where significant uncertainty is involved as to what the tasks should be, how they should be done, and what the implications are in time, cost and performance terms. Moreover, the inter-dependencies (covariances) ignored by simple PERT type approaches are of vital importance. Further, the issues and their relationships are so complex an approach employing separability is essential, gradually building up under-standing via partial analysis.

If the wider perspective discussed in the second section is relevant to port-folio management for a brokerage firm and the management of large engin-eering project risk, it clearly must have some relevance in other portfolio management contexts.

For example, marketing management can be viewed as a portfolio manage-ment situation, with associated pricing, promotion and production decisions involving correlated risks. A pair wise separability approach to such situations is attractive even without the risk issues: for example, see Chapman and Ward (1987). It is not difficult to visualize the operation of an approach to marketing management analogous to that of the fourth section, with brand managers assessing the impact of price and promotion changes, LP models optimizing production planning within constraints on price and promotion changes dic-tated by higher level management, related data acquisition, communication, feedback and feed-forward. Perhaps the key differences are the irreversibilities and lags associated with pricing and promotion decisions.

One of Ken Hilton's major concerns was the management of universities and associated financial control issues, as clearly indicated in his inaugural address republished in part in this volume. The allocation of budgets, buildings and student quotas by a university to faculties, schools or departments is a portfolio management problem in the general sense. Multiple criteria, many non-measurable, are important. Non-linearities analogous to E_{it} which are a function of X_{it} are important: give a department more resource and it may produce more research, but the rate of increase will not remain constant as more and more resource is applied. Lags and irreversible processes are important: give a department less resource and it may not be affected much for several years, after which the damage may be very expensive to repair. Politics and prejudice are important: A thinks B's discipline is less important, and vice versa, with similar differences between A and C . . . Z, so the decision taking processes used to attempt to achieve a reasonable and fair outcome are complex if not tedious. It would be a brave if not foolish person who attempted to implement an approach analogous to that of the fourth section in a university, but there are clear analogies, and a clear role for separability in such a process.

It is always dangerous to look for problems with a particular model or solution in mind. However, a set of issues of current concern to the first author of this paper suggest the framework discussed here may well prove of practical value. In any event the context is different enough to illustrate the nature of modifications necessary to adapt to different contexts.

These issues are concerned with the choice of type and timing of investment in sources of electric power by the Province of Ontario, Canada, for the next twenty-five years. The broad choice of balance between hydro, nuclear, coal fired and gas fired, the utility and non-utility (private) generation balance, and the balance between meeting demand and reducing or retiming (managing) demand are portfolio choice problems.

The issues are very complex. For example, the expected cost per kw hour of electricity from sources like non-utility co-generation are an increasing function of the amount required, while nuclear power expected cost per kw hour might be anticipated to decline as a function of the amount provided if a common design was used for all plant.

The current proposals, subject to an extensive review and enquiry (Ontario Hydro, 1990), for all practical purposes ignore risk, recommending nuclear power for the majority of all new base load, about ten 880 megawatt CANDU units in three stations, the exact number depending upon load growth.

The initial need, as the first author perceives it, is a simple demonstration of the benefits of reducing the economic risk faced by Ontario's population of a very high proportion of nuclear power in their energy portfolio. The proposed approach to this will use simple discrete probability tree/decision tree models to provide a simple enumerative comparison of example risk efficient portfolios, as discussed in Papers 13 and 22 of Chapman, Cooper and Page (1987). Avoiding the 'academic' flavour of this paper will be essential.

Assuming this initial need is met in a convincing manner, this will generate a need to suggest how Ontario Hydro might implement, or have imposed upon it, a suitable control system which will reflect an appropriate social view of economic and other risks. This will require recognition of the need to consider multiple objectives, provide information feedback and yield suitable incentives in an appropriate mechanism of control: the essence of financial control as discussed by Ken Hilton in his inaugural address (see also Hilton, this volume). This task will also require a simple clear exposition. However, most of the issues addressed earlier will need attention here, and the underlying framework can be used indirectly, if not directly. For example, the Ontario government might choose a set of target proportions for nuclear and non-nuclear utility power, and for demand met by more power and demand managed away, to be reviewed at five year intervals. The government might put bounds on those targets to give Ontario Hydro room to manoeuvre when dealing with shorter term decisions to bring new plant on and retire or mothball existing plant. The Department of the Environment might play the required decision support role, including, for example, auditing Ontario Hydro cost estimates and cost out-turns to assess associate risk and bias. Other roles may also be necessary, because different organizations are involved. For example, a government department may have to play a game-keeper role in terms of setting the price paid to non-utility generators by Ontario Hydro, and managing the conservation or demand management programme. The organizational issue are important and complex. For example, one conservation group associated with the review process enquiry is arguing for privatization, not for the reasons associated with CEGB privatization in the UK, but on the grounds that this should drive up prices and restrict nuclear development with the resultant (desired) effect of encouraging conservation.

REFERENCES

Brown, A. and Deaton, A. (1972) Models of consumer behaviour, *Economic Journal*, **82**, 1145–1236.

Chapman, C.B. (1974) Modular portfolio selection: an introduction, in *Portfolio Analysis: Book of Readings* (ed. J.P. Dickinson) Saxon House/Lexington Books, Farnborough.

Chapman, C.B. (1975) *Modular Decision Analysis: An Introduction in the Context of a Theoretical Basis for Consumer Demand Analysis*, Saxon House/Lexington Books, Farnborough.

Chapman, C.B. (1990) A risk engineering approach to project risk management, *International Journal of Project Management*, **8**(1), 5–16.

Chapman, C.B., Cooper, D.F. and Page M.J. (1987) *Management for Engineers*, John Wiley and Sons, Chichester.

Chapman, C.B. and Ward S.C. (1987) Modular decision analysis -a production scheduling illustration, *Journal of the Operational Research Society*, **38**(9), 803–14.

Hadley, G. (1964) *Nonlinear and Dynamic Programming*, Addison Wesley, Reading, Massachusetts.

Joyce, J.M. and Vogel, R.C. (1970) The uncertainty in risk – is variance unambiguous?, *Journal of Finance*, **25**, 127–32.

Markowitz, H. (1959) *Portfolio Selection: Efficient Diversification of Investments*, John Wiley, New York.

Ontario Hydro (1990) *Providing the Balance of Power: Ontario Hydro's Plan to Serve Customers Electricity Needs – Demand/Supply Plan Report*.

Pearce, I.F. (1964) *A Contribution to Demand Analysis*, Oxford University Press, Oxford.

Sharpe, W.F. (1963) A simplified model for portfolio analysis, *Management Science*, **9**(2), 277–93.

Wallingford, B.A. (1967) A survey and comparison of portfolio selection models, *Journal of Financial and Quantitative Analysis*, 85–106.

Ward S.C., Curtis, B. and Chapman, C.B. (1989) Roles, Responsibilities and Risks in Management Contracting. Report to the SERC on contract GR/E/48343, available from the authors, publication by CIRIA forthcoming.

Financial control of portfolio management decisions: Discussant's comments

CHRIS BURKE

In putting forward comments on Chapman's and Ward's paper (1992) I am very conscious of Ken Hilton's own highly personal discussant and seminar style. While appearing as often as not to have slept through an author's exposition of the work, he would nevertheless be first into the fray with questions that cut straight to the heart and purpose of the piece. Yet he always left speakers with a sense that there was value in what they had thus far accomplished and of his own continuing interest in what they might yet achieve. Chris Chapman and Steve Ward will have experienced this process on many occasions and indeed Ken Hilton will have commented on the genesis of this paper during his long and happy association with Chris Chapman. I am sure that the points I will make do not cut to the heart of the matter but I hope that I can at least emulate Ken by offering a positive note.

In their paper Chapman and Ward focus on two principal tasks:

1. A computationally efficient means of re-balancing a portfolio in accord with a target risk/return objective.
2. A computer-based decision support system to enable operationalization of their portfolio management method.

My discussion is focused on only the first of these tasks. Indeed even more narrowly than that, on the consequence of the particular modelling constraints established by the authors, and not at all on the computational feasibilty of the model. This even though it is the latter factor that prompted them to adapt the nested pair wise separability approach.

In the literature of finance, but not that of economics, the approach they advance is novel. However, the development of their model in a portfolio context can be graphically illustrated using the framework employed by Sharpe (1964, 1970) in his similar aim of reducing the computational complexity of the Markowitz (1952, 1959) mean-variance model. I draw parallels with Sharpe's work because of its central place in finance orthodoxy and because of its familiarity to those interested in portfolio models. I hope by recasting the Chapman–Ward model in this manner to make clear my concerns over the constraint definitions and the need for clarification of the direction (top down or bottom up) of the decision path used in their paper.

Consider a redrawn version of Figure 3.3, 'A Graph for Investment Selection using a Mean-Variance Approach'. In their figure the authors establish two boundaries; minimum risk and maximum return. Figure 3.5 below redrafts the original two asset Figure 3.3, now with return and risk measured on the axes. We can see from the Chapman–Ward discussion that their model, as outlined, does not allow for short sales and it therefore permits us to graph a simple efficient frontier. It has only one feasible minimum risk position and only one feasible maximum return position. The latter resulting from the investment of all the investor's initial capital endowment in the single asset offering the highest return. Chapman and Ward now seek to place the investment combi-

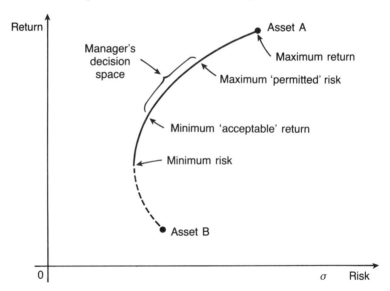

Figure 3.5 Operationalized Chapman–Ward mean-variance investment selection model.

nation somewhere between these two points in a manner that is consistent with investor/fund manager preferences. As shown in their Figure 3.4, further (subjective) constraints, e.g. minimum return and maximum risk, can be introduced to limit the decision space. I am not sure though that they actually achieve a place on the efficient frontier, nor indeed that such a simple single objective is truly what their model allows us to contemplate.

Where there are more than two assets available in which to invest, the efficient frontier is the result of determining risk/return efficent portfolios of assets. The frontier is efficient in the sense of meeting the 'minimum risk for any given return' objective noted by Chapman and Ward in the second section of their paper. To achieve this curvilinear shape of frontier the underlying assets should satisfy the requirement of being less than perfectly positively correlated one with another. At this point in order to determine which particular combination of assets will be held it is usual to introduce a positive return, risk free asset and thereby derive a unique (market) portfolio;[1] one in which all investors seek to place their capital, either entirely, or in combination with positive or negative holdings of the risk free asset. The opportunity set is very effectively extended by the introduction of the risk free asset and the positioning of a portfolio along the resulting 'capital market line' is then a simple matter of investor preference. There is no one particular combination of the market portfolio and risk free asset that is universally superior to any of the others. Minimum return and maximum risk boundaries can be brought into play as in the Chapman–Ward model to limit the decision space.

In a similar way the predominate theme of Chapman and Ward, is to move in risk/return space to an efficient point consistent with investor preferences. It is not clear to me that the Chapman–Ward model as specified necessarily achieves this, as I will outline below. However, it compensates by permitting a more complex investment decision to be considered through bringing aspects of investment other than risk and return directly into focus by incorporating these factors as constraints when allocating funds between any given pair, e.g. requiring a minimum holding for a market maker, or, giving a preference to the securities of 'green' companies.

Let us now consider in more detail how Chapman and Ward intend a decision maker to move towards the efficient frontier. The authors do not need to follow the familiar path of distinguishing between riskless and risky assets. They employ their paired approach, enabling the fund manager to make a series of funds allocations between paired assets. The procedure as they outline its operation in the fourth section of their paper, could start with a top down (possibly fairly arbitrary) allocation of funds into some broad category of investment, with lower managers making similar allocations. At these lower levels the decision to strike a balance of investment between a pair of individual assets is made in real time simultaneously with numerous similar decisions which collectively determine the balance of the portfolio. If the process is graphed using the axes risk and return, and assuming less than perfect positive correlation between any paired choice, we can build a picture as shown by the example in Figure 3.6 below:

In Figure 3.6 there are four assets, A, B, C and D, and constructed therefrom are three portfolios, AB, CD, and ABCD. As illustrated we have a world in which there are only four assets. For each pair of assets there is a subjectively restricted decision space, here shown as a solid line. The decision path leads to a specific portfolio combination, ABCD, that lies below the efficient frontier (here denoted by the dashed line). My concern is that the decision process moving from the bottom up does not obviously lead inexorably to the efficient frontier, unless restrictive assumptions concerning the assets' covariances are introduced. This is because a decision that is consistent with preferences at one level may be found to be sub-optimal when combined with decisions made independently at the same level. To limit this problem a more highly specified top down process than that envisaged by Chapman and Ward could be followed, but this then has the danger of becoming prescriptive, particularly if there are multiple objectives to be met, and of not affording individual managers the involvement that the authors seek to give them.

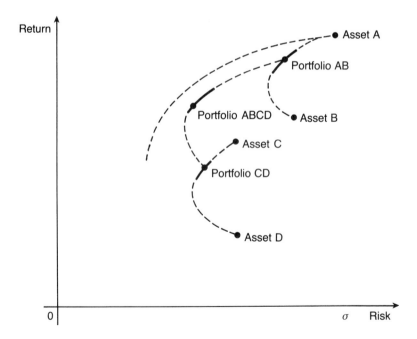

Figure 3.6 Aggregate portfolio selection using the Chapman–Ward model.

If my reading of the Chapman–Ward model is correct, it breaks from that notion of efficiency conventional in portfolio analysis and offers instead a means of pursuing a more complex target. This being the case should we expect this target to rest on the efficient frontier, in fact would anything less be acceptable when assessing managerial competence? There are really two ways to answer this question:

First at its simplest the answer is that if we speak only in terms of risk/return constraints imposed on individual managers, then it is likely that these impositions will deny the full range of possible asset combinations and thereby, as illustrated in Figure 3.6 leave the aggregate portfolio below the efficient frontier.

Second, slightly more complex is the answer that acknowledges that given their model permits the incorporation of constraints that are of themselves not defined in risk/return terms, it is to be expected that the resultant decision may not be risk/return efficient. Nevertheless, the programming support outlined in the latter half of their paper allows for managers, through shadow prices, to reflect on the consequences of any additional and binding constraint on return (as the suggested goal is return maximization) and on risk (through a review of shadow prices). It is an attempt to move more directly than does Sharpe to match a complex version of an investor's preference function directly to risky asset selection.

This it seems to me offers an opportunity to conclude on the positive note I promised at the start of this discussion. The Sharpe model is familiar to portfolio students and in placing the Chapman–Ward model alongside it I have sought to determine whether the latter affords new insights rather than computational gains. I think that in its capacity to incorporate additional constraints and to determine the risk and/or return consequences of such constraints, if any, the model allows a richer set of decisions to be addressed. In addition it enables a fund manager's performance to judged against more than one criterion.

Finally, I agree with the authors that while the resource allocation process between assets is analogous to resource allocations between university faculties and departments 'it would be a brave if not foolish person who attempted to implement' the model. I have given some thought to how it might work and finally admitted defeat. Still, these decisions have to be made and those of us who worked with Ken usually knocked on his door at such times and he would close his eyes and let us talk.

NOTE

[1] The market portfolio is effectively a holding of all the assets traded in the market, each weighted by its individual value relative to the value of the market as a whole. Readers will know that the diversification effect can be largely captured with a more narrowly based holding of securities.

REFERENCES

Chapman, C.B. and S.C. Ward (1992) Financial Control of Portfolio Management Decisions, in *Perspectives on Financial Control: Essays in Memory of Kenneth Hilton* (eds M.A. Ezzamel and D. Heathfield).

Markowitz, H. (1952) Portfolio Selection, *Journal of Finance*, March, 77–91.

Markowitz, H. (1959) *Portfolio Theory: Efficient Diversification of Investments*, John Wiley and Sons, New York.

Sharpe, W.F. (1964) Capital Asset Prices: A Theory of Market Equilibrium under Conditions of Risk, *Journal of Finance*, September, 425–42.

Sharpe, W.F. (1970) *Portfolio Theory and Capital Markets*, McGraw-Hill, New York.

4

*The management of working capital in multi-plant firms**

ALAN HAMLIN and DAVID HEATHFIELD

INTRODUCTION

Ken Hilton's early work as an economist with NEDO and subsequently at the University of Southampton included an examination of the inventory behaviour of the UK manufacturing sector. He was later to extend this work to international comparisons of stock/output ratios and to address the thorny problems of determining inventory behaviour when aggregating over several product lines (Hilton, 1968, 1974, 1976). Much of the work in this area concentrates on determining the optimum stocks of finished goods and of raw materials and fuels, either in terms of the 'transactions' and 'speculative' demands for inventories, or in terms of production smoothing models. There is also a growing literature on alternative methods of financing working capital. Ken's later work focused on aspects of managerial control, and on mechanisms by which such control could be exercised within organizations. Our intention in this paper is to attempt to bring together these two sets of concerns and discuss the implications for managerial control of recognizing the working capital dimension of the production process.

* An earlier draft of this paper was presented at a conference in honour of Kenneth Hilton, University of Southampton, 24–26 April 1991. We acknowledge the helpful comments of our discussant, Charles Sutcliffe, and other conference participants.

Perspectives on Financial Control: Essays in memory of Kenneth Hilton.
Edited by Mahmoud Ezzamel and David Heathfield.
Published in 1992 by Chapman & Hall, London. ISBN 0 412 40980 1.

However, in this paper we are concerned neither with financing issues nor with problems associated with stocks of finished goods and raw materials, we are concerned here solely with the remaining element of working capital – work-in-progress. Not only do we concentrate on this one aspect of working capital, we also ignore the transactions, precautionary and smoothing motives for holding stocks of work-in-progress. Our purpose is to focus on those issues which arise when we recognize the obvious but sometimes neglected fact that production takes time. Thus, even without storage and delivery costs it is always necessary to hold some work-in-progress and, therefore, some working capital.

We may distinguish two aspects of the time dimension of production; time as an element of costs and time as a productive factor. If we were concerned only with the former we might proceed by dating all inputs – so that a unit of labour employed today is identified as a different input, with a different price, from a unit of labour employed yesterday. With this expanded set of inputs the inter-temporal theory of production is formally analogous to the atemporal theory (see, for example, Hicks, 1946; Malinvaud, 1961). However, the complexity of dealing with such an expanded set of inputs will not commend itself to the more practical mind. The introduction of time as a directly productive factor requires still further modification of the standard approach since time itself (in the sense of elapsed) must now enter the production function alongside the time dated inputs. Nevertheless, it is possible to model decisions about production time as one of the choice variables of a profit maximizing firm, and we have presented such a model in Hamlin and Heathfield (1991) (other relevant aspects of the time dimension of production are discussed in Hamlin and Heathfield (1983, 1984) and references therein). The introduction of time also raises a number of interesting general equilibrium questions concerning the determination of the rate of interest and the rate of profit, but consideration of these would take us too far from our present purpose (see Pearce, 1970, appendix to Chapter 15)

It is our intention in this paper to present a simple model that includes both the cost and the productive aspect of the time dimension of production in order to analyse the case of a multi-plant, multi-shift firm, and to examine the consequences for the management of working capital in such firms.

A central point here is that even having stripped away all unnecessary detail, any model of the firm sufficiently rich to capture the necessity of working capital is already too complex to allow of simple conclusions concerning the appropriate managerial response to changes in the external environment. The economist may be happy to conclude that everything depends on everything else in a manner that is critically dependent on the precise details of the production function; but this is unlikely to be a satisfactory conclusion to the manager who needs to make decisions without detailed information on the production function and, equally important, to install a decision making process that will function well in a range of circumstances without necessarily being optimal in any of those circumstances.

By a decision making process here we mean an algorithm or set of rules which can be laid down to decentralize the management of the enterprise as a whole. Such a set of decentralizing rules might take the form of specifying the location of responsibility for decision making for each of a series of variables (overtime working, investment, etc.) and specifying the broad rules by which such decisions should be made (Ezzamel and Hilton, 1980). Again, the economist may typically think of all decisions being made simultaneously by a single agent, but the realities of management are different.

The structure of the remainder of the paper is as follows. The next section sketches the basic outline of the model and, in particular, the temporal structure of production. The third section then introduces fixed capital and the potential trade-off between fixed and working capital in the decision making of a multi-plant firm. This section also sketches the distinction between batch production and continuous flow production and points to a slight ambiguity in the measurement of working capital in the case of continuous flow producers.

The model developed in the second and third sections and, despite its simplicity, offers no direct guidance to managers. The fourth section then considers the possibility of generating reasonably robust managerial rules which capture the essence of the model. Such rules are presented and justified. Essentially, we argue that it is reasonable to separate decision making on the different aspects of working capital, and on the employment of factors more generally. And that such a separation points to some results which are not otherwise obvious. The final section contains some concluding comments.

A SIMPLE MODEL

In order to focus purely on the need for working capital deriving from the time structure of production, the simple model to be examined in this section will abstract from all other types of work-in-progress and stocks. Thus, we will assume that all finished goods are sold immediately, and that there are no physical stocks of either raw materials or work-in-progress. These last conditions will be met by the simple, if extreme, expedient of modelling a production process with labour as the only input so that there are literally no raw materials or unfinished goods (the introduction of raw materials does not affect the results of the analysis, see Hamlin and Healthfield, 1991). This device also sharpens the distinction between working capital and fixed capital. There is no fixed capital in the simple model of this section (it will be introduced in

67

the next section), but the necessity of working capital derives from the assumption that labour must be paid in advance of the receipt of sales revenue. In short, working capital is required to finance a wage fund.

Although labour is the only input in this first, illustrative model, labour is not itself a simple input. Rather, we separately identify three dimensions of labour. First, the number of workers present at a moment in time, which we term the crew size and denote L. Second rate of utilization of those workers, which may be thought of as the fraction of the day for which L workers (not necessarily the same L workers) are present. This variable we denote S. Third, the total period of time that elapses between workers arriving and output being produced, that is the duration of the production process in, say, days. This variable we denote T. The total amount of labour time involved in the production process is then LST. The production function then relates these three dimensions of labour input to the level of output:

$$N = f(L, S, T). \tag{1}$$

Where N is the size of the batch of output. This function will reflect the fact that while the number of workers present (L) and the duration of their presence (ST) are substitutes, they are not perfect substitutes so that, for example, increased speed can only be achieved by a more than proportional increase in L.

The total cost of producing a batch of N units of output by this technology is given by:

$$C = W_S LST(1 + r)^T. \tag{2}$$

Where W_S represents the average wage rate incurred when operating at the utilization rate S. The idea here is to model the fact, commonly known as a shift working premium, that the average cost of labour increases with the utilization rate of labour. Note that this utilization premium is not necessarily equivalent to an overtime premium; we are concerned with the proportion of the day that is worked rather than the hours worked by particular workers. Since all workers are assumed to be paid the same wage regardless of which shift they work, there will be no incentive to employ different numbers of workers on each shift. This indicates a possible extension to the model that would allow discussion of the introduction of unmanned shifts in some advanced manufacturing systems in Japan (Shah, 1983).

However, we shall simply specify:

$$W_S = g(S)$$

with $g' > 0$, and $g'' < 0$.

The $(1 + r)^T$ term in equation (2) indicates that wage payments are made in advance and so must be grossed up at the rate of interest (r) over the produc-

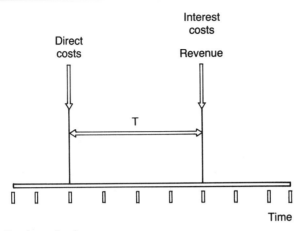

Figure 4.1 Batch production.

tion period (T). The simple time structure of batch production is summarized in Figure 4.1.

This discussion of the costs of the firm also allows the identification of the first of two possible meanings of working capital. That is the maximum indebtedness of the firm, which measures the financial resources which must be available to the firm if it is to meet its cash flow obligations. A second interpretation of working capital will be discussed in the next section when considering continuous flow, rather than batch, production. Given the structure of payments assumed here, it is clear that the firm must borrow its full cost, excluding interest costs. Essentially, the firm borrows its wage bill, and then repays this debt, plus interest, out of revenues T periods later. So the maximum indebtedness (I) of the firm is simply:

$$I = W_S LST. \tag{3}$$

We can now specify the profit maximization problem facing this firm when the output price (P) is parametric:

$$\max (NP - C) = NP - W_S LST(1 + r)^T, \tag{4}$$

by the choice of L, S and T subject to (1).

The first order conditions for this problem are:

$$Pf_L - W_S ST(1 + r)^T = 0 \tag{5}$$

$$Pf_S - LT(1 + r)^T (W_S + SW_S') = 0 \tag{6}$$

$$Pf_T - W_S LS(1 + r)^T (1 + T \log(1 + r)) = 0. \tag{7}$$

Manipulation of these first order conditions yields:

$$T = \left(\frac{Tf_T}{Lf_L} - 1 \right) \frac{1}{\log(1+r)} \tag{8}$$

$$S = \left(\frac{Sf_S}{Lf_L} - 1 \right) \frac{W_S}{W_S'} . \tag{9}$$

These two equations may be interpreted as follows. Equation (8) indicates that the optimal duration of the production process depends on the rate of interest, and on the properties of the production function – in particular the relative 'shares' of time and crew size at the equilibrium (in the notation of the model, the 'share' of time is Tf_T, and similarly for the other factors). So that, as one would expect, the higher is the rate of interest, the shorter is the production process. Equation (8) also shows that $Tf_T > Lf_L$ is necessary for $T > 0$. This restriction is natural, since, if it were not true, one could always substitute men for time and so save the interest element of the cost of labour – essentially one could avoid the need for working capital by producing output instantaneously. This restriction, then, embodies the idea that time is a cost effective input, and not merely a technically productive one.

Equation (9) then identifies S – the optimal rate of utilization of labour – in a similar manner. Essentially, S is determined by balancing the marginal cost of additional utilization (ie the 'shift premium' W_S') and the marginal benefit in terms of the productivity of utilization. Again, it is clear from (9) that $Sf_S > Lf_L$ is necessary for $S > 0$, since this condition embodies the idea that utilization is a cost effective input.

An important part of this story is that although S and T both relate to the time dimension of employment, the economic factors determining their optimal values are very different. A change in the rate of interest will have a direct impact on the duration of the production process, but no such direct impact on the rate of utilization; similarly, a change in the 'shift premium' will have a direct impact on utilization, but not on the duration of the production process. Of course, there may be indirect effects. In the case of an increase in the interest rate the direct effect, as we have already seen, will be a reduction in duration. If output is to be held constant, this will require an increase in employment; how this increase is divided between L and S then depends upon the properties of the production function as summarized in equations (8) and (9) above and, in particular, on the properties of the relative 'shares' of the three dimensions of labour input. This distinction between direct and indirect impacts will be a theme of the following discussion.

This simple model introduces some of the basic mechanisms at work in any consideration of the time dimension of production and, hence, in any consideration of working capital. It also points to a way forward to the analysis of more complex and realistic models. But in order to consider the multiplant firm, we need to introduce fixed capital. Each 'plant' may be considered as a block of fixed capital with certain capacity constraints and limited possibilities for capital – labour substitution. Thus the decision on the number of plants and on capital utilization will be intimately connected with the decisions already modelled in our simple model with no plants. The analysis of such a model is the subject of the next section.

MULTI-PLANT FIRMS

In introducing fixed capital and the possibility of multi-plant working into our simple model we wish to preserve as many features of the original model as possible while illustrating the potential trade off between fixed and working capital that is vital to our concerns. We model a plant simply as a block of fixed capital, so that the number of plants (k) is also a measure of the capital stock. Each plant is then manned by a crew of l workers, so that total employment is lk. The wage structure, utilization rate and duration of production are all as before. So, a firm produces output N according to the production function:

$$N = f(l, S, T, k). \tag{10}$$

Each 'batch' of output N is delivered to the market, and sold, at a point in time. To retain direct comparability with the simple model of the previous section we shall, for the moment, focus on the production of a single batch of output – we shall return to the case of continuous production below.

The cost structure of the firm is basically unchanged. Labour must be paid at the beginning of the production cycle, and there is now a rental cost of capital of q per plant per unit time. This cost must also be paid at the beginning of the cycle. We continue with the case of the maximization of the level of profits, but notice that the introduction of fixed capital would allow us to reformulate the firm's objective as the maximization of the rate of return on capital, as suggested by Pearce and Gabor (1958), For investigation of this and other maximands see Hamlin and Heathfield (1983). The *ex ante* maximization problem facing the firm is then:

$$\max(NP - C) = NP - (W_S \, Slk + qk)T(1 + r)^T \tag{11}$$

by choice of l, k, S and T and subject to (10).

The first order conditions for this problem are:

$$Pf_l - W_S STk(1 + r)^T = 0 \tag{12}$$

$$Pf_S - lkT(W_S + SW_S')(1 + r)^T = 0 \tag{13}$$

$$Pf_T - (W_S Sl + q)k(1 + r)^T (1 + T \log (1 + r)) = 0 \tag{14}$$

$$Pf_k - (W_S Sl + q)T(1 + r)^T = 0. \tag{15}$$

Manipulation of these conditions yields;

$$S = \left(\frac{Sf_s}{lf_l} - 1\right)\frac{W_S}{W_S'}, \tag{16}$$

which is identical to (9) in the case of the simple model, with l replacing L.

As before, then, the optimal rate of utilization of labour, and therefore also of capital, is determined by direct reference to the balance between the relative efficiency of more workers (l) and more intensive use of existing workers (S) on the one hand, and the elasticity of the wage rate with respect to utilization on the other hand. This result clearly reflects our assumption that the plant or capital costs (q) do not vary with the rate of utilization. It is straightforward to show that if $q = q(S)$ then the result equivalent to (16) is:

$$S = \left(\frac{Sf_s}{lf_l} - 1\right)\frac{W_S}{W_S'} - \frac{q_s'}{W_S'l}. \tag{16a}$$

So that, in this slightly more general case, the optimal rate of utilization is adjusted to allow for the impact of the cost of capital. However, for the remainder of this paper we shall return to the simpler case in which q is fixed.

The first order conditions also yield:

$$T = \left(\frac{Tf_T}{kf_k} - 1\right)\frac{1}{\log(1 + r)} \tag{17}$$

$$l = \left(\frac{(lf_l)^2}{(kf_k - lf_l)(S_s - lf_l)}\right)\frac{qW_S}{W_S'}. \tag{18}$$

Comparing equations (17) and (8) reveals that the incorporation of plant/capital in the model changes the time structure of production only to the extent that the 'share' of capital now enters in place of the 'share' of crew size. The duration of the production cycle still depends only on the interest rate and the structure of the production function, but now it is the relative productivity of time and capital that is significant. As before, this imposes a restriction on the model of $Tf_T > kf_k$, since, if this were not true, time would not be cost effective relative to capital.

Equation (18) then gives us a solution for crew size that depends on the wage function, the rental cost of capital, and the 'shares' of crew size, capital and utilization. Notice again that this equation places a restriction on the model; in this case, $kf_k > lf_l$. We may summarize the restrictions as:

$$Tf_T > kf_k > lf_l \quad \text{and} \quad Sf_s > lf_l. \tag{19}$$

The relationship between crew size and the wage rate in (18) is straightforward, although it should be remembered that we are concerned with crew size rather than total employment. The relationship with the rental cost of capital simply reflects the standard idea that capital will be more intensively 'utilized' as its rental price increases – although the increased 'utilization' here occurs through increased crew size rather than longer hours of operation.

Equations (16)–(19), together with the production function (10), completely characterizes the firm's *ex ante* optimum. But the characterization is by no means simple, even in this very simplified model. The optimal level of each of the variable inputs – the number of plants and the three dimensions of the labour input – depend directly or indirectly on all prices and the level of output and the detailed specification of the production function. This is a point that will be the focus of attention in the next section. But first we must deal with two further aspects of the model – the distinction between batch and flow production, and the distinction between short and long run decision making.

So far we have been concerned with the production of a single batch of output. In this simple context we have already noted that the working capital requirement of the firm is essentially the full cost of production (net of interest costs) since, on our assumptions, all of these costs must be paid at the outset. Thus the working capital requirement, is simply the maximum indebtedness of the batch firm as given by:

$$I = (W_S Sl + q)kT . \tag{20}$$

Clearly, given our focus on the time delay in production, batch production is a rather extreme case. We therefore wish to indicate that the extension to the case of steady state continuous flow production (in which the firm has cash flows – both receipts and payments – in each period) is straightforward. The structure of continuous flow production is illustrated in Figure 4.2.

The output of the firm is now N per period. But in order to produce at this flow rate the firm must essentially operate T batch lines side by side, with each at a different stage of production. Thus the firm must start a new batch of N each period in order to ensure a steady state flow of N units of output per period. On the same assumptions concerning the timing of payments as before, the firm must, therefore borrow sufficient funds to start T lines of production before any revenues accrue. Thus the maximum indebtedness of the flow production firm is simply:

$$I = (W_S Sl + q)kT^2. \tag{21}$$

And the flow producer can be seen as being simply T batch producers phased through time, with total employment given by lkT and the total number of plants given by kT.

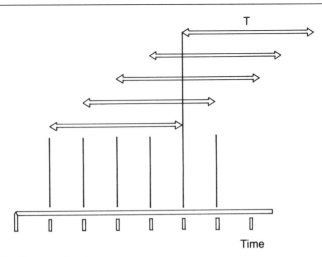

Figure 4.2 Flow production.

Thus all the discussion of the batch producer carries over directly to the case of the flow producer. However, the case of flow production also raises a second possible meaning for working capital – a cost centred meaning rather than a debt centred meaning. In steady state, expenditure in each period is given by the direct cost of starting a new line, plus the interest cost owing on the debt falling due. Together these clearly amount to the full cost of each line:

$$C = (W_S Sl + q)kT(1 + r)^T. \tag{22}$$

Alternatively, we may analyse the firm's costs per period in steady state into two components – the direct costs associated with labour and fixed capital, and the cost of servicing working capital (R) for one period:

$$C^* = (W_S Sl + q)kT + rR. \tag{23}$$

Clearly, in steady state, C and C^* must be equal, so that:

$$R = (W_S Sl + q)kT\left(\frac{(1 + r)^T - 1}{r}\right). \tag{24}$$

The comparison between (24) and (21) indicates that $R > I$ if $T > 1$, (and vice versa) so that the two interpretations of working capital coincide only when the duration of the production process and, therefore, the number of overlapping lines of production is exactly one. Whether the debt based figure (I) or the cost based figure (R) is the more appropriate measure of the concept of working capital will depend upon the purpose in hand.

We should also note a potential confusion between a plant and a line of production. We use 'plant' to indicate a unit of installed capital, whereas a 'line of production' is a group of plants operating on a particular time pattern. Thus a batch producer may have many plants but has only one line, whereas a flow producer must have sufficient lines (T) to ensure continuous production where each line may contain many plants.

Finally, we should emphasize that the discussion of this section has been concerned with the long run or *ex ante* planning decision faced by firms. Once capital is installed, and we move to consider the *ex post*, or short run, adjustment problem as firms attempt to accommodate changes in prices or demand with fixed capital, we return to the setting of the previous section. Thus, for example, once the manager has determined his plan along the lines discussed above, and installed the relevant capital, he must operate within the constraint of a short run production function as in equation (1). But here again there is a slight distinction between the batch producer and the flow producer.

The batch producer is straightforward. Installed capital is a fixed factor, and a short run production function defined on the variable factors is unambiguous in interpretation. But in the case of the flow producer, the installed capital, while fixed in total, retains a degree of flexibility in its allocation across lines of production. To put the point another way, the total number of plants is fixed but the number of lines is not. Total installed capital, in the case of a flow producer, is $k^* T^*$, where * denotes an *ex ante* chosen value. This quantity of capital may be re-allocated in response to changing conditions subject to the constraint:

$$kT \leq k^*T^*$$

So, the capital stock of each line of production, may be varied *ex post* only if variation in the number of lines offsets such variation. But the number of lines is also the duration of the production process. The forces at work here may be illustrated with a simple example. Suppose that the interest rate increases, what response is available to the flow producer in the short run? We have already seen that the principal direct effect of an increase in the interest rate is to reduce the planned duration of the production process. This in turn reduces the number of lines required to produce any given flow of output, so that the existing installed capital can be redistributed into fewer lines, each with more capital then before. Crew size and utilization can then be adjusted to produce the desired output on each line given k and T.

MANAGERIAL AND FINANCIAL CONTROL

The discussion to this point has been very much that of the economist concerned with the nature of the optimal (profit maximizing) allocation of resources in production. In this section, we turn attention to some of the issues raised by the need to design managerial and financial rules that may be expected to implement policies which approximate optimality in an environment that is more recognizably practical.

The essential point here concerns the distinction between the direct effects of prices on the factor employments and the indirect effects that work through changes in the factor 'shares' (recall that a factor's 'share' is the quantity of that input multiplied by its marginal product, Tf_T for example). It is clear that, in general, both the size and the sign of these indirect effects will vary with detailed variations in the specification of the underlying production function. For example, consider equation (16) repeated here for convenience:

$$S = \left(\frac{Sf_s}{lf_l} - 1 \right) \frac{W_S}{W_S'}.$$
(16)

The manager wishes to know how the choice of S should respond to changes in the underlying prices, but this is obscure in (16). A change in the interest rate will affect the choice of S to the extent that it determines the Sf_s and/or lf_l, but even the sign of the impact on the ratio of these shares is unclear since it depends on the elasticity of substitution between l and S in the production function. Thus, in the absence of detailed and accurate estimates of the parameters of the production function the manager is left with little guidance.

However, reasonably robust rules of thumb are available. We will consider two cases. The first concerns decisions of scale – that is the decision to expand

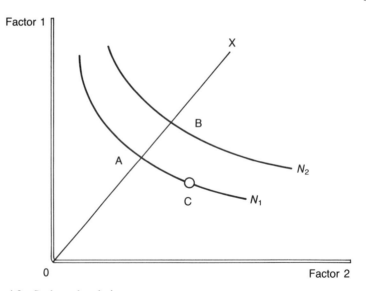

Figure 4.3 Scale and technique.

or contract output in the face of unchanged costs but some relevant shift in demand. The second concerns decisions of technology, that is decisions to alter the technology used to produce a given output as a result of a change in relative factor prices. These cases are illustrated in Figure 4.3 for the case of two factors of production. A decision of scale relates to a movement along a ray, such as the movement from A to B, expanding output from N_1 to N_2, while a decision of technology relates to a movement around an isoquant, such as the movement from A to C.

We will discuss decisions of scale first, and concentrate initially on the long run or *ex ante* management problem before considering the short run. Decisions of scale involve a movement along a ray such as OX in Figure 4.3. As a matter of definition homothetic production functions are those for which the ratio of 'shares' of any two factors is constant along any ray from the origin. Homotheticity of production functions has considerable empirical support, so that the assumption of homotheticity may be seen as a reasonable approximation. For homothetic production functions, equations (16), (17) and (18) simplify, respectively, to:

$$S = \frac{\alpha W_S}{W_S'} \tag{25}$$

$$T = \frac{\beta}{\log(1+r)} \tag{26}$$

$$l = \frac{\gamma q W_S}{W_S'}. \tag{27}$$

Where α, β and γ are positive constants. In this case, then, it is clear that l, S and T are independent of scale, so that the appropriate *ex ante* policy is to vary scale simply by expanding or contracting k. In other words, if the production function is homothetic, the optimal policy is to vary scale simply by replicating (or closing) plants, without varying the factor mix within plants.

While this rule is exactly optimal only for homothetic production functions, it may be seen as a managerial rule that may be appropriate in the absence of detailed information on the production function. Of course, the 'appropriateness' of the rule is essentially an empirical matter – relative shares may change in either direction along a ray, and so some change in factor mix may be appropriate, but in the absence of fairly detailed estimates of the production function it is not possible to identify the relevant direction of change, still less the extent of that change. Under these conditions a rule that offers simplicity without imposing an extreme assumption is clearly attractive.

This rule of relying on changes in k is clearly not applicable in the short run, since the short run is defined by reference to the fixity of k. But, reconsideration of equations (8) and (9) above indicates that the assumption of homotheticity implies that, even in the short run, T and S are independent of scale. So, in the short run decisions of scale involve only a scaling of crew size with no change in either the time duration of production or the rate of utilization of labour and installed capital. In the long run, however, crew size should be returned to its initial level and the change of scale should be accommodated by an appropriate scaling of the number of plants.

This rule of thumb is remarkable in that it suggests, for example, that even in the short run when installed capital is fixed, increases in output should not be produced by increased utilization – overtime working or the move to a two shift system – but by hiring more workers. Only in the very short run, when both installed capital and crew size are fixed, does the relevant managerial implement changes in scale via changes in the utilization rate with T held fixed.

We can think of this discussion as establishing a hierarchy of managerial responses to a desire for changes in the scale of operation. The immediate response is made in terms of utilization. But this is also the most costly response. In the medium term (when employment levels are variable but capital is fixed) it is appropriate to vary crew size and return the rate of utilization to its original level determined by the marginal cost of increased utilization. In the long run, installed capital should be adjusted so as to allow a return to the original manning and utilization levels. As we have seen, this hierarchy, with each step made up of clear and easily implemented policies suitable for managerial implementation, is optimal under a homothetic production function, but can be justified as an approximate managerial strategy when no detailed information on the production function is available.

We now turn to the case of decisions of technology. Here the problem is to respond appropriately, in both the short and long run, to a change in relative factor prices by changing the factor mix around an isoquant. As in the case of decisions of scale, we may begin by considering a special case – the Cobb-Douglas production function. The Cobb-Douglas function is a special case of a homothetic production function which involves constant factor shares both along rays (since it is a homothetic function) and around isoquants. Although the assumption of Cobb-Douglas technology is more restrictive than the assumption of homotheticity, it is still broadly consistent with a wide range of empirical experience, and can be seen as a sensible first approximation to an unknown production function.

In the Cobb-Douglas case, then, the simplified equations (25)–(27) apply everywhere, so that, in the long run, we have a separation of decision making in which T, the duration of the production process, responds only to the interest rate, S, the rate of utilization, responds only to the wage function, and l, crew size, responds only to the wage function and the rental cost of capital. The number of plants, k, then adjusts for scale, so as to keep to the same isoquant. An example may help. Let the interest rate increase, S and l should remain unchanged while T should be reduced (both the duration of the production process and the number of lines of production in the case of a flow producer). If k were left unchanged this would, in general imply a change in the rate of output, and so k must adjust if output is to stay constant.

As before, this separation of decisions is optimal only for the case of Cobb-Douglas technology, but it may form the basis of a more general managerial rule under uncertainty. Essentially, it amounts to an assumption of a constant and unitary elasticity of substitution between factors and can again be seen as a reasonable assumption in the absence of precise information on the production function.

In the short run equations (8) and (9) simplify to show that T depends only on the rate of interest and S depends only on the wage function, so that again we have a separation of decisions with crew size playing the role of compensating for other changes in order to hold output constant. Thus, to return to the earlier example, an increase in the rate of interest would reduce T, leaving S unchanged, and l could then be increased to hold output constant.

Clearly the Cobb-Douglas case is more restrictive than the homothetic case, but the resulting managerial rule of thumb is correspondingly more powerful. Homotheticity provides the basis for the hierarchy of decision making in respect of the scale of operation, but the Cobb-Douglas case provides a basis for a separability in decision making that extends to both matters of scale and matters of technology.

In short, accepting the Cobb-Douglas approximation allows managers to adopt simple and enforceable rules indicating which factors – including the three dimensions of labour taken separately – should be adjusted in response to any given change in factor or product prices. Such a set of rules is a necessary condition for decentralized management since, if all decisions are intimately inter-related (as is the case in general) they must all be made simultaneously.

Of course, a set of rules may be a necessary condition for effective decentralized management without the implication that any set of rules will do. We have argued that the structure of working capital in multi-plant firms is such that the particular set of rules outlined here form an appealing basis for decentralized management in the absence of detailed information concerning the production function.

CONCLUSION

Time is both costly and productive. The simple facts that production takes time, and that payments and receipts of income are not co-ordinated, is sufficient to generate a working capital requirement for firms. In this paper we have constructed a simple model that captures these aspects of the production process. The simplicity of the model is, however, more than just a pedagogic device. We are interested in the applicability of models to management; and it is clear that even the simple model developed here is too complex to provide the basis for a set of managerial rules that would allow of the decentralization of managerial control within the firm.

Further simplification is clearly required, and we have suggested particular simplifications which have the merit of delivering clear managerial rules without making extreme assumptions regarding the nature of the production process. These rules apply both to situations in which the scale of output is to be changed (perhaps in response to changes in demand), and to situations in which the technology of production is to be changed (perhaps in response to changes in relative factor prices). In each case the managerial rule of thumb identifies the variables which should react to any given change, and the appropriate direction of reaction. Thus each variable can be managed separately without the need for the simultaneous decision making that is optimal in principle but impossible in practice.

REFERENCES

Ezzamel, M. and Hilton, K. (1980) Can divisional discretion be measured?, *Journal of Business Finance and Accounting*, **7**(2), 311–29.

Hamlin, A.P. and Heathfield, D.F. (1983) Shiftwork and the choice of technique under alternative maximands, *Scandinavian Journal of Economics*, **85**, 283–94.

Hamlin, A.P. and Heathfield, D.F. (1984) Capital utilisation and investment in a mixed economy, *Recherches Economiques de Louvain*, **50**, 331–52.

Hamlin, A.P. and Heathfield, D.F. (1991) Competitive management and working capital, *Managerial and Decision Economics*, **12**, 207–17.

Hicks, J.R. (1946) *Value and Capital*, Oxford University Press, Oxford.

Hilton, K. (1969) The level of stocks in British manufacturing industry, *Applied Economics*, **1**(1), 17–36.

Hilton, K. and Cornelius, D.J. (1974) Planned stockholding: evidence from British company data, *Oxford Bulletin of Economics and Statistics*, **36**, 247–66.

Hilton, K. (1976) Inventory investment in *Topics in Applied Macroeconomics* (ed. D.F. Heathfield), Macmillan, London.

Malinvaud, E. (1961) The analogy between atemporal and intertemporal theories of resource allocation, *Review of Economic Studies*, **28**, 143–60.

Pearce, I.F. (1970) *International Trade*, Macmillan, London.

Pearce, I.F. and Gabor, A. (1958) The place of money capital in the theory of production, *Quarterly Journal of Economics*, **58**, 537–57.

Shah, R. (1983) Advanced manufacturing systems in Japan, *VDI International Magazine*, January, 103–10.

The management of working capital in multi-plant firms: Discussant's comments

CHARLES SUTCLIFFE

Research on working capital has been conducted from a number of different perspectives, and accountants have taken the lead in treating working capital as an important topic. Working capital can be defined using categories from the balance sheet as current assets less current liabilities, e.g. stock plus debtors and prepayments plus short term investments plus cash, less creditors, accruals and short term loans. Experience with bankruptcies and liquidations has taught accountants that overtrading, i.e. increasing sales above the level that can be supported by the available working capital, is an important cause of business failure. In consequence, businessmen usually consider working capital requirements as part of any new investment. Smith (1980) found that two-thirds of the firms he surveyed always included working capital in their capital budgeting procedures.

As well as viewing working capital in total as an investment that requires financing, accountants have also studied the individual components of working capital and how they can be controlled, e.g. cash budgets and ratio analysis. Many customers try to reduce their working capital requirements by delaying payment, and so credit control is seen as an important (possibly vital) aspect of a company's operations, while the introduction of just-in-time methods has reduced stocks and work in progress to a minimum. Management scientists have also become involved in optimizing company policy with respect to particular items of working capital. For example, the models for determining economic order quantities for materials, setting the size of cash discounts offered for prompt payment, choosing whether to take discounts for prompt payment, devising schemes for the investment of spare cash, analysis of the credit granting decision, treasury management, etc., Van Horne (1989).

Despite the obvious and considerable real world importance of working capital, economists have shown little interest. An exception is Vickers (1968, 1987), who showed that including working capital in the capital constraint of a firm does not alter the profit maximizing factor ratios, but does change the optimal values of the variables. Finance theorists have also shown little interest in working capital, even though it involves the features of risk and return. Cohn and Pringle (1980) have suggested that the limited analysis of working capital by finance theorists is because the assumption of perfect capital markets, which underlies many of the models used in finance (e.g. the capital asset pricing model), rules out working capital as an interesting problem. Only if there are market imperfections is liquidity of value. Thus, in the area of working capital, it appears that economic and finance theorists are lagging behind businessmen and the more applied disciplines of accounting and management science.

The paper by Hamlin and Heathfield (HH) has the admirable aim of trying to get away from the usual theoretical models of the firm built by economists. Such analysis generally treats the firm as a single decision making unit, and concludes that various sets of partial derivatives (whose numerical values are very difficult to estimate in practice) must be equated. Instead, this paper seeks to provide some simple decision rules for managers operating in a decentralized organization.

While time is clearly economically important in a world with non-zero capital and interest rates, the time required for production is usually not explicitly considered by economists. This is probably because they assume that, while the quantities of various inputs (e.g. labour and capital) can be varied, the time required for production is fixed. The paper by HH is welcome, in that it concentrates on the role of time in the production process, and incorporates production time as an endogenous variable. Economists have also largely ignored working capital. In the model developed by HH the main benefit from reducing production time is a reduction in the costs of financing the working capital. Hence, a strong link is established between the introduction of time and the introduction of working capital into the theory of the firm.

The paper by HH takes a very restricted view of working capital. It covers only the prepayment of wages, and so excludes debtors, short term investments, stocks of raw materials and finished goods, physical work in progress, cash, creditors and short term loans. While Hamlin and Heathfield (1991) show that the omission of raw materials does not affect the results, stocks of raw materials and finished goods are not included in the model used in Hamlin and Heathfield (1991). Much of the literature on the theory of the firm implicity assumes the manufacture of some product, e.g. the mythical widget. However, the assumptions used in this paper imply a rather strange production process in which the only inputs are labour and fixed capital; and the time required for production is non-trivial. I found it difficult to think of examples of manufacturing industries which meet these conditions, and could only come up with activities such as design, research, and software production. The model can be applied more easily to the production of services, e.g. training courses, medical services (such as psychiatry), legal services, auditing, etc.

While the production of services can meet the requirement for no variable inputs other than labour and take a non-trivial time period, the notion of work in progress in such cases may become problematic. This is because there might not be a well-defined moment when ownership of the 'output' is transferred to the customer. Often the service will be produced to the customer's specification, possibly in conjunction with the customer, e.g. psychiatry or training. In such situations there appears not to be any work in progress, although there may still be a need for working capital to finance prepayments for factor inputs, e.g. labour. Thus, while HH claim to be studying work in progress, it may be safer to interpret their work as dealing with prepayments.

HH make a number of powerful assumptions, some of which are implicit. These include the assumption that, for the multi-plant analysis, each plant is identical in all respects. It is also assumed that the number of workers present (L or l) can be varied, while the capital stock is fixed, i.e. the capital-labour ratio at a moment in time is variable. Similarly, if the number of production lines is reduced, it is assumed that the installed capital can be redistributed into fewer production lines, each with more capital than before. Thus, indivisibilities are assumed away. While it is a standard assumption of the neo-classical theory of the firm that the capital-labour ratio is continuously variable, the extent to which this ratio is actually variable in the short run is questionable.

A common, but unrealistic assumption made by HH is the absence of risk, (or that decision makers are risk neutral). They also assume that interest charges are the same (r) for paying the wages in advance and paying the rental charges at the end. The HH paper assumes that all wages are paid in advance, while the reality is that wages are paid in arrears. Of course, even if wages are paid in arrears, the producer may still have to pay out some wages before the product is sold, but the pattern of cash flows will be more complicated than is allowed.

An important assumption made by HH is that the average wage rate W_S is a function of labour utilization (S), while crew size (L or l) has no effect on the wage rate. This appears to be the only difference between labour utilization and crew size in the model, and so must be responsible for the conclusions which differentiate between S and L or l. These include the result that, in the short run, increases in output should be achieved by increasing crew size, not labour utilization; and the finding that T is a function of crew size (S) in equation (7), while in equation (17) T is a function of capital (k).

It is assumed by HH that interest is compounded each time period (possibly daily), but paid only at the end of the productive process, i.e. after T periods. This has implications for understanding the distinction which is drawn in this paper between two definitions of working capital: maximum indebtedness (I), and a cost-centred definition (R), where:-

$$I = (W_S Sl + q)kT^2 \qquad (21)$$

$$R = (W_S Sl + q)kT \left[\{(1 + r)^T - 1\}/r \right], \qquad (24)$$

and the terms are as defined in the paper. These two definitions differ unless $T = \{(1 + r)^T - 1\}/r$, which is only true when $T = 1$.

The reason for this difference between I and R is that the cost-centred definition (R) recognizes the interest charges at the end of each time period while, given the assumptions of the model, interest is not actually paid until the production process is complete; at which time interest must also be paid on the outstanding unpaid interest. This difference is related to the debate in accounting between recognizing an event when the payment is made (i.e. cash flow accounting) or when the legal liability is created (i.e. accrual accounting). In my view, given the assumptions of the model, the debt-based measure of working capital (I) is preferable as it allows for the need to pay interest on the interest. The cost-centred definition (R) could be revised to allow for the cost of interest on the interest, and then the two definitions would be identical. In which case equation (23) becomes

$$C^* = (W_S Sl + q)kT + \varphi R$$

where

$$\varphi = \left[\{(1 + r)^T - 1\}/T \right].$$

If $T = 1$, φ reduces to r. The term φ represents the arithmetic average interest rate per time period when allowance is made for the assumption that the interest rate is compound.

The equations derived by HH to give the optimal values of T, S and L or l (i.e. equations (8), (9), (16), (17) and (18)) have the property that the dependent variable is, in each case, a function of itself. This makes the task of solving these equations problematic.

This paper by HH makes two related contributions. One is the explicit consideration of production time as an endogenous variable, and this is associated with the introduction of working capital into the model. The second is the use of a number of powerful assumptions to devise simple decision rules for use by managers in a decentralized setting. The paper aims to open up a new area for study by economists (and finance theorists), by showing that the inclusion of working capital, even in a very limited way, can lead to interesting results.

REFERENCES

Cohn R.A. and Pringle J.J. (1980) Steps toward an integration of corporate financial theory, in *Readings on the Management of Working Capital*, 2nd edn, (ed. K.V. Smith), West Publishing Co., St Paul, pp. 35–41.

Hamlin, A.P. and Heathfield, D.F. (1991) Competitive management and working capital, in *Managerial and Decision Economics*, **12**, (3), June, 207–17.

Hamlin, A.P. and Heathfield, D.F. The management of working capital in multi-plant firms, (this volume).

Smith, K.V. On working capital as an investment by the firm, in *Readings on the Management of Working Capital*, 2nd edn, (ed. K.V. Smith), West Publishing Co, St Paul, pp. 609–24.

Van Horne, J.C. (1989) *Financial Management and Policy*, 8th edn, Prentice-Hall International, Englewood Cliffs.

Vickers, D. (1968) *The Theory of the Firm: Production, capital and finance*, McGraw-Hill, New York.

Vickers, D. (1987) *Money Capital in the Theory of the Firm: A preliminary analysis*, Cambridge University Press, Cambridge.

5

The use of data envelope analysis in measuring and diagnosing bank and building society branch performance*

JOHN CUBBIN

INTRODUCTION

In his inaugural lecture (see this volume), Kenneth Hilton referred to 'the doubling of output possible without technical progress in some industries merely by raising the level of efficiency in all firms to the current best practice firm'. There is a counterpart of this phenomenon within the firm – that is, raising the level of efficiency of all parts of the firm to that of the best-practice part.

Retail banks and building societies generate most of their business and incur most of their costs within their branch network system. The performance of this system is therefore a major element in determining profitability. All the clearing banks and the larger building societies have hundreds of branches and this is typically coupled with a highly centralized administration, which needs to make decisions about the branch location, closures, staffing levels, and

* I am very grateful to Stephen Rothwell, David Heathfield and participants in the conference in memory of Kenneth Hilton at the University of Southampton.

Perspectives on Financial Control: Essays in memory of Kenneth Hilton.
Edited by Mahmoud Ezzamel and David Heathfield.
Published in 1992 by Chapman & Hall, London. ISBN 0 412 40980 1.

reward systems, and which takes remedial action where particular branches are performing below their potential.

With hundreds of branches this is not an easy task. General attempts at improving performance – involving staff training, branch refurbishment, new product launches – are much easier to plan and implement within a centralized framework. However, the potential gains from bringing the worst-performing branches up to the level of the best-performing greatly exceed what any one of these general initiatives is likely to achieve. Figures of 25% or more in productivity gained for a region or system are not uncommon, judging from the results of calculations carried out for three deposit and loan institutions.

These gains roughly follow Pareto's law with 80% of the potential gains found in 20% of the branches. This means that improvement programmes targeted to this 20% will produce disproportionate gains. Data Envelopment Analysis (DEA) is a useful tool in helping to identify these branches. It uses data on resources employed and outputs generated to derive measures of comparative performance among the branches of an organization. Being multivariate, it avoids some of the difficulties of traditional ratio analysis, but it has weaknesses of its own which need to be understood properly in order to avoid drawing erroneous conclusions.

The origins of DEA can be found in an article published in 1957 by Michael Farrell. Although a number of applications building on Farrell's work were published by economists over the next 20 years the method only started to be widely employed after the publication of a paper by leading operations research academics (Charnes, Cooper, and Rhodes, 1979).[1] This led to its widespread use through the 1980s, with applications to military recruiting offices, schools, hospitals, electricity generating stations, fast food restaurants, university departments, and banks and building societies. Improvements were also introduced to relax some of the more restrictive assumptions implicit in the technique.

THE PRINCIPLES OF PERFORMANCE MEASUREMENT

Performance monitoring, which is one of the principle purposes of financial control, works to improve performance in the following major ways:

1. It allows management to identify the determinants of good performance. In the long run this leads to better decisions on such matters as the scale of branch operations, the input mix, and branch location policy.
2. By identifying the poorest performers, management can concentrate resources for improvement on those branches with the greatest unrealized potential (regardless of, for instance, *current* profitability.)

88

3. By fine tuning of the targeting and reward system the management can create better incentives for good performance. By contrast, a poorly-designed incentive system can create incentives towards efforts which may be counterproductive in the context of the whole organization.

Good performance is here defined in the context of the individual organization's goals. To be specific, if an organization uses scarce resources X to produce outputs Y, economic efficiency requires that the organization maximizes the surplus or profit $\mathbf{p}Y - \mathbf{c}X$. In a commercial context the vector $\mathbf{p}$ would be a set of output prices and $\mathbf{c}$ a set of unit factor costs. At the level where the branch operates $\mathbf{p}$ and $\mathbf{c}$ may involve transfer prices which are not fully known. Even where $\mathbf{p}$ and $\mathbf{c}$ are known and branch-level profit can be calculated there is still the problem of distinguishing actual from potential profitability.

In the public sector the valuations of different outputs may be controversial – as, for example in the case of kidney dialysis versus geriatric care in the National Health Service, and there may be reluctance to place explicit weightings on the outputs. Inputs may have scarcities not reflected in their market prices, and this creates further problems in measuring performance. The original appeal of DEA was that it seemed to offer a solution to this whole set of problems involving the valuation of inputs and outputs. As we argue below, this can be a dangerous assumption and may give rise to misleading assessments of relative performance. DEA does give estimates of the $\mathbf{p}$ and $\mathbf{c}$ implicit in each branch's operations, and these are used in the standard DEA measure of 'technical efficiency'. This measure ideally needs to be supplemented with other information, apart from the estimated $\mathbf{p}$ and $\mathbf{c}$ themselves.

THE NATURE OF DEA

By and large DEA operates in one of two modes – input shrinkage (or minimization) and output expansion (or maximization.) Figure 5.1 shows how DEA in the input minimization mode can use data on several inputs to produce a performance score that is independent of any imposed weighting system for the inputs. Branch D is producing the same amount (or less) of every output as branches A, B, and C. The fundamental assumption of DEA is that, if B and C are feasible then their linear combination E is also feasible. E is a radial contraction of D, using proportionately less of every input. The ratio OE/OD is the Farrell measure of technical efficiency. B and C are said to be the reference group for branch D.[2]

Figure 5.2 shows the equivalent measure in the output expansion mode. Branches I, J, and K are using the same (or less) of every input as branch G.

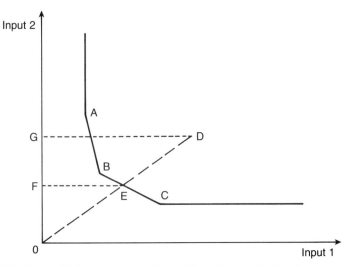

Figure 5.1 Input efficiency: a comparison of branches producing the same outputs. A, B and C are all technically efficient. B and C are the 'reference group' for unit D. Input efficiency for $D = OE/OD$.

I, J and K are regarded as technically efficient. The potential output vector for G is reckoned to be at H, the linear combination of I and J, which is a radial expansion of the point G. I and J are the reference group for G.[3]

With several hundred branches the number of potential reference group combinations is astronomical. DEA uses linear programming to achieve the calculation of these reference groups and the resultant performance scores. For example, suppose every branch uses one type of input, produces just one output, and has a certain market size. Then, in basic DEA the composite branch derived from the peer group or reference group for branch H have the following properties.[4]

1. They use no more of the input.
2. They produce no less of the output.
3. Their market environment is no more favourable.

Two standard *orientations* are typically adopted. The first ('input minimization') focuses on finding a peer group which uses less inputs. The second (output maximization) focuses on finding a peer group which produces more outputs. As the Appendix shows, different variations on the way these conditions are understood give rise to slightly different linear programming problems with different economic interpretations and give insights into different aspects of branch performance.

90

Table 5.1 shows an example of a report for a particular branch using software written by the author. This example assumes output maximization and constant returns to scale. Column (1) identifies the actual values of input used, outputs produced, and noncontrollable factors of the branch in question. Column (2) shows the weighted average of these variables for the peer group, etc. In one sense this can form the basis of a target for the branch and represents a point on the frontier such as H in Figure 5.2. The third column simply shows the ratio of column (2) to (1) (for inputs) or (1) to (2) (for outputs). This can be taken as a performance measure for the particular variable in question (OF/OG in Figure 5.1). The overall performance score is reported beneath the reference group comparison, along with some details of the reference group.

Data Envelope Analysis has, in some quarters, been promoted as a magical black box which solves all problems of performance measurement. Like all tools and like all measurement systems, DEA has its limitations, some of them are technical, others involve difficulties for implementation within an organization. The technical limitations are:

(a) technical efficiency is not the same as economic efficiency;
(b) DEA is sensitive to measurement errors; and
(c) the economic specification must be chosen carefully to reflect the objectives of the measurement exercise.

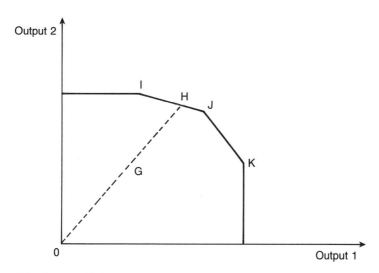

Figure 5.2 Output efficiency: a comparison of branches using the same inputs. I, J and K are all technically efficient. I and J are the reference group for unit G. Efficiency score of G = OG/OH.

Table 5.1 A basic report for Branch No. 234 Anytown

	Actual Ref. (1)	*Group* (2)	*Ratio* (3)
Resources			
Total com paid	86.33	84.50	0.98
Rent	23.10	23.10	1.00
Sales area	30.00	30.00	1.00
Tot staff	8.23	8.23	1.00
Production			
Gross Rec	14 868.52	23 429.49	0.63
Uncontrollable factors-additive			
Pop EFHJ	35.49	22.28	0.63
Tot competition	8.00	23.27	0.77
Uncontrollable factors-nonadditive			
Branch age	7.00	7.00	1.00
Unemployment (%)	7.00	7.00	1.00
Age closed a/c	3.19	3.23	0.99
Branch location	2.00	2.00	1.00
Performance score = 0.635			
Reference group branches			*Weight*
123 Firstown			0.2793
45 Secondplace			0.2689
678 Thirdville			0.2589
901 Fourthorpe			0.1704
234 Fiveborough			0.0614
567 Sixchester			0.0004
Relative scale			1.0392

These are examined in more detail below.

THE DIFFERENCE BETWEEN ECONOMIC AND TECHNICAL EFFICIENCY

Technical efficiency is a necessary, but not sufficient, condition for economic efficiency. In Figure 5.3 points A, B, and C, are all technically efficient but, given the relative price of inputs, A and C are higher-cost combinations which would become economically efficient only with substantial changes in relative input prices, (the ratio of the cost of A to the cost of B is called the *allocative* efficiency score for A). Indeed, a point like F, although it has a lower technical efficiency than A or C, is more economically efficient since its allocative efficiency outweighs its technical inefficiency.

Similarly, economic efficiency depends on the relative valuation of outputs. In Figure 5.4 A, B and C are all technically efficient but only B is economically efficient.

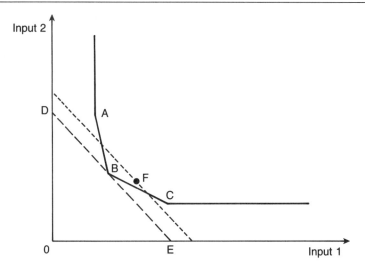

Figure 5.3 Input efficiency: a comparison of branches producing the same outputs. DE is the minimum attainable isocost line. Of the three technically efficient units only B is economically efficient. F is more economically efficient than A or C, though it is technically inefficient.

Indeed, as Farrell showed, a unit's overall efficiency can be broken down into its constituent parts since

Economic efficiency = allocative efficiency × technical efficiency

If data on relative prices are available this breakdown can be calculated using a series of DEA analyses. In Stage 1, costs and revenues (gross or net) are used as the inputs and outputs, and the noncontrollable factors are introduced in the normal way. This gives the overall measure of economic efficiency. In Stage 2, the physical inputs and outputs are introduced explicitly and this yields the measure of technical efficiency. Allocative efficiency is calculated by taking the ratio of these scores.

In practice the use of such exogenously determined prices (or variable weights) seems limited, the major reason being that DEA tends to be resorted to when some of the necessary weights are unobtainable, or when a shift in the ratios of inputs or of outputs is subject to constraints, so that the straight financial cost is not the same as the opportunity cost, which may be difficult to calculate. There may also be a presumption that allocative ineffi-ciency has been solved by other means, such as the use of standard ratios between different inputs. However, where exogenous prices are available, it is recommended that they are used so that a check on allocative efficiency can be made.

Technical efficiency itself can be broken into constituent parts. As we see in Figure 5.5:

Overall technical efficiency = pure technical efficiency × scale efficiency

By specifying both constant and variable returns one can get a breakdown of overall efficiency into 'technical' and 'scale' factors (see Banker, 1984). Overall technical efficiency (sometimes called technical and scale efficiency) is found by running a DEA model under the assumption of constant returns to scale. The pure technical efficiency component is found by running the same model under the assumption of variable returns, and scale efficiency is calculated by taking the ratio of these.

Input minimization (see Figure 5.5)

Technical and scale efficiency (CRS measure) $= \dfrac{GF}{GD} = S_1$

Technical efficiency (VRS measure) $= \dfrac{GE}{GD} = S_2$

Scale efficiency $= \dfrac{GF}{GD} \div \dfrac{GE}{GD} = \dfrac{GF}{GE} = \dfrac{S_1}{S_2}$

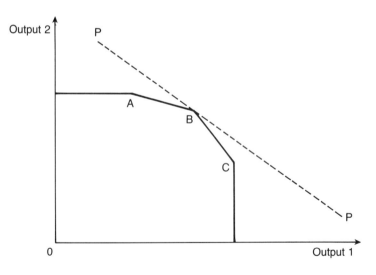

Figure 5.4 Output efficienty: a comparison of branches using the same inputs. Of the three technically efficient branches only B is economically efficient. PP is a line of equal value (e.g. revenue).

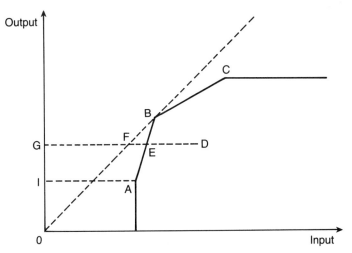

Figure 5.5 Technical and scale efficiency input minimization approach. A, B and C are technically efficient. Only B is technical and scale efficient. Scale efficiency of A = IH/IA. Ratios for D: Technical and Scale efficiency = GF/GD; Technical efficiency = GF/GD.

The measure obtained by the CCR (CRS) approach is based upon a scaling down of branch B to point F. The 'technical and scale efficiency score' is $S_1 = GE/GF$. The pure technical efficiency score is based upon A and B as the reference group producing a feasible point at E, so that $S_2 = GE/GD$. Finally, by taking the ratio $S_1/S_2 = S_3$ we obtain the degree of scale efficiency associated with the input level of D. S_3 will be less than one since the larger branch produces a greater ratio of output to input and is presumed to be at the most productive scale size (MPSS)[5]

The number of ways of breaking down economic performance into separate components is limited only by human ingenuity on the one hand and the needs of the situation on the other. For instance, to check whether the allocative inefficiency is on the input or output side is simply a matter of doing two separate sets of calculations. Input allocative efficiency should be calculated using the input minimization approach with and without a disaggregation of the cost elements into their physical components. Output allocative efficiency can best be calculated using the output maximization approach.

The disaggregation of performance in this way is intended to be more than simply an exercise in classification. In theory it should help a diagnosis of poor performance. If allocative efficiency is low it means that the wrong input combinations are being used or the wrong outputs produced. If scale efficiency is low it means that the unit is either too large or too small (and the scale indicator tells you which.)

95

For example, two branches may have identical overall scores but different breakdowns:

	Branch A	Branch B
Overall (economic) efficiency	0.504	0.504
of which:		
allocative	0.900	0.540
pure technical	0.800	0.933
scale	0.700	1.00
Scale indicator	0.500	1.00

Branch B's main problem is that it is using the wrong factor input combination (or possibly concentrating on unprofitable outputs). Branch A's main source of low efficiency appears to be its small size. The possible remedies to be considered are clearly different in the two cases. The full decomposition depends on a knowledge of relative valuations of outputs, or prices of inputs. In the absence of such prices it is advisable to carry out some disaggregated analysis to complement the overall measures. For example, building society branches can be analysed separately for their performance on deposits, mortgages, personal loans, etc., although this presents the danger of a super-abundance of measures familiar from ratio analysis.

Table 5.2 shows how the results of such multiple analyses can be presented in a compact form. This gives a profile of performance which identifies areas of strength and weakness. The only major drawback of the disaggregated analysis would seem to be that there can be no presumption that the implicit potential can be realized in all directions at once. On the other hand it might suggest priority areas for improvement in a more striking way than an aggre-

Table 5.2 Presentation of results of disaggregated outputs and other multiple runs

	No.	*ID number*	*Branch name*
	1	63	Sometown Northgate
	Score		
Description			
Gross receipts	1.000	********************************
Mortgages	0.706	*********************
Personal loans	0.447	*************
Average	0.718	+ + + + + + + + + + + + + +
	2	67	Elsewhere
Description			
Gross receipts	0.430	************
Mortgages	0.580	******************
Personal loans	0.427	************
Average	0.479	+ + + + + + + + + + +

gated analysis, and without the need for an explicit weighting of the different outputs.

SENSITIVITY TO MEASUREMENT ERRORS

DEA is really a sophisticated multivariate form of normalized performance ratio analysis. In the original Charnes, Cooper and Rhodes specification, the DEA measure is characterized as the maximum of a ratio of inputs (denoted by the vector Y) to inputs (denoted by the vector X):

$$\frac{vY}{uX}$$

subject to the normalization constraint that this ratio not exceed 1.00 for any other branch when the weight vectors v and u are applied to all other branches. In practice we tend to use the linear programming dual of CCR's formulation which produces the v and u as shadow prices rather than variables in their own right.[6] The measure of efficiency can thus be considered as a ratio of two ratios:

$$\frac{vY}{uX} \bigg/ \frac{vY^*}{uX^*}$$

where the * indicates values of Y and X for members of the reference group of the branch in question. Sources of measurement errors may therefore be:

(a) errors in X and Y;
(b) errors in X^* and Y^*;
(c) errors in the selection of the reference group; and
(d) errors in the selection of v and u.

Every system of measurement is limited by the accuracy of the raw data employed and DEA is no exception. A 1% error in X and Y will produce an error in X/Y of roughly 1.4% if X and Y are uncorrelated, less if they are positively correlated, and more if negatively correlated. A major component of any project involving DEA is therefore the validation of data to be used. This involves the analysis of outliers, the testing for consistency of alternative means of deriving the same information, checks for unexpected patterns in time series, and the carrying out of spot checks on individual items. Since DEA can be sensitive to errors in outliers, the initial runs of any model will normally be tested against prior expectations. Discrepancies may be due to an incomplete DEA model, to the limited power of unaided intuition, or to data errors. By looking at such cases in detail the initial model can be improved and many sources of data error can be tracked down. Whatever method of analysis is subsequently used it can be no better than the underlying data.

The need to ensure that the underlying data are accurate turns out to be a side benefit of DEA in some cases. In both public and private sector applications, databases which management had been using for decision making have been found to be: inadequate in coverage; using definitions sometimes not well understood; and highly variable in accuracy. This has forced a re-evaluation of which items to concentrate upon in order to derive meaningful performance measures, and a clearer understanding of the limitations of particular measures. In one case a major public body decided to completely overhaul its management information after a DEA study.

One frequently-mentioned benefit of regression analysis is that it 'allows' for measurement error, and that frontier econometric methods create a breakdown between measurement error and deviations due to performance. This is slightly misleading. It is true that the calculated equation relating expected output to inputs assumes errors *in the outputs*, but:

1. Errors in the inputs produce bias in the estimated equation.
2. There is no known way of separately identifying which part of a branch's deviation from the calculated equation is due to measurement error and which is due to efficiency differences.
3. Econometric 'frontier' methods of calculating seem to be sensitive to the assumptions made, not only about the functional form of the underlying equation, but also about the form of distribution of the 'errors'.

In the light of these considerations, a method which encourages data accuracy would seem to have much to recommend it. The old adage of 'garbage in, garbage out' applies equally to econometric results and data envelope analysis.

SCORES ONLY 'UNIQUE' FOR A GIVEN SPECIFICATION

The results are also sensitive to specification. By specification we mean not only constant or variable returns, but whether specific variables are included or not. Generally speaking, scores will be higher:

(a) when variable returns to scale are specified;
(b) when more variables are included; and
(c) when there are fewer other branches available for comparison.

This means that it is important to use the appropriate specification for the purpose in hand, and that a complete picture of the reasons for a particular level of performance might require several sets of analysis on the same branches. For example, by adopting a sequential approach one may use DEA to identify the reasons for poor raw or unadjusted performance.

In one study a sequential analysis was carried out with four output variables[7] after grouping the input and noncontrollable variables in the following way:

1. Group A – resources which represent a major item of cost to the building society. These are typically controllable at some level of the organization.
2. Group B – market factors describing the environment in which a particular branch operates. This may include the demographic breakdown and a measure of activity in the local market. These are only controllable in the sense that the society can, by opening and closing branches in different locations, affect branch market conditions. Normally these would be classified as noncontrollable inputs.
3. Group C – branch factors describing the internal appearance, location, etc. of the branch. These are typically noncontrollable in the sense that the local management may have no control over them, although regional and national management make decisions which affect them.
4. Group D – this is a miscellaneous collection of factors which are of perhaps dubious relevance to branch performance in actuality but may be possibly regarded as plausible reasons for poor performance on further investigation.

In Stage 1, only Group A variables are employed. This gives a datum point from which to measure the importance of the other factors. Branches which appear to be poor performers in Stage 1 are essentially those with consistently poor ratios of outputs to cost elements. The central question is whether this poor performance is remediable. Branches with a poor score on Stage 1 but a good score on Stage 2 (where group B factors are introduced) are those where the poor performance is attributable to a poor local environment – for example, a high proportion of poor quality older terraced housing, to use an ACORN classification. In such cases it may be worth considering closing down or relocating the branch, if the poor market potential of the area is expected to persist.

Branches which have a poor score on Stage 2 have a market potential higher than they are currently achieving. It then becomes desirable to identify the cause of the poor score. Stage 3 introduces the local branch conditions. If the score rises at this stage the branch has relatively unfavourable branch conditions which may be remediable. Detailed analysis of the report for the branch and further investigation may suggest practical ways of improving performance.

Branches which improve their scores at Stage 4 (introduction of Group D variables) are the most problematic. Here something beyond DEA is required to find out whether the newly-introduced factors are a plausible reason for low

Table 5.3 A sequential approach to specification the effect of varying the number of   input and noncontrollable variables

Group	No. of variables	No. of efficient branches	%	Gross advances	Further advances	Personal loans	Gross receipts
					Potential Increase (%)		
A	7	6	6.2	76	68	87	63
B	11	23	23.7	36	34	40	31
C	15	51	52.6	21	20	18	15
D	19	70	72.2	11	10	10	8

performance or simply a coincidence. The sensitivity analysis discussed below has a role to play here since it shows how much weight has been attached to each factor in arriving at the performance score.

Branches which remain low scorers even after the introduction of the Group D variables are those with a strong case to answer. By definition, it is a factor which has been left out of the DEA which is causing poor performance. Whether this is poor management practice or a new flyover being built outside the front door does need some investigation. In the absence of flyovers or other explanations, an improvement in branch management practices is the recommended course of action.

Table 5.3 summarizes the results for one set of ninety-seven branches. The variables included were the standard four output variables plus the following inputs:

    Group A: Total staff
                    Sales area
                    Notional rent of branch premises
    Group B: Population in ACORN[8] groups E, F, H, J
                    Households in ACORN groups E, H, I, J
                    Households in ACORN groups D and G
                    Average age of closed accounts (inverse indicator of
                    housing market activity)
    Group C: Branch inspection grade
                    Total number of competitors
                    Branch location quality indicator
                    Commission paid
    Group D: Percentage unemployment
                    Number of counselling pods
                    Number of automatic teller machines
                    Manager's length of service in branch

The allocation of the variables to categories was subsequently revised in later versions of the model. The level of unemployment was later reclassified to group B, for instance, following discussions with line management.

The first row of this table suggests an enormous potential for performance increase, of the order of 75%. Row 2, however, shows that much of this improvement would not be available because of the limited markets where many of the apparently poor performers are located. Once account is taken of market limitations the potential gains fall to around 35%. The seventeen branches which achieve a score of 1.00 only because of their poor catchment area could perhaps be reviewed with a view to closure or radical relocation. The twenty-eight branches which become 'efficient' only when account is taken of local branch factors need to be examined for ways to ameliorate poor siting or other facilities.

The '10% variation' column in the full report (see Table 5.5) can be checked to identify the key variables which are responsible for the high score. When such an analysis was carried out, Total competition was a key variable in twenty-five of the twenty-eight cases, Total commission in twenty cases. Branch location within the town was relevant in seventeen cases, but the inspection grade achieved emerged as relevant only in the case of fourteen branches. Subsequent discussion and clarification of the way the inspection grade was defined led to the dropping of this variable from the analysis.

Nineteen branches achieve a score of 1.00 with the addition of the Group D category of variable. Some of these variables should, with the benefit of hindsight, be classified with groups B and C. For example, percentage unemployment should probably be grouped with category B and the rest to C. The reason for putting these in Group D was that there was some doubt about their relevance as valid reasons for poor performance. The question of the best grouping of categories will be investigated further in Phase 4.

Even if the group D variables are accepted as valid reasons for poor performance this leaves twenty cases out of ninety-seven where, even taking account of fifteen input factors, the branch is performing poorly in comparison with other branches. These should be a priority for further investigation with a view to discovering and correcting the source(s) of the poor showing of these branches.

Given the sensitivity of performance scores to specification, the numerous possibilities can be confusing. When would one assume constant, and when varying, return to scale? This depends on whether one wishes to know S_1, S_2, or S_3. S_3 is obviously very useful in getting a fix on whether a branch is too large or too small *given its input mix and given its noncontrollable factors*. Such measures feed into decisions of a fairly long-term nature.

However, if one wishes to use DEA as a basis for setting performance targets – that is as part of a financial control system – the S_1 and S_3 measures are

Table 5.4 Sensitivity to specification

Specification		Branch F	Branch G	Branch H
1. Base model:				
Inputs:	Staff			
	Floor area			
Outputs:	Mortgages	0.35	0.35	0.40
	Loans			
	Deposits			
2. Add:	Catchment area characteristics	1.00	0.40	0.50
3. Add:	Local market activity	1.00	0.45	0.60
4. Add:	Branch location indicator	1.00	1.00	0.65
5. Add:	Variable returns to scale	1.00	1.00	1.00

possibly less relevant. If a manager is saddled with a branch that is too large or too small he cannot be expected to attain targets such as G, based upon extrapolations, unless the overall analysis shows that there are no systematic scale effects, or that they are small enough to be ignored or taken into account in an informal way. Table 5.4 shows sensitivity of score to specification for three branches.

Branch F's score improved substantially once we take into account the effect of the catchment area – for example, demographic measures based upon housing types, unemployment rates, and so on. Insofar as the variables that matter may be thought to be permanent to the catchment area it may be sensible to close down Branch F – although the decision should not be made on the basis of DEA alone.

For Branch G a small rise in score once local housing market activity is taken into account means two things. The base model peer group had a higher level of activity than Branch G and thus the raw score was being unfair to Branch G on this account. The new peer group will probably have the same activity level as G. A poor catchment area does not seem to be a valid excuse for G's low performance since the score does not rise once this is taken into account.

However, the score rises to 1.00 once we take into account branch location. This means that the previous peer group had a better branch location than G. Arguably the reason for G's poor performance is therefore its relatively poor location.

Branch G, therefore, needs not so much closing down but is potentially a candidate for relocating to a better spot. Since this can be expensive DEA should not be the sole basis of this decision. It might be that the branch is badly run as well as being in a poor location, the poor location is merely a factor that provides an excuse.

Branch H remains inefficient until a variable returns to scale assumption is incorporated. In this case DEA is suggesting that the branch is either too small or too large for the scale of its operations (the scale indicator shows which). H is thus a possible candidate for amalgamation (if too small) or splitting up (if too large).

The solution for the LP to each branch contains much diagnostic information and this can be presented in a form such as Table 5.5. For example, column (3) compares each variable for the branch with its value for the reference group.

Information on the sensitivity of a particular specification to changes in variables is contained in the simplex tableau associated with the solution to the LP programme and this can be incorporated into the report which is generated for each branch.

For output maximization, the overall score represents the best of the ratios for the outputs (for input minimization the overall score corresponds to the best of the input ratios). This illustrates the principle that DEA chooses its measure in a manner which shows the branch in the best possible light.

The outputs where the ratio is lower than the overall score are said to be 'in slack' because the constraints such as (2), (8) and (12) are not operating. As there is only one output in the example above this possibility cannot occur. Ratios of 1.00 for the inputs indicate a constraint which is binding and which therefore will have a nonzero shadow price, information on which is contained in column (6) of Table 5.5.

The shadow prices are contained in the simplex tableau which is used to solve the LP and can be used in two ways. The less interesting way is as an alternative method of calculating the performance score.

$$\mu = \frac{\Sigma \, V_i \, Y_i}{\Sigma \, U_i \, X_i}$$

This corresponds to the original Charnes, Cooper, and Rhodes way of presenting DEA, of which the approach presented here is the linear programming dual. In the case of output maximization $\Sigma \, V_i \, Y_i = 1.00$ and $\Sigma \, U_i \, X_i = 1/\mu$.[9]

A more interesting application is to make use of the notion that, under the assumptions implicit in DEA the U_i represent the marginal products of the inputs and the V_i represent the resource cost of the outputs. In production theory terms, the ratios of the U_i are isoquant slopes and the ratios of the V_i are slopes of the production frontier.

This information is useful in individual branches to indicate where savings can be made at little or no cost to output. By examining the scores for the

Table 5.5 Report for Branch No. 999 Someplace The Square

	Actual (1)	Ref. group (2)	Ratio (3)	Minimum (4)	Maximum (5)	10% change (6)
Resources						
Total com paid	137.25	137.25	1.00	127.16	150.72	− 0.0150
Rent	73.30	71.73	0.98	71.73	No limit	0.0000
Sales area	90.00	80.87	0.90	80.87	No limit	0.0000
Tot staff	30.50	30.50	1.00	28.60	31.14	− 0.1205
Production						
Gross Rec	55 483.32	72 332.13	0.77	0.00	72 323.13	0.1000
Uncontrollable factors-additive						
Pop EFHJ	89.73	49.99	0.56	49.99	No limit	0.0000
Tot competition	75.00	75.00	1.00	72.06	90.33	0.0052
Uncontrollable factors-nonadditive						
Branch Age	39.00	21.62	0.55	0.00	No limit	0.0000
Unemployment (%)	10.10	10.10	1.00	9.55	14.33	0.0215
Age closed a/c	4.63	4.63	1.00	4.53	4.85	0.0251
Branch location	3.00	3.00	1.00	2.84	3.10	0.0116
Performance score = 0.767						
Reference group branches						
345 Here			weight			
			0.6907			
678 There			0.6508			
987 Uptown			0.1458			
654 Downtown			0.0549			
321 Midtown			0.0124			
Relative scale			2.6066			

whole branch network, one can get a handle on the productivity of particular inputs, or the opportunity cost of generating outputs, or the extent to which noncontrollable factors limit performance. For example, suppose we find from the analysis of shadow prices that type A staff have the same marginal product as type B staff yet the employment costs of type B staff are 30% higher, it would make sense to investigate the practicality of substituting type A for type B personnel.[10] This is an indication of allocative inefficiency.

The shadow prices, or variable-weights are indicated in Table 5.5 in the '10% change' column. This shows the effect on efficiency measures of a 10% change in the value of the numerator or denominator of μ on the assumption of no change in the reference group. This '10%' formulation is chosen since the raw weights all have different dimensions and depend on the units of measurement of each variable, and are thus difficult to interpret.

Those variables that are currently 'in slack' have zero weights, since they would have no effect on the measured score. The 10% ratio column tells us which variables the branch would wish to emphasize to put itself in the best possible light.

Columns (4) and (5) (headed minimum and maximum) are the closest equivalent to *t* values familiar to users of regression analysis. Actually they are more like the confidence intervals that one might construct from '*t*' values. These are derived from the interior of the simplex tableau. In the same way as Wald-type statistical tests (such as Student's '*t*') they are derived from information available at the estimated point in parameter space. The upper and lower limit figures indicate by how much a variable would have to change before the slack associated with it entered or left the LP basis – which corresponds to the shadow price on the relevant constraint jumping between a zero or non-zero value (one obvious distinction for a confidence interval is that the range indicated here is open ended). A wide range before a variable's optimal weight (i.e. the shadow price corresponding to its constraint) jumps indicates the following:

(a) where a variable has a non-zero optimal weight this will still be important for a large change in the variable; and
(b) where a variable has a zero optimal weight the variable will still be treated as unimportant for a large change in the variable.

One distinction from regression analysis is that these sensitivities are calculated for each branch, since they differ from branch to branch. Variations of DEA exist which put lower and upper limitations on these variable weights. This is not difficult technically – the main difficulty is finding an appropriate basis on which to set these limitations. One effect of setting limits on the *U*s and *V*s is to reduce the number of branches which come out with a score of 1.00, since some people regard it as a difficulty when a large proportion of branches appear to be 'efficient'.

DEA has many other technical limitations – for example, the assumptions of convexity, strong disposability, and non-stochastic frontiers – and these may mean that sometimes DEA is not appropriate or needs further elaboration in particular circumstances. The fundamental need is to understand when these limitations are likely to lead to false deductions. Any project involving DEA needs to have built into it some mechanism for verifying the particular DEA model being applied, i.e. the carrying out of sensitivity analysis as a matter of course as part of the validation procedure.

PRACTICAL DIFFICULTIES

Some of the practical difficulties have already been touched upon – for example, the need to ensure accurate data. The choice of variables to be taken into account in deriving conditional performance scores is another major time consuming problem. However, the major practical difficulty is the transfer of the DEA technology to the organization making use of it.

The practical limitations are:

(a) several iterations will be required before the evolution to an acceptable DEA 'model' for the organization;
(b) the data requirements of DEA may necessitate an overhaul of the infor- mation available to management; and
(c) there can be major problems of acceptance of such a performance meas- urement system if the details are seen to be imposed from above.

The managerial literature on successfully implementing change in organiza- tions seems quite clear.[11] In addition to the inventor of ideas, five roles need to be filled:

1. The entrepreneur, with the flare to spot good opportunities.
2. The integrator, who can co-ordinate efforts.
3. The expert, to ensure it is technically correct.
4. The manager, who keeps things on track.
5. The change sponsor, who provides support from above.

One person can fulfil more than one of these roles, but not usually all of them. Typically the DEA entrepreneur is on the staff of the organization's headquar- ters with some responsibility for measuring performance, or (s)he may be in a planning or strategy function. The technical specialists in the headquarters may regard DEA as a sophisticated way of solving a perennial line manage- ment problem (for example, target setting). It is essential to keep expectations realistic – to spell out at an early stage that DEA is not a magic black box, but has important limitations, and that if the project is to succeed there must be understanding by those who are going to use it and acceptance by those who are going to be affected by it.

Understanding can be achieved by working as closely as possible with the ultimate operators of the DEA software. This is as important as providing good training and manuals. *Acceptance* depends upon consultation with representatives from branch management from the earliest stages of setting up a DEA model and through the process of validating the model(s) eventually to be used for performance assessment. This will not only ensure that criticisms are taken into account at an early stage but is also a valuable source of information and ideas on the correct specification to be used. The biggest danger is that a half understood and poorly validated DEA model is introduced for performance assessment. Poor models inevitably produce some performance ratings which are regarded as unfair. Since fairness, (and its ability to take into account factors which other methods cannot) is one of the appeals of DEA, failure to consult on the appropriate specification will defeat the major objective of performance assessment.

Such consultation with the line functions may be unfamiliar and perhaps uncomfortable at first to people in staff positions, who may not wish to expose half-developed systems to critical scrutiny. In extreme cases this may be a symptom of severe management problems which need to be tackled before systems of performance measurement can achieve their full potential. Having set up a co-ordinating committee and project plan which makes sure as far as possible all the above roles are filled and there is suitable representation from line management it is possible to start with an initial model. Previous experience with DEA models is obviously useful here, but each organization has its own style, its own strategic aims, and its own perception of the factors limiting branch performance.

The initial model generates data requirements which may need several weeks of elapsed time to meet, especially given the probability that most of the data initially available require certain errors to be corrected. The initial model generates results and initial performance rankings which can then be scrutinized by members of the co-ordinating committee. Although many of the rankings will be regarded as basically correct, at first there will normally be some obvious discrepancies between DEA scores and what is known about particular branches. This is typically due to the omission of one or two factors from the analysis, which were perhaps discarded in early discussions or for which data were not immediately available. This discussion should lead to the second phase model with a reduction in the number of discrepancies between the DEA results and existing perceptions.

The cycle of assessment and refinement is part of what Kenneth Hilton referred to as 'information feedback' in the context of evaluating control systems.[12] This needs to be carried out four or five times. By this stage the

DEA results should be leading to revisions of line managements' perceptions of performance, rather than vice versa. The contribution of DEA is to make comparisons systematically and objectively, to show areas of strength and weakness, to identify limiting factors on performance, and to pick out particular branches for more detailed consideration. There will always be factors outside those included in a DEA model which will need consideration, and these are frequently specific to a branch. For this reason it is not recommended that DEA be used on its own in a mechanical way to set targets, but rather be considered as an input into the target-setting process. The other uses of DEA, for example in examining scale effects or factor productivities, are not so dependent on individual branch characteristics. Nevertheless, where strategic decisions are to be taken, such as setting policy on the amalgamation of branches or the closure of agencies or sub-branches, DEA findings would normally be supplemented by other kinds of evidence.

The process of moving to an acceptable model will, in many cases, lead to the collection of new items of data. The discussion of what should be in the DEA model is also an opportunity to reassess, and perhaps cut down, the number of items which are collected but which are never used to inform any decisions. This may have beneficial side effects, since whatever is measured is perceived to be important (the main danger afflicting all quantitative performance systems is that measurable aspects of performance drive out the unmeasurable aspects, but this applies much more to public sector and non-profit organizations than to banks and building societies).

MATHEMATICAL APPENDIX

The reference groups used in DEA have the following properties:

1. They use no more of the input

$$\sum_{1}^{N} \lambda_i Y_i \leqslant Y_K \tag{1}$$

The K subscript refers to the branch whose performance is being measured. N is the total number of branches in the analysis. The reference group is those branches for which λ is nonzero. The number in the reference group is less than or equal to the number of constraints in the linear program minus 1.[13]

2. They produce no less output

$$\sum_{1}^{N} \lambda_i Y_i \geqslant Y_K \tag{2}$$

3. Their noncontrollable factors are no more favourable

$$\sum_{1}^{N} \lambda_i Z_i \leqslant Z_K \tag{3}$$

An example of Z would be a measure of market size, such as the population in certain demographic categories (eg "Pop EFHJ" in Tables 5.1 and 5.5). The program used to produce the results of the tables actually allows for 'negative noncontrollables' where the inequality in equation 1 is reversed. In Tables 5.1 and 5.5 'Total competition' is such a variable, on the basis that an increase in total competition will reduce the ability of a branch to make loans or collect receipts.

Two standard *orientations* are typically adopted. The first ('input minimization') focuses on the finding a peer group which uses less inputs.

Different versions of DEA make different assumptions about the λs (which we call the 'branch weights'), but all require that

$$\lambda_i \geqslant 0 \text{ for all } i \tag{4}$$

i.e. that the branch weights are either zero or positive.

The original Charnes, Cooper and Rhodes (1978) formulation made no further limitation on the λs. The Banker, Charnes, Cooper varying returns to scale (VRS) approach requires that

$$\sum_{i=1}^{N} \lambda_i = 1 \tag{5}$$

Another version, the non-increasing returns to scale (NIRS), which is equivalent to the original Farrell (1957) formulation of the problem, imposes the condition that

$$\sum_{i=0}^{N} \lambda_i = 1 \tag{6a}$$

where λ_0 is the weight accorded the null vector (i.e. zero input and zero output). This condition is equivalent to

$$\sum_{i=1}^{N} \lambda_i \leqslant 1 \tag{6b}$$

while producing at least as much output (in a no-more-favourable environment). This produces the linear programming problem (with constraints on λs imposed as appropriate).

Program 1 (input minimization)

Minimize μ (7)

Subject to:

$$\Sigma \lambda_i X_i \leqslant \mu X_K \tag{8}$$

$$\Sigma \lambda_i Y_i \geqslant Y_K \tag{9}$$

$$\Sigma \lambda_i Z_i \geqslant Z_K$$

$$\mu, \lambda_i \geqslant 0$$

μ is typically referred to as the input efficiency or performance score (OE/OD in Figure 5.1). A separate LP is calculated for each branch which has its own performance score and reference group.

The second standard orientation is output maximization:

Program 2 (output maximization)

Maximise φ (10)

Subject to:

$$\Sigma \lambda_i X_i \leqslant X_K \tag{11}$$

$$\Sigma \lambda_i Y_i \geqslant \varphi Y_K \tag{12}$$

$$\Sigma \lambda_i Z_i \geqslant Z_K \tag{13}$$

$$\varphi, \lambda_i \geqslant 0$$

$1/\varphi$ is the output efficiency or performance score (OG/OH in Figure 5.2).

However, these are not the only possible orientations. Another possibility maximizes the sum of input and output scores.

Program 3 ('productivity maximization' – for want of a better term)

Maximize $\varphi - \mu$ (14)

Subject to:

$$\Sigma \lambda_i X_i \leqslant \mu X_K \tag{15}$$

$$\Sigma \lambda_i Y_i \geqslant \varphi Y_K \tag{16}$$

$$\Sigma \lambda_i Z_i \leqslant Z_K \tag{17}$$

$$\varphi, \mu, \lambda_i \geqslant 0$$

Implementing these programs as they stand using standard, commercially available linear programming software will produce values for efficiency scores etc. as part of the output. In order to make much use of the results, however, purpose-built DEA software such as that produced by the author, is preferable. This will:

- feed in data from a standard source such as a spreadsheet;
- set up an LP for each branch in turn according to user-defined specifications, including variable selection, returns to scale, the set of branches to be analysed, etc.;
- solve the LP for every branch taking into account the high frequency of degeneracy in large DEA LP problems – since degeneracy is extremely uncommon in most normal applications of LP some general-purpose LP software is subject to problems of endless cycling or rounding error once the program gets above a certain size;
- produce a series of output files giving reports for individual branches, summary statistics, shadow prices, etc.; and
- contain additional programs to summarize the results of several analyses and to present results in an easy-to-interpret format.

NOTES

[1] The main reason economists were so slow to take up the method is probably as a result of their pre-occupation with multiple regression analysis as the major method of data analysis. Most economics training involves only cursory reference to linear programming.

[2] Note that, although there is no imposed weighting system for the two inputs, DEA uses an implicit weighting system which is the slope of the line segment BC, i.e. the weights are generated by the algorithm.

[3] The implicit relative valuation of the outputs is the slope of the line segment I J.

[4] The mathematical expression of these conditions is contained in the Appendix.

[5] The *scale indicator* is the ratio OF/OB and shows the extent to which the reference group is scaled up or down. If the scale indicator is less than 1.00 we are in the region of increasing returns, and in the region of decreasing returns if greater than 1.00.

[6] This is purely a normalization constraint which ensures that all scores lie between zero and one.

[7] These were mortgage advances, further advances and secured personal loans, unsecured personal loans, and gross receipts.

[8] ACORN is an acronym for 'A Classification Of Residential Neighbourhoods' produced by CACI Ltd. This gives a demographic breakdown of each branch's catchment area based upon a detailed analysis of Population Census and other information collected at the household level. The ACORN classifications used in the DEA were based on a regression analysis to identify which demographic groupings were the prime sources of different types of business.

[9] Except in the variable returns to scale case and where there are *nonadditive* variables, in which case an extra constraint gives another shadow price which is included in the denominator.

[10] In recent years, police forces have substituted civilian for police staff in some functions, at a considerable saving to the public purse. DEA shows that civilians appear as effective, at the margin, as non-civilian police (see Levitt and Joyce, 1987).

[11] See, for example Dalziel and Schoonover (1988); but see also Tomkins and Colville, (this volume).

[12] See p. 11 of Kenneth Hilton's Inaugural Lecture (also this volume).

[13] This arises as follows. The number of basic (i.e. nonzero) variables in an LP is equal to the number of constraints. The performance score measure will be basic and there may be some slack variables in the basis. Hence the number in the reference group is {number of constraints – 1 – number of constraints which are slack.}

REFERENCES

Aly, H.Y., Grabowski, R., Pasurka, C., and Rangan, N. (1990) Technical, scale, and allocative efficiencies in US banking: an empirical investigation, *Review of Economics and Statistics*, 211–18.

Banker, R.D. (1984) Estimating most productive scale size using data envelopment analysis, *European Journal of Operational Reesarch*, 35–44.

Charnes, A., Cooper, C.C., and Rhodes, E. (1978) Measuring the efficiency of decision making units, *European Journal of Operational Research*, **2**(6), November, 429–44.

Dalziel, M.M., and Schoonover, S. C. (1988) *Changing Ways: A practical tool for implementing change within organisations*, American Management Association (AMACOM), New York.

Farrell, M. J. (1957) The measurement of productive efficiency, *Journal of the Royal Statistical Society*, Series A, General, **120**, Part 3, 253–81.

Ferrier, G.D. and Lovell, C.A. Knox (1990) Measuring cost efficiency in banking: econometric and linear programming evidence, *Journal of Econometrics*, **46**, 229–45.

Field, K. (1990). Production efficiency of British building societies, *Applied Economics*, **2**, 415–26.

Ganley, J.A. and Cubbin, R. (1991) *Public Sector Efficiency Measurement: Applications of data envelopment analysis*, Elsevier, Amsterdam.

Goberna, M.A., Lopez, M.A., and Pastor, J.T. (1990) *Performance and Location of Bank Branches: A methodological approach*, Institute of European Finance, Research Papers reference number RP90/15, University of Wales, Bangor.

Hilton, K. (1975) *Control Systems for Social and Economic Management: An inaugural lecture*, University of Southampton.

Levitt, M. and Joyce, M. (1987) *The Growth and Efficiency of Public Spending*, Cambridge University Press, Cambridge.

Tomkins, C. and Colville, I., Financial control and devolved management in central government, this volume, pp. 255–80.

Vassiloglou, M. and Giokas, D. (1990) A study of the relative efficiency of bank branches: An application of data envelope analysis, *Journal of the Operational Research Society*, **41**(7), 591–7.

The use of DEA in measuring bank and building society branch performance: Discussant's comments

DAVID F. HEATHFIELD

Data Envelope Analysis grew out of economists' attempts at modelling empirical production functions (Farrell, 1957). Economists followed the regression route and developed stochastic frontier function models (Forsund *et. al.*, 1980) which made best use of their econometric expertise and which yielded functional forms conducive to further mathematical expression, application and analysis.

Others, typically those working in Business Schools, followed the more prosaic path of DEA. Theirs was an interest in performance measurement rather than an interest in production functions *per se*. This 'application driven' research tended to ignore the stochastic nature of the problem and to minimize the need for a clear mathematical functional form for the production function. The emphasis instead was on determining the 'frontier' or 'best practice' performance from observations of actual performance. The frontier was simple. It was to be convex and had to cover all the actual observations. Even so there were (and are) many conceptual and practical problems to be overcome before it would yield a valuable addition to the management toolkit.

As has been well established by Salter (1966) there is throughout the economy much catching up to be done by the poorest performers if they are to match the most efficient, and the gains to be had from this catching up far outweigh those possible from across the board improvements or from technical progress.

To identify and to realize any such potential gains must be a major management interest and DEA provides them with a means of moving towards this ideal.

This paper considers some of the strengths and weaknesses of DEA in the context of its application to measuring 'performance' in a multi-product, multi-input service industry. Comparisons of performance are simple enough if each performer uses the same combination of inputs and produces the same combination of outputs since this is tantamount to the single input, single output case but complications arise when there is a variety of input combinations, output combinations and levels of activity. For all practical problems these conditions rarely apply and DEA offers a way of comparing unlike with unlike by choosing convex combinations of other branches so as to construct a best practice replica of the branch under scrutiny.

There are various ways of measuring the distance between the branch and its frontier equivalent and these, following Farrell, are interpreted as allocative efficiency, technical efficiency and their product – total efficiency. The first of these typically requires data on prices of outputs and inputs but these are often not available. Were they available the problem could again be reduced, albeit with some loss of insight, to a single input, single output case. What is suggested here is that the shape of the frontier should provide the relative values (shadow prices) and so total efficiency can be decomposed into its components even in the absence of price data.

The author is well aware of the shortcomings of the analysis and spells them out for the reader. Of particular moment is the neglect of the stochastic nature of the model. Performance indicators are highly sensitive to measurement errors which could nullify the results. In this regard the stochastic frontier approach seems to have been too readily dismissed. Very flexible functional forms are available as are standard estimation packages e.g. Limdep.

On the other hand it is clear from this application that DEA provides a useful method of precipitating, directing and informing discussions between the central management and the branches. Techniques which are transparent and flexible enough to engage people in this way have important advantages over more esoteric ones.

The step-by-step approach to establishing the frontier by progressively introducing more and more variables, offers branches a way of explaining away some or all of their shortcomings but the bottom line is that any residual – unexplained departure from the frontier – is put down to managerial failures. This seems to be a poorly established attribution of cause. It is simply assumed that having nowhere else to go it must go to management. This is reminiscent of the economists' explanation of economic growth. All growth that can be

114

explained by labour, capital, etc. is subtracted from actual growth and the unexplained residual is put down to technical progress. This is therefore little more than a definition of technical progress – that which cannot be otherwise accounted for. This cannot be the case of managerial incompetence which could clearly be defined in terms of which actions were taken (or not taken) by unsuccessful managers. Performance in all walks of life lacks consistency and such chance departures from an ideal cannot fairly be used to judge individual managers – at least not without some explicit link between his/her actions and the results of the DEA.

REFERENCES

Farrell, M.J. (1957) The measurement of productive efficiency, *Journal of the Royal Statistical Society*, Series A, General 120, 253–81.

Forsund, F.R., C.A. Knox Lovell and Peter Schmidt (1980) A survey of frontier production functions and of their relationship to efficiency measurement, *Journal of Econometrics*, **13**, 5–25.

Salter, W. (1966) *Productivity and Technical Change*, Cambridge University Press, Cambridge.

6
Adjustment costs and organizational change

HILARY INGHAM*

INTRODUCTION

In his opening paper to this volume, Ezzamel (1992) defines financial control as a mechanism designed to promote the smooth functioning of an organization in line with the basic objective of that organization. Defined as such, financial control forms part of a wider spectrum of organizational control mechanisms available to the firm since it focuses specifically on control systems founded on financial criteria. In modern corporations financial control systems abound – performance related pay systems being one example.

Of course financial control systems are an important facet of the management of economic activity within the firm, in particular via its choice of organizational structure. Since the seminal contributions of Chandler (1962) and Williamson (1970) attention has been focused on the organizational innovation of divisionalization; in particular the pure multidivisional (M-form) firm. Central to the much espoused efficiency advantages of the M-form organizational structure are its superior financial control mechanisms; in particular divisional control via the establishment of an internal capital market.

However the establishment, and operation, of formal financial control systems are problematic. In his inaugural lecture, delivered in 1975 (see also this

* I am grateful to John Cable, Mahmoud Ezzamel and Steve Thompson for comments on earlier drafts of this paper. The usual disclaimers apply.

Perspectives on Financial Control: Essays in memory of Kenneth Hilton.
Edited by Mahmoud Ezzamel and David Heathfield.
Published in 1992 by Chapman & Hall, London. ISBN 0 412 40980 1.

volume), Kenneth Hilton highlighted the difficulties inherent in economic and social control systems which are absent in control systems found in the physical sciences. Among the points he notes are the mixture of optimizing and non-optimizing business objectives, the paucity and deficiency of the data and uncertainty about the effects of the system. Such sentiments suggest that the establishment of formal control systems which are to remain operational over time is likely to be beset with difficulties. Thus it may be conjectured that optimal control in a business environment will require flexible, adaptive, mechanisms.

Since the time of this lecture much empirical research has been conducted on the performance effects of the M-form organizational innovation; the evidence is surveyed in the next section. In much of the early work fairly crude M-form categorizations were employed thereby, to a degree, overlooking the wide diversity of financial control systems operational within divisionalized companies. The major focus of these studies was the existence, or otherwise, of superior performance for M-form firms. Latterly, however, research in this area has widened and scepticism has been voiced concerning: the universality of superior M-form performance, the existence of pure M-form firms and, also, the suitability of this organizational structure for other than pure conglomerate concerns. As discussed in the next section, central to this current debate are the global problems of financial control systems addressed by Kenneth Hilton in 1975.

Following this review of existing empirical work, the third and fourth sections of this paper present a model of organizational change which permits an examination, at the firm level, of the intertemporal nature of any performance improvements generated by organizational change. As such, the model presented is very much in the spirit of the work of Ezzamel and Hilton (1980) since, this work excepted, the dynamic nature of the performance effects of organizational change remain under researched. It is therefore hoped that this paper will provide further evidence on this dimension of the relationship between organizational structure and performance.

INTERNAL ORGANIZATION AND THE M-FORM HYPOTHESIS

The economics of internal organization emanates from the concept of the transaction as the ultimate unit of economic analysis (Commons, 1934). The use of transactions costs to determine the relative efficiency of firm versus market provision was discussed in the now widely cited paper by Coase (1937). Latterly Williamson (1970, 1975, 1981, 1986) has extended this work by considering the efficiency of different governance structures as means of overcoming market failure.

Williamson's work also draws heavily on Chandler's (1962) exposition of the organizational innovation of the multidivisional administrative structure. Historically companies were administered within functional, unitary (U-form), governance structures wherein activities were demarcated by functional specialisms such as finance, marketing etc. and decision making was centralized; the benefits of such a structure clearly derive from the gains from specialization. However, as the firm's operations increase in complexity via growth and, more importantly, diversification, the suitability of the U-form organizational structure declines. Thus if, as the firm grows, additional layers are added on to an existing hierarchy the result is a cumulative loss of overall control (Williamson, 1967). Furthermore, as the firm diversifies, the increasing complexity of the information which the central decision maker needs to store and process exacerbates the problems of bounded rationality (Simon, 1955) thereby preventing effective centralized management. Of course, in the majority of cases, it is the conjunction of the volume and the complexity of information which hinders management. As a consequence of these informational problems, long term planning tends to be crowded out by day-to-day operational decision making.

The weaknesses of the M-form structure for the management of large US enterprises are detailed in Chandler (1962). To circumvent these problems many large corporations responded by divisionalizing their organizations and employing a M-form structure. Within a multidivisional company the organization is decomposed into divisions – quasi-autonomous firms – which are granted profit centre status. Normally, in a diversified company, divisions tend to be product based although decomposition can alternatively be achieved via geographic groupings or a mixture of both. One advantage of such divisionalization is that it permits decentralization of decision making since, whilst corporate strategy matters are still determined at peak co-ordinator level, operational decision making can be devolved to divisional managers. In addition, the establishment of divisions increases the quality of the information available to top management by providing more detailed information on the performance of constituent parts of the organization.

Of course divisionalization *per se* will not necessarily produce any tangible performance benefits for the firm. In order to reap these it is necessary that the firm establishes an effective control system; within M-form firms the emphasis is on financial control tools which maximize performance. One mechanism commonly employed is the use of incentive payments for divisional managers based on the performance – relative or absolute – of their division. Additionally, within a multidivisional enterprise, the capital allocation function is internalized with Head Office chanelling funds to the divisions on the basis of performance. Both these control systems are designed to curb the opportunism of divisional managers and ensure goal congruency throughout the organization. Thus only firms which establish both autonomous divisions and effective monitoring and reward systems can be viewed as pure multidivisionals. For such companies Williamson (1970) notes:

> The organization and operation of the large enterprise along the lines of the M-form favours goal pursuit and least-cost behaviour more nearly associated with the neoclassical profit maximisation hypothesis than does the U-form (functional) alternative. (Williamson, 1970, p. 134)

This has become known in the literature as the multidivisional hypothesis.

Over the past two decades there have been a number of studies to test the validity of this hypothesis.[1] Many different empirical models have been employed; the diversity of the approaches are doubtless due to the difficulty over the quantification of organizational structure and the alternative indicators of performance which can be used. Early studies for the UK and USA (Armour and Teece, 1978; Steer and Cable, 1978) employed accounting measures of performance in regression models – pooled and cross-sectional respectively – which included organizational structure in the exogenous variable set. As Cable (1988) notes, the chosen time period can be critical in studies of this nature. Thus differential M-form performance is only observable during the diffusion period; the selection of a suitable sample period therefore requiring that certain companies have adopted divisionalization while others have not undertaken any organizational change. However it may also be that performance during this diffusion period of the early adopters of the M-form structure may itself be abnormal. Thus, during this transitional period, adjustment costs may be incurred during the introduction of the new administrative structure (Ezzamel and Hilton, 1980). Alternatively change, *per se*, may positively impact upon performance – the so-called Hawthorne effect.

These problems notwithstanding, these two early studies did provide support for the multidivisional hypothesis; however the magnitude of the organizational structure effect of Steer and Cable (1978) – nearly 50% of the average return on capital – is viewed as suspiciously large. To circumvent the well-documented limitations of accounting measures of profitability – in particular when used in intra-firm comparison – following studies by Teece (1981) and Thompson (1981, 1983b) chose alternative performance measurement. In the first of these, although he employed accounting data, Teece (1981) subjected these data to various non-parametric tests and only using a matched pairs test did he find support for the multidivisional hypothesis. In a radical departure from existing work, the two studies by Thompson, using abnormal share price returns as a performance indicator, used an event-based study to measure the impact of organizational change. One of the interesting findings of this research was that the positive performance benefits of the M-form structure

120

were partly due to the abnormally poor performance of the holding company form (H-form) companies in the sample.

Thus far the work discussed relates only to the UK and USA, the two countries possessing active capital markets providing external finance. Interestingly studies conducted on German data (Cable and Dirrheimer, 1983; Bühner, 1985) produced no support for the superiority of the multidivisional structure. This, it is suggested (Cable, 1988), may be due to institutional differences such as bank representation on supervisory boards. Likewise in Japan, where similar institutional arrangements exist, no M-form gains were empirically proven (Cable and Yasuki, 1985).

An additional dimension of the debate which merits attention is the issue of classification. Hill (1985), for example, posits that corrupted multidivisional companies are far more prevalent than pure M-form firms. Using data from the same questionnaire, this issue is addressed more fully in Hill and Pickering (1986). Thus these authors found considerable differences in management practices amongst divisionalized companies. In particular they highlighted the failure of top management to relinquish power over operational decision making and the internal allocation of capital on non-competitive grounds. In more recent work the applicability of the M-form structure to companies other than pure conglomerates has also been questioned (Hill, 1988; Ingham, 1992). Such work suggests that intra-firm business necessitates that top management fulfil a co-ordination role and thereby are more involved in operational decision making than would be the case in a pure multidivisional company. In such situations optimal divisionalization will not be pure M-form, instead financial control systems will need to be designed specifically to take into account intra-firm interdependencies. This need to tailor control systems to optimal divisionalization is discussed in Ezzamel (1985).

The final issue of organizational change, and that which is the focus of this paper, is its temporal effect on performance. Thus, the majority of the extant empirical works pays little, if any, attention to the intertemporal nature of any performance benefits resulting from reorganization.[2] Even those studies which have focused on the impact of reorganization on performance (Thompson, 1981, 1983b) have only considered a short post-reorganization period. This shortcoming certain of the authors concede:

> Our results do not, of course, indicate how long the transitional period is and hence the total reorganization cost. In the course of our classification exercise, however, some firms were observed in a transition phase over several years. (Steer and Cable, 1978, p. 24)

To contribute to the empirical findings in this area, this paper seeks to address the intertemporal nature of the effects of organizational change on performance by viewing the firm's governance structure as a capital good which, if changed, incurs the firm in adjustment costs. As such this study adopts a similar approach to that of Thompson (1983a) which shows that the diffusion process of the M-form structure resembles that of a physical capital innovation.

ORGANIZATIONAL CAPITAL AND ORGANIZATIONAL CHANGE

Any organizational structure employed by a firm represents a significant human capital investment by that company. Prescott and Visscher (1986) discuss the ways in which the firm invests in this organization capital. Essentially such capital consists, in part, of what the firm knows about its employees in so far as this permits efficient monitoring and optimal job matching in addition to the human capital of its employees.[3] The past investments that any firm has made in such capital represent a sunk cost. If a firm wishes to augment this capital stock in any way it will face present period costs which must be weighed against the future expected benefits arising from such an investment. Such costs are termed adjustment costs; these are defined, by Nickell (1978), as follows: 'productive implementation of capital goods over and above the basic costs of those goods' (Nickell, 1978, p. 25).

Two distinct types of adjustment costs are commonly identified in the literature on physical investment. First, there are those costs which are external to the firm; for example firms may face rising supply curves for capital goods, particularly if faced with a monopsonistic supplier. Second, there are those adjustment costs which are internal to the firm; the installation of capital goods, for example, causes a dislocation in production as well as imposing a burden on managerial and administrative staff which may well impair their current work.

Likewise a firm will incur costs if it wishes to adjust its stock of organizational capital. Certain of the human capital embodied in the firm's management becomes obsolete when the firm changes its administrative structure. The tasks of managers, both at the divisional and Head Office levels, will change significantly if, say, the firm moves from a functional to a multidivisional structure. In particular the increased decision-making responsibility which divisional managers in M-form firms face will require new skills and additional training may be required for this purpose. Alternatively the firm may lack the necessary managerial capital and be forced into outside recruitment; thus adjustment costs which arise via the need to increase managerial capital may be internal and/or external to the firm.[4]

However, in addition, the establishment of a new administrative structure may itself incur costs for the firm. Channon (1973) notes that many UK companies employed American consultancy companies to design M-form

122

structures. Furthermore, if the maximum gains from any reorganization are to be realized, then an effective monitoring and control system must be implemented. The requisite changes in the information channels within the firm are a further source of internal adjustment costs.

The existence of these adjustment costs of organizational change therefore imply that, in addition to the expected benefits of reorganization, there also exist non-trivial costs. Ignoring the potential effects of these could introduce considerable bias into any empirical work. The following section therefore develops the idea of the intertemporal nature of the performance effects of organizational change.

THE ORGANIZATIONAL LIFE CYCLE

The discounted profit stream of the firm can be decomposed into three distinct phases to represent an organizational life cycle

$$\pi_t = \left(\int_{t_0}^{t_1} (R_t - X_t) + \int_{t_1}^{t_2} (R_t^* - X_t^* - C_t^*) + \int_{t_2}^{\infty} (R_t^{**} - X_t^{**}) \right) e^{-rt} dt \tag{1}$$

where:

π_t = Profit
R_t = Revenue
X_t = Operating costs
C_t = Adjustment costs (assumed strictly convex)[6]
* = Value of variable during transitional period
** = Value of variable post-reorganization
r = Discount rate (assumed constant)
$[t_0, t_1]$ = Pre-reorganization period
$[t_1, t_2]$ = Transitional Period
$[t_2, \infty)$ = Post-reorganization period

Of course with such a representation is it necessary to consider what factors cause differing epochs over the company's lifespan. The first 'break', t_1, is the date at which companies choose to reorganize; likely factors influencing this decision are imitation of competitors or, alternatively, as a response to a crisis (see Chandler, 1962; Thompson, 1981). As given the model includes a further shift at t_2 since it is assumed that any reorganization will be subject to adjustment costs, i.e. a period of time – (t_1, t_2) – must elapse before the firm realizes the benefits of the new organizational structure.

Considering first the firm's revenue stream it is assumed that $R_t^* < R_t$. Thus it is assumed that, due to the non-separability of adjustment costs, during the transitional period revenue falls below that which the firm would have achieved had it not undertaken organizational change. This occurs for two reasons; first, resources which could have been used for current production are diverted towards the reorganization process. Second, there are also opportunity costs of organizational change since there exist alternative ways in which a firm may seek to improve its performance, capital expenditure being one possibility. No *a priori* expectation is attached to the relative size of R_t and R_t^{**} although the work of Ezzamel and Hilton (1980) suggests that divisionalization may cause revenue to increase.

On the operating cost side it might seem appropriate to assume that $X_t^{**} < X_t$ reflecting the elimination of organizational slack post-reorganization. However, to ensure performance increases, it is not sufficient that the firm is divisionalized; sufficiency requires that the appropriate control mechanisms are present within the company. Given that monitoring is not costless it is not possible to unambiguously determine the relative magnitude of X_t^{**} and X_t.[6]

It is simple, within this framework, to isolate the gross gain from reorganization. This is given by:

$$E\left(\int_{t_2}^{\infty} \{(R_t^{**} - X_t^{**}) - (R_t - X_t)\}\, e^{-rt}\, dt\right) \tag{2}$$

where $E(\dots)$ denotes an expectation.

If the firm moves from a sub-optimal organizational structure to an optimal one then this gain will be positive. It is the existence, and magnitude, of this gain which has been the focus of certain empirical studies (Ezzamel and Hilton, 1980, Thompson, 1981).

However, the inclusion of adjustment costs, via the transitional period, complicates the issue since, in addition to the expected benefits of reorganization, there also exist expected costs. Thus, during the transitional period, the firm faces a decline in its performance:

$$E\left(\int_{t_1}^{t_2} \{(R_t - X_t) - (R_t^* - X_t^* - C_t^*)\}\, e^{-rt}\, dt\right) \tag{3}$$

With non-separable adjustment costs it is assumed that $R_t > R_t^*$ and that $X_t^* > X_t$ reflecting both dislocation of production and the additional production costs that may occur during reorganization. The existence of adjustment costs implies that $C_t^* > 0$.

The net gain from reorganization is therefore given by:

$$E\left(\int_{t_2}^{\infty} \{(R_t^{**} - X_t^{**}) - (R_t - X_t)\}\, e^{-rt}\, dt\right)$$

$$-E\left(\int_{t_1}^{t_2} \{(R_t - X_t) - (R_t^* - X_t^* - C_t^*)\}\, e^{-rt}\, dt\right) \tag{4}$$

The foregoing analysis suggests that any inference about the relative performance of optimally organized firms based on empirical results with a limited temporal dimension must be viewed with a certain degree of scepticism. Any perceived performance differentials may simply be due to the fact that companies are at different stages in their organizational life cycles.

Before proceeding to empirically examine the above model, one further aspect of the transitional period must be mentioned. Thus far it has been assumed that the instantaneous effect of reorganization is a deterioration in performance and that it is only in the longer term that any benefits are realized. However there exists an alternative hypothesis that the reverse may be true. Thus change itself may positively impact on a firm's performance; this is, of course, the Hawthorne effect. Furthermore, given that in the longer-term divisional managers, and other employees, will become familiar with the workings of any administrative structure, opportunistic behaviour may well return as individuals learn ways to 'beat the system'. These alternative hypotheses are examined in the empirical work contained in the following section.

METHODOLOGY AND EMPIRICAL RESULTS

This section contains an intertemporal analysis of the impact of organizational change on performance. The most salient feature of organizational structure is that it is unobservable; at best, companies can be classified along the lines proposed by Williamson (1975). In reality this classification exercise is far more tenuous than that associated with other, commonly employed, qualitative variables. One of the most problematic areas concerns the between a pure M-form company and a corrupted one with evidence suggesting that the incidence of pure multidivisional companies is low (Hill and Pickering, 1986). In addition, the optimality of the pure M-form structure outwith the domain of the pure conglomerate is also questionable (Hill, 1988).

The empirical analysis of this paper centres on an examination of the impact of organizational change on a company's performance. The organizational structure variable which is necessary for this approach is a time series of observations indicating the company's structure over the entire estimation period. As such the results are free of any bias introduced by inaccurate inter-company classification which may plague cross-sectional studies. However the classification problem concerning when in time a company should be categorized as multidivisional etc. remains. An additional facet of the approach adopted here is that it permits an examination of whether organizational change *per se* has an unambiguous affect on performance (positive, negative or zero) or whether this impact depends on the nature of the change (U-form to M-form, U-form to H-form, etc.).

The statistical model employed is:

$$\pi = f(\text{OS}, \ \mathbf{Z}) + e \tag{5}$$

where the dependent variable, π, the performance measure, is the return on net assets.[7,8] To isolate firm-specific profitability the dependent variable is deflated by the industry rate of return to remove any variability in performance caused by macroeconomic factors. The inadequacy of accounting data is well documented, but, despite its shortcomings, is still widely used as a performance measure. In the current context only intra-firm profitability is used thus problems such as different firms' treatment of depreciation is not a major concern.

The exogenous variable set contains all those factors deemed to influence a firm's profitability including organizational structure (OS). $\mathbf{Z}$ is a vector containing additional explanatory variables; those included in the specification are size, market power, growth, capital investment, capital intensity and the debt/equity ratio. A full description of the components of $\mathbf{Z}$ is given in the Appendix to this paper along with a summary of the empirical results. e is a white noise error term.

Empirically the organizational life cycle of the company is modelled via the inclusion of a spline function in the statistical specification; this technique has been used to a limited degree in the analysis of structural change (Poirer, 1976). It is the residual variation, i.e. that which is unexplained by the explanatory variable set, $\mathbf{Z}$, in profitability that is therefore attributed to organizational structure.

The full model becomes:

$$\pi = \alpha_1 D_1 + \alpha_2 D_2 + \alpha_3 D_3 + \beta_1 D_1 t + \beta_2 D_2 t + \beta_3 D_3 t + g^T \mathbf{Z} + e \tag{6}$$

which is estimated subject to the restrictions:

$$\alpha_1 + \beta_1 w_1 = \alpha_2 + \beta_2 w_1 \tag{7}$$

$$\alpha_2 + \beta_2 w_2 = \alpha_3 + \beta_3 w_2$$

For each company, D_1, D_2 and D_3 are 0/1 dichotomous variables which take the unitary value during the pre-reorganization, transitional and post-reorganization periods respectively. The two linear restrictions ensure that the function is continuous at the two join points, w_1 and w_2, these points being the dates at which a company enters the new phases of its organizational life cycle. The advantages of ensuring this continuity are discussed in Boyce (1986) with the major benefit of this approach over a discontinuous one being that it makes use of information for the entire time period when estimating a given sub-period.

Via simple substitution restricted least squares estimation yields an estimating equation since, from (7)

$$\alpha_1 = \alpha_2 + \beta_2 w_1 - \beta_1 w_1$$

$$\alpha_2 = \alpha_3 + \beta_3 w_2 - \beta_2 w_2$$

$$\therefore \ \alpha_1 = \alpha_3 + (w_1 - w_2)\beta_2 - \beta_1 w_1 + \beta_3 w_2 \tag{8}$$

substituting for α_1 and α_2 in (6) yields:

$$\pi = \{\alpha_3 + (w_1 - w_2)\beta_2 - \beta_1 w_1 + \beta_3 w_2\} D_1 + (\alpha_3 + \beta_3 w_2 - \beta_2 w_2) D_2 +$$

$$\alpha_3 D_3 + \beta_1 D_1 t + \beta_2 D_2 t + \beta_3 D_2 t + g^T \mathbf{Z} + e \tag{9}$$

which can be rearranged to give:

$$\pi = \alpha_3(D_1 + D_2 + D_3) + (D_1 t - w_1 D_1)\beta_1 + (w_1 D_1 - w_2 D_1 - w_2 D_2 + D_2 t)\beta_2 +$$

$$(w_2 D_1 + w_2 D_2 + D_3 t)\beta_3 + g^T \mathbf{Z} + e \tag{10}$$

which can be rewritten as:-

$$\pi = \alpha + \beta_1^{**} X_1 + \beta_2^{**} X_2 + \beta_3^{**} X_3 + g^T \mathbf{Z} + e \tag{11}$$

where

$$\alpha = \alpha_3(D_1 + D_2 + D_3) \text{ and } D_1 + D_2 + D_3 = 1$$
$$X_1 = D_1 t - w_1 D_1$$
$$X_2 = w_1 D_1 - w_2 D_1 - w_2 D_2 + D_2 t$$
$$X_3 = w_2 D_1 - w_2 D_2 + D_3 t$$

The sample used is that employed by Channon (1973) and, additionally, used in the work of Steer and Cable (1978); it is comprised of the UK's top 100 manufacturing companies as of 1970. The reasons for the choice of this sample are twofold: first, Channon (1973) provides reasonably detailed case histories for each of the companies which permits the extraction of information such as the date of organizational change and the precise form of structure adopted. Second, as the aim of this particular study is to examine the temporal aspect of organizational change, it was necessary to choose a sample for which a post-reorganization period was available. The data on organizational structure and the date of change were supplemented by business histories and the financial press. Clearly a questionnaire survey could not be conducted as it

127

would not be feasible to expect accurate answers concerning events occurring two decades ago, even if personnel changes did not render such an exercise impossible. For certain companies it was not possible to obtain data on the length of the transitional period. For these companies the time path of profitability was examined to see whether a switch of regime could be identified for up to five years after reorganization; this was then tested using a Chow test. Fortunately, it was only necessary to use this procedure in a minority of cases. Due to attrition for reasons such as acquisition, the final sample size used for estimation was sixty-one companies. Companies for which the number of available observations was less than thirty are excluded. All the quantitative data was taken from the Cambridge/DTI databank.[9]

Table 6.1 Nested testing procedure

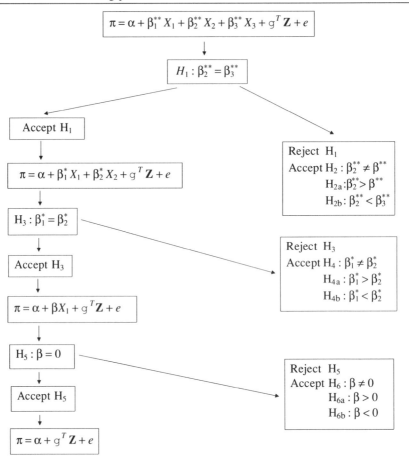

A schematic representation of the testing procedure employed is given in Table 6.1. Embedded in the general model are a number of nested hypotheses which are of interest. The first hypothesis of interest involves testing the restriction that $\beta_2^{**} = \beta_3^{**}$, this determines the existence, or otherwise, of a transitional period following reorganization.[10] If H_1 is accepted then the impact of organizational change is instantaneous and sustained. If, however, equality of the two coefficients is rejected by the data then two alternative possibilities exist; first, if $\beta_2^{**} > \beta_3^{**}$ (H_{2a}) then the Hawthorne effects dominates whereas if $\beta_2^{**} < \beta_3^{**}$ (H_{2b}) adjustment costs dominate.

Returning to the acceptance of H_1 it is then necessary to consider the possibility of the equality of β_1^{*} and β_2^{*} (H_3). If H_3 is accepted then there is no discernible difference in the influence of organizational structure on profitability across organizational regimes. If however the data rejects the equality of the coefficients then two alternative hypotheses can be investigated; if $\beta_1^{*} > \beta_2^{*}$ (H_{4a}) then adjustment costs are present, furthermore these costs do not disappear in the long-run. Alternatively if $\beta_1^{*} < \beta_2^{*}$ then the Hawthorne effect is dominant; organizational change brings about an instantaneous improvement in profitability and this is sustained.

Finally, if H_3 is accepted, it is necessary to test whether or not $\beta = 0$ (H_5). If this restriction is accepted then the data support the hypothesis that organizational structure exerts no, independent, influence on profitability. If this restriction is not accepted by the data then H_{6a} and H_{6b} respectively test the sign of β.

The empirical results, estimated over the period 1948–82, for the sixty-one sample companies are summarized in Table 6.2 below.[11] The information contained in this table relates only to the organizational structure variables; details of the full empirical specifications are provided in the Appendix. Overall the explanatory power of the chosen statistical models is acceptable with over 50% of the variation in profitability being explained for the majority of companies in the sample. The evidence on the impact of organizational change is mixed; the existence of an organizational life cycle is statistically upheld for twenty of the sample companies with the evidence equally divided as to whether adjustment costs or the Hawthorne effect dominate the transitional period.

For twenty-one of the sample companies the impact of organizational change was instantaneous and sustained throughout the post-reorganization period. For thirteen of the companies the new organizational structure positively affected performance although for eight the effect was negative. No discernible impact of organizational change was uncovered for twenty of the companies. This does not, however, necessarily mean that organizational structure does not affect profitability. For seven of these firms the residual variation in performance attributed to organizational structure was significant;

Table 6.2 Summary empirical results for organizational life cycle model

Industry	Number of companies Hypothesis							
	H_{2a}	H_{2b}	H_{4a}	H_{4b}	H_5	H_{6a}	H_{6b}	N
Food	2	1	1	3	3	0	1	11
Brewing	2	1	0	1	1	0	0	5
Tobacco	0	0	1	0	0	1	1	3
Chemicals	0	2	1	1	1	1	1	7
Metal manufacture	0	0	0	1	2	0	0	3
Non-electrical engineering	1	1	1	2	0	0	0	5
Electrical engineering	2	2	0	2	0	0	1	7
Motor vehicles	1	0	1	0	1	0	0	3
Metal goods n.e.s.	0	1	1	0	1	0	0	3
Textiles	1	0	1	0	2	0	0	4
Bricks, pottery and glass	0	0	0	1	0	0	1	2
Paper and publishing	0	1	1	2	1	0	0	5
Miscellaneous manufacturing	1	1	0	0	1	0	0	3
N	10	10	8	13	13	2	5	61

however this influence was positive in only two cases. This latter finding is somewhat surprising since it might be conjectured that optimal organizational change should, to some degree, be continuous in the sense that firms should continually improve their control systems. Finally for thirteen companies no independent influence of organizational factors was discernible.

Of course, if firms are concerned only with the long term gains from organizational change, then the relevant issue of concern is the relative influence of organizational structure on performance pre-reorganization and after any transitional period, if such exists. This matter is addressed in Table 6.3; results are presented only for those companies for which the data supported differing impacts of organizational factors across regimes. Three groups of subsidiary hypotheses are considered. H_1, H_2, and H_3 represent those cases where the influence of organizational factors on profitability pre-reorganization was found to be negative, zero and positive respectively. The subscripts a and b indicate whether reorganization improved or worsened the impact of organizational structure on performance.

The evidence shows that for approximately half of the companies reorganization appeared to have a positive effect. What is, however, interesting is the fact that it is only for the sub-set of those companies for which $\beta_1 < 0$ where the majority enjoyed this gain. Such a finding therefore suggests that crisis induced reorganization is the most likely to produce positive benefits for the firm. The evidence presented shows that for the majority of the remaining companies the change in organizational structure did not improve performance.

Table 6.3 Long term effect of organizational change on performance

	H_1		H_2		H_3	
	$\beta_1 < 0$		$\beta_1 = 0$		$\beta_1 > 0$	
	/ \		/ \		/ \	
	H_{1a} H_{1b}		H_{2a} H_{2b}		H_{3a} H_{3b}	

Industry	Hypothesis					
	H_{1a}	H_{1b}	H_{2a}	H_{2b}	H_{3a}	H_{3b}
Food	2	3	1	0	1	1
Brewing	1	1	0	1	0	1
Tobacco	0	2	0	0	1	0
Chemicals	2	1	1	0	1	1
Metal manufacture	0	1	0	0	0	0
Non-electrical engineering	2	0	1	2	0	0
Electrical engineering	2	1	1	0	0	3
Motor vehicles	0	0	0	0	0	1
Metal goods n.e.s.	1	0	0	1	0	0
Textiles	0	0	0	2	0	0
Bricks, pottery and glass	1	1	0	0	0	0
Paper and publishing	2	0	0	0	1	1
Miscellaneous manufacturing	0	0	0	1	1	0
N	13	10	4	7	5	8

A further point of interest is the relationship between the nature of organizational change and its net effect. Some slight evidence does exist that for those companies which moved to a M-form structure, such as those in the chemical industry, the performance effects of reorganization were positive. Conversely, for the brewing companies, which tended to adopt fairly loosely controlled H-form structures, the dominant effect was negative. Likewise for the textile companies, where divisionalized structures resembled the corrupted M-form, any observed impact on performance was, once again, negative. Thus, overall, the results are supportive of the hypothesis that the adoption of a pure M-form structure can yield performance benefits but, in addition, suggests that these benefits are not forthcoming when more hybrid organizational structures are employed.

SUMMARY AND CONCLUSIONS

This paper has attempted to assess the intertemporal nature of the impact of organizational change on profitability. As such the approach adopted is complementary to existing empirical work in this area. Via the examination of an organizational life cycle an attempt has been made to model the independent influence of organizational factors on performance across different administrative structure regimes. Of particular interest is whether or not the data would support the notion that a firm's organizational capital was quasi-fixed in a manner akin to physical capital and, thus, that any change, i.e. reorganization, would incur the firm in adjustment costs.

The evidence presented is interesting; the results suggest that for almost one-third of the sample companies there was no differing impact of organizational factors across the life cycle. Furthermore the data only upheld the existence of any transitional period for a further third of the companies in this particular sample. For the companies for which an adjustment period was found to exist then the results are divided equally as to whether adjustments costs or the Hawthorne effect dominate. The empirical results have, therefore, provided only weak support for the notion of the quasi-fixity of organizational capital.

Although the adoption of a pure M-form structure did lead to improved performance, the results generated are thus less supportive of the benefits of divisionalization than certain of the earlier empirical studies. Of course what may be reflected here is that organizational change should, to a degree, be viewed by the firm as a continuous process; as such, no structural instability would, therefore, be anticipated. It remains true, however, that the evidence presented here lends no support to the view that organizational change provides unambiguous performance benefits for the firm.

APPENDIX

The complete list of exogenous variables included in **Z** is as follows:

Z1: Size
Z2: Market power
Z3: Growth[+]
Z4: Growth via retentions
Z5: Growth via external finance
Z6: Capital intensity
Z7: Capital investment[+]
Z8: Debt/equity ratio

[+] Indicates that these variables were also included lagged one period.

Obviously in the interests of parsimony and the minimization of problems of multicollinearity only a subset of these variables was included in the final specification chosen for each company. Table 6.A1 shows which variables were found to be significant determinants of profitability for each of the sample companies and, in addition, the sign of the relevant coefficient. The companies are grouped according to their industrial classification at the end of the estimation period (1982). Where companies were classified differently over the estimation period the appropriate deflator for the dependent variable was varied accordingly.

132

Table 6.A1 Summary of empirical results

Industry	Company	S	Z1	Z2	Z3	$Z3_{-1}$	Z4	Z5	Z6	Z7	$Z7_{-1}$	Z8	$\overline{R}^2$
Food	Associated British Foods	2	—	—	+						—		0.76
	British Sugar	0		—	+				—**			—**	0.36
	Cadbury Schweppes	3		—**	+**								0.75
	Heinz	2		+	+**	—**			+**		—**		0.69
	Lyons	3		—**	+*				+				0.76
	Rank Hovis McDougall	2		+	—	—**					—		0.76
	Rowntree	0			+**						+*		0.51
	Spillers	2			+**						—*		0.77
	Tate & Lyle	1		—	+**				—**			+**	0.75
	Unilever	0		—**	+**						—		0.65
	United Biscuits	3		—*	+**				—**			+	0.55
Brewing	Allied Breweries	3		—**	+**				+**			+**	0.63
	Distillers	2		—	—								0.43
	Guinness	3			—				—			+**	0.79
	Scottish & Newcastle	1		—	+							+*	0.15
	Whitbread	3		—*				+				—	0.85
Tobacco	Gallaher	1		+**	+				+			+**	0.67
	Imperial Tobacco	2		+**	+				—*			+**	0.91
	Rothmans Carerras	1		+	+				—*				0.33
Chemicals	Albright & Wilson	2			+				+**				0.70
	Beecham	1		—**					—*				0.67
	British Oxygen	3		—**	—				—**			+	0.72
	Esso	2		+**		—**							0.76
	Fisons	1		+	+**								0.13
	Glaxo	3		—	+**				+**		—*		0.74
	ICI	0		+	+				—**			—*	0.24

Independent Variables

Table 6.A1 (cont.)

Industry	Company	S	Z1	Z2	Z3	Z3₋₁	Z4	Z5	Z6	Z7	Z7₋₁	Z8	$\overline{R}^2$
Metal manufacture	Birmid Qualcast	0		+**	+							−**	0.40
	Delta Metal	0		−	−						−		−0.04
	Tube Investments	2		−	+				−*			+	0.16
Non-electrical engineering	Babcock & Wilcox	3		+	+*				−*		−		0.68
	John Brown	2		−**	+**	−			+*			−**	0.74
	Henry Simon	2		+**	+				+**			−	0.21
	Smiths Industries	3		−		−*			−**				0.69
	Vickers	2		−	+**		+		+				0.21
Electrical engineering	BICC	3		+**		−**			−*			+**	0.68
	EMI	3		−								+	0.44
	GEC	3		−**	+**	+*			−*			−*	0.88
	ICL	0		−**	+**	−**			−*				0.68
	Lucas	1					+**						0.93
	Plessey	2		−**	+**	−**							0.52
	Thorn	2				−*			+**				0.74
Motor vehicles	Associated Engineering	2		+**	−				−			+**	0.28
	Chrysler	0		+	−							+*	−0.04
	Vauxhall	3		−*	+**						−	+*	0.95
Metal Goods	GKN	2		−**	+**							−	0.71
	Johnson Matthey	3		−	+**							+*	0.46
	Metal Box	1		−*	+**	−*			−*		+		0.65

Industry	Company	S							
Textiles	Coates Patons	1	—**	+**	+**	—**		+	0.30
	Courtaulds	0	+	+**	+**			—	0.48
	Tootal	3	—**	+**	+**			—	0.50
	Turner & Newall	2	+**	+	+			—	0.81
Bricks, Pottery & glass	Associated Portland Cement	1	—			—**		—	0.85
	Marley	2	+**		—**			—	0.45
Paper and publishing	Bowater	2	—**	—				—	0.68
	British Printing Corporation	2	+**	+**	—**		—**	—**	0.85
	Reed	2	+**	+			—**		0.65
	Thompson Organization	3	+**	+**	—	+**	+**	+**	0.89
	Wiggins Teape	0	—	+**		+**	+**	+**	0.88
Miscellaneous manufacturing	Burton	3	+**	—	+**	—**	—**	—**	0.69
	Dunlop	3	—	+	—**	—**	—**	—	0.88
	Swan Hunter	0	—	—				—	-0.05

Notes:

1. The exogenous variable set for each individual company was determined via a series of Likelihood Ratio Tests.
2. The column 'S' relates to the Spline coefficients. 3 indicates that 2 breaks (i.e. a transition period) were supported by the data; 2 indicates 1 break (instantaneous adjustment); 1 indicates 0 breaks (no discernible change in the impact of organizational structure throughout the estimation period) and 0 indicates that the inclusion of an organizational structure variable was not supported by the data.
3. + = variable included in final specification and positive.
   — = variable included in final specification and negative.
   ** = significant at 5%
   * = significant at 10%

NOTES

[1] For a review of these empirical studies see Cable (1988).

[2] To allow for an adjustment period certain firms are classified as transitional in the majority of empirical studies.

[3] Further discussion of the aspects of human capital can be found in Becker (1975).

[4] In the context of growth, adjustment costs have been considered by Penrose (1959) and Slater (1980).

[5] Convexity implies that rapid change is always costly. The validity of this convexity assumption is discussed at length in Nickell (1978).

[6] Interestingly in their questionnaire survey Ezzamel and Hilton (1980) found that the primary impact of divisionalization was on increasing revenues rather than decreasing costs.

[7] See Steer and Cable (1978) for results generated using alternative accounting measures of performance.

[8] Despite the shortcomings of accounting measures of performance, this measure was felt to be preferable to the use of a market model. One of the major limitations of the latter approach is ascertaining the precise announcement date of impending reorganizations; such information is not highlighted in the financial press to the same degree as takeover bids for example. In addition, Teece (1981) argues that the reaction of the market to information about reorganization is typically to ignore it. Finally, given the time period used, there may well be additional problems concerning the stability of beta over such a number of years.

[9] I am grateful to A. Goudie and G. Whittington for providing this data.

[10] The restrictions of the equality of coefficients across regimes were tested using Likelihood Ratio tests.

[11] The estimation procedure was restricted least squares; where the data indicated the presence of serial correlation a Beach-MacKinnon technique was used.

REFERENCES

Armour, H.O. and Teece D.J. (1978) Organizational structure and economic performance: a test of the multidivisional hypothesis, *Bell Journal of Economics*, **9**, 106–12.

Becker, G.S. (1975) *Human Capital* 2nd ed, National Bureau of Economic Research.

Boyce, J.K. (1986), Kinked exponential models for growth rate estimation, *Oxford Bulletin of Economics and Statistics*, **48**, 385–91.

Bühner, R. (1985) Internal organization and returns: an empirical analysis of large diversified German corporations, in *Industry Structure and Performance* (ed. J. Schwalback), wzb, Edition Sigma.

Cable, J.R. (1988) Organizational form and economic performance, in *Internal Organization, Efficiency and Profit* (eds R.S. Thompson and M. Wright), Philip Allan.

Cable, J.R. and Dirrheimer M.F. (1983) Hierarchies and markets: an empirical test of the multidivisional hypothesis in West Germany, *International Journal of Industrial Organization*, **1**, 43–62.

Cable, J.R. and Yasuki M. (1985) Internal organization, business groups and corporate performance: an empirical test of the multidivisional hypothesis in Japan, *International Journal of Industrial Organization*, **3**, 401–20.

Chandler, A.D., Jr (1962) *Strategy and Structure: Chapters in the history of the industrial enterprise*, MIT Press.

Channon, D.F. (1973) *The Strategy and Structure of British Enterprise*, Graduate School of Business Administration, Harvard University.

Coase, R.H. (1937) The nature of the firm, *Economica*, (new series), **4**, 386–405.

References

Commons, J.R. (1934) *Institutional Economics*, University of Wisconsin Press.

Ezzamel, M.A. and Hilton K. (1980) Divisionalisation in British industry: a preliminary study, *Accounting and Business Research*, **38**, 197–214.

Ezzamel, M.A. (1985) On the assessment of the performance effects of multidivisional structures: a synthesis, *Accounting and Business Research*, Winter, 23–34.

Ezzamel, M. (1992) Corporate governance and financial control, in this volume.

Hill, C.W.L. (1985) Internal organization and enterprise performance: some UK evidence, *Managerial and Decision Economics*, **6**, 210–16.

Hill, C.W.L. (1988) Internal capital market controls and financial performance in multidivisional firms, *Journal of Industrial Economics*, **XXXVII**, 67–83.

Hill, C.W.L. and Pickering J.F. (1986) Divisionalisation, decentralisation and performance of large UK companies, *Journal of Management Studies*, **23**, 26–50.

Hilton, K. (1975) Control systems for social and economic management, Inaugural lecture, University of Southampton, also in this volume.

Ingham H.C. (1992) Organizational structure and the internal economy of the firm: the UK insurance industry, *Managerial and Decision Economics*, forthcoming.

Nickell, S.J. (1978) *The Investment Decisions of Firms*, Cambridge University Press, Cambridge.

Penrose, E.T. (1959) *The Theory of the Growth of the Firm*, Basil Blackwell.

Poirer, D.J. (1976) *The Economics of Structural Change*, North Holland.

Prescott, E.C. and Visscher M. (1986) Organization capital, *Journal of Political Economy*, **88**, 446–61.

Simon, H.A. (1955), A behavioural model of rational choice, *Quarterly Journal of Economics*, **69**, 99–118.

Slater, M. (1980) The managerial limitation to the growth of the firm, *Economic Journal*, **90**, 520–8.

Steer, P. and Cable J.R. (1978) Internal organization and profit: an empirical analysis of large UK companies, *Journal of Industrial Economics*, **XXVII**, 13–30.

Teece, D.J. (1981) Internal organization and economic performance: an empirical analysis of the profitability of principal firms, *Journal of Industrial Economics*, **30**, 173–200.

Thompson, R.S. (1981) Internal organization and profit: a note, *Journal of Industrial Economics*, **XXX**, 201–11.

Thompson, R.S. (1983a) Diffusion of the M-form structure in the UK: rate of imitation, inter-firm and inter-industry differences, *International Journal of Industrial Organization*, **1**, 297–315.

Thompson, R.S. (1983b) M-form adoption and M-form performance: an empirical investigation, *Recherches Economique de Louvain*, **49**, 3–24.

Williamson, O.E. (1967), Hierarchical control and optimum firm size, *Journal of Political Economy*, **75**, 123–38.

Williamson, O.E. (1970) *Corporate Control and Business Behaviour: An inquiry into the effects of organizational form on enterprise behaviour*, Prentice-Hall, Englewood cliffs, NJ.

Williamson, O.E. (1975) *Markets and Hierarchies: Analysis and antitrust implications*, Free Press.

Williamson, O.E. (1981) The modern corporation: origins, evolution, and attributes, *Journal of Economic Literature*, **19**, 1537–68.

Williamson, O.E. (1985) *The Economic Institutions of Capitalism: Firm, Markets and Relational Contracting*, Free Press.

Williamson, O.E. (1986) *Economic Organization: Firms, markets and policy control*, Wheatsheaf Books.

Adjustment costs and organizational change: Discussant's comments

JOHN CABLE

Do adjustment costs matter? Economists often assert or imply not: that they do not affect equilibrium choices. At the height of merger waves one may be tempted to think the economists have a point; and as long as perceived gains at the new equilibrium are reasonably large, relative to the returns at the old, their expected long term nature may in itself be enough to ensure that, even after discounting, it is perfectly rational for agents to ignore transitory effects. Yet, at the margin, there must be cases where the (discounted) long term benefits and the immediate costs are finely balanced; at a personal level, few will not at some time have resisted moving for no other reason than that the improvement in situation does not warrant the costs, the effort and the distractions of the journey to get there. And, to determine how wide is the margin within which the trade-off between long term gain and short term costs operates, we clearly need to know about the magnitude of transition costs. Thus, Hilary Ingham's analysis directs us to an important, and neglected, area of enquiry.

In the context of organizational change, perhaps as elsewhere, there are at least two separate questions concerning adjustment costs. First, for reasons outlined above, there is the question of their magnitude. Second, in interpreting empirical estimates of the performance effects of alternative organizational forms, we need to be sure when we are looking at equibrium changes or differences, undistorted by the intrusion of short run factors, and when we are not. Previous writers have been concerned about these issues rather more, perhaps, than Hilary's discussion (at para 2, p. 122 and Note 3) might suggest. Thus, subject as always to accuracy of classification, the inclusion of 'transitional' categories in cross section studies, if appropriately modelled, can offer at least partial answers to the first question, and reassurance on the second. The fact that the length of the transition period may be indeterminate, as her quotation from Steer and Cable (1978) notes, does not impair the effectiveness of the relevant categorical variables in normalizing for the fact that some firms are in transition over the period observed; and while, as stated, the *total* transition cost cannot be calculated (since this does require knowledge of total transition time), this does not mean that the instantaneous or *per period* cost during the transition phase will be irrecoverable from the parameters. Moreover, the fact that studies using the market model and share price measures of performance, notably by Thompson, 'have considered only a short post-reorganization period' is irrelevant; the whole attraction of the market model approach is that, if one buys the efficient markets story at any rate (as opposed to the short-termism, fads and bubbles alternative), both short run transition costs and long run returns will be fully, and accurately, reflected in share price adjustment around the time the news of reorganization breaks. Of course the market model approach will not yield estimates of transitions costs themselves, since the market has netted these out; but, if the underlying assumptions hold, we do know it is the (market's view of the) discounted equilibrium shift in future profit streams that is being captured. Before leaving this aspect of the previous literature, and in view of Hilary's own results (of which more later), it is pertinent to note the generally rather mixed results on transition effects previously reported: Armour and Teece (1978), for example, finding no evidence of them, whereas Steer and Cable (1978), for example, reported firms in transition exhibiting only 46–56% of the full equilibrium gain, in returns to equity and returns to long-run capital equations, though insignificant deviations from the equilibrium gain when performance was measured in terms of the profit margin.[1]

If Hilary's analysis does not quite boldly go where none has gone before, it certainly strikes out into pretty unchartered territory, and is all the more welcome for that. Bold, certainly, is the route selected, modelling the corporate life-cycle in just three phases – pre-, during and post-reorganization. Of course the world is more complex than this. The major companies included in the sample will, over the thirty-four-year period, inevitably have been subjected at various times to demand and technology shocks, been involved in mergers and/or capital restructurings, been affected by changes in management and corporate direction, and so forth. Abstracting from these and other perturbations in order to focus on the single organizational change may have its price, but this will become clear only in the light of the results, and arguably should not influence the *a priori* modelling. I am however somewhat less convinced, *a priori*, of the spline-function aspect of the empirical model. The effect, if I understand it right, is to produce a piecewise linear function with discontinuities of slope, but not of level, at the predetermined critical points of time. In the particular circumstances of the present analysis, given the nature of the corporate change being investigated, might there not be a case for allowing a discontinuity of *level*, i.e. an intercept shift, at least at the time of organizational change, and possibly at the end of the transition period also? A suitable combination of intercept and slope dummies would accommodate this less restricted model within a single estimating equation using all the available observations, and would at minimum provide a basis for comparison. Finally, so far as specification is concerned (apart from inevitable niggles about the specification of the **Z** vector), one might question the treatment of organizational form (OS) as exogenous, not least in the light of the well-known crisis-response hypothesis for organizational change that is referred to a number of times in the paper. While the feedback from profit to structure on this hypothesis would naturally operate with a lag, treatment of the system as recursive in order to justify the quasi-exogeneity of OS would also, as always, require independence of the error terms across equations in all time periods. In the eventuality of an omitted variable problem, this might well not be the case, thereby bringing back into play the vexing question of the **Z** vector.

With respect to the results, the main question is inevitably how to account for their extraordinarily mixed nature, with no discernible impact of organizational factors in twenty companies; evidence of a transitional period in twenty companies, but with as many showing temporary gains as losses; and instantaneous and sustained effects in twenty-one, in this case breaking roughly 60:40 in favour of gainers. Two points raised earlier may perhaps help towards an explanation for this diversity. First, the 'bold' model, excluding any normalization for other factors and events disturbing profits within the three subperiods, may simply be letting through too much noise for any clear signal to emerge. Second, the restrictive, spline-function formulation may be squeezing out evidence of effects that would be caught by other types of discontinuity and within-period time paths. Other possibilities also come to mind. Among the equations for individual companies listed in the appendix table, explanatory power is in some cases rather low (by normal standards for time-series estimates), with R^2 below 0.25 in nine cases, below 0.5 in a further six, and so low in a handful of the former group as to raise doubts about overall significance. It would be interesting to know what the overall picture would become with these weaker results omitted. Perhaps, too, it would help to place more emphasis than at present, in estimation and in interpretation, on distinguishing the specific form of organizational change – whether to M- or H-form, etc. – and also whether or not the change can be regarded as *optimal* in each specific case. Clearly, if one is attempting to aggregate even over one specific type of organizational change, in a small sample where there are some 'errors', a confusing overall picture is only to be expected. Alternatively, perhaps, there may be problems with the dating of the transitional period, in particular its end. Presumably, a common pattern is for heavy adjustment costs at the beginning of the transition period, tapering off thereafter.[2] Detecting precisely that the end has come would then be difficult, even for insiders. Moreover, it might well be the case that risk-averse managers, financial analysts and the like would only declare the end of the adjustment after the return to normalcy was in fact well established over (say) two or three reporting periods. If so, reliance by researchers on evidence from this source might lead to exaggerated transition periods and, ultimately, downward bias in estimates of adjustment costs. There could also be a systematic bias towards exaggeration of transition periods in cases of 'mistakes', or moves resulting in eventual *declines* in equilibrium performance. In these circumstances it might be interesting to experiment by imposing *fixed* transition periods in estimation (or perhaps a series of experiments with fixed periods of varying length) or, alternatively, finding some way of modelling decay into the adjustment costs over the transition period.

In sum, Hilary's analysis raises important issues, and points out a way in which to tackle them. I have a feeling that there is more in the data than has yet emerged, and various directions for further work in estimation and interpretation are suggested or implied in what has already been said. If, in the course of further work it is possible to extract from these models estimates of the *magnitude* of adjustment costs, where present, as well as merely their presence or absence, our understanding would be greatly enriched.

NOTES

[1] For firms in transition to M-form in the Steer – Cable analysis, the overall shift due to organizational form is the algebraic sum of the M-form *(OF)* and transitional *(T)* dummy parameters: 0.0847 plus − 0.0454, and 0.1047 plus − 0.0462 in returns to equity equations with and without interaction terms, and 0.0626 plus − 0.0316 in the returns to long-run capital equation; hence the figures quoted in the text here. In passing, comment on what Hilary describes as the 'suspiciously large' estimate of *OF* on performance in the S-C analysis – nearly 50% of the average return on (equity) capital – is irresistible. I have myself long held the view, not apparent to Peter Steer and myself at the time of our article, that the estimated M-form gain is subject to positive specification bias, due to the omission of variables controlling for the quality of management. The argument is as follows. In the diffusion period within which the gains from adoption of M-form are observable, it is on average the better-run firms which will have adopted early, and the less well run firms which should have adopted, but have not, against which the M-form differential is mainly observed. Thus, the M-form dummy systematically also selects well run firms, and its estimated coefficient conflates M-form and quality of management effects. Note, however, that while this qualifies the *magnitude* of estimated M-form gains, it is not actually bad for the M-form hypothesis itself; for only if M-form is a good thing would it be systematically chosen early by well-run firms.

---

2 I assume that the period is of the order of many months, and possibly years, given the magnitude of the M-form reorganization. Supporting evidence for this view might be cited from D.J. Teece (The diffusion of an administrative innovation, *Management Science*, 26, (1980), 464-70) who finds the half-life for the diffusion of M-form is of the order of 14–41 years compared with Ed Mansfield's 0.9–15 years for technical innovations (*Industrial Research and Technological Innovation*, W.W. Norton, NY, 1968); and from Thompson (1983a) whose finding that symmetric diffusion curves dominate others in the M-form diffusion process indicates its resemblence to *major* as opposed to routine technological innovations.

7
*Agency costs, incentives and management buyouts**

STEVE THOMPSON

INTRODUCTION

In his introductory paper to this volume, Mahmoud Ezzamel (Paper 1) explores the nature of financial control within organizations. He shows that the locus of that control influences the choice of financial mechanisms which may be used to induce appropriate behaviour within the organization. Thus, for example, in multi-level systems the instruments of financial control exercised by the central headquarters over the operating units tend to stress formal, output goal achievements. In contrast, local control focuses upon 'softer' objectives and upon 'behaviour rather than output'.

One of Kenneth Hilton's research interests was an examination of the benefits of decentralization within large, multi-output firms (e.g. Ezzamel and Hilton, 1980 a, b). His work complemented that of O.E. Williamson (1975) and others which had proposed an efficiency rationale for divisionalized firms based upon a vertical separation of responsibilities between the headquarters and operating divisions. In such a multi-divisional (M-form) firm the corporate HQ takes responsibility for strategic planning whilst using formal financial controls to motivate the quasi-autonomous product divisions. This arrange-

* This paper draws upon joint work with Mike Wright and Ken Robbie, some of which is published in Thompson *et al.* (1992), to whom I owe a considerable debt. The paper also benefited from comments by Mike Page, Mahmoud Ezzamel, Hilary Ingham and John Cubbin.

Perspectives on Financial Control: Essays in memory of Kenneth Hilton.
Edited by Mahmoud Ezzamel and David Heathfield.
Published in 1992 by Chapman & Hall, London. ISBN 0 412 40980 1.

ment, Williamson suggested, allows transactions to occur in informationally efficient internal markets, whilst minimizing the incentives for the pursuit of non-profit goals by senior management. Such an arrangement also facilitates a mixture of formal and informal controls. For example, while an external lender traditionally has no role to play unless and until the borrower defaults, in the M-form's internal capital market the central financier can monitor project progress and offer expertise as required.

The early empirical studies (Steer and Cable, 1978; Ezzamel and Hilton, 1980a; Armour and Teece, 1978; Thompson, 1981) provided some confirmation of the apparent performance superiority of divisionalized firms – at least around the time of reorganization, see Ingham's contribution to this volume. However, subsequent empirical work has questioned the robustness of these findings. It appears that many divisionalized firms fail to achieve the M-form's separation of activities and level of incentives. Hill and Pickering (1986), for example, report that central office over-involvement distorts internal competition for funds in many cases. The same study also reveals that a substantial minority of divisionalized firms went to the opposite extreme with the central office abdicating responsibility for capital allocation and allowing the divisions to retain and reinvest their earnings. Furthermore, even where an appropriate distribution of responsibilities is achieved, the resulting corporate structure may not contain incentives sufficient to motivate senior management and divisional managers to play their roles in the interests of shareholders. While Williamson (1975) recognized the existence of these non-optimal M-Forms, this subsequence research suggests they are widespread.

It follows that recent research on the internal organization of the firm has tended to concentrate upon incentives. The firm's structure is usually presented as a multi-level principal-agent problem in which the shareholders (as ultimate principals) need to motivate the peak-tier managers to take value-maximizing decisions and to monitor the activities of their subordinates, the divisional managers, and so on down the hierarchy. This view is reflected in current research interest in issues such as profit-sharing, executive compensation, stock options, labour participation, entrepreneurship, etc.

This paper is intended as a contribution to such a literature. It examines the management buyout (MBO) as a response to the failure to resolve corporate problems within some form of divisionalized structure. The typical MBO involves the divestment of a division or subsidiary in which incumbent managers hold a substantial equity stake. The result is to replace financial control, as exercised by the hierarchy, with a set of market-dominated relationships between managers and their financier/investor principals. This produces radical changes to the incentives faced by the managers. Mounting empirical evidence suggests that the managers' response to these incentives raises operating efficiency, at least in the short-to-medium term.

The second section discusses the characteristics of MBOs in the UK. The third section examines the changes in agency costs involved when a division is divested to a debt-financed company substantially owned by managers. The empirical evidence is reviewed in the fourth section and the fifth section reports some results of a performance study of UK buyouts. A brief conclusion follows in the final section.

MBO CHARACTERISTICS

The details of MBO tractions have been described elsewhere (Thompson *et al.*, 1989; Robbie *et al.*, 1991) by the present author and others. In consequence a brief review of the characteristics relevant to the present work appears sufficient:

• MBO activity increased sharply in the early 1980s – see Table 7.1 – when it was particularly associated with sales from under-performing business during the industrial recession. More latterly MBO deals became commonplace during the long phase of industrial recovery and growth. The value of MBO deals both in aggregate and as a percentage of all corporate control activity, also grew substantially over the period, but with a more erratic path reflecting the irregularity of very large transactions.

Table 7.1 The growth of MBOs in the UK

Year	Number (includes buy-ins)	Value (£m)	Value as % of the Total Market for Corporate Control
1980	35	28	0.0
1981	145	193	9.0
1982	246	663	23.3
1983	241	372	13.7
1984	243	406	7.0
1985	290	1180	14.3
1986	301	1485	9.3
1987	427	3529	18.5
1988	450	4923	18.3
1989	504	7521	22.4

Source: Business Monitor and CMBOR, University of Nottingham.

• Very few UK MBOs have involved the private acquisition of publicly-held companies. (Unlike the US, where 'going private' leveraged buyout (LBO) transactions are frequent). A substantial majority of UK deals (usually 60–70% year) continue to involve the voluntary divestiture of one or more divisions or subsidiaries by a public or privately-held company. In addition, there has been a steady flow of MBOs from state-sector companies, a consequence of the government's privatization policy.

147

- Most UK MBO deals leave the management team with a substantial proportion of the voting shares – usually a majority in all but the larger deals – although in some cases the managers' holding varies with the *subsequent* performance of the new company, according to a so-called 'ratchet' mechanism.
- The management's disproportionately large shareholding is made possible by the use of assorted debt and quasi-debt instruments. However, the extent of leverage is usually more cautious in the UK than in US deals. Furthermore, bank credit and syndicated bank loans are more important in the UK while marketed debt dominates in the USA.
- The principal financing institution – whether this provides debt, equity or some combination – frequently plays an active role in supervising the new company. For example, it might provide a non-executive chair to the new board or hold the right to nominate one or more directors. The lead financial institution will normally insist on more detailed and more frequent (i.e. monthly) reporting than would ordinarily be provided to the external market.
- As in the USA, most UK MBOs occur in mature, cash-generating industries. However, there is a substantial minority of deals in other sectors where new product development is essential – such as computer software and electronics – and even (as Wright and Ennew, report in this volume) some in financial services.
- Michael Jensen (1989) recently described the US LBO as an enduring organizational form, with only 5% of 1300 cases recorded between 1981 and 1986 having returned to quoted status. In the UK, by contrast, MBO companies appear to retain their independent private status for a relatively short period. By 1990, 36% of identified deals had experienced a change of status – either through acquisition (17%) or stock market flotation (19%) – and all but one such deal identified before 1985 has ceased its independent private life.

MBOS: INCENTIVE AND FINANCIAL CONTROL ISSUES

The conventional publicly-quoted company has a potential agency problem in that senior management may be merely weakly motivated to engage in value-creating actions for their shareholders (Jensen and Meckling, 1976). The latter, who may be presumed to hold balanced portfolios and hence typically small holdings in any one share, face a free rider problem in acquiring information about managerial deficiencies and acting upon it. Hence given high monitoring costs to outsiders, the managers may enjoy the discretion to follow their own preferred interests. A recognition of this problem may lead the board of directors, on behalf of the shareholders, to introduce performance-related pay, stock options, etc. for senior management. Furthermore, the latter, nearing the peak of their careers, may be encouraged to hold a significant proportion of their wealth in the form of the company's equity.

In multi-business firms, however, motivating divisional managers will be more problematic. Stock market or profits-based schemes are ineffective if a large number of divisions creates a free rider problem. Similarly, schemes based on divisional performance will be flawed where divisions operate in entirely different market environments or where intra-divisional vertical relations create problems of administering transfer prices. Particular difficulties might be expected in motivating managers in charge of divisions with good cash flow potential but poor growth prospects. These managers may find that increases in their efforts merely raise earnings for reinvestment elsewhere in the firm. Furthermore, promotions to corporate headquarters may be facilitated by the initiation of successful projects not by the introduction of economies. Hence, divisional managers in low growth, 'cash cows' may be particularly difficult to motivate.

The divestment of a division to a new company in which management has a substantial equity holding – the essence of a MBO – replaces hierarchical control with market-based incentives. These include incentives for the firm's managers to act in a value-maximizing manner and for the suppliers of debt and equity capital to become involved in an active monitoring role.

As noted above, the members of a MBO team typically become major shareholders in the new company – thus reducing the traditional manager-investor agency problem. Furthermore, this ownership interest is frequently reinforced by a 'ratchet' mechanism – whereby the equity share is made performance-dependent – and by the bonding commitment made by individual managers to finance it; that is, the manager's own investments are generally financed by loans, second mortgages, etc., increasing his/her vulnerability to failure.

UK MBOs also leave outside investors and lenders with strong incentives to monitor management behaviour, usually by taking non-executive directorships/chairmanships, etc. Since the new company is *unquoted* the outside equity is typically held in large blocks by institutions with little scope for easy exit. Hence the need to exercise 'voice' (Hirschman, 1970) in ratifying decisions. A similar situation occurs on the debt side, where again the financing institutions tend to hold substantial positions but have an obvious interest in restraining high risk behaviour. Even where diversified loan portfolios are obtained by syndicating debt, the lead institution(s) has a reputation to defend by maintaining monitoring on behalf of the syndicate.

Following the insights of Jensen (1986, 1987), in particular, it has been noted that the use of debt itself may reduce agency costs in MBOs. It is commonplace that many buyouts occur in profitable but low-growth industries – locations where the opportunities for reimbursement may be limited. Jensen suggests that the 'free cash flow' generated frequently becomes the target of managerial indolence or misuse. Leverage has the effect of committing managers to meet the company's interest obligations or else jeopardize its survival – i.e. it lowers managerial discretion to engage in non-value-maximizing diversions.

It is, of course, possible that MBOs achieve financial success by transferring value from another group to the investors rather than creating value via efficiency improvements. In US 'going private' deals, for example, the company's existing bondholders may face increased risk as a consequence of extensive issue of new unsecured debt (Asquith and Wizman, 1990). Similarly, the favourable tax treatment accorded to debt interest means that any increase in leverage will tend to transfer benefits from the exchequer to the company.[1]

In the case of the UK MBO where, as noted above, the typical transaction involves the divestment of a division to its managers, the issue of transfers from bondholders or tax authorities is not particularly relevant. The two obvious categories who could lose by an MBO are parent shareholders and divisional employees.

In the early 1980s there were some spectacularly successful MBOs where it was apparent *ex post* that the division has been badly underpriced. However, it would be surprising if generalized underpricing were to persist. It appears reasonable to expect that vendors' price expectations would rise as MBOs received more favourable publicity.

Shleifer and Summers (1988) have pointed out that hostile takeovers frequently change the employees' terms and conditions of employment and, as such, represent a 'breach of trust'. of the implicit work contract. In a similar vein it is conceivable that MBOs alter the terms of employment in ways injurious to the interests of labour – perhaps by requiring higher effort levels or by lowering non-monetary rewards. Conversely, it is entirely feasible that MBO deals improve employee welfare either by the introduction of participation/shareholding schemes or via the sharing of increased efficiency in higher wages.

PERFORMANCE EFFECTS OF BUYOUTS: RECENT EVIDENCE

Until recently there were very few published studies of buyout activity. However, in the past three or four years there have been a number of US articles and – unlike the rather ambiguous findings of the comparable merger literature – these studies indicate that the changed incentives do induce performance improvements. The research on 'going private' LBO deals (see De Angelo *et al.*, 1984, Marais *et al.*, 1989 and Lehn and Poulson, 1989 in Table 7.2) indicates that existing shareholders receive a bid premium at least as high as in conventional tender offers and that, furthermore, this totally dominates any losses to existing bondholders. The American research also suggests the market approves of divestment to manager-led companies: a study of divisional buyouts by Hite and Vetsuypens (1989) found small but significant positive announcement effects for the vendor's shareholders.

Table 7.2 US empirical studies of buyouts

Study	Sample	Findings
De Angelo *et al.* (1984)	72 Going private 1973–80	Significant positive wealth effects for shareholders in bought-out firms
Marais *et al.* (1989)	113 Going private 1974–85	Wealth gains to shareholders exceeding any bondholder losses
Kaplan (1989)	76 MBOs 1980–6	Operation performance and asset utilization improvements
Lehn and Poulson (1989)	263 Buyouts 1980–7	Substatial premium to pre-buyout shareholders
Muscarella and Vetsuypens (1990)	72 Reverse LBOs	Improved profitability and lowered costs
Hite and Vetsuypens (1989)	Divisional buyouts	Small, significant gains to vendor's shareholders
Smith (1990)	58 MBOs 1977–86	Improved cash flow to assets and employees
Lichtenberg and Siegel (1990)	c. 1000 plants involved in MBOs	Improved further productivity
Singh (1990)	55 LBOs and MBOs which made a public offering	Bought-out companies outperformed their industry averages three years prior to an IPO

In addition to these market-based studies, there are some recent articles which use accounting data to examine post-MBO performance. Kaplan (1989) documents substantial improvements in operating performance and indicates a very substantial return to total capital in the years immediately following a buyout. Muscarella and Vetsuypens (1989) find improvements in profitability and lower costs among their sample of LBOs which subsequently returned to quoted status. Similarly, Smith (1990) reports improvements in cash flow to assets and cash flow per employee. Plant level analysis by Lichtenberg and Siegel (1990) suggests that bought-out companies do not engage in extensive lay-offs but the authors do find evidence of total factor productivity improvements in the three years following buyouts and a lowering of the ratio of white collar to blue collar workers.

Research outside the US is much more limited in scale and scope. Two surveys conducted by Nottingham University's Centre for Management Buy-Out Research (CMBOR) of UK MBOs up to 1983, (Wright and Coyne, 1985) and of MBOs completed between 1983 and early 1986 (Thompson *et al.*, 1989) found evidence of improvements in turnover and trading profits. The earlier survey, which principally involved deals arising during the 1980s recession, indicated that 18% of jobs were lost immediately after the transaction.

By the time of the later survey initial job losses had fallen to 6%, with evidence of some subsequent employment gains. Both surveys revealed that MBOs were often accompanied by improvements in internal control systems.

It has been suggested that the incentives in UK MBO deals encourage an undue emphasis on the short-term. For example, the level of gearing is normally at its highest immediately after the creation of the new company and the existence of ratchets, etc. gives managers a strong interest in out-performing their targets. A study of the longer-term performance consequence of buyouts (Warwick Business School, 1989) has suggested that the profitability improvements of the first three years are not, on average, sustained beyond that time. However, these conclusions were based on small sample sizes.[2]

UK BUYOUT PERFORMANCE: SOME RESULTS

The latter part of this paper seeks to respond to the paucity of systematic UK evidence by introducing some results from a study of those MBOs which have returned to the stock market via an initial public offering (IPO) of shares. This approach avoids two of the difficulties which have beset previous UK work in the field. First, the offering requires detailed provision of information which is otherwise hard to obtain for *private* companies. Second the lack of an extended time series on performance data is overcome if it is assumed that the market valuation after flotation *fully reflects* the anticipated future earnings of the company.[3]

Sample

An examination of all flotations on the London Stock Exchange between January 1982 and March 1989 indicated that approximately 180 former MBOs had achieved a quotation. However, a large majority of these represented relatively small deals for which financial and ownership data were generally unavailable. In consequence, the sample was restricted to those MBOs floated between 1982 and 1989 with a market capitalization > £10m and ownership data relating to the MBO deal itself. This yielded a total of thirty-one cases bought-out between 1982 and 1987 and floated between 1984 and 1989, see Table 7.3 with an average lag between MBO and IPO of 21.8 months. The initial deal price varied between £3.8m and £260m (mean £51.08m), while the subsequent equity value on flotation ranged between £12.1m and £840.0m.

It was recognized, of course, that there is some selection bias in using a sample of MBOs which have returned to the stock market. Such companies, almost by definition, are among the more successful buyouts. However, since this research was concerned with an inter-firm analysis and did not seek to quantify the benefits of an MBO per se, an entire sample drawn from among the more successful firms did not appear to be inherently problematic. Furthermore, some selection bias is inevitable when dealing with MBOs: for example, unsuccessful cases will tend to fail or to be acquired *before* they have generated sufficient published data for the outside researcher to use them.

Table 7.3 Timing of sample MBOs and flotations

Year	1982	1983	1984	1985	1986	1987	1988	1989
MBO	3	2	1	9	8	8	–	–
IPO	–	–	3	–	5	9	11	3

Average lag between MBO and IPO = 21.8 months

The derivation of an excess return to capital across the interval between buyout and IPO, that is between times T_1 and T_2 in Figure 7.1, required a comparison between the actual outcome and the return on an asset of equivalent riskiness. The excess return to investors' equity alone was initially considered as a performance measure but rejected on the grounds that it would be inflated by the purely mechanical effects of leverage. Instead, following Kaplan (1989) the return to total capital (i.e. equity + debt) was used as a better proxy for the efficiency with which the firm uses its assets. Adjusting for risk was problematic, precisely because the newly bought-out company is private, and therefore the only equity beta estimates available are those *after* the IPO. Hence it was necessary to make certain assumptions above the appropriate systematic risk. A number of alternative excess return measures were derived, but the preferred alternative, following Kaplan (1989),[4] was the excess return (XRETI) on *total* capital defined as:

$$\text{XRETI} = \frac{\left(\begin{array}{l} 1 + (\text{Equity}^* + \text{Interim Principal and Interest Payments}^2 \\ \quad + \text{Debt}_2 - \text{Total Capital}_1)/\text{Total Capital}_1 \end{array} \right)}{1 + R_f + B_a (R_m - R_f).} - 1$$

where the '*' denotes market value, book value otherwise;
subscripts 1 and 2 denote beginning and end period values, respectively;
R_f is the risk-free rate proxied here by the three-month Treasury Bill return;
R_m is the market return, using the FT 500 index;

and B_a is a measure of the asset beta $= \dfrac{B_e}{1 + (1 - t) \cdot \dfrac{D}{E}}$

for equity beta (B_e), using the London Business School Risk Measurement Service estimate of the immediate post-float beta, where t is the corporation tax rate and D/E is the debt/equity ratio at the time of the IPO.[3]

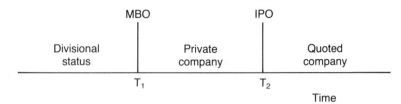

Figure 7.1 Evolution of an MBO.

Since data on the debt replacement schedule *between* the MBO and IPO were generally unavailable, the interest paid had to be estimated. EXRET1 was calculated assuming the whole debt had to be serviced across the complete interval at the rate of LIBOR + 2% (widely quoted by institutional sources as the typical MBO rate) – as such it represents an upper bound estimate. The total capital excess return was then re-estimated omitting interest paid entirely (EXRET2).

Model specification

It was expected that the post-float market capitalization would capture the effects of any performance improvements between MBO and IPO *and* the projected performance of the newly-quoted company. However, an abundant literature on public offerings suggests that the initial market capitalization also depends upon agency and signalling factors associated with the offering itself. After Jensen and Meckling (1976) it might be anticipated that any dilution of the management's equity holding will influence monitoring efforts within the firm so as to reduce its value. Similarly, in an environment of uncertainty and asymmetrically distributed information any reduction in management's holdings may *signal* an anticipated downturn in the firm's prospects. This suggested the need to control for agency and signalling factors, including the change in management equity holdings, present at the float.

These considerations suggested a model of the basic form:

Excess Returns $= f$ (Incentives incorporated in the MBO; Agency and signalling factors association with IPO; firm controls)

where the explanatory variables were as follows:

Incentive factors

The manegerial equity ownership effect was initially measured as the percentage of equity (MANI) subscribed by the management team at the time of the MBO. Preference shares were initially included as debt capital, but an alternative management ownership measure (MAN2) was employed when preference shares were re-classified as equity.

154

A binary variable (RATCHET) was used to identify any performance-related equity ratchet for managers.

To control for the bonding effect of debt on the distribution of free cash flow (Jensen, 1986) the debt-equity ratio at the time of the deal (DEBTEQ1) was used. An alternative (DEBTEQ2) was used where preference shares were included as equity.

IPO factors

To control for the agency/signalling effects of a partial management exit the change is management equity (CHANGEQ) was included.

The IPO literature (Downes and Heinkel, 1982 etc.) suggests that signalling difficulties may be countered by hiring leading professional firms as brokers, auditors, solicitors, etc. for the new issues. The reputations of these agents serve as hostages against misrepresentation in the offer documents. An attempt was made to control for the use of 'leading' professionals. However, it appeared to be the case that almost all full LSE listings used these better-known firms such that no satisfactory binary classification could be made.

The period of our sample IPOs 1984–9 did contain a sub-period of intense activity in the new issues market, dating perhaps between LSE deregulation ('Big Bang') in October 1986 and the market crash of October 1987. A Bank of England (1990:252) analysis identifies this as a 'hotspot' of activity with new issues typically moving to a 25% premium after one week's trading. While our market capitalization measure was taken a month after flotation – to avoid any initial underpricing effects – it was recognized that market behaviour in this period may have been atypical. In consequence, a binary variable (PRECRASH) was included for those IPOs occurring in the year preceding October 1987.

Firm controls

A firm size variable, deal price or total capital (SIZE) of the new company, was included to control for any small company effect by which unusually rapid growth by some small companies might – given a negative correlation between MAN1 and size – appear to inflate the incentive role.

Five MBOs in the sample resulted from sales out of the public sector. Privatization may be associated with under-pricing (Thompson *et al.*, 1990), particularly since the vendor's management have no direct interest in the outcome. A binary variable (PRIVAT) was used to distinguish these cases.

Industry sources suggested to us that under-pricing was a frequent feature of the earlier buyouts on divestment when vendors were unaware of the potential of management ownership to raise value. As this appeared plausible, we included a binary variable EARLY for those MBOs that occurred between 1982 and 1984.

155

The full model, with the predicted signs over the coefficients may be summarized as follows:

$$EXRET1 = a_0 + \overset{+}{a_1} MAN1 + \overset{+}{a_2} DEBTEQ1$$
$$+ \overset{-}{a_3} CHANGEQ + \overset{+}{a_4} SIZE + \overset{+}{a_5} PRIVAT$$
$$+ \overset{+}{a_6} PRECRASH + \overset{+}{a_7} RATCHET + \overset{+}{a_8} EARLY$$
$$+ Ei \tag{1}$$

Results

Descriptive summary statistics for the continuous and binary variables are provided in Table 7.4. Equation (1) was estimated by OLS, using the alternative versions of the dependent variable, and the results are shown in Table 7.5. In each specification using either EXRET1 or EXRET2 as dependent variable, the management ownership effect emerged as positive, large and statistically significant. The magnitude of the coefficient estimates was surprising: for example, with EXRET1 as dependent variable it appears that a 10% increase in management equity ownership (MAN1) would increase the returns to total capital by at least 25%. (Subsequent tests revealed no indication of either non-linearities or structural breaks in this seemingly robust finding.)

Table 7.4 Sample characteristics: summary statistics

(a) Continuous varibles

Variable name	Range Min.	Max.	Mean	Standard deviation
MAN1	0.0008	1.0	0.30	0.29
MAN2	3.80	81.7	34.3	21.99
DEBTEQ1	0.41	238.0	22.0	44.07
DEBTEQ2	0.41	235.0	10.81	41.83
CHANGEQ1	0.0	0.66	0.30	0.19
TCAP1	3.80	260.0	51.99	64.01
XRET2	− 0.026	5.51	1.35	1.23
XRET1	− 0.039	6.34	1.45	1.42

(b) Binary variables

Variable	% = 1
RACHET	52
PRIVAT	16.1
PRECRASH	29.0
EARLY	19.35

By contrast the debt-equity ratio carried a negative – if insignificant-coefficient, giving no support to the free cash flow argument for the incentive effects

Table 7.5 Determinants of the excess returns[a] to total capital: OLS estimates (£ *statistics in parentheses*)

	Explanatory variables													
	MAN1	MAN2	DEBTEQ1[b]	DEBTEQ2	EARLY	RATCHET	CHANGEDQ	PRECASH	PRIVAT	SIZE[c]	CONSTANT	R^2	$\overline{R}^2$	n
EXRET1	2.56	—	1.20	—	0.44	—	0.30	0.15	0.10	1.46	0.26	0.54	0.39	28
	(3.15)		(1.19)		(1.04)		(0.31)	(0.39)	(0.19)	(0.03)	(0.50)			
EXRET1	—	3.55	—	−8.03	0.32	0.42	0.41	−0.05	0.15	−44.86	0.82	0.52	0.26	26
		(2.93)		(1.58)	(0.68)	(1.02)	(0.42)	(0.14)	(0.65)	(1.22)	(1.74)			
EXRET2	2.32	—	−1.06	—	0.32	—	0.54	0.03	0.10	−2.24	0.31	0.51	0.34	28
	(2.95)		(1.09)		(0.77)		(0.58)	(0.08)	(1.19)	(0.06)	(0.62)			
EXRET2	—	2.90	—	−6.46	0.25	—	0.57	−0.16	0.33	−45.28	0.85	0.45	0.26	28
		(2.40)		(1.27)	(0.53)		(0.58)	(0.42)	(0.62)	(1.24)	(1.80)			

a = EXRET measure normalized by means; b = $\times 10^{-2}$; c = $\times 10^{-4}$.

of debt.[5] Similarly, including a RATCHET dummy variable (which caused the sample size to fall to twenty-six) failed to reveal any support for incentive effects of ratchets.

It had been conjectured that underpricing in early MBO deals, when vendors were perhaps unaware of the scope for improving under-performing divisions, would be reflected in higher returns. In the event EARLY, though positive, was insignificant. The privatization variable PRIVAT was also positive and insignificant – perhaps reflecting the relatively small number of privatization sales (five) in the sample. The PRECRASH variable failed to show any evidence of inflated returns for 1986-87 floats, while the inconsistent coefficient signs pattern for SIZE indicated an absence of any 'small firm' effect.

There are potentially important factors which have been omitted for our analysis. First, the monitoring role of the investing and lending institutions could not be analysed on a comparative basis. (In every deal in the sample institutions appeared to take boardroom representation, allowing little basis for comparison). Along with the re-concentration of equity in management hands there tends to be a concentration in outside ownership by a small number of institutions. These shareholders and the new company's loan suppliers have strong monitoring incentives. Second, the analysis does not consider *vendor* performance after the MBO. It is assumed that the potential improvements in performance are not fully captured, *ex ante*, in the deal price. Third, the need for comprehensive ownership data unfortunately restricted the sample to large deals and necessarily reduced its size. A large sample, which embraced more small deals, would be both more representative and, arguably, better suited for an examination of the motivational consequences of debt: in smaller MBO deals the management equity ownership tends to be very high and it might be expected that other factors exert a stronger influence on performance outcomes. Further research is being carried out to try to remedy these deficiencies.

Despite these caveats the size, significance and robust nature of the MAN1 and MAN2 coefficients are clear. The results are entirely consistent with the view that management equity ownership represents a major motivational factor. Evidence elsewhere suggesting that divestment from a divisionalized firm to a new management-led company raises performance, leaves open several possible sources of gain. For example, it could be that the act of divestment – by reducing the height of the vertical hierarchy – improves decision-making; or again it is possible that management responds to its new autonomy with more enthusiasm. Without ruling out these general factors, the results reported here of a *continuous* relationship between performance and management ownership point to the considerable importance of financial incentives in determining managerial behaviour.

CONCLUSION

Elsewhere in this volume (for example in the paper by Ezzamel) it has been shown that the literature on financial control usefully complements the rather general economic analysis of internal organization. This literature describes the devices which are used to translate organizational objectives into achieved results. However, the success of MBOs over the past decade or so indicates the existence of a useful alternative to internal control apparatus. The divestment of a subsidiary or division to a new company in which existing managers have a major ownership involvement substitutes a market-based relationship between the firm and its capital suppliers, for one based on internal hierarchy. Provided that the new entity is technologically and economically separable from its parent, and provided that its activities allow a substantial measure of debt finance, it may substitute the powerful incentive effects of equity ownership for a complex set of administrative devices. Evidence presented here and elsewhere indicates that such ownership involvement exerts an important positive influence on performance.

NOTES

[1] The overall picture is more complex since the purchase of the company will *ceteris paribus* increase the tax obligations of the vendors, Jensen *et al.* (1989).

[2] The limitations of the UK evidence on MBOs are discussed in Wright *et al.* (1991), Chapter 7.

[3] The IPO of any larger company subjects it to detailed scrutiny by professional share analysts. MBO flotations have a particular significance because of venture capitalists' exist concerns. The IPO itself allows a partial exit for institutional holders of equity and also puts the company into the public arena for a possible third party takeover, Muscarella and Vetsuypens (1990).

[4] This section draws upon Thompson *et al.* (1992).

[5] The debt-equity ratio *was* significant when the return to equity investors was substituted to return to total capital. However, this is unsurprising among a sample of successful buyouts, i.e. a group of companies for whom leverage has worked:

Return to Equity $= 0.02 + 1.33$ MAN1 $+ 2.35$ DEBTEQI $- 0.21$ EARLY
$\quad\quad\quad\quad\quad$ (0.06) (2.26) $\quad\quad$ (3.23) $\quad\quad\quad\quad$ (0.67)
$\quad\quad\quad\quad\quad + 0.33$ CHANGEQ $- 0.02$ PRECRASH $+ 0.54$ PRIVAT $- 25.72$ SIZE
$\quad\quad\quad\quad\quad\quad$ (0.48) $\quad\quad\quad\quad$ (0.09) $\quad\quad\quad\quad$ (0.139) $\quad\quad$ (0.88)
$R^2 = 0.56$, t-statistics in parentheses, where return to equity is the proportionate change in equity value between MBO and IPO relative to the change for the FTSE index, assuming a beta of unity – see Thompson *et al.* (1992).

REFERENCES

Armour, H. and Teece, D. (1978), Organizational structure and economic performance, *Bell Journal of Economics* **9**, 106–22.

Asquith P. and Wizman, T. (1990), Event risk, covenants and bondholder returns in LBOs, *Journal of Financial Economics* **27**(1), 195–214.

Bank of England (1990) New equity issues in the UK, *Bank of England Quarterly Bulletin*, May, 243–52.

Cable, J. (1985) Capital market information and industrial performance: the role of West German banks, *Economic Journal* **95**, 118–32.

De Angelo, H., De Angelo, L. and Rice, E. (1984) Going private: minority freezeouts and stockholder wealth, *Journal of Law and Economics* **27**, 367–401.

Downes, D. and Heinkel, R. (1982) Signalling and valuation of unseasoned new issues, *Journal of Finance* **37**, 1–10.

Ezzamel, M. (1992) *Corporate Governance and Financial Control*, in this volume, pp. 3–26.

Ezzamel, M. and Hilton, K. (1980a) Divisonalisation in British industry: a preliminary study, *Accounting and Business Research* Spring, 197–213.

Ezzamel, M. and Hilton, K. (1980b) Can divisional discretion be measured? *Journal of Financial and Business Accounting*, **2**, 311–27.

Hill, C. and Pickering, J. (1986) Divisionalization, decentralisation and performance of large UK companies, *Journal of Management Studies* **23**, 26–50.

Hirschman, A.O., (1970) *Exit, Voice and Loyalty* Cambridge University Press, Boston, MA.

Hite G. and Vetsuypens, M. (1989) Management buyouts of divisions and shareholder wealth, *Journal of Finance* **44**, 953–70.

Ingham, H. (1992) Adjustment costs and organisational change, this volume.

Jensen, M.C. (1986) Agency costs of free cash flow, corporate finance and takeovers, *American Economic Review: Papers and Proceedings* **76**, 323–36.

Jensen, M.C. (1987) The takeover controversy: analysis and evidence, in J. Coffee, L. Lowenstein and S. Rose-Ackerman (eds.) *Knights, Raiders and Targets: The impact of hostile takeovers*, Oxford University Press.

Jensen, M.C. (1989) The eclipse of its public corporation, *Harvard Business Review*, September/October.

Jensen, M.C. and Meckling, W. (1976) The theory of the firm: managerial behaviour, agency costs and ownership structure, *Journal of Financial Economics* **3**, 305–60.

Jensen, M.C. Kaplan, S. and Stiglin, L. (1989) Effects of LBOs on tax revenues of the US Treasury, *Tax Notes* **42**, 727–33.

Kaplan, S. (1989) The effects of management buyouts on operating performance and value, *Journal of Financial Economics* **24**, 217–54.

Lehn, K. and Poulson, A. (1989) Free cash flow and sharehaolder gains in going private transactions, *Journal of Finance* **44**, 771–88.

Lichtenberg, F. and Siegel, D. (1990) The effects of LBOs on productivity and related aspects firm behavior, *Journal of Financial Economics* **27**, 165–94.

Marais, L., Schipper, K. and Smith A. (1989) Wealth effects of going private on senior securities, *Journal of Financial Economics* **23**, 155–9.

Muscarella, C. and Vetsuypens, M. (1990) Efficiency and organizational structure: a study of reverse LBOs, *Journal of Finance* **45**, 1389–413.

Robbie, K., Thompson, R.S. and Wright, M. (1991) Managerial buyouts: incentive and ownership efforts, *Business Strategy Review* 2.

Shleifer, A. and Summers, L. (1988) Breach of trust in hostile takeovers, in A. Auerbach, ed., *Corporate Takeovers: Causes and Consequence*, University of Chicago Press.

Singh, H. (1990) Management buy-outs and shareholder value, *Strategic Management Journal*.

Smith, A. (1990) Corporate ownership structure and performance: the case of management buyouts, *Journal of Financial Economics* **27**, 143–64.

Steer, P. and Cable, J.R. (1978) Internal organization and profit: an empirical analysis of large UK companies, *Journal of Industrial Economics* **27**, 13–30.

Thompson, R.S. (1981) Internal organization and profit: a note, *Journal of Industrial Economics* **30**, 201–12.

Thompson, R.S. and Wright, M. (1990) UK management buyouts: debt, equity and agency cost implications, *Managerial and Decision Economics* **12**(1), 15–26.

Thompson, R.S., Wright, M. and Robbie, K. (1989) Management buy-outs, debt and efficiency: some evidence from the UK, *Journal of Applied Corporate Finance* **2**(1), 76–86.

Thompson, R.S., Wright, M. and Robbie, K. (1990) Privatisation via management and employee buyouts: ownership forms and incentive issues, *Fiscal Studies* **13**(3), 71–88.

Thompson, R.S., Wright, M. and Robbie, K. (1992) Management equity ownership, debt and performance, *Scottish Journal of Political Economy*, in press.

Warwick Business School (1989) *The Long Term Performance of Management Buyouts*, Touche Ross.

Williamson, O.E. (1975) *Markets and Hierarchies* (Free Press).

Wright, M. and Coyne, J. (1985) *Management Buyouts*, (Croom-Helm: Beckenham, England).

Wright, M., Thompson, S., Chiplin, B. and Robbie, K. (1991) *Buy-ins and Buy-outs: New Strategies in Corporate Management*, Graham and Trotman.

Wright, M. and Ennew, C. and Starkey K. (1992) Control, Internal Organisation and Divestment: Experimentation and the Boundaries of Financial Services' Firms. Chapter in this volume.

Agency costs, incentives and management buyouts: Discussant's comments

MICHAEL PAGE

The MBO is a surprising phenomenon. If a division of a business has failed to perform in the past, much of the blame would appear to lie in the hands of the managers who have been running it. It seems paradoxical that a popular solution to the problem has been to sell apparently under performing companies with large burdens of debt to the self-same managers who have been running them in the past.

If management buyouts work, a plausible explanation is provided by Agency Theory which hypothesises that there are large inefficiencies in divisional organization which can be eradicated by selling off businesses into a 'market-dominated' environment where a revised incentive structure enables efficiency gains to be realized. Steve Thompson's paper is a welcome attempt to measure the gains from buyouts for a sample of firms and to test the explanatory power of various sources of gain. Limited evidence exists about UK buyouts and they have occurred in a very different environment from the USA, where the bulk of buyout research has been done.

This discussion examines agency cost and alternative explanations for buyouts and comments on the methods and results of Thomson's paper.

Alternative (not mutually exclusive) explanations of why buyouts succeed include:

1. Information asymmetry – managers are assumed to have superior information about the potential performance of divisions in comparison with the

* Halpern and Woolf Professor of Accounting, Portsmouth University

information available to head office and shareholders of the holding company.

2. Wealth transfers are possible in the new organization away from some stakeholders, such as employees, towards others such as managers and shareholders.

3. The parent organization may also procure wealth transfers which would not have been possible while the MBO was still part of the parent group.

Mechanisms for achieving improved returns from MBOs include:

(a) operating efficiencies;
(b) reduction in agency and transactions costs; and
(c) avoiding implicit contracts (chiefly with employees) of the old organization.

Thompson suggests that problems of the divisional form which cause MBOs are:

(a) motivation of managers;
(b) divisional performance measurement; and
(c) transfer pricing.

There may be genuine motivational problems; it is difficult to give divisional managers the prospect of very large rewards, which would exceed the likely rewards of top management. This may be particularly the case in the UK where profit-related bonuses are not a traditional feature of compensation packages. But divisional performance measurement and transfer pricing do not appear to be insuperable problems. If financiers can work out performance-related debt contracts for MBOs and if, as frequently occurs, buyouts pre-negotiate long-term contracts with components of the parent organization, then there seems to be no *a priori* reason to believe that similar arrangements would not be possible within a divisional structure.

Likewise, the reason that 'cash cows' are sold off is framed, on theoretical grounds, in terms of the difficulty of motivating managers where promotion to headquarters is not likely from such operations. This suggests a rigidity of organizational promotion patterns which is unsupported. One can think of a number of organizations where aspiring high-fliers have often been placed in just such cash cows (frequently in hazardous and unpleasant locations) because the cash cows are highly valued and because high-fliers can be motivated by the promise of future promotions in a way which more mundane managers cannot.

An alternative explanation of divestment of cash cows is that the parent wishes to invest in higher present value but riskier projects. If the parent has substantial, risky debt the additional risk imposed on the debt may result in a wealth transfer to the parent's shareholders.

The empirical part of the paper investigates the cross-sectional variations in abnormal return of a sample of MBO firms which achieved a listing subsequent to buyout. As the author acknowledges the population is a somewhat special one, and is further restricted to consider only 'large' deals (market capitalization over £10m). The average length of time between MBO and initial public offering (IPO) is surprisingly short (22 months). So short as to make one suspect that flotation was commonly planned at the time the MBO took place and that few fundamental changes in the MBO's business, products or technology occurred in the period, although considerable cost savings might have been achieved.

Return of the MBO to public ownership is a puzzling phenomenon if agency costs are the cause of the original MBO. If the original buyout was designed to free the company of agency costs by giving managers a stake, how does flotation not reintroduce agency costs by diluting the managerial stake? Thompson suggests that the cause of reduction of agency costs is replacement of 'financial control exercised by a hierarchy' by the imposition of 'market-dominated relationships between managers and their financier/investor principals'. While this proposition may have some validity in the USA, in the UK one must ask whether the MBO discipline is really 'market-dominated'. MBOs are rarely financed by marketable debt: bank debt is the rule. Similarly equity not held by banks is generally in the hands of venture capitalists, and prior to IPO, the control they exercise is arguably similar to that exercised by a holding company (board representation, receipt of regular reports etc.) rather than a market-based discipline.

The one sense in which the discipline can be said to be market-based is that the company is forced to seek any additional finance it requires through the market. As Rozeff (1982) and Easterbrook (1984) have suggested forcing companies into the market for new capital can have agency benefits which are sufficient to explain apparently tax-inefficient dividend payments. Similar benefits may be achieved in removing the MBO from the financial discipline (or otherwise) which results from head office financing. Market-based debt is likely to be less 'forgiving' (Williamson, 1988) than head office.

The other source from which agency benefits might arise in the UK is the equity stake of management. Greed has a place in the management of buyouts which it did not in divisional management and in this Thompson's results are instructive. On the basis of cross-sectional regressions using excess returns as the dependent variable he finds significant coefficients attaching only to variables related to management ownership. A 10% proportional increase in managements' equity stake gave rise to a 25% increase in the excess return variable. Even though this is not an annualized figure but across the period MBO to IPO it is nevertheless an astonishing figure.

Because Thompson's gearing variable turns out to be insignificant and of opposite sign to that expected, it provides no support to the hypothesis that debt restrains managerial consumption of free cash flow. The data do not include a measure of the quantity of 'new' money raised by flotation for the company, as opposed to replacement finance for debt and sale of managerial claims. The extent to which companies were being forced to market for finance for new projects might have given an insight into whether agency gains arose from disciplining companies to raise new capital in the market.

CONCLUSION

MBOs are not only interesting in themselves, they are a useful test bed for new theories of the firm, particularly agency based theories which have explanations for a number of classic financial puzzles. It would have been unrealistic to expect the paper to quantify the contribution of alternative sources of gain in buyouts (information asymmetry, agency costs, wealth transfers) or of the mechanisms bringing them about. Nevertheless Thompson's findings provide some interesting indicative results and future researchers may give less weight to explanations relating to particular market and institutional factors such as the crash or pricing failures in an emerging market and correspondingly more weight to matters of continuing interest. Thompson did not use a particularly rich data source. There are a lot more data available in company financial reports than used in the paper. Future studies may be expected to gain more insight into the sources of gains – market expansion, labour shedding, technological improvement etc. It would also be instructive to compare MBOs with other IPOs and to track the subsequent history of the floated companies. For many companies flotation is an intermediate stage between private ownership and eventual takeover by a large public group. If this is apparently applicable, or even especially applicable, to MBOs, added to the high proportion of direct acquisitions of MBOs, it would imply a need to re-evaluate criteria for success. If the MBO is only a transitory phase with a high probability of leading to eventual acquisition and return to divisional status, does an agency cost explanation of the phenomenon based on supposed deficiencies in divisional organization stand up to examination?

REFERENCES

Easterbrook, F.H. (1984). Two agency-cost explanations of dividends. *American Economic Review* **74**, 650–59.

Rozeff, M.S. (1982) Growth, beta and agency costs as determinants of dividend payout ratios *Journal of Financial Research* **5**, 249–59.

Williamson, O.E. (1988) Corporate finance and corporate governance *Journal of Finance* **XLIII**, 3, 567–91.

8

Control, internal organization and divestment: experimentation and the boundaries of financial services' firms

MIKE WRIGHT, CHRISTINE ENNEW and KEN STARKEY

INTRODUCTION

Organizational structure is influenced by both the nature of a firm's operating environment and by the strategy which is developed to enable the firm to perform in that environment. This operating environment can be seen to have both internal and external dimensions, although it is in the external environment that the most rapid change is likely to occur. The importance of rapid changes in the external environment in generating major strategic change is widely recognized; these changes have equally important consequences for organizational structure, since major strategic change is likely to require a re-evaluation of existing organizational arrangements and control systems. The form of the links between organizational structures and control systems is highlighted in Ezzamel (this volume) who makes use of the framework developed by Ouchi (1981). For example, various performance measures,

Perspectives on Financial Control: Essays in memory of Kenneth Hilton
Edited by Mahmoud Ezzamel and David Heathfield.
Published in 1992 by Chapman & Hall, London. ISBN 0 412 40980 1.

incentive mechanisms, monitoring of the takeover market, etc. may be applicable in hierarchical organizations, whereas the price mechanism (perhaps augmented by closer managerial control in certain relationships) is the principal means by which markets operate. Hence formal delegation may not be a prerequisite for a system of control (Hilton, 1975, and also this volume).

Decision-making structures, corporate culture and tradition and the changing needs of the market are all presented as influencing the nature of the control system that is employed and that in turn can affect the overall performance of the business. Some of the earliest work on the link between organisational structure and performance was undertaken by Ezzamel and Hilton (1980). Since then, the issue of the appropriateness of particular organizational structures and the factors determining the boundaries between firms has received considerable attention in the lierature (see for example, Thompson and Wright, 1988).

Increasingly, a key issue in this literature is the understanding of organizational responses to major internal and external changes. Appropriate organizational structures and control systems are dynamic phenomena, influenced by changing environmental conditions and the different endowments of firms' competences and capabilities (Prahalad and Hamel, 1990; Teece *et al.*, 1990). In the limit, these factors influence the spread of activities owned by a firm and the boundary between internal (hierarchical) and (external) market relationships. In dynamic conditions, firms may need to take action to re-establish the appropriate boundary between these relationships. That is, the control mechanism becomes some form of market relationship rather than just an internal panoply of financial control devices. Divestment, the sale in some form of certain activities, is the means by which this action may be effected.

The analysis of the role and functions of divestment as a mechanism for organization and control is a relatively new area of study. The current state of the literature has been reviewed by one of the authors elsewhere (Wright *et al.*, 1991). Much of the attention has either been devoted to general strategy (e.g. Duhaime and Grant, 1984; Harrigan, 1985) or has focused upon the measurement of the effect on stock market prices of the announcement of a divestment. The number of sector-specific studies is limited and this paper attempts to rectify this balance by focusing upon financial services, a sector which has hitherto been largely neglected in the areas of both control and divestment.

The financial services sector is of particular interest for two main reasons. First, it is undergoing a period of rapid environmental change which is likely to have important implications for strategy and organization. In part this change was demand-driven as a result of both an increase in the volume of personal savings and a requirement for increasingly sophisticated products from a more financially aware consumer. However, many of the most visible developments were supply-driven, in the form of extensive deregulation, developments in information technology and the associated globalization of financial markets. The main consequence of these developments was the gradual erosion of the traditional boundaries which had existed between different types of institution and between different types of market. The opportunity to expand into new markets and new products was quickly exploited by a large number of firms. The second reason for addressing financial services concerns the generally important level of asset specificity observed in the provision of intangible products, such as the specific skills embodied in human assets and the brand name (and hence trust, quality, etc.) associated with a particular provider of financial services.

Diversification into new areas, either by acquisition (external growth) or organic (internal growth) methods, may be expected to produce a need to adapt control mechanisms. Concern has been expressed by, among others, one of the industry's regulators that insufficient control has been exerted in undertaking many of these developments. The Building Societies' Commissioner, for example, has emphasized that, while developments were to be encouraged, there was a need for better forward planning, evaluation of alternative proposals to develop into new areas, and better management to deal with these issues if they were not to end in failure (Bridgeman, 1989). At the start of the 1990s, there were signs that such problems were forcing financial services firms to reconsider their spread of activities and resolve control problems through, among other things, divestment.

This paper examines the extent and nature of diversification and organizational changes in financial services firms. It seeks to identify the major control problem areas facing financial services firms and to consider the role and extent of divestment in dealing with these issues. The following section summarizes the conceptual arguments for divestment. The third and fourth sections examine the external and internal pressures, respectively, which may lead to divestment in the financial services sector. The fifth section reviews the extent and nature of divestment in this sector. Little evidence is available on the extent of mergers and acquisitions in financial services, there being no regularly published series of data in this area. Accordingly, the trends presented in the fifth section represent new evidence collected by the authors. The final section presents some conclusions.

RATIONALE FOR DIVESTMENT

Divestment is one particular method of organizational restructuring which entails an alteration in the boundaries of the firm. These boundaries may be influenced by a variety of internal factors and external pressures as is illus-

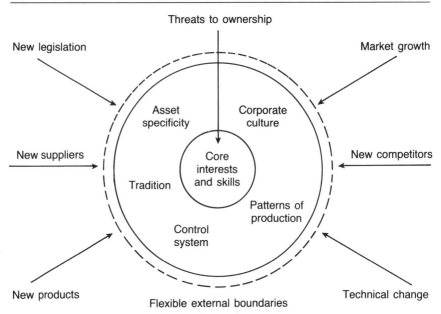

Figure 8.1 Pressures on organizational boundaries and control systems.

trated in Figure 8.1. Internal factors are concerned primarily with culture, corporate tradition, asset specificity (the extent to which physical and human assets are dedicated to a particular task) and the nature of the production process. These factors do change over time, although the pace of change within the organization's core is likely to be gradual. Nevertheless, these elements may play an important role in the restructuring process. For example, future strategic developments may be incompatible with existing structures and thus necessitate adjustments in the boundaries of the firm. Rapid change is more likely to be a characteristic of the external environment. Sudden changes will alter the 'fit' between the organization and its environment, provoking a re-examination of strategy and as a consequence, possible adjustments in the boundaries of the firm.

The various approaches towards organizational structures based on the 'transactions costs' model (e.g. Williamson, 1975, 1979 and Ouchi, 1981) seek to explain the development of particular organizational forms according to the degree of such factors as asset specificity, transaction frequency and transaction complexity. For example, the transactions cost model emphasizes the suitability of internalization where there are frequent requirements for the specialist application of proprietary knowledge, where physical assets are indivisible and where there is a lack of trust in complex transactions (Teece,

170

1980). In the opposite situation, market relationships would be preferable, while the intermediate case would call for some form of quasi-market arrangement. In the context of this model, the multi-divisional structure (M-form) of organization is seen as offering a potentially advantageous compromise between the pure spot market transactions and the administered vertical hierarchy. In the strict multi-divisional form of organization, divisions compete for investment funds in an internal capital market, with the head office overseeing this process. The existence of an internal labour market ought to permit better-informed recruitment to senior positions and the possibility of internal promotion and enhanced job security ought to encourage employee commitment to the organization.

Despite the apparent attractions of the M-form to a diversified business, there are some problems. In practice, there is evidence to suggest that many firms apparently organized on a strict multi-divisional basis do not meet the necessary conditions on resource allocation and incentives (Wright and Thompson, 1987). Empirical evidence indicates that USA and UK firms organized on strict multi-divisional lines have superior performance to those which are not (see Thompson and Wright, 1988 for a review of the evidence). There is also evidence to suggest that internal capital markets do not always function effectively and that internal labour markets may also be problematical. The inability to write complete employment contracts raises the possibility of opportunism on the part of both employees and management. Such problems have led to various forms of rethinking the relationship between the centre and the division (Goold and Campbell, 1986).

Moreover, many firms which may meet the theoretical conditions for a multi-divisional form of organization do not move in this direction. The reasoning lies in the notion of the firm as a specific bundle of resources and mechanisms for adaptation and learning (Prahalad and Hamel, 1990; Teece *et al.*, 1990). The boundaries of the firm are not arrived at in a deterministic manner but rather are influenced by their different competences and capabilities. Hence, the learning systems in some firms may prevent them adapting adequately. The problems may be exacerbated in dynamic markets by the types of external pressures seen in Figure 8.1, which relate to new legislation, new suppliers, new products, technological change, new competitors, market growth and development, and threats to ownership from the market for corporate control. The difficulties are further compounded in dynamic markets as the 'value' of the firm's specific bundle of capabilities and competences becomes uncertain.

Where a given firm adjusts to such new developments through either internal growth or acquisition appropriate control systems and integration may not be achieved. In any uncertain environment firms may be conceived as being engaged in a constant process of search for a set of assets which fits their given competences (Cable 1977). Success in such experimentation is a function of external factors themselves and the firm's learning processes. Organizational change can thus be understood in part as a process of experimentation with various forms of management structures. As part of this process, subsidiaries may be acquired which are subsequently found not to fit with the parent firm's overall objectives. Poor fit may mean unsatisfactory performance, but it may also relate to mistakes in acquiring an entity which cannot economically be integrated into the group as a whole. The degree of fit may be influenced by changing environmental and technological conditions (Chiplin, 1986), the size of the subsidiary, and the life cycle of product markets (Pashley and Philippatos, 1990), so that something which was originally compatible is no longer (Harrigan, 1980; Duhaime and Grant, 1984). In respect of financial services, these types of negative synergy argument were mentioned by Gardner (1990) in the context of US investment banking, and to a lesser extent in the context of the UK experience post 'big-bang'.

Failure to achieve economies of scale and scope through internal growth or merger activity, coupled with the impact of technical change, is likely to influence the appropriate configuration of assets for the firm. Technical change may both erode natural monopoly-type arguments for economies of scale and modify views about joint production of certain goods and services (Chiplin, 1986). Hence, divestment may become economically efficient, leading to production by two or more separate entities or possibly by means of joint venture. Pashley and Philippatos (1990) find different patterns of divestiture according to whether a firm was in one of four life-cycle groups: late expansion/early maturity, regenerating maturity, late maturity/early decline and decline. For firms in the late expansion/early maturity stage, divestment was found to be associated with reducing debt from the high levels incurred during expansionary phases. Late maturity/early decline firms were found to use divestment primarily to improve profitability by selling-off poorly performing units, and this was also the case for those firms in the regenerating maturity group. For the decline group, divestment was mostly associated with improving liquidity.

The agency cost argument suggests that where ownership and control are separate, management may resist sell-offs where they would bear the effort-costs but reap few rewards and hence have no incentive to undertake the changes. The introduction of greater managerial equity, closer monitoring by a small group of institutional shareholders, the use of high levels of debt to introduce a commitment to perform in order to meet interest payments and the greater threat of hostile takeover may provide both incentives and pressure on managers to improve performance. Hence firms may sell-off or spin-off unwanted subsidiaries and/or engage in various forms of capital restructuring (Wright *et al.*, 1991).

The above factors may often be interrelated, but, at the same time, their specificity means that the same factors do not necessarily explain a particular level of divestment in a given firm. To the extent that firms need to change their strategic direction as markets change and adjust incompletely, subsequent divestment may be anticipated. Divestment may be favoured in circumstances of inadequate control when there are serious difficulties in the assimilation of acquisitions into a group structure where the corporate cultures of the two entities are incompatible (Arrow, 1974; Jones, 1985) or where problems arise in respect of internal trading (vertical integration) where the appropriate way to manage one part is not suitable for the other, or where one part of an internal production process is able to exploit an adjacent stage through the benefits to entry against outside suppliers provided by common ownership. In the latter case, as long as care is taken in deciding which parts are to be sold, divestment and control through the market may improve overall efficiency (Wright, 1986b). Whether divestment is by sale to another group, to incumbent management or in the form of other options (such as asset swaps, demergers, management buy-ins, etc.) depends on a variety of factors (Wright *et al.*, 1991), including speed of sale, local reputation, information availability and management co-operation.

COMPETITIVE ENVIRONMENT DEVELOPMENT IN FINANCIAL SERVICES

The external pressures on the internal and external boundaries of financial services firms may be elaborated as follows. Competition between firms is an important factor in effecting change but is itself influenced by the degree to which profitable opportunities are perceived to be available, the regulatory framework which places constraints on what firms may legally undertake, and changes in information technology which may reduce costs and introduce new methods of distribution (Wright, 1990). Changes in these environmental factors may require changes in both the external and internal boundaries of financial services firms. By redrawing their internal boundaries through emphasizing product categories and by changing external boundaries through acquistions and joint ventures, firms may be better placed to formulate new strategies, in both a proactive or reactive manner, and to achieve efficient delivery of their range of products. Changing external boundaries through divestment presents itself as an option when growth strategies go wrong (Harrigan, 1985).

The recent changing environment for financial services has had several dimensions: changes in the nature of personal assets and liabilities, changes in the regulatory framework, the trend towards globalization, the effects of fundamental changes in information technology, and the redrawing of the boundaries of financial services firms. Competitive action has been influential in exerting pressure for regulatory change at a time when several governments have been predisposed towards market forces. The regulatory changes which have been introduced both reflect new market conditions and permit further developments. The history of the regulation of financial services up to the beginning of the 1980s was one of restrictions upon both the range of products that a particular firm may offer and constraints upon the geographical area in which services can be sold. The Building Societies Act 1962 tightly restricted the activities of societies. In addition, Stock Exchange rules placed limits on the investment of outside capital in member firms and maintained the single capacity dealing system whereby brokers conducted all their business through jobbers who did not deal directly with market customers. Many of these restrictions developed in order to offer some degree of protection to consumers, but were not always consistent with market efficiency and may well have hindered innovation. Competition can be limited by the exclusion of firms from one product market from providing services allocated to institutions in another sector.

Developments in information technology have radically altered delivery systems for many products, (e.g. automatic teller machines frequently replacing traditional bank tellers for deposit and withdrawal services), while deregulation has forced the financial services sector to move away from a traditional 'product/institutions' view of the market to a more consumer-orientated approach (Wright, 1990). Both developments in information technology and the competitive effects of deregulation have also had a profound effect upon the life cycle of financial services products.

Deregulation, while not eliminating boundaries between different organizational groups, causes those boundaries to become increasingly blurred. The traditional barriers between markets are also being eroded (Clarke *et al.*, 1988); retail customers can gain access to wholesale financial markets while the development of securitization (e.g. mortgages) means that distinctions between money and capital markets are no longer clear cut. The process of deregulation presented a number of new opportunities to financial services firms, but also poses a number of threats. New areas of the financial services market have been opened up, but firms now face increasing competition in their more traditional areas of business. For example, The Building Societies Act 1986 offered new market opportunities by considerably extending the range of products which could be offered by societies to include unsecured lending, integrated home buying packages, estate agency services, a wider range of insurance broking services and the provision of full personal banking services (Wright *et al.*, 1986). Additionally, the Social Security Act gave financial services firms the opportunity to provide personal pensions, although such services were to be provided through a separate subsidiary.

The Financial Services Act 1986 introduced a new framework for the regulation of investment business, with particular focus on the protection of the interests of consumers, including new rules for the marketing of financial products, the regulation of firms providing such products and requirements for firms to choose whether to be independent intermediaries or tied to a particular investment firm's products.

Domestic deregulation has had a major impact on the market for financial services in the UK. Further developments are likely with the implementation of the EC Single Market Programme. The process of harmonizing a regulatory framework across Europe will, for many organizations, require careful analysis and a re-evaluation of strategies to maintain or extend competitive advantage. Once again, organizations looking to exploit the opportunities created by the single market may look to acquisition as a possible mechanism for market entry. Indeed there is already evidence of an increase in the number of cross border acquisitions in financial services (Wright and Ennew, 1990). Nevertheless, it is important to remember that the organization and control issues which have led to domestic divestments are potentially much greater in the case of cross border acquisitions, suggesting that a further wave of divestments is likely in the wake of 1992.

Alongside deregulation, increased competition has placed pressure on many institutions' previous dominant positions. For example, competition for building societies was heightened by the greater market presence in mortgage provision by the banks (and the entry of new types of mortgage providers) and their use of interest-bearing cheque accounts. The former resulted in the Building Societies' share of the new mortgage market falling to its lowest point of 50.3% in 1987, though it has recovered since. The overall mortgage market itself has been subject to severe fluctuations in the period since the introduction of the Building Societies Act, with the sharp rises in both house prices and lending in the middle of 1988 being subsequently reversed as a result of high interest rates and a slowing in the growth of real personal disposable incomes.

INTERNAL ORGANIZATION AND CONTROL IN FINANCIAL SERVICES

As both internal and external environments change, internal structures must adjust as the business seeks to identify, possibly by a process of experimentation, the organizational structure which is most appropriate to its circumstances. In order that the process of divestment in the financial services sector may be understood, this section addresses the extent to which both externally-related actions (strategy) and internally-related actions (organization structure and control) have developed and problems have arisen in association with the environmental changes noted earlier.

Strategy

The strong link between strategy and internal organization has been a major focus of research since the seminal work of Chandler (1962). Using Porter's (1980) classification of strategy according to competitive scope (broad or narrow) and competitive advantage (cost or differentiation), we can examine the current and future directions selected by financial services firms and then link strategy to structure. For current purposes, a broad competitive scope is represented by the decision to serve many market segments and a narrow competitive scope (a 'focus' strategy) by the decision to serve only a few. Cost competitive advantage is taken to entail a narrow (typically standardized) product range while differentiation competitive advantage requires a broad

Table 8.1 Current corporate strategy

	All firms	Insurance companies	Insurance brokers	Banks	Unit investment trusts	Building societies	Stock brokers
Cost focus Narrow product Range	111	27	11	6	18	20	17
Small number of sectors	(42.0)	(42.2)	(23.9)	(27.3)	(42.9)	(43.5)	(63.0)
Cost lead Narrow product Range	59	18	7	3	12	14	4
Large number of sectors	(22.3)	(28.1)	(15.2)	(13.6)	(28.6)	(30.4)	(14.8)
Differentiation focus Broad product Range	52	11	14	5	9	8	2
Few sectors	(19.7)	(17.2)	(30.4)	(22.7)	(21.4)	(17.4)	(7.4)
Differentiation lead Broad product Range	42	8	14	8	3	4	4
Broad sectors	(16.0)	(12.5)	(30.4)	(36.4)	(7.1)	(8.7)	(14.8)
Total respondents	264	64	46	22	42	46	27

Note: Figures in brackets are percentages.

product range. The data for this analysis are drawn from a mail questionnaire survey of institutions' new product developments, problems in diversification etc., conducted by the Nottingham Institute of Financial Studies (NIFS) in 1987/8 details of which are described elsewhere (Ennew, Wright and Watkins, 1990). The survey focused attention on how firms expected their strategies to evolve over the period up to 1992. The results of the strategy survey are presented in Tables 8.1 and 8.2.

Table 8.2 Future corporate strategy

	All firms	*Insurance companies*	*Insurance brokers*	*Banks*	*Unit investment trusts*	*Building societies*	*Stock brokers*
Cost focus							
Narrow product Range	56	10	7	3	10	9	7
Small number of sectors	(22.0)	(16.4)	(16.7)	(14.3)	(25.0)	(19.6)	(44.0)
Cost lead							
Narrow product Range	61	22	7	2	13	9	5
Large number of sectors	(24.0)	(36.0)	(16.7)	(9.5)	(32.5)	(19.6)	(21)
Differentiation focus							
Broad product Range	57	12	11	5	8	11	5
Few sectors	(22.5)	(19.7)	(26.2)	(23.8)	(20.0)	(23.9)	(20.0)
Differentiation lead							
Broad product Range	80	17	17	11	9	17	4
Broad sectors	(31.5)	(27.9)	(40.4)	(52.4)	(22.5)	(37.0)	(16.0)
Total respondents	254	61	42	21	40	46	25

Note: Figures in brackets are percentages.

Comparing current and future strategies the survey results show that 64% of firms currently rely on cost-based strategies with a narrow product range and the bulk of these are focus strategies in a limited number of market segments. However, over the five years following the survey we observe a significant shift in favour of differentiation strategies with 54% of respondents planning to pursue this route, thus taking advantage of the removal of restrictions on product ranges. It is interesting to note that the biggest increase appears to occur in the category representing differentiation leadership.

177

There is little evidence of firms opting for major strategic shifts over the five years following the survey (e.g. cost focus to differentiation leadership). The number of cost focusers declines; 44.8% seek to retain their existing strategy, 23.8% opt for cost leader-ship and 21% for differentiation focus. Among cost leaders the most common change in strategy is made in order to take advantage of deregulation to broaden product ranges; 51.6% of cost leaders retain that strategy but 31.6% anticipate moving to differentiation leadership. Among those firms currently pursuing a differentiation based strategy there is no evidence of any significant move away from this source of competitive advantage.

Growth and diversification

Different approaches to diversification have been followed by different sized institutions. In respect of building societies, for example, the smaller ones have generally adopted a cost focus strategy, concentrating on only a few, typically, regional market segments, while a larger proportion of the medium and larger societies have opted for more extensive market coverage. Small societies are those with assets less than £100m at the time of the survey, medium societies had assets between £100m and £5000m, and large societies had assets of more than £5000m. Among the group with assets greater than £100m, there will be many medium-sized societies who may be limited in their strategic responses by constraints on the composition of the asset side of their balance sheet or by capital composition requirements. The largest societies might be thought to experience the fewest constraints and as such be best placed to compete over the full range of the market. Wrigglesworth (1989) reports on a survey of forty building societies in 1988/9. The asset limits requirement for balance sheets was seen to have greatest impact on the smaller societies as was the constraint on capital requirements. Restriction on per-mitted new activities were generally considered unimportant and the only noticeable difference between medium and large societies came in the form of the capital requirements constraint. There remains the issue of internal resource constraints which may tend to reinforce this notion of strategic group-ings. Given the costs and the risks associated with strategic adjustment and diversification, the larger societies, through having access to large pools of resources, may be better placed to take advantage of the opportunities presented to them.

The survey evidence tends to support this conclusion with the smaller societies tending to concentrate on their traditional areas of business and diversification being more popular among the medium and large societies (Ennew and Wright, 1990). For many of the medium-sized societies this entails following, at a more regional level, the strategies pursued at a national level by the larger societies. For the larger societies, personal banking (including loans and overdrafts) and investment packages are similarly important areas of expansion; insurance services less so because most of the larger societies are already involved in the provision of such facilities. Other important areas for the larger societies include estate agency, Electronic Funds Transfer at Point of Sale (EFToS), secondary mortgages and personal financial planning.

The general strategic moves, and the particular product developments discussed above have important implications for the financial services market. Given the environmental pressures noted earlier, it is by no means certain that the personal financial services sector will be able to support such a large proportion of differentiation leaders and such an extensive introduction of new suppliers of existing product types. These responses may reflect some initial over-optimism on the part of a number of participants. Indeed, a subsequent study of building societies by Edgett and Thwaites (1990), notes a less strong movement towards differentiation. This would seem to indicate some change on the part of societies. Edgett and Thwaites (1990) also note that societies face a conflict between their growth objectives and their profit and capital adequacy based means of assessing performance. One may thus expect to see adjustments in corporate strategic direction with some firms reducing the extent of their differentiation. Once the full effects of deregulation have been realized, institutions may have to readjust their strategic position in the market in order to deal more effectively with the new situation. This shift may also be heavily influenced by financial services' organizations competences and capabilities, which as will be seen below, reduce their ability to adapt.

Mergers, mutualization and conversion

With the increase in competition and the pressures towards diversification many financial services firms may perceive an increased need to merge in order to provide a viable base for even a limited increased range of services. Wrigglesworth (1989) suggested that mergers among building societies, for example, might be one way of easing the impact of asset constraints on expansion. Alternatively, mergers may be necessary to make it worthwhile for another type of institution (e.g. an insurance company or finance house) to consider a joint venture arrangement. The problems of searching and finding a compatible partner ought not to be ignored.

The issue of ownership form, that is mutual or non-mutual, is of particular importance to both building societies and insurance companies. The contentious issue of conversion to plc status, which has been raised in building societies especially, also has implications for the strategies which firms wish to pursue. Short of merger with other large societies, those large-middle ranking societies wishing successfully to pursue a differentiation strategy may need to consider conversion to make it viable. Such a move has its costs in that conversion may need to be linked directly to merger with another type of institution.

The agency relationship between shareholders and managers differs markedly between mutual and non-mutual firms. The ability of claimholders in mutuals to withdraw resources on demand may present a low cost mechanism for controlling agency costs, which outweighs the adverse effects of minimal direct control (Fama and Jensen, 1983). However, the extent to which managers have discretion to engage in unproductive investments before the threat of residual claimants (owners) taking action becomes effective is unclear. The retention of mutual status may enable experimentation without the threat of takeover from another type of institution and may encourage over-diversification. Ultimately, the price of retaining mutual status for all but the largest of societies may be the need to adopt a more focused strategy emphasizing narrow market segments. However, a survey by Ingham (1991) finds that the 'average' mutual insurance company now operates in more product markets than does the median proprietary company.

Organizational structure and culture

Major strategic changes will also impose stresses on traditional management structures and skills which are likely to extend beyond simple adjustments in the head office/branch relationship. Where product innovation is an important component of strategy, it seems likely that success will require dynamic management structures, integration of the activities involved in innovation and a more conducive corporate culture (Johne and Harborne, 1985). Additionally, as the range of products extends, organizations, and their branch networks in particular, will need to consider the development of appropriate (and typically new) delivery systems. These pressures for organizational change will be present whether the product is introduced internally or by acquisition.

Evidence from the NIFS survey sheds light on the extent of organizational changes taking place to deal with new product introductions and the managerial problems involved. Respondents were asked to state which changes had occurred for products introduced in the last year, and what was expected in the coming five years (Table 8.3). Most notable in both respects is the recruitment of specialist management, a need which is expected to increase substantially in the next five years. A similar increase is expected in changes in the highest level of managers. Part of this change, of course, may be due to retirement, but the magnitude of the increase may indicate a perceived need to introduce senior management with a broader strategic perspective than traditionally associated with senior managers in this sector. The actual and

Table 8.3 New products and organizational changes

Type of change	For products introduced in last year %	Expected in next 5 years %
Changes in highest level managers	16.9	30.2
More flexible organizational structure	18.0	22.7
New tier of management	9.7	15.8
Introduction of divisionalization	12.2	13.7
Removal of a tier of management	1.4	1.4
Recruitment of specialist management	19.8	35.3
Change in head office-jargon relations	5.0	10.1

Bases for percentages 265.

perceived need for a more flexible organizational structure also figures very strongly and keys-in with expected changes. Changes in head-office branch relations, however, figure relatively lowly. These differences may reflect an emphasis upon strategic thinking, but a key issue is the extent to which branch networks fully respond to the new directions expected of them. There may be perceived managerial problems in introducing new products. The survey distinguishes between products introduced by acquisition and those developed internally (Table 8.4). For those institutions having introduced new products by acquisition, difficulties in combining different management styles and in combining different computer systems are both seen to be important, as might

Table 8.4 Managerial problems in introducing new products

		Important %	Quite important %	Not important %	Not answered %
(a)	Products introduced by acquisition				
	difficulties in combining different management styles	23.4	21.2	8.6	46.8
	difficulties in combining different computer systems	26.6	19.4	9.0	45.0
(b)	Products introduced by internal product development				
	difficulties in recruiting specialist staff	35.6	32.4	11.9	20.1
	difficulties in dealing with change in the organization	20.5	38.1	19.1	22.3
	difficulties in reacting quickly to competition	30.6	27.0	19.8	22.6

Bases for percentages 265.

181

be expected. For those institutions introducing products by internal development, difficulties in recruiting staff is noticeably the most important problem, followed by difficulties in reacting quickly to competition.

The manner in which change is introduced into an organization has long been recognized as having an important bearing on whether or not change succeeds (for example, see Tomkins and Colville, this volume). Moreover, there is a need to match the process of change to the particular organizational context. In some cases this may require a change in organizational culture to match a particular new strategy. As noted earlier, the concept of an organization's capabilities and competences has an important role in analysing how change is to take place and at what speed. As noted in our discussion of divestment perspectives, organizations tend to have well-developed codes by which they function and established ways in which they adapt. Changing those codes and learning systems, and hence the organization's culture, may be difficult. Successful product innovation, in commercial banks, has been found to be dependent upon the existence of a flexible management structure which stimulates and progresses efficient product innovation, good internal integration of all activities involved in innovation and a corporate culture receptive to innovation. Further difficulties may be raised with new products introduced by acquisition rather than internal development, as our survey evidence shows. Question marks over the realization of gains from merger are well known.

Key problems are caused in the integration of different cultures and management styles. There may be a need to introduce a monitoring system for a newly acquired subsidiary which is consistent with other parts of the organization. However, different management styles and organization structures may be appropriate for different circumstances. Moreover, managers and employees operating in different market sectors may need to be remunerated differently to give them the incentive to perform. For example, estate agency activities may require a more flexible mode of operation and a more entrepreneurial remuneration package than traditional bank or building society branch functions. Failure to take account of these factors may provoke resistance to change and difficulties in meeting competition in the market.

Evidence from the insurance industry (Ingham, 1991) indicates that firms adopted sub-optimal divisionalized structures to deal with diversification and that they subsequently recentralized their administration when no benefits were forthcoming. As Ingham, (1991) points out: 'This reaction may have been incorrect; with a higher degree of coordination by head offices to exploit the benefits of interdependencies a form of divisionalised structure may have been optimal'.

The provision of new products is not simply concerned with whether they should be generated internally or acquired. As our discussion of the economics of internal organization literature indicated, an important strategic question is whether an activity or product should be provided within the firm itself or through an arrangement with another firm. If the latter approach is preferred, further examination of the appropriate nature of the relationship is needed. In some cases, a pure market relationship will be appropriate. In others, some kind of collaboration may be necessary, through such mechanisms as joint ventures, minority shareholdings, franchizing, etc. For example, the Building Societies Act 1986 enables societies to offer unsecured loans for the first time. The vast majority of societies choosing to offer unsecured loans are doing so through links either with one of the Scottish clearing banks or the Co-op Bank or (more common) with a Finance Company. These links may provide benefits to both societies and finance houses. They enable smaller societies, in particular, to enter the market, and provide ready access to the necessary expertise. For finance houses, the advantages relate to access to a wider branch network and reduction in vulnerability to losing customers if societies supplied the product on their own. Indications are that greater attention could have been paid to more flexible links than has actually occurred.

Distribution strategies, of course, have important organizational dimensions. The manner in which building societies, for example, operate in offering insurance products may be heavily influenced by the costs involved, especially the training of staff to acquire the requisite skills. The polarization decision involves distributors of investment products opting either to be tied representatives or to offer independent advice or as an introducer to someone who will provide advice. Institutions have made their polarization decisions, and the majority have now opted for tied status many switching from originally deciding to be independent. The impetus for this change has come first from the realization that many customers did not appreciate the significance of 'independent financial advice', and second that there were considerable efficiency gains to be made from dealing with only a single supplier, including avoidance of training costs. It is also important to note that societies may adopt a dual approach, with the society itself being 'tied' and a separate subsidiary offering 'independent' advice. National Westminster is the only major bank to offer independent advice through its branches. Evidence from other sectors indicates changing forms of relationships over time. Those insurance companies with more mediocre performance still relying on referrals by independent agents may, in time, need to further revise their distribution decisions. Those with tied arrangements may need to question how effective their agents have been and what effects there are on company reputations. Agents themselves may come to compare remuneration levels between suppliers.

DIVESTMENT TRENDS IN FINANCIAL SERVICES

The second half of the 1980s witnessed the most significant merger wave in history in terms of the real value of transactions in both the UK and the US

(Wright *et al.*, 1991). This upsurge in transfers of ownership was marked by greater size of individual deals, new forms of transaction (particularly buy-outs and buy-ins), new financing instruments and a greater level of acquisition activity in the financial services sector. Information concerning acquisitions in the financial services sector is difficult to come by. Official series published by the Bank of England ceased in 1979 and the Business Monitor QM7 series does not cover financial services. The only systematic information now available is that collected by Acquisitions Monthly in respect of acquisitions and divestments and by CMBOR in respect of management buy-outs. The Acquisitions Monthly data is only available from the mid-1980s onwards and in any case does not involve regular publication of trends in financial services acquisitions and divestments. What follows is the result of the authors' specific analysis of the Acquisitions Monthly and CMBOR data.

The number of acquisitions of independent firms in the financial services sector trebled between 1985 and the peak year of 1987 (Table 8.5), and subsequently declined to a level little above that of 1985 in 1990. The value of such acquisitions fluctuated throughout the period, reaching a peak of £6.8 billion in 1989. As a proportion of all acquisitions of independent firms, the peak year was 1987, when financial services accounted for one-sixth of transactions. Market share fell in the following two years, but increased again in 1990 to reach 13.2%. In terms of the value of transactions, the highest share was also achieved in 1987, with the share being maintained at around a fifth in 1989 and 1990.

Table 8.5 Independent acquisition of financial firms in the UK

	No.	Acquisition of independent firms (%)	£m	Acquisition of independent firms (%)
1985	67	6.9	553.3	5.6
1986	144	10.9	2356.22	9.6
1987	190	16.1	4539.04	26.0
1988	140	10.5	2577.02	12.6
1989	87	7.1	6793.5	22.6
1990	74	13.2	2907.0	19.1

Source: AMDATA

In respect of divestments, the Acquisitions Monthly information shows an average of about twenty divestments per year in financial services from 1984 to 1988 (Table 8.6). There is some indication of a sharp increase in divestments in 1989 and 1990, reflecting major restructuring in the sector following failed diversification strategies.

184

Table 8.6 Parent-to-parent divestments (sell-offs) in financial services in the UK

	No.	*£m*
1984 }	47	666.1
1985 }		
1986	20	659.0
1987	23	724.1
1988	18	146.0
1989	32	712.4
1990	47	1356.7

Source: Acquisitions monthly

Over one hundred management buyouts have now been recorded of firms in the financial services sector (Table 8.7), accounting for 4% of all buyouts ever recorded and some 6.7% of their value. Such buyouts tend to be more highly represented amongst larger transactions, with 8.3% of all buyouts completed for a transaction price in excess of £25 million being in this sector. A further nine management buy-ins have been completed amongst financial services firms.

Table 8.7 Management buyouts in financial services

	No.	*Prop of all MBOs by no.*	*Prop of all MBOs by value*
Pre 1982	7	3.2	7.0
1982	2	1.0	0.6
1983	6	2.8	12.6
1984	11	5.1	15.1
1985	16	6.4	6.5
1986	10	3.3	3.9
1987	15	4.5	8.2
1988	17	4.6	2.6
1989	12	3.3	6.7
1990	24	5.2	12.8
Total	120	4.1	7.0

Source: CMBOR

An indication of the shift in importance of divestment in the financial services sector is shown in Table 8.7. In 1985, there were almost as many sell-offs and buyouts as independent acquisitions. However, between 1986 and 1988 the proportion of sell-offs and buyouts to independent acquisitions fell to between a fifth and a quarter. By 1990, the proportion had again reached the level seen in 1985.

Table 8.8 Divestment and buyouts as a proportion
of independent acquisitions in financial services

	By No.
	%
1985	94.0
1986	20.8
1987	20.0
1988	25.0
1989	50.6
1990	95.9

In the United States studies (e.g. Duhaime and Grant (1984)) which addressed the strategic rationale behind sell-offs in general concluded that they were likely to involve more peripheral businesses and that it was unusual for divested units to have had a vertically integrated relationship with their parent group. Evidence from UK divestments by sell-off (Thompson and Wright, 1988, ch 10) indicates that about one-third had a horizontal relationship with the former parent, that is were in the same market sector, a fifth were unrelated, a tenth were related in a vertical manner, and the remainder were divestments by financial companies, breweries, hotels, etc. In respect of buyouts, the evidence (Wright, 1986b), shows that almost two-fifths of buyouts of divisions or subsidiaries sold their products and services to the former parent, and in some cases the buyouts were very heavily dependent upon their former parent. General studies of both sell-offs (Porter, 1980) and buyouts (Thompson and Wright, 1988) show extensive evidence of search activity as corporations sell-off on average more than half of their acquisitions in new fields and more than three-fifths of their acquisitions in entirely new fields, and that the majority of subsidiaries divested as buyouts had been owned for a small proportion of their lives by the parent. Of course, the sale of a subsidiary does not necessarily imply that the divestor is exiting completely from a sector, but may be reducing his commitment or altering the balance of his presence.

Within the financial services sector, exit from the provision of certain product areas may be by divestment or by rationalization and reversal of earlier decisions. In respect of the latter, the Leeds Permanent for example, has opted to reduce its service range in order to concentrate on more traditional building society activities. Many societies have switched from being an independent intermediary under the Financial Services Act 1986 to a tied arrangement. The running of the EFTPoS system introduced on an experimental basis by the Anglia (prior to its merger with Nationwide) has been taken over by Barclaycard. Economies of scale have also encouraged the linking of initially separate ATM networks.

186

A detailed examination of the sell-offs and buyouts in financial services in the last two years (Table 8.9) provides insights into the kinds of areas where firms are changing their spread of activity. There are some marked differences between divestments and buyouts, especially in respect of investment and fund management, but both show high levels of transactions involving insurance brokers. To some extent the divestments involve the sale of operations to become tied parts of larger groups (e.g. the sale of RAC Motoring Services insurance broker to Provident Financial), in parallel to the extensive acquisition of small independent brokers in the light of the polarization requirements of the Financial Services Act.

Table 8.9 Main product groups for divestments and buyouts (1989–1991Q1)

	Divestments	*Buyouts*
Investment management/fund management	13	1
Insurance broking/consulting	11	19
Stockbroking/securities	9	3
Insurance	9	1
Leasing/HP	8	2
Estate agency	7	–
Retail/merchant banking	7	1
Financial services	6	1
Life asurance	5	1
Credit card operator	3	–
Consumer credit	3	–
Underwriting	3	–
Trust	3	–
Mortgage finance/administration	2	4
Other	7	3

Source: AMDATA/CMBOR

A major area of diversification by financial services firms, particularly building societies and insurance companies, was estate agency services. However, in the period covered by the table some seven divestments occurred. Estate agents occupy an important position at the front of the house-buying process and in principle provide obvious vertical integration benefits for the provision of mortgages by societies and for the selling of endowment and contents policies by insurance companies. Entry by societies and insurance companies into estate agency took one or more of various forms – acquisition, cold starts, franchizing, partial acquisitions, joint ventures and branch conversions. Acquisition enables a network to be constructed quickly, but carries with it the problems of integration and incentivization of former owners who are now wealthy after being bought-out. Cold starts and branch conversions provide the means by which gaps in acquired networks may be filled and enable some of the problems of acquisition to be avoided. However, they are a slow means of market entry. Links with other institutions, partial acquisitions and franchizing enable risk-sharing and may enable improved control to be achieved through the provision of greater incentives to franchise-holders and managers who are significant equity-holders. Against these benefits must be set the problems in establishing a brand image, ensuring an adequate quality of management performance, and in ensuring adequate control so that quality reputation and trust relationship with customers are not harmed.

Serious issues need to be addressed in relation to using estate agents as a distribution route. Estate agents have traditionally had a poor reputation in the eyes of the public, as surveys regularly show. Hence, societies and other institutions face an important task in changing the image of estate agents in order that their own reputations are not damaged. A second major problem arises in integrating a large number of acquisitions made in a short period of time, particularly as the managerial skills required in estate agency are very different from those involved in running financial institutions. These problems may be overcome by recruiting estate agency people whose skills may now be at a premium because of the increased demand for them to undertake the task. However, there remains a problem in motivating managers of estate agents who have just become very wealthy as a result of being bought-out and whose entrepreneurial style is at variance with traditional financial institutions approaches to business. The franchise route avoids the high premia being paid on acquisitions (and hence implications for profitability) and the internal managerial issues just noted. However, there are major issues involved in establishing a brand image, in ensuring adequate quality of management performance (especially given the recent wave of acquisitions in which a large proportion of the better estate agents have been incorporated into groups) and in ensuring adequate control so that the institution's quality reputation is not harmed.

The problems involved in integration, which have been particularly exacerbated by adverse market conditions and a level of cross-selling of products below expectations, have provoked extensive subsequent divestment and closure of acquired estate agency businesses. Of the first financial services firms to enter estate agency, Provident Financial, sold its Whitegates estate agency chain in 1989 to Legal and General, and Lloyds Bank sold its Black Horse estate agency to Abbey Life. The most notable exit has involved the Prudential, which had built up the largest estate agency network and which has now exited. Prudential is shifting its diversification from upstream (i.e. sources of new policyholders such as house buying services) integration to downstream integration (i.e. those individuals with policies reaching maturity who are seeking further investments) as it considers that greater growth can be generated from policy holders wishing to invest the proceeds of matured policies than from the cross-selling of insurance products to house buyers. In addition to Prudential, major networks such as Royal, Hambros Countrywide, Nationwide-Anglia, Black Horse, and Abbey National have all rationalized their estate agency networks through the closure of several hundred outlets in total. Other notable divestments include the sale of credit card operations by Burton Group (acquired by General Electric US), Storehouse (acquired by Yorkshire Bank) and Chase Manhattan (acquired by Alliance and Leicester Building Society). TSB has announced its decision to withdraw from the mortgage market, following its earlier divestment of its Target Life insurance acquisition.

As with firms generally, some financial services organizations have been more intensive divestors than others (Table 8.10). The most intensive has been the failed British & Commonwealth. There are also other indications of retrenchment from financial services by non-financial services firms, for example Burton Group has, besides selling its credit card operations, disposed of Debenhams Investment Services (Stockbroking) and Bell Noble Elliott (Fund Management). Boots has also divested its life insurance interests. Other financial services firms have focused their core activities through divestment, e.g. Hogg Robinson. We noted earlier the particular problems in cross-border diversification and expected divestments here. This process is beginning but as yet is not as well advanced as in the UK.

Table 8.10 Multiple divestors in financial services (1989–1991Q1)

	Sell-offs	Buyouts	Total
British & Commonwealth	6	4	10
Berisfold International	5	–	5
Burton Group	3	–	3
Hogg Robinson	3	–	3
LIT Holdings	3	–	3
Bromsgrove Ind.	2	1	3
Chase Manhattan	2	–	2
Elders	2	–	2
EFT	2	–	2
Hong Kong and Shanghai Bank	2	–	2
Newman Birts and Partners	2	–	2
Post Office	2	–	2
Prudential Corp.	2	–	2
Standard Chartered	2	–	2
Steel Burrill	2	2	4
York Trust	2	2	4
International City Holdings	1	1	2
Dominion International	–	3	3

Source: AMDATA and CMBOR.

CONCLUSIONS

The discussion in this paper demonstrates the applicability of general perspectives on control and divestment to the case of financial services. As in the management control literature generally, the issues increasingly do not relate simply to the optimal levels of delegation. The appropriate levels of delegation, and hence organizational structures and management control systems, important though they are, are a subset of the wider issue of the appropriate boundaries of the firm.

A key issue in the design of financial and organizational control systems is the barriers which prevent firms moving in a deterministic manner to the system which may theoretically be the most appropriate for a given set of contingent factors. These factors concern the organization's specific core competences and capabilities. Hence, for a given individual organization it may be preferable to divest certain activities rather than attempt to design increasingly complex internal control systems which may not in any case have the desired effect. Where a trading relationship is to persist, this may then be carried out through some form of managed market activity. This type of control arrangement may be most appropriate where the nature of activities is significantly different, particularly in relation to the specific skills and incentive mechanisms which are involved. The need for divestment may arise most notably in uncertain environments where firms are seeking to enter new markets by means of acquisition. The well-recognized problems of integrating and controlling new acquisitions may be exacerbated by poor performance resulting from either the market itself or from mistakes in acquiring a particular firm.

This paper has addressed the problems of financial control in the specific context of the financial services sector which has been neglected by researchers but yet has experienced substantial reorganization and restructuring through assets sales in the early 1990s. The nature of this restructuring highlights the problems of integrating very different activities (e.g. traditional financial services with estate agency) in an uncertain market environment.

At present, research focusing on financial services is still at an early stage, and we would suggest that possible fruitful areas for further study in the light of the discussion in this paper might include:

- An assessment of the conditions under which some form of managed market or dynamic network of operations may be more appropriate than straightforward ownership where there are uncertain environments and where experimentation and flexibility are important.
- An assessment of the nature of individual firms' core capabilities and competences and how this has influenced both the nature and success of diversification activity.

190

- An examination of the link, if any, between ownership form and the extent to which 'excessive' diversification occurs.
- The extent to which cross-border diversification is more problematical and needs to take different forms in order for flexibility and future exit to best accommodated.
- An estimation of the success of diversification as measured by the relationship between the number of units retained and the number of units divested by the financial services firm, an approach similiar to that proposed by Porter (1987) in respect of diversification in the United States.

ACKNOWLEDGEMENTS

Financial support from Barclays Development Capital Limited and Touche Ross Corporate Finance for the Centre for Management Buy-out Research is gratefully acknowledged. Thanks are also extended to *Acquisitions Monthly* for the provision of data on acquisitions and divestments in financial services.

REFERENCES

Arrow, K. (1974) *The Limits of Organisation*, Norton.
Barnes, P.A. (1985) UK building societies – a study of the gains from merger, *Journal of Business Finance and Accounting*, **12**(1), 75–92.
Bridgeman, M. (1989) Retrospect and prospects, *Building Societies Gazette, Conference 1989*, 18.
Cable, J. (1977) A search theory of diversifying merger, *Recherches Economique de Louvain*, **43**, 225–43.
Carter, R.L. *et al.* (eds) (1986) *Personal Financial Markets*, Philip Allan, Oxford.
Chandler, A.D., Jr (1962) *Strategy and Structure*, MIT Press, Cambridge MA.
Chiplin, B. (1986) Information technology, in *Personal Financial Markets*, (eds R.L. Carter *et al.*), Philip Allan, Oxford.
Clarke, P.D. *et al.* (1988) The genesis of strategic marketing control in British retail banking', *International Journal of Bank Marketing*, **6**(2), 5–19.
Duhaime, I. and Grant, J. (1984) Factors influencing divestment decision making: evidence from a field study, *Strategic Management Journal*, **5**, 301–18.
Easton, G. (1988) Competition and marketing strategy, *European Journal of Marketing*, **22**(2) 31–49.
Edgett, S. and Thwaites, D. (1990) The influence of environmental change on the marketing practices of building societies, *European Journal of Marketing*, **24**(12), 35–47.
Ennew, C. and Wright, M. (1990) Building societies in transition: strategy in a new market environment, *Managerial Finance*, 14–25.
Ennew, C., Wright, C. and Watkins, T. (1990) The new competition in financial services, *Long Range Planning*, **23**(8), 80–90.
Ennew, C., Watkins, T. and Wright, M. (1990) *Marketing Financial Services*, Heinemann, Oxford.

Ezzamel, M.A. and Hilton, K. (1980) Divisionalisation in British industry: a preliminary study, *Accounting and Business Research*, Spring, 197–213.

Fama, E. and Jensen, M.C. (1983) Agency problems and residual claims, *Journal of Law and Economics*, **XXVI**, 327–50.

Gardner, E. (1990) A strategic perspective of bank financial conglomerates in London after the crash, *Journal of Management Studies*, **27**(1), 61–73.

Goold, M. and Campbell, A. (1986) *Strategies and Styles: The role of the centre in managing diversified corporations*, Blackwell, Oxford.

Harrigan, K. (1980) *Strategies for Declining Businesses*, Lexington Books, Lexington MA.

Harrigan, K. (1985) *Strategic Flexibility*, Lexington Books, Lexington MA.

Hilton, K. (1975) Control systems for social and economic management, *Inaugural Lecture*, University of Southampton (also in this volume), pp. 27–40.

Ingham, H. (1992) Organisational structure and the internal economy of the firm: the UK insurance industry, *Managerial and Decision Economics*, forthcoming.

Johne, A.F. and Harborne, P. (1985) How large commercial banks manage product innovation, *International Journal of Bank Marketing*, **3**(1), 54–70.

Jones, C.S. (1985) An empirical investigation of the role of management accounting systems following takeover or merger, *Accounting, Organizations and Society*, **10**, 177–200.

Ouchi, W.G. (1981) Markets, bureaucracies and clans, *Administrative Science Quarterly*, March, **25**, 129–41.

Pashley, M. and Philippatos, G. (1990) Voluntary divestitures and corporate life-cycle: some empirical evidence, *Applied Economics*, **22**, 1181–96.

Porter, M.E. (1980) *Competitive Strategy: Techniques for Analyzing Industries and Competitors*, Free Press, New York.

Prahalad, C. and Hamel, G. (1990) The core competence of the corporation, *Harvard Business Review*, May/June, 79–91.

Teece, D. (1980) Economies of scope and the scope of the enterprise, *Journal of Economic Behavior and Organisation*, 223–44.

Teece, D., Pisano, G. and Shuen, A. (1990) *Firm Capabilities, Resources and The Concept of Strategy*, CCC Working Paper No. 90–8.

Thompson, R.S. and Wright, M. (1988) *Internal Organisation, Efficiency and Profit*, Philip Allan, Oxford.

Thwaites, D. (1989) The impact of environmental change on the evolution of the UK building society industry, *Service Industries Journal*, 40 60.

Williamson, O.E. (1975) *Markets and Hierarchies: Analysis and antitrust implications*, Free Press, New York.

Williamson, O.E. (1979) Transaction cost economics: the governance of contractual relations, *Journal of Law and Economics*, **22**, 233–62.

Wrigglesworth, J. (1989) *Building Societies Research*, UBS Philips & Drew.

Wright, M. (1986a) Housing finance and consumer credit, in *Personal Financial Markets* (eds R.L. Carter *et al.*), Philip Allen, Oxford.

Wright, M. (1986b) The make-buy decision and managing markets: the case of management buy-outs, *Journal of Management Studies*, **23**(4), 434–53.

Wright, M. (1988) *Redrawing the Boundaries of the Firm*, in *Internal Organisation, Efficiency and Profit* (eds Thompson, R.S. and M. Wright), Philip Allen, Oxford.

Wright, M. (1990) The changing environment of financial services, in *Marketing Financial Services* (eds C. Ennew, T. Watkins and M. Wright), Heinemann, Oxford.

Wright, M., Chiplin, B. and Thompson, S. (1991) The market for corporate control: divestments and buy-outs, in *Mergers and Merger Policy* (eds J. Kay *et al.*), 2nd edn, OUP.

Wright, M. and Diacon, S.R. (1988) The regulation of the marketing of long term insurance, in *Marketing Insurance* (eds N. Dyer and T. Watkins), Kluwer.

Wright, M. and Ennew, C. (1990) 1992 and bank strategic marketing, *International Journal of Bank Marketing*, Special Issue on 1992, 5–10.

Wright, M. and Thompson, S. (1987) Divestment and the control of divisionalised firms, *Accounting and Business Research*, Summer, No.67, 259–68.

Wright, M. and Watkins, T. (1987) Deregulation and the strategies of building societies, *Service Industries Journal*, April, 7(2), 216–31.

Wright, M., Watkins, T., Price, C. and Hughes, J. (1986) *The Future of the Building Societies*, EIU Special Report 1057.

Control, internal organization and divestment: Experimentation and the boundaries of financial services' firms: Discussant's comments

STEVE THOMPSON

In recent years there has been an increasing degree of interaction between the disciplines of economics, accounting and business strategy/marketing as academics have sought to understand the organization of firms. Unfortunately, however, despite the rise to predominance of the service sector in the modern economy most analysis is still centred on the manufacturing firm: that is most authors discussing the firm's internal structural arrangements still work with an explicit or implicit model of an entity producing units of physical output. Mike Wright and his co-authors are thus to be congratulated for presenting this treatment of the particular factors influencing the structuring of financial services firms and for showing how deregulation has encouraged new structural configurations. The authors' approach is explicitly inductive. They have collected data from a number of sources – some of them primary – and they then generalize about their findings. This is a useful first stage – both in interpretation and in opening up the area to further enquiry. The next step is for the authors, or others, to formulate and test specific hypotheses relating to service industry organization and performance – perhaps along the lines suggested in Ingham (1992).

The authors identify key stages in the development of new organizational structure and then draw upon their knowledge of the financial service sector to illustrate the process. In essence the authors describe a sequence in which *environmental change* occurs creating the need for a *strategic response*. This brings about a new configuration of *activities* and hence *capabilities* within the firm giving rise to the need for *structural adaptation*. In most industries during 'normal' periods environmental change will be relatively gradual. Of course, there are industries – such as entertainment and clothing – where demand is subject to very large, unpredictable fluctuations, similarly many industries go through abnormal periods of rapid technological change. However, relatively gradual market and technological change is probably the norm for most firms. What creates the extremes of stability and turbulence is governmental regulation. Government regulation can create an environment in which competition and innovation are suppressed and in which new entry is blockaded. Once such constraints are removed or amended, the environment frequently becomes extremely turbulent – with participants rushing to exploit new opportunities or to forestall moves by rivals. In the resulting scramble decisions are taken and investments made which the firms subsequently regret – hence each initial rush for new opportunities in a deregulatory regime tends to be followed by a period of shake-out and retrenchment.

Historically, financial services have been subject to intense supervision and regulation – largely to promote stability. This is true in the USA – where banking and, at least in some states, insurance are subject to pervasive regulation – as much as it is in the more interventionist economies of Western Europe. It has been particularly the case in the UK, where stability and monetary policy goals were pursued at the cost of encouraging cartels in the banking and building society sectors and discouraging firms from diversifying across financial product boundaries.

During the 1980s deregulation policies were pursued right across the financial services sector and banks, building societies, securities trading, investment provision and insurance companies all experienced measures of liberalization. As Mike Wright *et al.* point out the immediate consequence was to allow firms the opportunity to exploit economies of scope – through cross-selling products, offering packages of related services, utilizing brand name advantages, etc. – previously denied to them. This, for example, the building societies which had been previously largely restricted to providing residential mortgages began to diversify into other lending, current account services, money transmission, insurance marketing, pension provision, estate agency, etc. Similarly, the merchant banks diversified into market making, share analysis, etc.

There were three particular difficulties associated with diversification decisions in such an environment. First, individual management teams faced considerable pressures to follow expansionary diversifications – even if their own purely commercial judgements questioned the wisdom of so doing. Second, the identification of significant multi-product economies – economies of scope – is never straightforward *ex ante* and was extremely difficult where individual service firms and their rivals were coming to completely new areas. Third, rapid diversification often involved the takeover of other financial service companies; undertaken against similar acquisitive strategies on the part of rivals this frequently resulted in the payment of a considerable premium over the target company's tangible asset valuation. These difficulties may be considered in turn.

The removal of a regulatory constraint on the scope of a firm's activities presents it with a problem comparable with the decision whether or not to adopt a new innovation. If the innovation is non-drastic the firm may gain by its adoption in the absence of too many rivals doing the same; if too many others also adopt it, the gains may be insufficient to justify the costs of introduction. A drastic innovation may leave the firm no choice: if others adopt the firm must follow or face eclipse – thus the innovation may be successful even if it leaves the whole industry's profits at a lower level.

Now consider industry i which is permitted, for the first time, to diversify into industry j. Suppose firm Ai believes there to be moderate economies of scope resulting from the joint production of i and j. It has to take a decision whether or not to enter industry j at the same time as it knows its rivals Bi, Ci etc. must take the same decision. Suppose Ai considers three possible outcomes of its rivals' behaviour – *most enter, some enter* and *none enter*. If *none enter*, Ai enjoys the competitive advantage afforded by the economies and gains positive profits. However, if *most enter* there will be excessive competition in j and severe losses. Alternatively, if Ai decides not to enter j it will experience some pressure on margins in i if at least some rivals choose to enter. Let Ai assign an equal probability to each of the three rival outcomes and let the pay-off structure be as shown:

		Most enter j	Some enter j	None enter j
		Rivals in i		
Ai	Enters j	− 3	0	+ 1
	Does not enter	− 1	− 1	0

Ai's pay-off matrix

As drawn, the expected outcome from each strategy is equal (− 2/3). However, since the dispersion of pay-offs is greater for the *enter* strategy, rational risk-averse players would be expected *not* to enter. But would managers?

Heavy financial losses may result if everyone enters – overbidding to join and then cutting margins in the face of excess capacity. However, if all firms face similar difficulties it seems unlikely that Ai's management will be singled out for blame. Thus Ai's managers may downgrade this negative pay-off – particularly if they operate in financial mutuals *without* conventional stock market monitoring. Furthermore, managers' concerns with size – a natural pre-occupation given that remuneration correlates more strongly with size than profitability (Berger and Humphrey, 1991) – and professional desire to be seen as active initiators rather than passive respondents together reduce the attraction of the non-entry strategy. Therefore, even when the managers' perceptions of the profit pay-offs indicate no entry, their own evaluation of the actions may lead to diversification.

Economies of scope arise where the cost of producing i and j together is less than that of producing them separately; thus:

$$C(i, \ j) < C(i) + C(\ j).$$

These savings usually result from the more intensive use of some input common to the production of i and j. In manufacturing, where inputs and outputs tend to be well-defined and easily quantifiable, a would-be diversifier should be able to locate and estimate the potential of under-utilized inputs. In services, by contrast, the difficulty of separating production and delivery stages frequently means that it is difficult to distinguish inputs from outputs. For example, consider two banks with different levels of counter-staffing: is the more heavily staffed one less efficient or producing a superior service? Input measurement problems are compounded because service industries tend to depend upon human capital inputs rather than physical ones.

In the case of financial services the normal rationale for diversification is to utilize more intensively the firm's organizational and marketing assets – for example, its branch network, brandname, goodwill or client list – and to generate sales by lowering customer search costs in a so-called 'one-stop shop' facility. However, the extent to which these advantages will generate profits in an entirely new industry is very difficult to predict. For example, will a building society branch network, established to handle savings accounts, prove an adequate base for the provision of full retail banking services?

Evidence from the USA, where piecemeal financial deregulation has been occurring over the past decade, is not particularly helpful. For example, tests for multi-product economies across large samples of American banks have yielded inconsistent results (a recent large-scale study (Berger and Humphrey, 1991) even suggests that within sample efficiency variations totally dominate economy of scope effects). Furthermore, even where the evidence on multi-product economies is well-determined, it indicates that their magnitude depends strongly on the overall scale of the firms operations (Hunter and Timme, 1990). In short, therefore, neither past experience nor academic research provides the financial services manager with a clear prediction about the success of new product diversifications.

The obvious route to rapid diversification lies in the acquisition of existing suppliers. This is particularly likely, as in the case of deregulation, where market participants are conscious that rivals are following a similar strategy. However, the obvious danger is that rivalry leads to over-bidding. The recent history of UK financial services provides several examples of such takeover scrambles – particularly the bank/building society/insurance company rush for estate agents and the merchant banks' acquisitions of stockbrokers/market makers.

The danger of over-payment is particularly strong because of the intangible nature of the assets involved. The production and selling of financial services depends upon human and organizational skills, but these may be incompletely transferred in a merger. Wright *et al.* point out that effective estate agency depends upon determined selling, but the agent who is bought out by a building society subsidiary is not necessarily as motivated as branch manager as he was as owner. Similarly, the acquiring firm can lose personnel or find that they have overpaid for a brand name to be subsumed within their own.

When a manufacturing firm is acquired in a takeover a new management team may be thought of as gaining control over several categories of assets: physical plant, product patents, market share etc. However, it appears that in service company acquisitions these assets are all too frequently intangible. (Even market share is not transferable in a business characterized by irregular demand – such as estate agency?) These difficulties point to the need for a more systematic study of the ways in which service sector mergers differ from their widely investigated manufacturing counterparts.

The authors produce some interesting and largely novel evidence to support their contentions. To this reader the most fascinating piece of evidence was the indication in Table 8.8 that large-scale divestment followed acquisition with such a short lag (why is the private sector so forgiving in cases of unsuccessful acquisition?). It is to be hoped they now subject this to careful analysis to determine not merely the distinguishing characteristics of financial services as economic activities, but also that final disguised cost of regulation – that is the cost of removing it!

REFERENCES

Berger, A., and Humphrey, D.B. (1991) The dominance of inefficiencies over scale and product mix economies in banking, *Journal of Monetary Economics*, **28**(1), 117–48.

Hunter, W.C. and Timme, S.G. (1990) Does multiproduct production in large banks reduce costs?, *Federal Reserve Bank of Atlanta, Economic Review*, May – June, 2–11.

Ingham, H. (1992) Organisation structure and the internal economy of the firm, *Managerial and Decision Economics*, (forthcoming).

PART THREE
The social and organizational implications of financial control

9

Financial control in the financial services industry: The case of Lloyd's of London

DAVID GWILLIAM, KEITH HOSKIN
and RICHARD MACVE

INTRODUCTION

During the last decade there have been many changes in the regulation of UK financial institutions designed both to increase competition and, through 'self-regulation', to improve accountability to clients and providers of capital. Much of the regulatory framework imposed by the state is embodied in the Financial Services Act 1986 (FSA) and in the related legislation for individual financial sectors, and the associated reporting and audit requirements emphasize the central importance of adequate financial reporting and financial controls.

This paper focuses on the regulatory changes at Lloyd's, which in many respects parallel those that have taken place in other sectors of the financial services industry. But Lloyd's also has many unique features.

In the remainder of this paper we first set out the basic framework of the management and operation of Lloyd's, and give the history of the more significant changes relating to financial control and accountability that have taken place at Lloyd's. We focus on the unique importance at Lloyd's of the role of accounting in sharing out risks and rewards, and critically examine some of

Perspectives on Financial Control: Essays in memory of Kenneth Hilton.
Edited by Mahmoud Ezzamel and David Heathfield.
Published in 1992 by Chapman & Hall, London. ISBN 0 412 40980 1.

the conceptual and practical limitations of the main accounting performance measures now being reported. In the light of these limitations we review an attempt that has been made to measure the cost of the self-regulatory framework that has been established and ask why such a competitive market, exhibiting in a literal way the relations of 'principal' and 'agent', has needed external pressure to develop its 'self- regulation'. This leads us finally to ask how a Foucauldian perspective on the regulatory discourses and practices, and the relations of knowledge and power might be developed to provide a historico-theoretical framework for understanding the processes of change that acknowledges, but goes beyond, an economic cost–benefit framework.

THE LLOYD'S INSURANCE MARKET

Names and syndicates

The basic structure of the Lloyd's insurance market is that individuals, 'Names', write insurance for various types of risks, the security for the policyholders ultimately being the personal assets of these individuals. Originally, each Name wrote insurance on his (women Names were not permitted until 1970) own behalf, judging what risks to accept, the rate to be charged, whether to reinsure a proportion of the risk, etc. As the scale of the business to be written expanded groups of Names would come together in 'syndicates' to cover particular risks, each Name having liability only for his stated percentage share of the risk (not joint liability with the other syndicate members). Over time syndicates grew larger and, importantly, not all Names were active in the market. The business is written by the syndicate's 'active underwriter'.

Non-active Names (usually termed 'external Names' or 'external members') are in many, although not all, respects like investors in the insurance market. They provide the market with capacity (the amount of premium that can be written by each Name is restricted and therefore the capacity of the market is effectively a function of the number of Names) and obtain in return their share of the profits or losses of the syndicates to which they belong. Numbers had more than tripled between 1975 and 1985, and today Lloyd's has approximately 27 000 Names of whom fewer than 20% are working Names. Since 1969 overseas Names have been admitted and today make up more than 15% of the total.

Names can and do spread their risks by belonging to more than one syndicate (there are more than 400) and on average each Name is a member of about ten syndicates. Syndicates are managed by agents, 'managing agents'. Managing agents (who may be responsible for more than one syndicate) appoint the active underwriter for their syndicate and are responsible for managing the affairs of that syndicate. Although syndicates are controlled by managing agents it is a rule of Lloyd's that each Name must have a 'members' agent' to look after his or her affairs. These agents have a role that is becoming increasingly comparable to that of intermediaries who act on behalf of 'naive' investors in the capital market (e.g. Beaver, 1989; 10). Managing agents may and often do act as members' agents as well. Names' membership is personal and not transferable, and carries unlimited liability, although 'personal stop loss' and 'estate protection' insurance may be purchased.

Apart from a few syndicates writing short-term life business, syndicates are presently classified according to whether their principal lines of business lie in one of four 'markets': marine, non-marine, motor and aviation, although these 'market barriers' are now being progressively demolished. Syndicates vary in size, the largest now numbering their Names in thousands, but until recently there were also significant numbers of quite small syndicates – in 1982 17% of the marine syndicates had less than fifty members. Some of these were niche syndicates specializing in a particular type of risk; others wrote parallel business to larger syndicates managed by the same managing agent and were often termed 'baby' syndicates.

Regulation at Lloyd's

The first Lloyd's Committee was elected in 1771. At first it had limited powers but its authority was greatly enhanced by its first formal constitution, the Trust Deed of 1811, and even more by the Lloyd's Act of 1871 which gave the Committee authority, sanctioned by Parliament, to control the members of Lloyd's. Subsequent Acts of Parliament in 1911, 1925, 1951 and 1982 have allowed Lloyd's to retain its self-regulatory status. It was this combination of self-regulation and the fact that syndicates are not companies (in fact they have no separate legal status) which led to the relative (but not complete) absence of compulsory requirements for accounting and audit in the period before 1982.

At that time, Lloyd's was itself considering a number of reforms of accounting and audit arrangements, following the report of the Fisher Working Party in 1980, but these were overtaken by a series of scandals in 1982 in which it was revealed that syndicate assets had been misappropriated by a number of agents (Hodgson, 1984, p. 328). Funds had been channelled through connected brokers and connected insurance companies (often overseas in tax havens) acting as reinsurers. Another source of temptation was the opportunity to cream off the more profitable and less risky business to the 'baby' syndicates on which managing agents and their associates participated, leaving the less attractive business in the 'main' syndicates in which the external Names also participated (Hodgson, 1984, p. 319).

Following the appointment of Ian Hay Davison as Deputy Chairman and Chief Executive in 1983 (at the request of the Governor of the Bank of England), a series of reforms was introduced both to remove conflicts of interest (including the divestment of managing agencies from brokers, and tight control over authorization of connections with insurance companies and of parallel syndicates) and to improve accountability. Since 1984 syndicate accounts have been required to be published on a central file at Lloyd's, and since 1986 auditors have been required to give a 'true and fair' opinion on those accounts comparable to that required by UK company law for limited companies. The accounting and audit requirements are now set out in a series of Lloyd's byelaws, of which the chief is the latest Syndicate Accounting Byelaw (No. 11 of 1987) and its subsequent amendments (SAB).

Accounting at Lloyd's

The particular characteristics of the Lloyd's market have meant that syndicate accounts have certain unique features. Syndicate accounts for any one year are normally kept open for three years so as to allow time for the majority of claims to be notified and processed. At the end of each of the first two years (the 'open years') an underwriting account reflecting premiums and claims to date (i.e. those policies and claims processed through the central Lloyd's Policy Signing Office (LPSO)) together with expenses and income from investments is produced, but there is no attempt to estimate the amount of any outstanding claims (or premiums and reinsurance recoveries). At the end of the third year the account is closed and the syndicate pays to transfer liability for all future claims (and premiums and reinsurance recoveries), this payment usually being termed the 'reinsurance to close' (ritc). This payment is arranged by the active underwriter/managing agent and in practice is nearly always arranged with the identical syndicate (subject to any membership changes) operating in the following year.

If it is impossible to determine with reasonable accuracy the appropriate amount of ritc then it may be necessary to keep the underwriting account open until such time as it is possible to determine the amount. (Under the Run-off Years of Account Byelaw of 1989 this decision can only be taken after obtaining reports from independent actuaries and the syndicate auditors, and after seeking 'quotations' from other syndicates for the price they would require for taking on the liabilities.) Syndicate accounts kept open in this way are usually termed 'run-off' accounts and are often associated with very unsuccessful underwriting. In recent years the importance of the ritc calculation has if anything increased as the proportion of business in which claims may not be notified for many years ('long tail' business) has increased. Once the result is determined and the account is closed, the whole of any balance of profit is distributed to Names according to their percentage participation in the syndicate – if there is a loss, Names will have to make good the deficiency.

DEVELOPMENTS IN SYNDICATE REPORTING

There has been a remarkable overall change in climate at Lloyd's, where 'openness and disclosure are now the order of the day as against exclusiveness and secrecy' (Macve 1986, p. 4). In particular, among all the changes made during his period as Chief Executive, Davison (1987, pp. 6–7) has deemed the publication of the previously private syndicate accounts to be the most important change of all:

> The most important, irreversible thing that I did was to establish disclosure: once the accounts of syndicates were properly prepared, audited and published to the world the external members of Lloyd's could be their own police force.

It was thus a major change of approach when the requirement was introduced, with effect from the 1983 accounts (i.e. those in which the 1981 year was closed), that fully audited syndicate accounts (together with a managing agent's and underwriter's report) be filed at Lloyd's each year and available for public inspection. Included in these annual reports was a statement of 'Disclosures of interests' which gave details of any transactions or arrangements in which those connected with the management of the syndicate had an interest, and in particular gave financial details of situations of parallel underwriting, including 'baby' syndicates. The primary purpose of these reforms was to provide better information to the large number of Names who are now remote from the market's day-to-day operations – and it is with the protection of Names that the Neill enquiry was also concerned in introducing further disclosures and refinements of presentation. By contrast, in the case of insurance companies the increase in regulation and demand for information over the last twenty years or so has resulted primarily from the DTI's concern for the security of insurance company policyholders (e.g. Harte and Macve, 1991).

The Neill report

The accounting reforms at Lloyd's that were introduced following Ian Hay Davison's appointment as Chief Executive were taking place at a time when government policy was opening up capital markets in the City and institutions generally to greater national and international competition, and at the same time strengthening the framework of regulation and supervision in order to increase public understanding of and confidence in the operations of the financial sector, so as to promote wider investment participation. The FSA provided the government's framework for protecting investors, and Parliament debated whether Lloyd's should come under the provisions of that Act. In the event the government decided that Lloyd's should be exempted from the Act but that a committee of inquiry, chaired by Sir Patrick Neill, QC, should consider whether the regulatory arrangements at Lloyd's would provide protection for Names comparable to that proposed for investors under the FSA. The Committee agreed that the public filing of syndicate accounts was 'an innovation the importance of which cannot be over-estimated given the traditional secrecy surrounding syndicate affairs' (Neill, 1987, para 5.3, p. 22).

But the Committee, while readily acknowledging the major programme of reform that had already been achieved, concluded that in a number of respects the arrangements in place or being implemented at Lloyd's did not offer the same standard of protection as would be available elsewhere in the financial services field, and made seventy recommendations for further action or consideration by Lloyd's (Neill, 1987), all of which were immediately accepted in principle by the Council.

We shall focus on some of these that relate in particular to disclosure and accounting. But first we examine the distinctive problems that arise in determining the results and performance of Lloyd's syndicates.

CONCEPTUAL PROBLEMS OF SYNDICATE ACCOUNTING

In addition to their role in providing information for investment-type decisions and in demonstrating honesty of agents, syndicate accounts have another crucial role. They provide the irrevocable basis for sharing out the results of the syndicate's business between Names and this role gives accounting at Lloyd's a unique importance. The need for 'equitable' methods of accounting – and equity is enshrined as a basic principle in SAB – arises not solely in relation to the division between Names in any one underwriting year: the combined investment of premiums received and the sharing of expenses require equitable allocation between Names on different underwriting years. Above all the need to 'hand over' the business of the closing year to succeeding years through the ritc requires that the basis of its calculation be equitable as between different generations of Names. In addition to disclosure of what has been done it is therefore also vitally important that the accounting principles by which results are measured be those that are most equitable in the circumstances: especially as there is no alternative mechanism at Lloyd's for sharing results equitably. Whereas in a listed company, if the dividend distribution is too cautious or profits are ploughed back, investors may still get their fair return through share price appreciation, if a Name leaves a syndicate at the end of an underwriting year the cheque he receives when the account is closed is his final settlement. He cannot sell his membership, and there is no 'efficient market' to remedy any defects of the accounting.

Neill gave little attention to this 'measurement' aspect of syndicate accounting, apart from the recommendation that there should be a clear statement of policy for allocation of expenses between agents, syndicates and years of account. But its importance has been made clear in two distinct ways, both by the continuing discussion over the role of discounting in relation to the ritc and the use of 'time and distance' reinsurance policies, and by the concern over the large number of 'run-off' accounts. Both of these reflect the problems of arriving at an 'equitable' result after three years in relation to business which may develop over many years to come.

The reinsurance to close (ritc)

The determination of the ritc is central to accounting at Lloyd's, both in assessing 'solvency' for the protection of policyholders and in determining Names' share of the results.

Estimates of the outstanding insurance liabilities are required for two purposes:

1. to calculate the ritc in order to settle the result of the closed year;
2. to estimate whether the balances on the open years are likely to be sufficient to cover the future development of their premiums and claims (including the further development of the closed years reinsured into them).

Essentially it is the comparison of the liabilities determined under point 2) with their available assets (including personal assets) that determines the 'solvency' of the Names, and Lloyd's, with the approval of the DTI, lays down certain minimum requirements for the calculation of these liabilities in the annual solvency test. However, the primary objective with regard to giving a 'true and fair view' of the result and to determining the ritc is to arrive at an equitable amount, based on the information available, at which the outstanding liabilities of the closed year should be transferred to the Names in subsequent years – it is therefore important not only that the amount should be adequate but also that it should not be excessive. The Inland Revenue share this concern, and the redefinition of ritc in the Finance (No. 2) Act 1987 as an expense, not a premium, has enabled them to mount a stronger challenge and to require a much fuller justification of the amounts provided. Whereas in the past anecdotal evidence indicates that the provision in some syndicates was merely agreed between the active underwriter and the auditors 'over the telephone', both Lloyd's rules in SAB and the demands of the Inland Revenue now require comprehensive written documentation of the assumptions and calculations underlying the amount provided. There has also been an increasing involvement of consulting actuaries in the projection of outstanding losses and the provision needed for 'incurred but not reported' claims (IBNR).

One of the most important improvements in accounting (recommended in Macve, 1986) that has now been introduced following Neill is the requirement to split the result for the closed year into the amount relating to the 'pure' underwriting year and the amount representing the impact of the prior years reinsured into the closed year. Taken together with the requirement that the underwriter should identify in his report the major factors that have produced a surplus or deficiency on the prior years this enables readers of the accounts to interpret the results more sensibly and to understand the margin of error within which estimates have to be made. This analysis has revealed that prior years generally have a significant impact on closed year results, even when the amount of the adjustment to the ritc itself is relatively small (see Table 9.1 in the Appendix). Some agents give a detailed analysis of the individual prior years (as is required of insurance companies in their DTI returns). However the effect on underwriting results cannot be viewed in isolation from the impact of the funds provided by the ritc on the closed year's investment earnings.

Discounting and 'time and distance' reinsurance

The interrelationship of the provision for ritc and the investment earnings on the funds thereby set aside raises fundamental issues about the basis on which results are determined and shared between Names. There is the general issue of whether the ritc should be discounted for future investment earnings (which is not allowed for solvency test purposes, but is for syndicate accounting purposes, although no syndicate accounts at present include it); and the specific issue of the role of 'Time and Distance' reinsurance policies (T&D) under which a reinsurance premium is paid now for stated amounts of recovery at stated future dates at a price reflecting the discounted present value of the future cover. These policies have a similar effect to discounting and are used by a number of syndicates. Both affect the balance of risk and reward as between present and future Names, and both are controversial. The present differences in practice by different syndicates are confusing and unsatisfactory.

Measurement of results is, however, not only an issue for the equitable division of those results between Names. It also enters into the appraisal of syndicate 'performance' which is relevant for the investment-type decisions they need to make about where to continue, where to increase and where to decrease their underwriting commitments for the future – i.e. to assist them with decisions relating to potential risks and rewards that are comparable to those facing investors. The importance attached to providing Names with measurements of performance is clear both from Neill recommendation 4, implemented in the Members' Agents (Information) Byelaw, prescribing the disclosure of a members' agent's average performance for his Names, based on syndicate results, and from the commercial success of the 'League Tables' published by Chatset (Rew and Sturge, 1990) and by the Association of Lloyd's Members (ALM, 1990). In this respect it is perhaps surprising that Neill did not comment on what further reforms might be needed in respect of syndicate accounting principles – although following the model of the FSA, and the SIB's rules, those would be matters that would more naturally be regarded as matters for Accounting Standards. Given the terms of reference of the Neill committee – to compare the position of Names with that of investors under the FSA – it is not surprising that the main focus of Neill's recommendations has also been on additional disclosures, as well as on arrangements for the restructuring of the market relationships.

ACCOUNTING BASED CONTROLS AND PERFORMANCE INDICATORS

Premium income

The longest serving control used by Lloyd's regulatory authorities has been the level of premium income written. The intention is to monitor the level of risk being assumed. Names are given an authorized limit on the basis of their declared wealth (means) and the premium written by syndicates is monitored by Lloyd's to guard against 'overwriting'.

It is difficult to see what other measure could be used, but given that the objective of the control is to limit the volume of risk assumed, it is clear that the level of premium income (which combines price and volume of business) may not reflect this. When competition is fierce and underwriters cut rates they may be accepting a lot more risk for a given amount of premium income. Further practical difficulties arise in handling business written in US or Canadian dollars and in specifying an appropriate exchange rate for monitoring purposes given the three year period of account.

Premium income has at least the merit of simplicity as a statistic. Two more complex accounting measures which have been developed as performance indicators following the Neill recommendations are the 'calendar year investment yield' and the calculation of members' agents' performance.

Calendar year investment yield

Following recommendation No. 9 of the Neill report (1987), that annual reports should include the information necessary to enable Names to judge the

211

competence with which agents' investment management functions are being handled, Sch 4, para 6 of the revised SAB now requires (but only with effect from the 1988 reports) an analysis of the 'calendar year investment yield', to comprise:

(a) the average amount of the syndicate funds available for investment during the year ended on the reference date;

(b) the aggregate gross investment return in respect of syndicate investments during that year;

(c) the amount specified in (b) above expressed as a percentage return on the average amount of the syndicate funds available for investment as specified in (a) above (the 'calendar year investment yield');

(d) where a material amount of the syndicate funds available for investment is invested in more than one of the prescribed currencies referred to in paragraph 2 of Schedule 2 to this byelaw, an analysis of the calendar year investment yield so as to identify separately the yield attributable to each such currency; and

(e) in respect of each item required by the preceding provisions of this sub-paragraph, the corresponding amount for the previous year.

The Explanatory Notes (paras 89-92) indicate that the average fund should normally be 'determined on a monthly basis at a point during the month which itself represents a reasonable reflection of the average value of funds. This point, once identified, should be used consistently thereafter.' The managing agent's report 'should comment on the basis adopted for computing the average amount of funds available for investment'.

There have been criticisms of the requirements (e.g. from the ALM) for giving agents too much flexibility, and suggestions that there should be a requirement for analysis by the three major currencies, together with investment valuation in each of those currencies; a reconciliation between the calendar year return and the return allocated to the underwriting accounts; and, because of the different tax effects, separate disclosure of the 'income' and 'capital gains' elements of the return. Professional investment managers have also made representations as to ways of further standardizing the basis of measurement.

It is clear that comparisons of return can only be meaningful if they are adjusted for the risks of the portfolios held (which are also influenced by the risks of the insurance business underwritten), as well as for time. So although the calculation of yield that is now reported may give some indication of performance, the difficulties of specifying a conceptually sound basis for the measurement of yields inevitably means that comparisons with other syndicates and with other forms of investment cannot be precise (e.g. Tippett, 1990).

Members' agents' average return

Following the Neill Committee's recommendation (1987, No 4) that there should be better disclosure of members' agents' performance, the Members' Agents (Information) Byelaw (No.7 of 1988) now requires each members' agent to publish a Members' Agent Information Report (MAIR) showing, *inter alia*, its average performance for each year of account. The average performance is derived from the sum of the aggregate results of the Names for whom the agent acts, expressed as a percentage of the total allocated capacity of those Names.

The comparable performance statistic for the market as a whole is shown in Lloyd's 'Global' accounts. The statistic is presumably intended to convey similar information to the 'earnings per share' statistic prescribed by SSAP 3 for listed company accounts, but it has certain distinctive features. The capital invested by the shareholders of a company depends for its rewards on the performance of the company's business, and the earnings per share calculation attempts to indicate how successful the company's performance has been in generating profits for shareholders.

It should be noted that the Lloyd's performance measure relates to allocated capacity (the amount of premium income Names are potentially allowed to write) not to 'capital', as the Name's capital backing for their underwriting is also free to earn a return elsewhere. The measure therefore reflects two related but separate components of underwriting judgement: how profitable is the business written, and how much capacity is being utilized. In other words, the result as a percentage return on allocated capacity comprises the result as a percentage on the premium written, multiplied by the premium written as a percentage of the premium limit.

While Names would, other things being equal, prefer more rather than less of their permitted capacity to be utilized to produce profitable business, an underwriter who utilizes all his capacity on business returning 15% on premium income will show the same performance as an underwriter who utilizes only half his capacity, but on business returning 30% on premium income. The latter has also ensured that he has capacity still available should market conditions unexpectedly improve, without the danger of running up against the premium limits that are controlled and monitored closely by Lloyd's.

This information is of course provided in each of the syndicate reports, together with underwriters' comments, and the overall average performance measure is comparable to an average of the returns as calculated in the syndicate League Tables (Rew and Sturge, 1990; ALM, 1990). Nevertheless, decomposition of the overall average performance measure into these two elements could provide additional useful insight for Names in assessing their members' agent's performance in placing them on the 'best' syndicates and the 'quality' of their earnings. But even the more detailed analysis would still suffer from the limitations inherent in the determination of syndicate results that have already been discussed.

BENEFITS AND COSTS OF THE NEW INFORMATION

In the previous sections, we have looked at the underlying uncertainties and range of subjective judgements inherent in the determination of syndicate results, and considered some limitations of the various performance indicators derived from these results. The numbers now made available may indeed provide useful information for economic decision making by Names and potential Names. But their value – as with so much accounting information – seems likely to lie more in the way they expose areas of the underlying business activity to further intelligent questioning and analysis (and thereby modify the behaviour of those now made accountable for them), than in any precise measurement that unambiguously classifies and ranks alternative choices with minimum error. Ken Hilton warned of the danger that 'without a proper framework, the analysis of financial data may yield rather silly results; and a little knowledge in this field may yield positively the wrong results' (1975, p. 23). Nevertheless, as with so much accounting information, the imposition of a standardized requirement for a particular measure across all relevant enterprises inevitably leads to such simplistic classifications and rankings. Numbers which reveal new truths by generally being broadly or approximately 'right' are often precisely, and in some circumstances perversely, wrong: yet they can come to be treated as if they were always precisely right. As we have argued, at Lloyd's the structure is very different from that found in stock exchanges, futures exchanges, foreign currency exchanges or commodity exchanges, where the conditions that might create an 'efficient market' that could compensate for such misprocessing of information can be identified.

How are the advantages and disadvantages of such a regime to be assessed? How has the balance been decided? Why has regulation focused on the reporting of such inherently problematic performance measures? Is there a clear calculus of economic costs and benefits? In the remainder of this paper we first review a recent appraisal of the costs and benefits of Lloyd's self-regulatory regime, and then ask how appropriate the regulatory apparatus appears from the viewpoint of an agency theory framework. This leads us to argue that the nature of the changes that have taken place, while having enormous economic effects, goes beyond the limits of economic cost/benefit analysis, and that a broader political, social and historical framework needs to be developed for understanding the ways in which these changes have been implemented and the form they have taken.

The burden of regulation

The continuing reforms of syndicate accounting and reporting, together with the monitoring of their effectiveness, have imposed a considerable regulatory burden on Lloyd's and the agents. The cost of this regulation must ultimately be borne by policyholders in more expensive insurance, or out of the profits of agents and Names, and it is important to ask whether such regulation is cost-effective (Morris, 1987). Moreover, regulation that may be agreed to be necessary may nevertheless be administered ineffectively, so as to fail to achieve its objective, or inefficiently so as to impose unnecessary additional costs.

Those involved with regulation at Lloyd's (as is common with those involved with regulation under the FSA generally (Seldon, 1988)) have generally paid little attention to the economic cost-benefit analysis of the regime. But increasing concern over such questions prompted the commissioning of a study on the costs of compliance with Lloyd's regulation, which was completed in December 1988 (KPMG Peat Marwick McLintock, 1988). The study reviewed both the costs of regulation within the Corporation of Lloyd's, which had risen from £3.6m in 1981 to £17.2m in 1987 (representing a real growth, after allowing for inflation, to about $3\frac{1}{2}$ times the 1981 level), and also attempted to estimate the compliance costs falling on agents. No estimate was made of how much the cost of preparing the annual reports had risen since the introduction of publication and the rules of SAB, nor of the extra audit cost being incurred, but compliance costs of the agencies completing the consultants' case studies classified under the heading of 'accounts' (as shown in Appendix V of the report) amounted to a total of £33 000, and under 'solvency and globals' to £48 000, which represented 5% and 7% respectively of total compliance costs (excluding LPSO charges), and 0.12% and 0.17% respectively of total agency and syndicate expenses. However an individual agent (questioned by Duguid in Seldon, 1988, p. 60) has estimated that 5% of total syndicate expenses relate to the auditing and production of underwriting accounts.

The broad conclusion of the study was that, while regulatory costs have risen greatly in recent years, and are perceived by agents as a real burden in some respects, a substantial proportion of the direct costs are commercially necessary and consistent with sound business practice. The opportunity costs incurred through senior time being diverted from finding new business to compliance with regulation are felt to be more significant, but regrettably no satisfactory ways of quantifying such costs could be found.

A number of areas were identified in the study where the implementation and administration of the regulation could be more efficient and cost effective, but the objectives of Lloyd's regulation were broadly endorsed by agents, and there was recognition that there is also a cost in not having regulation, given the examples of past regulatory failures such as the scandals of the early 1980s where the cost to the Lloyd's market ran to many millions of pounds (Neill, 1987, p. 13 gives estimates of the amounts wrongfully appropriated in the three leading cases subsequently subjected to disciplinary investigation, which total at least £55m, although substantial amounts were recovered). However, agents also expressed doubts as to whether the limitations of regulation are properly understood and were concerned that a false confidence might be generated among Names and policyholders that they were thereby guaranteed against incompetence or loss. Recent events have shown that while regulation may reduce fraud or impropriety, it cannot prevent the consequences of poor underwriting judgement.

Agency theory: competition versus regulation

In discussing the costs and benefits of regulation of accounting and auditing (e.g. the requirements for limited companies to publish audited accounts) agency theory has been developed (see e.g. Jensen and Meckling, 1976; Watts and Zimmerman, 1986), to focus on the relationship between investors as 'principals' and managers as 'agents'. The theory seeks to explain the costs and benefits to each party of different 'monitoring' arrangements whereby the principals are able to restrict agents from acting in their own rather than in the principals' interests. Under certain assumptions it can be shown, for example, that it is in the interest of managers wishing to obtain investors' capital at the cheapest cost to voluntarily arrange for monitoring to take place, e.g. by hiring an auditor to report on the accuracy of the managers' reporting of their performance.

This insight is closely related to the views expressed by agents in the KPMG Peat Marwick McLintock study (1988, paras 3.3, 7.2) that many regulatory requirements are commercially necessary to the successful operation of the Lloyd's market. The theoretical analogy of principal and agent is particularly forceful in the context of Lloyd's where the legal relationship between Names and agents is in fact governed by the law of agency. The fundamental question therefore arises whether the degree of control required for the protection of Names would not best be settled by leaving it to Names and their agents to agree between themselves what arrangements are needed, in the light of a rational economic and commercial appraisal of likely costs and benefits (including the potential losses in an unregulated market), rather than incurring the costs of regulation that is imposed on the market, whether by Lloyd's or from outside. Developing that line of argument one might question whether much of the central regulatory and monitoring apparatus now in place is necessary, as Names would have put pressure on agents directly to introduce equivalent safeguards insofar as they were thought to be needed.

There are however a number of reasons why the insights offered by simplified, abstract models of agency relationships may not capture even all the economic conditions, let alone the political and wider social considerations that underlie modern structures of regulation and self-regulation. In real-world markets it is not possible to replicate fully the ideal competitive conditions of theoretical economics, and some of these imperfections may justify the imposition of regulation. Thus the KPMG Peat Marwick McLintock report (1988, paras 3.3, 7.6) draws attention to the role of regulation in replacing market forces to a certain degree in the special circumstances at Lloyd's, where competition is limited since Names are not free to move between members' agencies and syndicates in the way that shareholders can move their holdings from company to company. At Lloyd's the relationships ideally need to be long-term (given the problems of equitable determination of individual years' results). Agents control access to syndicates and Names are not able to sell their place on a syndicate in the way that a shareholder can sell his shareholding in order to realize its value. If the structure of the market could be made more competitive, there might be a lesser need for regulation.

There are other complexities in the relationship between Names and agents that may have hindered the direct expression by Names of what reforms they would wish to see (Gwilliam, 1989). For example, Names on a syndicate each have several liability and no real corporate identity and, unlike company shareholders or partners, have no functions exercisable as a body in general meetings. This is one practical reason why the appointment of syndicate auditors remains *de jure*, as well as *de facto*, the responsibility of the managing agent: organizing collective action on behalf of Names is a difficult process. Until the recent reduction in taxation rates and withdrawal of certain tax concessions, there have also been very substantial tax advantages through membership of Lloyd's (Aczel *et al.*, 1990) which, combined with the club-like manner of operation and image of privilege associated with being a Name, may have reduced the incentive of external Names in the past to 'rock the boat' by seeking more stringent monitoring of agents' activities.

The changes in the structure of the market also occurred fairly rapidly – so that although more formalized reporting and monitoring arrangements now appear, with hindsight, to be a necessary concomitant of the enormous growth in the number of external Names and their increasing remoteness from day-to-day operations in the market, the process by which change would have occurred would almost certainly have been much slower if events had not brought external pressure and the threat of government intervention. Both

Davison (1987, e.g. pp. 3, 87–8) and Neill (1987, e.g. para 3.22) comment on the widespread ignorance that they found among agents of their responsibilities under agency law, and it is only since 1986 that the ALM, a Names 'pressure group', has been given facilities by Lloyd's to make its existence known to Names.

The reforms of accounting and auditing arrangements are not only for the benefit of existing Names in relation to their own syndicates. The public filing of accounts assists Names in making comparisons between syndicates, but it is not possible for agents to calculate any precise relationship between the disclosing of their own syndicates' results in company with those of other syndicates, and the costs or benefits in terms of their reputation with their own and potential Names. There are also wider public policy arguments for mandatory disclosure, e.g. in ensuring the confidence of Names in the market as a whole (as with investors generally in the case of the wider company disclosures: Lev, 1988), or in enhancing the confidence of the public generally in the operation of major institutions of the economy (e.g. Edwards, 1938). Lloyd's is a major contributor to the UK's international earnings and there is a high degree of public interest in seeing that its self-regulation is effective. Apart from any direct interest of Names in the results of individual syndicates, the availability of their accounts and the related disclosures is an important means for informing the public as to how that self-regulation is operating. At this level of consideration it becomes almost impossible to separate the economic and commercial aspects of regulation from the political advantages and disadvantages. Thus the Neill recommendations already discussed are a direct result of a political decision that Lloyd's must meet standards comparable to those already set by the FSA.

TOWARDS A FOUCAULDIAN ANALYSIS?

The import of standards from other arenas suggests that there are wider social forces at work too. The history of accounting and auditing from the nineteenth century onwards shows that it is not simply the calculus of economic costs and benefits that brings change and adaptation in reporting and monitoring activities. Corporate crises (e.g. Tricker, 1982) have frequently triggered new demands for accountability. However, the adoption of accountability as the appropriate remedy may itself be seen as a product of more wide-ranging shifts in knowledge about and attitudes to society, which have developed rapidly over the last 200 years and have created modern forms of power and control which are rooted, not so much in physical coercion and punishment by those in authority, but in a mutual reciprocal surveillance of individuals up and down the hierarchy of command in business as well as in other organizations (Foucault, 1977).

Thus, although the limitations of the accounting-based results and related performance indicators may cast doubts at the level of a 'cost-benefit' analysis on the effectiveness of the continuing reforms, it is inadequate to hope to assess the nature and effectiveness of regulatory intervention in wholly cost-benefit terms. The new regime of accountability has transformed the nature of Lloyd's in many ways, some obvious, some subtle. Is there a deeper explanation for the way in which the ideas of self-regulation have taken hold at Lloyd's and produced such an extraordinary change in outlook in such a relatively short period? We see the developments at Lloyd's as reflecting a continuing expansion of the power of accountability that has developed since the nineteenth century (when banks and insurance companies were among the first to be regulated by compulsory accounting and audit arrangements (Edey and Panitpakdi, 1956)).

In recent years there have been a number of studies which have explored changes *within* organizations from a Foucauldian perspective. The Foucault derived analysis (e.g. Hoskin and Macve, 1991) sees change as an exercise in power–knowledge relations, where it is the power of expert knowledge that plays the crucial role. The key practices are identified as examination and calculation (both financial and non-financial). Thus changes to be looked for would include the introduction of new expert knowledge systems and the increasing dominance of a discourse centred on control and accountability, emphasizing constant examination and measurement of performance. The focus of the analysis is on delineating the power/knowledge interactions, including the emergence of resistances to the new power of knowledge and the internalization of control as self-control.

There have as yet been few attempts to use this perspective to understand changes in the external control and monitoring of organizations (see Robson, 1991; Ibrahim 1990). The case of Lloyd's offers an opportunity to attempt such an appraisal, which will require investigation of the interaction between external influences and power-relations and the internal reforms introduced to promote efficiency and accountability among agents.

Discourses

The discourses of accounting and accountability have recently been brought to bear on the (attempted) transformation of management and control of a range of social institutions – not just City institutions such as those directly affected by the FSA, but also institutions whose objectives have not hitherto been seen as primarily 'financial', including government agencies, hospitals, schools and universities. The recourse to accounting to justify changes across so many different organizations underlines the special power which accounting – particularly the practices of private sector management and financial accounting – is perceived to confer. In the 'Anglo-Saxon' tradition of account-ing (articulated primarily in the USA and UK) the focus is on 'standardizing' calculations of profit as measures of performance, despite the underlying conceptual difficulties which make impossible any unambiguous definition of the concept of profit (see Macve, 1981).

This is the mode of discourse that has been explored in the accounting reforms at Lloyd's: a mode which is justified as focusing on the needs of 'investors and creditors' and which is increasingly expressed in 'standards' of accounting practice issued by authoritative bodies such as the ASC (and now ASB) following the model imported from the USA. Thus the emphasis at Lloyd's has been on making the accounting as close as possible to the require-ments for limited company accounting and audit, and the normal SSAPs apply except where the individual unique features of Lloyd's prevent this. Names are treated as if they were 'investors', even though in many respects they are quite unlike shareholders in the 'normal' capital market. A major aim of the reforms has been to undermine the notion that 'Lloyd's is different', a notion which has been seen as creating in the past a culture of secrecy and a mystique exploited to deter outside scrutiny. A new hierarchical mode of control has now been imposed on a group whose prevailing 'clan culture' had deviated from the cultural norms of society generally (see Ouchi, 1980).

Practices

In the company sphere financial accounting focuses on the bottom line profit as *the* performance indicator, together with its derivatives, such as 'earnings per share', and decompositions into 'current' and 'prior year adjustments'. Reflecting the power of this discourse, we see at Lloyd's the development of accounting practices that focus on 'bottom line' performance indicators such as the standard results calculated for the League Tables, and the average rate of return to be calculated for members' agents' performance measurement (apparently seen as a close parallel to 'earnings per share', even though, as argued above, the analogy is imperfect). There is now also a splitting of the 'pure' and 'prior' years results. While this is extremely effective in revealing the inherent uncertainties in the estimates, those very uncertainties mean that each element is itself fundamentally a matter of subjective estimates and re-estimates so that the 'realism' of the split in an underwriter's overall appraisal of his 'book' of business may be dubious. For the present Lloyd's has kept its 'three-year accounting' system, although there are emerging pressures to change to 'one year' accounting to be 'like the insurance companies'; but as a first step the syndicates are now required to give the rate of return achieved on their investments year by year (crude though that measure has also been argued to be).

The whole apparatus of Companies Act and standard accounting requirements has been applied as far as possible in the byelaws, backed up with requirements for the keeping of proper 'accounting records', including documentation of conflicts of interests, of reinsurance arrangements and of policies for charging expenses to syndicates. There are specified formats for accounts and required details of note disclosures. The audit practices too have been changed to be as similar as possible to those carried out by the major accounting firms for listed company clients (Gwilliam, 1989). There is the whole self-regulatory apparatus laying down Codes of Practice for charging expenses, and for avoiding conflicts of interests and disclosing those conflicts that remain. And now there are summary annual reports too, just like listed companies. The financial press is better informed and freely comments on events at Lloyd's, and on the problems facing individual syndicates and their Names, as it does on other financial institutions and companies in other industries. From a power–knowledge perspective these are all practices which promote a new level of surveillance and judgement by or on behalf of Names, paralleling the apparatus for surveillance by shareholders in companies.

Power–knowledge relations

The impact of these discourses and practices has been to create changed relations of power between those directly involved in running Lloyd's market – the working Names who run the agencies and act as active underwriters, and who previously dominated the Committee and the Council – and those outside: the external Names, and the other 'major players' – the state (as legislator and tax collector), the institutions of the City, and the professions – whose declared role is to bring their knowledge and expertise to bear on behalf of the external Names and in the 'public interest'. In the first wave of reforms, it was the Governor of the Bank of England who 'appointed' a senior member of the accounting profession (then Chairman of the ASC) to the new role of 'Deputy Chairman and Chief Executive' (Davison, 1987 p. 68); in the second wave it was the government that required the appointment of a committee of inquiry under an eminent lawyer, Sir Patrick Neill, QC (who had been Chairman of the Council for the Securities Industry, and was later to become Vice-Chancellor of Oxford University) to see that the state's apparatus of self-regulation, as devised in the FSA, was brought to bear on Lloyd's as on other City institutions.

So the Council of Lloyd's now includes not only representatives of external Names, but representatives of the 'financial experts' whose qualifications and knowledge give them power in the City, such as the Chairman of the SIB and senior partners of accounting firms who have been active in audit standard setting (Lloyd's of London, Annual Report and Accounts 1990, p. 2). The Inland Revenue has established an expert cadre of tax inspectors who adopt a more aggressive, interventionist stance and also demand fully documented written evidence to justify the level of the ritc being provided – which they also more frequently 'disallow'. The Press is provided with the information to make public comment; and in the background waits the EC Commission that also wishes to make Lloyd's 'comparable' to the other 'insurance enterprises' that it seeks to regulate, and to bring it tidily into its proposed directive on the annual accounts of insurance undertakings (published in 1988, revised in 1989 and 1991).

The changing relations of power among these external interests has also changed power relations within the market. This shift in real power to a new breed of managers, unlike the old 'owner managers', is precisely that which Chandler has traced in *The Visible Hand* (1977) as the origin of the modern corporation. This kind of shift does not occur primarily to promote economic efficiency (Ezzamel *et al.*, 1990): the managers who increasingly gain power are those with expert knowledge. This has arguably been happening at Lloyd's, in the first instance at the global level of the market and its regulation. At this level the appointment of independent experts to revise the market's philosophy has led to the creation of a cadre of regulatory staff employed by the Corporation of Lloyd's. In turn this has begun to change the nature of the managers within the agencies.

As in so many other arenas there is a new breed of accountable (and above all self-accountable) managers – many of whom are not themselves Names – who are increasingly acquiring power and authority as the 'managers of change' and who are ready to articulate the new-found objectives and achievements of their activities to regulators, politicians and the public at large. We have not gathered systematic evidence of the extent of this process, but, for example, one of the largest agencies, Sturge & Co, recruited as its Chief Executive one of the partners from Ian Hay Davison's firm who had been part of the team devising the new regulations, and who has now moved on to become Chief Executive of the Stock Exchange. The recently appointed finance director of the same agency is a former partner of another 'Big 6' firm who is also Deputy Chairman of the Abbey National Building Society.

From our perspective, it is therefore certainly no surprise to find that one of Neill's recommendations (1987, no. 46) was that:

examinations should be instituted which all those intending to become active underwriters would be required to pass. The syllabus should include the law of agency and insurance law and practice, Lloyd's own regulatory requirements and relevant accounting and management techniques associated with the conduct of insurance business. Consideration should also be given to requiring the principals of members' agents to take some appropriate form of examination.

This 'managerial' knowledge – sensitive to being 'accountable for the numbers' – is of a different kind from the knowledge, based on a network of intelligence gathering about ships and their movements, which originally gave Lloyd's its powerful pre-eminence in marine insurance in the eighteenth and nineteenth centuries.

Some implications

At Lloyd's we have identified a new emphasis being placed on accounting and accountability, even though the precise outputs of the process – the accounting profits and related performance indicators – may be subjected to critical scepticism as to how far they can provide Names with the key information they need for deciding which syndicate to join or leave, or how to change their participations. The importance of accountability as it has developed in other arenas and other organizations since the nineteenth century, lies primarily in the way in which the disclosures and performance measures constitute a detailed coherent written archive of organizational structure, policies and practices that may be critically examined both internally, through 'management accounting', and externally by the expert audit of its 'financial accounting'. It establishes norms of performance for comparisons within and without the organization and these become internalized by those who have become newly accountable (Hoskin and Macve, 1986). At Lloyd's the new accountability – even though the very definitions of the accounting categories are disputable – has already significantly changed the whole culture of their operations from one which prized secrecy to one which is more open to questions and where those who are skilled in the expert knowledge underlying the new disciplinary regime are becoming increasingly powerful.

One might also draw on such a Foucauldian analysis of the forces of change to understand how resistances to the new 'visibility through the numbers' might emerge. Take for example the emphasis on managing agents' positions in the League Tables of results, on the 'average percentage return' calculated for members' agents, and on the rate of return being achieved on investments. Studies of pension fund managers currently being undertaken are beginning to suggest that a gaming approach is adopted towards such 'leagues' in order to ensure that managers do not 'conspicuously' fail – which requires aiming to be a 'good average' and thereby equally avoiding conspicuous success. Will Lloyd's agents similarly find ways to try to 'beat the system' to protect their own best interests rather than those of Names?

Another expectation from a Foucauldian perspective might be that the surveillance on behalf of Names will in turn develop into a greater surveillance *of* Names in a reciprocal system of control and accountability. There have indeed been some discussions within the market about a need for more rigorous examination and testing of evidence of the continuing capital adequacy of Names (i.e. beyond the initial documentation of their wealth at the time they join), although these have not as yet been taken further. But the increasing interest of the EC in 'understanding' Lloyd's, together with the possibility that some of the recent serious cases of underwriting losses may bankrupt significant numbers of Names, could put such a strain on Lloyd's outstanding record for 'security' ('no valid claim has ever not been met') that Names will no longer be protected from view by the reputation of Lloyd's as a whole.

The impact of discourses and practices stressing visibility, accountability, etc., and decisively realigning the power within the market towards the knowledge experts, also renders it increasingly likely that Lloyd's should become a limited liability market. For the new accounting and appraisal discourses and practices treat the accountable entities as if they were already equivalent to those in a limited liability market. At a discursive level, unlimited liability may well have started to become 'abnormal', since the discourse of modern accounting, managerial and financial, is concerned with articulating limited liability business concerns and takes limited liability for granted as the framework within which all decisions and evaluations are made. If this is so, then the day comes nearer when it will appear 'inevitable' that Lloyd's should adopt the limited liability route. Indeed discussion of the possibility has already begun as Lloyd's undertakes a fundamental review of its structure for survival into the next century. It can already be seen that, perhaps as a consequence – and certainly in parallel – the more Names are treated like investors the more they are coming to be regarded as, and behave like, investors in other respects. For example there are already proposals for 'unitization' of allocated capacity across a portfolio of syndicates to increase diversification of risk.

One may also speculate that the intense focus on devising measures to protect the interests of Names over recent years may have distracted Lloyd's from another of its 'fundamental' problems. Now that the tax advantages of Lloyd's as an 'investment club' have been whittled away, and much of its cost advantages reduced through the high costs of operating ever more like an international corporation and less and less like a street market, it has needed to focus more sharply on its primary role, namely the running of a successful insurance business in the face of national and international competition. In the wider insurance market – as in the world of business generally – the dominant mode of discourse is nowadays that of product competition, of marketing, and of the 'customer as king'. Of course that wider market is dominated by limited liability entities, the insurance companies, who are accountable in the first instance to a different constituency, being directly regulated by governmental bodies. In Britain that monitoring is conducted by the DTI, whose primary concern is to ensure the security of policyholders but which also has concerns to promote adequate competition for policyholders' benefit. It is doubtful whether the accountability required by the DTI in that regard can guarantee that security (Harte and Macve 1991), but that is not the point. The point is that the business strategy of these enterprises – steered by the bias of regulation – probably starts by facing in a different direction, emphasizing the primacy of policyholders' needs and thus providing the spur to the managements of companies to focus on competing to attract customers by meeting their needs and preferences with new products. It would seem prudent for Names to ask themselves what is being done in the name of *their* interests. They might wish to consider whether Lloyd's has been resting too much its reputation for first class security. This too can only be speculation, but points to the need *inter alia* for a greater understanding of the relationships between the dominant discourses of business life, the regulatory environment and actual business practices, priorities and organizational changes.

CONCLUSIONS

There has been continuing rapid change at Lloyd's, as in many other institutions in the City and beyond. The focus of these changes has been on the protection of Names who have been viewed as in many respects 'equivalent' to investors. In the process the 'clan' culture of Lloyd's as a club has been overlain by the 'hierarchical' culture of the regulated public company. Many unique features of Lloyd's, and the particular role of its accounting in determining absolutely the shares of risks and rewards that Names receive, have been partially submerged under the company orientated discourses that portray accounting and audit as providing 'useful information for investors' decisions'. The accounting-based performance indicators that are now disclosed share not only the limitations of the measures of financial control generated for other kinds of businesses, but the additional limitations that arise from the nature of Lloyd's business and market structure. The regulatory changes go beyond the compass of a wholly economic cost-benefit analysis.

It may be premature to see a wider Foucauldian analysis as either necessary or sufficient for understanding these forces of change. Perhaps the import of company accounting and auditing practices to Lloyd's was simply the most convenient 'off-the-peg' solution in an emergency. But then one must ask how the regime of accountability for companies generally has developed and why it takes its present form. The answer to that must await a larger-scale examination of the development of financial accounting and auditing, and the interrelationships of state, financial institutions ('the City') and the professions from the mid-nineteenth century to the present day. But one can perhaps begin to see where the particular piece of the jigsaw that is Lloyd's could fit into such a larger scale Foucauldian picture of the nature of the historical 'conditions of possibility' from which has developed the present regime of financial accountability and financial control of financial institutions, as well as of non-financial companies and other organizations.

ABBREVIATIONS

ALM   The Association of Lloyd's Members
ASB   The Accounting Standards Board
ASC   The (former) Accounting Standards Committee of the CCAB
DTI   The Department of Trade and Industry
E&O   Errors and Omissions (insurance cover)
FSA   Financial Services Act 1986
IBNR   'Incurred but not reported' claims
LPSO   Lloyd's Policy Signing Office
MAIR   Members' Agent Information Report (Lloyd's)
RITC   Reinsurance to close (Lloyd's)
SAB   Authors' abbreviation for The Syndicate Accounting Byelaw, i.e. Lloyd's Byelaw No. 7 of 1984, replaced by No. 11 of 1987 (as amended)
SIB   Securities and Investments Board
SSAP   Statement of Standard Accounting Practice
T&D   Time and Distance (reinsurance policy)

APPENDIX

Development of prior years' reinsurance to close

The margin of error in estimating the necessary ritc is brought out by information on how prior years reinsured into the current year of account have developed. Figures calculated for the market as a whole (Rew and Sturge, 1989, pp. v and xxii) are shown in Table 9.1.

Taking Lloyd's Global figures for the 1986 account a mere 5% difference on the ritc brought forward of £3 666m would be £183m, equivalent to 25% of the underwriting result for the 1986 year and almost the whole of the underwriting result for the 1985 year. The figures shown in the table illustrate the nature and effect of the 'margin of error' very clearly and are essential information in aiding Names' understanding of the risks they bear.

Table 9.1 Development of prior year's reinsurance to close: market results

	1 Pure Profit/ Loss (£m)	2 (Shortfall) Release (£m)	3 Net Profit/ (Loss) (£m)	4 2 as % of 1
For closed year 1986				
Marine	228	(24)	204	(10.5)
Non-marine	438	(131)	307	(29.9)
Motor	(18)	11	(7)	61.0
Aviation	111	(8)	103	(7.0)
For closed year 1985				
Marine	172	(18)	154	(10.5)
Non-marine	294	(175)	119	(59.5)
Motor	(51)	16	(35)	(31.4)
Aviation	30	15	45	50.0

Note: These figures exclude the run-off years; life and other syndicates are included in non-marine. The pure profit/loss is calculated after syndicate expenses and profit or loss on exchange.

REFERENCES

ALM (1990) *Lloyd's Syndicate Results 1987*, ALM, London.

Aczel, M., Broyles, J. and Masojada, B. (1990) Participation in the Lloyd's insurance market as a portfolio investment, *Journal of Business Finance and Accounting*, **17**(5) Winter. 609–33.

Beaver, W. (1989) *Financial Reporting: An accounting revolution*, 2nd edn, Prentice-Hall, Englewood Cliffs, NJ.

Chandler, A. (1977) *The Visible Hand* Harvard University Press, Cambridge, MA.

Davison, Ian Hay (1987) *A View of the Room: Lloyd's, change and disclosure*, Weidenfeld & Nicolson, London.

Edey, H.C. and Panitpakdi, P. (1956) British company accounts and the law 1844–1900, in *Studies in the History of Accounting* (eds A.C. Littleton and B.S. Yamey), Sweet & Maxwell, London.

Edwards, R.S. (1977) The nature and measurement of income, *The Accountant*, July–October 1938; reprinted in (eds W.T. Baxter and S. Davidson) *Studies in Accounting*, ICAEW, London.

Ezzamel, M., Hoskin, K.W. and Macve, R.H. (1990) Managing it all by numbers, *Accounting and Business Research* 153–66.

Foucault, M. (1977) *Discipline and Punish*, Allen Lane, London.

Gwilliam, D.R. (1988) Agency theory and audit: insights from the Lloyd's insurance market, presented at the Ernst & Young Accounting Research Symposium, UCW Aberystwyth, July.

Harte, G. and Macve, R. (1991) The Vehicle and General Insurance Company, in *Cases in Financial Reporting and Auditing* (eds S. Turley and P. Taylor).

Hilton, K. (1975) Control systems for social and economic management, Inaugural Lecture, University of Southampton.

Hodgson, G. (1984) *Lloyd's of London: A reputation at risk*, Allen Lane, London.

Hoskin, K.W. and Macve, R.H. (1986) Accounting and the examination: a genealogy of disciplinary power, *Accounting, Organizations and Society*, 105–36.

Hoskin, K.W. and Macve R.H. (1991) Boxing clever: for, against and beyond Foucault in the battle for accounting theory, paper presented at the Interdisciplinary Perspectives on Accounting Conference, University of Manchester, July.

Ibrahim, I.A.G. (1990) *The analytics of relations of power between regulated companies in the UK and the ASC*, PhD thesis, University of Sheffield.

Jensen, M.C. and Meckling, W.H. (1976) Theory of the firm: managerial behavior, agency costs and ownership structure, *Journal of Financial Economics*, **3** (October) 305–60.

KPMG Peat Marwick McLintock, (1988) *Lloyd's Regulation: Costs of compliance*, December.

Lev, B. (1988) Towards a theory of equitable and efficient accounting policy, *Accounting Review*, January 1–22.

Macve, R. (1981) *A Conceptual Framework for Financial Accounting and Reporting: the possibilities for developing an agreed structure*; a report prepared at the request of the Accounting Standards Committee, ICAEW, London.

Macve, R. (1986) *A Survey of Lloyd's Syndicate Accounts* ICAEW, Prentice-Hall, London.

Macve, R. and Gwilliam, D. (1992) *A Survey of Lloyd's Syndicate Accounts*, 2nd edn, Prentice-Hall/ICAEW, London.

Morris, R. (1987) Review of *A Survey of Lloyd's Syndicate Accounts, Accounting and Business Research* (Autumn) 361–2.

Neill, Sir Patrick, QC (Chairman) (1987) *Regulatory Arrangements at Lloyd's: Report of the Committee of Inquiry*, London: HMSO.

Ouchi, W.G. (1980) Markets, bureaucracies and clans, *Administrative Science Quarterly*, **25**, 129–42.

Rew J. and C. Sturge (eds.) (1990) *Lloyd's League Tables–1987* Chatset, London.

Robson, K. (1991) On the arenas of accounting change: the process of translation, *Accounting, Organizations and Society*, **16** 547–70.

Seldon, A. (ed.) (1988) *Regulation – or Over-Regulation?* Institute of Economic Affairs.

Tippett, M. (1990) Estimating returns on financial instruments – stochastic analysis, working paper, Australian National University.

Tricker, R.I. (1982) Corporate accountability and the role of the audit function, in *Auditing Research: Issues and opportunities*, (eds A.G. Hopwood, M. Bromwich and J. Shaw), Pitman, London, pp. 53–68.

Watts, R.L. and Zimmerman, J.L. (1986) *Positive Accounting Theory*, Prentice-Hall, Englewood Cliffs, NJ.

Financial control in the financial services industry: The case of Lloyd's of London: Discussant's comments

DAVID OTLEY

The paper falls into two rather distinct parts, the first of which is primarily concerned with accounting techniques and the second of which is about the regulation of an institution. However, the two parts are only loosely connected, and I will therefore discuss them separately.

To me, one of the most striking aspects of the accounting part of the paper is that it describes a situation where the result of accounting calculations actually matters to those involved. Although this is not unusual in management accounting, it is comparatively rare in financial accounting. Because much private sector accounting is concerned with companies whose shares are traded, it can be argued that errors or biases in financial accounting procedures are of little substantive significance. Any errors made in accounting valuation will be corrected in the prices paid for shares which are transferred from one owner to another. This is true, par excellence, for companies with a Stock Market listing where accounting numbers serve only as a backstop in determining share prices – and most financial accounting theory concerns itself primarily with such listed companies.

But Lloyd's is much more akin to a close company. When a Name wishes to withdraw from a syndicate, the accounts determine the terms on which such withdrawal is permitted. If the accounting valuations are inaccurate, then either the withdrawing party or the remaining Names will be disadvantaged.

Thus, central to this issue is the fundamental Accounting problem of establishing a profit figure for a period before all the consequences of the period's actions have become apparent. Particularly interesting to an outsider is the use of 'Time and Distance' policies to circumvent the need for discounted cash flow evaluations of future events. This seems to be a case of the development of a market mechanism to permit sensible practices which go beyond generally accepted accounting principles. Here, issues of accounting practice are avoided by the use of a traded insurance policy.

But does the accounting system actually achieve an equitable result between past, present and future Names? The evidence would seem to suggest that it does not. The increasing rate of disallowal by the Inland Revenue of 'reinsurance to close' provisions would indicates that there has been a systematic bias against leavers. This is perhaps not an unexpected situation as the balance of power lies with the managing agent who will continue to remain with a syndicate. Overall one is forced to the conclusion that the accounting procedures provide only a weak level of protection to Names.

The use of this accounting information to provide control and performance indicators is even weaker. The use of premium income as a measure of risk can surely only be justified on the basis of it being a relatively objective figure, rather than it being closely related to the phenomenon of interest. Further, the performance indicators derived from those used in the company sector appear to miss their mark almost entirely. Their use perhaps best indicates the dominance of public company-based accounting techniques over other possibilities.

The discussion now shades into issues of regulation. Here I would agree that the issue requires a sociological interpretation, although I would not necessarily progress down the Foucauldian track taken by the authors. The first question that arises is why the recently introduced controls were not required in the past. Here I would identify two complementary suggestions. First, there was a social catchet and status associated with being permitted to act as a Name; it indicated substantial wealth and social acceptability. Furthermore, it did not require the use of that wealth directly in the syndicate; the wealth acting solely as asset backing and would hopefully never be required. Thus it offered the chance of an income stream (as a reward for risk-bearing) without demanding the sole use of the capital. Second, and probably more important, there were significant tax advantages to the Name which added to the attractiveness of the 'investment'. All in all, membership of a Lloyd's syndicate provided a tax-shielded income stream for some of the wealthiest people in the establishment.

The second question of interest is what caused this happy situation to change? I am not adequately informed to provide an answer, but the need for substantially increased levels of asset backing as business grew coupled with the decline in the numbers of seriously wealthy individuals must provide a

230

partial answer. New Names might only be available if some more formal assurances about the performance of syndicates and if protections were established to protect 'remote' Names from unscrupulous (although not incompetent) agents. The nature of Lloyd's had begun to change from a club to a business.

The final question that is raised concerns why private sector control techniques were imported and applied, in a situation to which they were not well-suited, rather than more appropriate techniques being tailored to the specific circumstances. Again, I think two factors were paramount. First, such techniques were available. They might not be perfect, but they would be quick to install and also (relatively) cheap. Second, the techniques possessed a great deal of credibility. They were used in the private sector and were considered to provide appropriate protection to Stock Market investors – why should they not provide equivalent protection to Lloyd's Names? Additionally, the level of financial understanding of potential Names might not be high. Alternatively, their power base might be relatively weak. I don't know, but the questions provide a fascinating hunting ground for the business sociologist.

The authors have provided a fascinating description of an institution and topic that was previously unknown to me. In so doing, they have opened up a series of questions about both accounting measures and the regulation of financial institutions that deserve further questioning. In a sense, they have begun to develop a contingency theory of financial controls (i.e. what controls are appropriate to which circumstances). But, even more importantly, they have raised questions about how regulatory instruments become demanded and accepted within our business and social culture. Much further work is required, but they have set an important direction for future scholars.

10

Reforming financial controls in the NHS – or is the NHS a 'deviant' organization?

IRVINE LAPSLEY*

INTRODUCTION

Since the mid-1970s, the NHS has been subject to a series of financial management initiatives. As explored further below, these are comprehensive in nature, including recommendations on systems of budgetary control, capital investment decisions and reforms of capital accounting. These initiatives stem from central government exerting influence in its pivotal role as the provider of funds with overall statutory responsibility for the delivery of NHS health care. As noted below, certain facets of the above aspects of financial control have been developed by others interested in the NHS, but these non-governmental developments have tended to be sporadic and fragmentary. This is quite distinct from central government intervention in NHS financial controls, in which these initiatives are seen as *national* policies or the precursors to the development of national policies (as in the case, for example, of trial sites for management budgeting).

* The author gratefully acknowledges helpful comments from Sue Llewellyn, Falconer Mitchell and Robin Roslender.

Perspectives on Financial Control: Essays in memory of Kenneth Hilton.
Edited by Mahmoud Ezzamel and David Heathfield.
Published in 1992 by Chapman & Hall, London. ISBN 0 412 40980 1.

The merits of these developments are explored in this paper from the perspectives of:

(a) whether, in accounting terms, they are technically sound and whether they have had or will have a significant impact on accounting practices; and
(b) the extent to which such developments are consistent with the context of the NHS.

These issues are elaborated upon further, below.

THE CONTEXT

The importance of the social and the organizational context in the study of accounting information is now well established (see, for example, Burchell *et al.*, 1980; Laughlin *et al.*, 1989). This study takes the perspective of 'labelling theory' or the 'labelling perspective' in analysing the organizational and the wider social setting in which NHS financial reforms take place. This perspective originated with the work of Lemert (1951) and was developed subsequently by Becker (1963), among others. It can be described as the process of identifying behaviour which is regarded as deviant and classifying or labelling it as deviant. This tends to form a three-stage process:

1. primary deviance (the identification phase);
2. labelling as abnormal and deviant; and
3. secondary deviances, in which there are changes in behaviour arising from the labelling process.

The labelling perspective depicts deviance not simply as *actual* violations of norms for behaviour, but also as behaviour which is *defined* as deviance. Further, the act of identifying deviant behaviour by decision makers (e.g. policy makers, corrective or regulatory agencies) is with a view to controlling or eliminating it. However, labelling theorists would suggest that there may be unintended consequences in that the labelling process may actually *accentuate* the activities defined as deviant at the first stage (i.e. secondary deviance). Therefore, the identifying agency's (e.g. policy maker, regulator) aim of control will not be achieved.

Much of the work of labelling theorists has been addressed at explaining the behaviour of individuals in society. This includes studies of criminal behaviour and of illness and disability. For example, Piliavin and Briar (1964) on criminal behaviour, Goffman (1961) on the mentally ill, Scott (1969) on blindness, Davis (1963) on disability and Higgins (1980) on deafness. However, despite the interesting explanations of behaviour which it offers, 'labelling' has not been beyond criticism to the effect that it is not rigorous enough to be considered a theory in its own right; that the act of 'labelling' does not produce uniform negative consequences in the form of secondary deviance; that individuals so categorized actually wish to behave as deviants (Davis, 1972; Bordua, 1970; Young, 1975; Mankoff, 1971). Nevertheless, despite such reservations over the labelling perspective, and its previous focus, on individuals, it is suggested here that it offers interesting insights into the *raison d'etre* of central governments' identification of what it perceives to be weaknesses in NHS financial control systems and the response of the NHS to these recommendations.

There are numerous facets to the suggestion that not only has the NHS come to be regarded as 'deviant' by central government, but that the effects of central government efforts to redress this (i.e. 'labelling') have accentuated the factors, attributes and characteristics by which the NHS might be regarded as 'deviant' in the first place (i.e. secondary deviance). This might be seen as part of a general process by which central government has sought to reduce the public sector, and to change the practices of those public services which remain in the public sector to what might be regarded as 'best practices' in the private sector (see, for example, Pollitt, 1986). The specific factors which might have prompted central government to regard the NHS as 'deviant', when compared to the private sector, apart from the fact of its public ownership, include the nature of its management systems and its accounting practices, the ambiguity of its objectives and the particular problem of measuring its output.

In this regard, the most important dimension of the NHS management system, which has long attracted considerable attention (see, for example, Perrin *et al.*, 1978) and which the government might consider 'deviant' or 'abnormal', from what might be expected in the private sector, is that of the role of hospital doctors in the NHS. Hospital doctors, in general, and consultants, in particular, are well recognized as major consumers of resources, within the NHS. However, while they are key decision makers in the use of hospital resources, they, nevertheless, have little formal financial responsibility. This differs markedly from what might be expected in the world of the private sector, in which managers in production and other functions would have explicit budgetary responsibilities. This state of affairs has led to numerous attempts to involve hospital doctors in financial management, as discussed further below.

This circumstance is also a factor in the introduction of general management (Griffiths, 1983) which seeks to challenge the power and influence of the various professional groups within the NHS by replacing them with a private sector concept of the 'ideal' management structure. The existence of such an influential group within the NHS has led to the comment that, in effect, clinicians exert a form of 'clan control' over the NHS (see Bourn and Ezzamel, 1986).

This distinctive aspect of the NHS is further complicated by the overlay of both the ambiguous nature of its objectives and problems of measuring NHS output. The initial objectives of the NHS were based on the principle of equity, namely health care was to be made 'available to everyone regardless of financial means, age, sex, employment or vocation, area of residence or insurance qualification' (*The NHS Bill: A summary of the Proposed Service*, Cmd. 6761, HMSO, 1946, p. 3). However, to operationalize these objectives has proved difficult. In part, this can be attributed to the economic circumstances of the NHS, in which there is an absence of pricing systems to ration its activities in the face of an increasing demand for its services.

This excess demand is fuelled by the changing nature of the population, with a high proportion of elderly who make greater demands on the health care system and by medical advances which create further demands for services (see, for example, *Royal Commission on the National Health Service* (Merrison Report), 1979). This elusive nature of the objective of equity is also accentuated by the resource iniquities which have existed within the various health authorities/boards since the inception of the NHS and the failure of successive resource allocation systems to redress such iniquities (see, for example, Noyce *et al.*, 1974). This, in turn, is heightened by the finite amount of resources available for health care expenditure, all of which makes the original objectives of the NHS difficult to attain.

These circumstances are aggravated further by the various meanings which can be attributed to the means of achieving these objectives. For example, does equity of access entail self-sufficiency in provision at all levels and areas of the NHS? The basic ambiguity of these aims has been explored by Bourn and Ezzamel (1986). They have demonstrated that the fundamental aim of equity does not translate well into operational objectives, not only for the NHS, overall, but also for the various elements of its hierarchy.

This situation is complicated further by uncertainties over means-end relationships in the delivery of health care. In the absence of a pricing system for health care services, there is a well known problem of measuring the worth of its output. A principal difficulty with available indicators is their *partial* nature, i.e. they are specific to particular categories of health care (e.g. acute, geriatric) and do not permit comparisons across medical specialties. At best such comparisons can be achieved by relying on the expert views of clinicians. However, such comparisons merely emphasize the importance of the *providers'* role in determining health care priorities. This set of circumstances has led to numerous attempts at deriving surrogate measures of health care outcomes (see, for example, Fanshel and Bush (1974), Rosser and Watts (1978), Torrance *et al.*, 1982). Despite such efforts, there is as yet no generally accepted surrogate, or sets of partial indicators, of the quality of health care provided.

All of the above fits Hofstede's (1981) analysis of situations of management control, in which the effects of management intervention are unknown because of such uncertainties over ambiguities in objectives, and because of difficulties of measuring output. Hofstede's analysis suggests that the *rationalistic* procedures adopted/adapted from the private sector will not be appropriate in achieving or improving management control in the NHS. As an alternative, the NHS might be recognized as a *distinctive* form of organization, with distinctive financial and management controls, rather than as a *deviant* one. This implies that reversion to the system of 'clan control' by medical professionals alluded to above, in which accounting information does not have a dominant role, may be a superior method of managing and controlling the activities of the NHS than the recent round of financial management initiatives. This issue is addressed in the conclusion to this paper after a review of (a) the changing role of the Treasurer in the NHS (his status, changes in the managerial context in which he operates, reflections on the nature of old style financial controls in a situation of 'clan control') and (b) the major financial management initiatives, and the extent to which they have extended or improved the techniques of financial control available to the Treasurer, or merely accentuated the distinctive nature of the NHS.

THE CHANGING ROLE OF THE TREASURER

In the early days of the NHS the title of Treasurer was given to the principal accountant within the (then) regional hospital boards. While this remains in use today, there has been a general switch to the title of Director of Finance. This is not mere semantics. The original title of Treasurer has distinct connotations as regards role and function within the organization. This is exemplified by the duties of these Treasurers in the early (1950s) and middle (1960s) years of the NHS. The major role of the then Treasurer was that of *paymaster*, with responsibility for payroll (the largest item of NHS running costs at c. 70%), creditors and the overall aim of maintaining financial equilibrium, as depicted by balancing income and expenditure in any given financial year. The source of income was as today, i.e. almost entirely grants from central government. This was accounted for by a statutory return, which, when aggregated for the entire NHS, formed the basis of Appropriation Accounts which were laid before Parliament. These are still prepared and have changed little in content or structure for decades. As a source of information for local management they were (and are) of little use – too late, and lacking in management focus on performance achievement.

In this situation major capital expenditure was controlled tightly by the DHSS and Scottish Home and Health Department (SHHD), by a system of permission being granted to undertake major projects ('control by starts'). The major financial criterion in such decisions was size of capital outlay plus estimates of the revenue consequences of capital schemes (RCCS). This might be seen as a variant on the accountant's rate of return. At the level of the regional hospital board or individual hospital, there was minor capital expenditure and little capital appraisal, with certain exceptions (e.g. replacement of boilers).

This absence of useful accounting information for capital planning was mirrored by a similar situation in the control of revenue expenditure. Health boards and hospitals were funded by allocations from central government and, with no revenue-raising powers of their own (as is the situation, today) there were no budgets, as such. The major source of management accounting information was that of costing returns. These set out subjective analyses of the costs of operating individual hospitals and of hospital boards. These persist in Scotland but in a different format in England, as discussed further below. The major drawbacks with such information were its lateness and its focus on actual running costs, without comparing them to budgets.

In this world in which the medical profession exerted a form of 'clan control' over key policy developments, the Treasurer was regarded as a 'mere bookkeeper'. He did not have the same status within the NHS as the medical and nursing professions. However, the Treasurer *was* in a position to best exert control from the centre to maintain his objective of overall financial balance. This he would achieve by strong establishment control, in which appointments to vacancies could be delayed (or, possibly, frozen) and payments to creditors could be delayed (or accelerated, as the case may be) and stocks of materials could be run down or built up, all with the objective of achieving a break even position at the financial year end. A similar informal pressure to control the prescription of drugs by the medical profession was (and still is) exerted by pharmacists in hospitals. In terms of financial control, the Treasurer may have appeared as a 'shadowy figure' – in effect, financial management by stealth.

However, this situation did not persist. While the NHS had always enjoyed a successful position in terms of its claim on the public purse in the 1950s and 1960s it was already becoming evident that (a) there was a substantial growth in the demand for, and nature of, services provided by the NHS and (b) the original stated aim of equality of access to health care for all of the population was not being achieved. The major response of central government to this set of circumstances was the creation of a new management structure (DHSS, 1972) based on the concept of consensus management, which had been widely recommended within the management literature of the 1960s as 'best practice' (see for example, Bennis, 1966; Leavitt, 1965). This was a central government initiative which resulted from an (indirect) labelling of the NHS as inefficient and incapable and which launched the NHS on a path towards the adoption or adaptation of a set of management accounting techniques which were and are used widely in the private sector.

As far as the role of the Treasurer was concerned, this revised management structure resulted in a change of status, with formal recognition of the accounting function on a par with other professions, such as medicine and nursing. The 'financial management by stealth' in a situation of clan control by the medical profession, as described above, was to be abandoned. Instead, there was an expanded, more visible, role for the Treasurer. This new role was welcomed by leading practitioners of the day, such as R. Brinley Codd (1971), the then Treasurer of South-East Thames Regional Health Authority, who identified the need for greater use of 'fundamental techniques of management accounting' (p. 247), which, in his view, had not been utilized fully, at that time. This view was reinforced by the then Association of Health Service Treasurers (1979), which recognized and supported the new financial/managerial role of the accountant, as opposed to the traditional treasury/paymaster function. The following section of this paper explores the extent to which this abandonment of the old style of financial control based on balancing the books (allied to the clan control of the medical profession) has resulted in new improved financial control systems, by considering the impact of recent and current financial management initiatives in the NHS.

THE FINANCIAL MANAGEMENT INITIATIVES

The financial management initiatives within the NHS take a variety of forms. These might be grouped conveniently, as follows:

(a) management control;
(b) capital accounting; and
(c) the operating environment.

Both (a) and (b) refer to financial management initiatives designed to improve internal management information systems within the operational branches of the NHS. These extend over the past sixteen years or so.

The major distinguishing feature of these various initiatives, which are discussed in some detail below, is that of central government's desire to reform NHS financial controls by replicating private sector accounting information systems. The use of the private sector as a reference point for these reforms takes different forms, as noted below. For example, the recruiting of a senior industrialist (Griffiths) whose remit led, inevitably, to recommendations for reforms based on 'best commercial practice'. Or the explicit statement in the central government White Paper on capital accounting that its recommendations were to achieve comparability with the private sector. All of this is supportive of the notion that the NHS is regarded by central government as a 'deviant' organization over which control might be exercised in a better fashion if it adopted the management and financial control procedures of the norm – the private sector. However, according to the labelling perspective, the inappropriate categorizing of behaviour as 'deviant' may have the consequence of accentuating the original 'deviant' factors (i.e. secondary deviance). In this regard, we examine the extent to which these private sector recommendations on accounting practices translate effectively to the NHS or whether they serve to merely demonstrate the distinctive nature (or, alternatively, 'deviance') of the NHS.

The third category refers to the government's most recent proposals which seek to create an entirely new environment in the NHS, in which financial management should have a significant role. This particular set of proposals is also consistent with the 'labelling' perspective outlined earlier. However, they represent a different order of magnitude from the reforms of management control and capital accounting. As root and branch reforms, these seek to replace the provider-driven ('clan control') nature of the NHS with a market-orientated approach in which consumers/patients have a central role to play in determining the mix, level and quality of health care services.

This particular reform can be seen as the ultimate manifestation of the NHS (in its original form) as a 'deviant' organization, on the grounds that its operating environment differs markedly from the norm of the private sector. While the NHS has been dominated from the outset by considerations of equity of access to health care, the 'norm' of the private sector is seen to be motivated by considerations of efficiency. This attribute of the private sector is most marked in the existence of markets for products and services. Therefore, (as the labelling perspective would predict), a market in health care must be created to conform to the desired norm. These differing aspects of NHS financial management initiatives are considered, in turn, below.

Management control

There have been five major developments within the area of management control in the NHS since the mid-1970s. (For a detailed discussion of these see Perrin *et al.*, 1988). While pursuing the same basic theme of devolved management accountability, these developments offer differing, but, in some senses, parallel, attempts to solve the issue of management control in the NHS. These were as follows:

(a) Functional Budgetary Control (1974), with the subsequent development of Unit Budgeting;
(b) Clinical Budgeting (Wickings, 1974 on);

(c) Specialty Costing (Magee, 1978 on, plus Korner, 1980 on);
(d) Management Budgeting (1983), Griffiths Report; and
(e) Resource Management (1986 to date), DHSS.

The first of these addressed the problem of the NHS having allocations and not formal budgeting systems, within the constraint of the absence of revenue-raising powers. However, its major focus was that of ancillary and support services (domestic, estates and buildings, radiography) with no impact on the clinical aspect of service, save for nursing. In effect this system was based on the familiar accounting notion of responsibility accounting but, it failed to take account of the most important decision makers and users of resources, i.e. the medical profession. This defect of functional budgetary control was recognized by Wickings, among others. He initiated a series of attempts to involve clinicians in budgeting. However, these attempts at 'clinical budgeting' were not widespread and were not embedded in the basic budgetary control system, which was geared to functional control, as depicted above, although, by this time, efforts were being made to devolve budgets to units (groups of hospitals and related services).

In the face of these developments a separate, parallel development which built on the earlier notions of costing statements was taking place. This had begun, on a pilot basis, in Wales under Charles Magee. It was given considerable impetus by the Korner report of 1980. This tackled the problem of 'what to do' with clinicians by proposing the compilation of regular costing information on clinical specialties. This development was not pursued in Scotland.

However, when the Griffiths report (1983) pronounced its verdict that NHS management lacked direction and the ability to respond to change, it also recommended that 'cost awareness' (as, for example, typified by the Korner proposals) was not sufficient for management control. It recommended that a system of management budgeting should be introduced, in which clinicians assumed formal management responsibility for their activities. This can be seen as a failure, for a variety of reasons. One particular reason was the failure of the Griffiths report to understand the behaviour and training of health care professionals which was (and is) geared to caring for patients rather than financial management. An alternative interpretation of this failure is that the 'clan control' of the medical profession resisted its introduction, with some considerable success. It was thought that this would be resolved by renaming this initiative (to the Resource Management initiative) and broadening the nature of the information used beyond the financial to include patient care data (DHSS, 1986).

However, even now, such systems are not operational in the vast majority of UK hospitals. It would appear that both technical and cultural/behavioural factors have contributed to this failure. There has been a major miscalculation of the amount of time and resources required to make such systems operational. This is accentuated by the need to reconcile two, quite different, information systems: the financial information system and the patient administration system. This, in turn, is not helped by the lumpiness of NHS computing investment, with different, non-compatible systems, (Willcocks and Mark, 1988). Added to this are the issues of how to gain acceptance by the medical profession who, at least initially, appear to have viewed such exercises as 'cost cutting' rather than for the benefit of patients. Furthermore, such developments do not sit well with the new NHS organizational structure with multiple sources of authority (informal and formal), even although the General Manager is deemed to be the ultimate authority within the various units and Health Boards/Authorities. A contrasting view to this was expressed by the Secretary of State for Health, William Waldgrave, in which he referred to the 'efficient and intensive period of work' which led up to the NHS reforms and referred to these changes in NHS management practices as 'the most thorough-going changes since the foundation of the NHS' (as reported in the NHS *Management Executive News*, April, 1991, p. 1). However, this viewpoint may only serve to underline the detachment (remoteness?) of policymakers from the operational services. For example, the above statement almost coincides with the publication of the DHSS sponsored evaluation of resource management (Health Economics Research Group, 1991) which has confirmed that, not only were the costs and timetable for implementation optimistic, but there was little evidence of positive benefits for patient care arising from resource management at the official pilot sites.

Overall, therefore, it can be seen that there are various strands to the present state of the art in accounting information systems for management control in the NHS. The outright adoption of private sector practices (in the manner recommended by Griffiths) has not proved to be a widespread success. There are, as outlined above, technical reasons for this. It could also be argued that the NHS is in transition and that, ultimately, such information systems will function effectively. However, more fundamentally, it can be seen that these proposals to implement private sector practices (to make the NHS conform) have not succeeded because they are based on a particular (rational, logical) mode of organizational behaviour and failed to take account of the distinctive nature of the NHS. In particular, the nature of the service provided and the distinctive role played by health care professionals in the delivery of this service. Further, in terms of Hofstede's (1981) analysis of management control, this should take the form of political/judgemental control for many levels of NHS management because of ambiguity over objectives and difficulties of output measurement.

In terms of the perspective adopted in this paper, these repeated initiatives to reform this particular aspect of NHS financial controls might be seen as a series of attempts by central government to make the NHS conform to private sector practices. That is, the government has defined a situation of deviance which may not, in fact, exist. And, because the NHS has been labelled, as or is seen as, 'out of control' or deviant, the labelling perspective would suggest that this 'deviance' has become more pronounced with each distinctive variant of financial management control which emerges, as the NHS fails to respond to central government's efforts to control the NHS by making it conform to its norm of private sector practices. The extent to which this view can be supported depends, of course, on the merits of alternative systems of managing and controlling the NHS, such as a reversion to a culture-based control system. This issue is taken up further in the conclusion.

Capital accounting

There are two aspects to the capital accounting problem within the NHS:

(a) how best to make decisions about capital developments; and
(b) how to account for such capital expenditure.

The first of these refers to the familiar investment decision. However, there are longstanding issues which make such decisions particularly difficult within the NHS. In the absence of a system of pricing for health care provided, NHS managers are confronted with difficult decisions in considering alternative investment. For example, how is a trade off established between (a) a new accident and emergency unit, (b) improved accommodation for psychogeriatric patients and (c) equipment for renal dialysis? One approach is the identification of 'quality-adjusted' life years, in which the number of years of normal life which can be expected to benefit a particular patient or group of patients is used as the yardstick, (see for example, Drummond, 1991, and Mooney and Olsen, 1991). These difficulties over investment decisions are exacerbated by the capital rationing situation which prevails in the NHS.

In an attempt to resolve this problem the DHSS (1982) and SHHD (1986) have introduced a new variant of the traditional investment appraisal, called *options appraisal*. This stresses the need to (a) focus on the alternative proposals, (b) evaluate these in the context of a strategic plan and (c) use discounting techniques rather than the old style 'revenue consequences of capital schemes' approach to investment. There is evidence that such procedures are now being employed within the NHS (Lapsley, 1986; Ferguson and Lapsley, 1988).

However, this evidence is based on surveys of NHS personnel (often finance) with a particular responsibility for the development of capital expenditure proposals. There is a need for a greater understanding of how such information generated by the adoption of the options appraisal technique is used within the organization, not only by managers, but also by others affected by, and involved in, the investment decision. It is interesting to note, for example, that two economists with considerable experience of the NHS have expressed concern about the lack of, and need for, rational procedures and processes in dealing with options appraisal (Mooney and Henderson, 1986). This observation is indicative of the kinds of difficulties encountered in the implementation of management control systems in the NHS, in which 'rational, logical' systems do not fit into the realities of organizational life. This is an area worthy of further research.

The matter of how the NHS accounts for capital expenditure has only recently been tackled by government (as part of the NHS reforms) despite repeated suggestions by interested commentators that some form of depreciation accounting should be adopted by the NHS. In essence, until now, the NHS has not had any form of capital asset accounting – no asset registers, no depreciation, no accounting number for assets held in its balance sheet. One particular consequence of not having capital asset accounting has been the absence of information on the geographical distribution of assets held. For policy makers and other interested parties, this has meant that it was not possible to detect if the original NHS aim of equality of access to health care was being met, at least as regards assets held by the different health authorities/boards.

The form of capital accounting which is being introduced into the NHS, in 1991, as part of the NHS reforms, is quite distinctive. It has two parts:

(a) a depreciation charge based on net current replacement cost; and
(b) a finance charge based on the Treasury discount rate (the 'opportunity cost' of capital) which is charged against the net current replacement cost of assets held.

It has been introduced with the stated aim of achieving comparability with the private sector. However, the above system is markedly different from typical private sector practices, on a number of counts. The use of current cost accounting, when this has been abandoned by the private sector (save for some recently privatized organizations) is one aspect of this. The introduction of a notional finance charge is also evidently distinct from private sector practice. Furthermore, the concept of depreciation may serve a number of purposes (as in income measurement and capital maintenance). However, the object of the NHS capital charge is quite distinct. It is to make managers sensitive to capital costs which, at present, may be regarded as a free good in their decisions.

There are difficulties of both a conceptual and a practical nature with this system of capital charging. In the first instance, the logic of using a uniform rate (the Treasury discount rate) as a proxy for the costs of servicing capital is, at least, questionable. The capital stock of assets held by individual health authorities will reflect the history of that particular authority. This will have been influenced by the initial stock of assets held when the NHS was created and exacerbated by the failure of successive resource equalization policies. Given that this is so, this charge against inherited assets cannot be held as a measure of the efficiency of any particular NHS management's asset utilization. Furthermore, there is a well established and voluminous literature (see for example, Thomas, 1974) on the dysfunctional effects of apparently arbitrary cost allocations on management's behaviour. In this regard, this composite capital charge, which could be seen as introducing more rational capital accounting in the NHS, may have unintended dysfunctional consequences in terms of NHS management's response.

Indeed, this particular capital asset accounting system and the government-recommended processes and procedures for making investment decisions might be seen as examples of 'secondary deviance'. That is, in response to government initiatives to improve capital accounting systems, the NHS has derived systems for both *ex ante* and *ex post* capital accounting which differ from the private sector norm and which emphasize the distinctive nature of the NHS. For example, the difficulties over output measurement and ambiguity of objectives are accommodated, to a degree, within the options appraisal framework. Also, the selection of replacement cost for the basis of accounting can be seen as reflecting the continuity of supply in a public service which does not price its output. Indeed, the use of the Treasury's opportunity cost of capital as a signal to managers for the capital cost of servicing assets held merely emphasizes the reliance of the NHS on the Exchequer for funds. In short, the recommended techniques for both aspects of capital accounting serve to accentuate the distinctive nature of the NHS. Furthermore, there is a need for research to explore the extent to which such techniques do improve management processes and fit the realities of NHS organizational life.

The operating environment

The most dramatic of the proposed reforms of the NHS (DOH, 1989) is that of the creation of an internal market for health care. This is to be achieved by the creation of *purchasers* and *providers*. Health authorities will be purchasers of services from directly managed (NHS) hospital facilities or from self-governing hospital trusts within their authority, or from such facilities outside their authority, or from the private sector. In addition, where there are GP fund-holders within districts, these practices will have the right to purchase services from any of the above alternatives set out above. The allocation of funds to GP budget holders to permit them to operate in this way will be deducted from the health authority's funds, as the authority will no longer be responsible for purchasing services for patients in these practices.

The purchasers can enter into three types of contract with providers, (a) cost per case, (b) cost and volume and (c) block contracts. In (a), the contract is agreed on a specific patient treatment cost. In (b) the provider receives a sum for treating a specified minimum number of patients, plus cost per case up to a maximum activity level. The block grant will entail the provision of an agreed activity level in exchange for a fixed sum of money. It might be assumed that categories (a) and (b) above would be the typical cases in a genuine internal market. However, available costing information in health authorities is not sufficiently precise to provide patient treatment costs. At present, the best available information is average costs for specialties. However, within specialties, costs may vary with different treatments which require different resources. Given the inadequacies of existing costing information for agreeing contracts, it is likely that a high proportion of purchaser/provider contracts will be on a 'block grant' basis, at least in the immediate future. This suggests that the internal market will not function, as intended.

Furthermore, the design of the internal market is based on a mechanism in which health authorities are not only *purchasers* but they are also responsible for *providers* (i.e. directly managed hospital units). It may be that, ultimately, more and more hospitals will opt out for self-governing hospital trust status, but, at present, the health authorities have a dual role which does not square with the idea of a market in which arms length negotiations take place. Also, the introduction of GPs as *purchasers* is something of an uncertain factor. By giving budgets to GPs and allowing them to 'shop around' for treatments for their patients the internal market breaks the traditional links between referrals from GP to hospital consultants. However, there are unanswered questions about how GPs will behave. They may act differently from their colleagues in hospitals (see, for example, the above discussion of management control), but this remains to be seen.

Furthermore, to allow informed decisions to be made by purchasers there is a need, not only for accurate costing information, but also for quality of care received. Given their nature, as outlined above, the tariff rates used for settling purchaser/provider contracts cannot be accepted as proxies for the 'willingness to pay' of the private sector and market place. This leads back to the familiar problem of output measurement in health care.

In terms of the labelling perspective, the above aspects of the internal market – the inability of health authorities to generate costing information to facilitate the operation of the market; the (expected) reliance on block grant contracts; the lack of genuine arms length relationships between principal purchasers and providers; the need for information on both costs and quality of care and their relationship to allow informed decisions to be made; the uncertainty over the behaviour of the GP as a fund-holder suggest that it will not function as intended. In short, in moving towards the private sector norm of the market place, the NHS has emphasized the distinctive nature of its activities, which might be interpreted as 'secondary deviance', i.e. the implementation of the internal market accentuates the characteristics of its operations which are different (or 'deviant'?) from the private sector.

CONCLUSION

This paper has examined the reform of financial controls within the NHS. It has sought to do so by considering the technical merits of a series of financial management initiatives and by adopting the labelling perspective to provide a contextual analysis of the settings in which such changes are taking place.

One evident, major outcome of these changes in financial management has been a new, more powerful, more visible role for the accountant in the NHS. In terms of changes to, and refinements of, the accounting techniques available to him, there would also appear to be substantive change. One notable aspect of this is the development of options appraisal as a more sophisticated approach to the investment decision. However, while there is evidence of the use of such techniques, there is need for greater knowledge of how their use fits into the NHS. Indeed, the distinctive nature of the NHS – the ambiguity of its objectives, the difficulties of measuring output, the uncertain effects of management intervention and the existence of competing values (notably between the medical profession and finance/management) – have all placed limitations on the development of management control systems. These developments have also been constrained by a lack of expertise and of resources and because of inadequate and differing systems of information technology. Of the other major changes, time will tell if the new capital accounting system will achieve its aim of improving managerial sensitivity to capital costs and if the internal market will result in greater efficiency in health care provision. However, doubts have been expressed over both of these, at least in the short run.

The labelling perspective adopted suggests that the government does not regard the NHS as a distinctive (unique?) organization but has identified it as 'deviant' when compared to its norm of the private sector. This 'deviance' applies to NHS accounting and management practices and to the very nature of the organization, itself. This perspective suggests that such labelling may lead to 'secondary deviance', in which the characteristics/behaviour identified as deviant become more pronounced. In effect, this has happened with the NHS. The various attempts to reform its financial controls by government have resulted in substantive modifications to the private sector norm, which serve to underline the distinctive nature of this organization.

This raises the question of whether it might have been better if the NHS had not embarked upon their extensive series of financial reforms but had, instead, remained with the system of control in which the finance function was essentially of a 'paymaster/treasury' variety, in which the major function of the finance officer was to balance the books and break even. In this situation, the priorities of the NHS were dominated by the views of the medical profession, which exerted a form of clan control. It could be argued that this arrangement was more economical and that it better fitted the aims and nature of the NHS. However, one major caveat to the reversion to this form of control is the fact that the medical profession had its own pecking order of medical specialties. In particular, acute services were given a higher priority than the Cinderella services of the mentally handicapped and geriatric care (see, for example, SHHD, 1980). Indeed the motives and behaviour of the medical profession have not escaped criticism. For example, Zeckhauser (1974) alleges that the medical professions adoption of an ethical code is a device to avoid regulatory constraint; Kennedy (1983) has also described the medical profession's stance on ethics as essentially a means of exploiting its position of power while neglecting the interests of consumers. These arguments cast doubt on the suggestion that the reversion to a 'clan control' system dominated by the medical profession would be in some sense 'superior' to the attempts to create an internal market. Nevertheless, it has yet to be demonstrated that the various NHS reforms (including the creation of the internal market) will actually deliver greater patient care. Indeed, according to the labelling perspective, the possible failure of such reforms is likely to lead to even more 'reforms' to make the NHS conform to (become a part of?) the private sector.

REFERENCES

Association of Health Service Treasurers (1979) *The Role of the Treasurer in the National Health Service*, CIPFA, London.

Becker, H.S. (1963) *Outsiders: Studies in the Sociology of Deviance*, Free Press, Glencoe.

Bennis, W. (1966) *Changing Organisations*, McGraw-Hill, New York.

Bordua, D. (1970) Recent trends: deviant behaviour and social control, in *Crime and Delinquency*, (ed. C. Bersani) Macmillan, London.

Bourn, M and Ezzamel, M. (1986) Organisational culture in hospitals in the National Health Service, *Financial Accountability and Management*, 2(3), 203–26.

Burchell, S., Clubb, C., Hopwood, A.G. and Nephapiet, J. (1980) The roles of accounting in organisations and society, *Accounting, Organisations and Society*, 1(8), 244–51.

Codd, R. Brinley (1971) Costing and efficiency in the Health Service, *Public Finance and Accountancy*, 1(8), 244–51.

Davis, F. (1963) *Passage Through Crisis*, Bobbs-Merrill, Indianapolis.

Davis, N. (1972) Labelling theory in deviance research, *Sociological Quarterly*, 13, 447–74.

DHSS (1972) *Management Arrangements for the Reorganised National Health Service*, HMSO, London.

References

DHSS (1982) *Investment Appraisal in the Public Sector*, DHSS, HN(82) 34.

DHSS (1986) *Resource Management (Management Budgeting) in Health Authorities*, DHSS, HN(86)34.

DOH (1984) *Working for Patients, the Health Service: Caring for the 1990s*, CM 555, London, HMSO.

Drummond, M. (1991) Output measurement for resource – allocation revisions in health care, in McGuire *et al.*, *Providing Health Care*, Oxford.

Fanshel, S. and Bush, J.W. (1970) A health-status index and its application to Health Services outcomes, *Operations Research*, **18**, July–December.

Ferguson, K. and Lapsley, l. (1988) Investment appraisal in the National Health Service, *Financial Accountability and Management*, **4**(4), 281–7.

Griffiths, R. (1983) *NHS Management Inquiry*, DHSS, London.

Goffman, E. (1961) *Asylums*, Penguin, Harmondsworth.

Health Economics Research Group (1991) *Final Report of the Brunel University Evaluation of Resource Management – Summary*, Brunel University, Uxbridge.

Higgins, P.C. (1980) *Outsiders in a Hearing World*, Sage, London.

Hofstede, G. (1981) Management control of public and not-for-profit activities, *Accounting, Organisations and Society*, **6**(3), 193–216.

Kennedy, l. (1983) *The Unmasking of Medicine*, Paladin, London.

Korner, E. (1984) *A Report on the Collection and Use of Financial Information in the NHS* (6th Report), DHSS, London.

Lapsley, I. (1986) Investment appraisal in UK non-trading organisations, *Financial Accountability and Management*, **2**(2), 135–51.

Laughlin, R, Hopper, T. and Miller, P. (1989) Contextual studies of accounting and auditing: an introduction, *Accounting, Auditing and Accountability Journal*, **2**(2), 4–7.

Leavitt, H. (1965) Applied organisational change in industry, in *Handbook of Organisations*, Rand McNally, Chicago.

Lemert, E.M. (1951) *Social Pathology: A Systematic Approach to the Study of Sociopathic Behaviour*, McGraw-Hill, New York.

Magee, C.C. and Osmolski, R.J. (1978) A comprehensive system of management information for financial planning decision making and control in the hospital service, University College, Cardiff.

Mankoff, M. (1971) Societal reaction and career deviance: a critical analysis, *Sociological Quarterly*, **12**, 204–18.

Merrison Report (1979) *Royal Commission on the National Health Service*, Cmnd. 7615, HMSO.

Mooney, G. (1986) *Economics, Medicine and Health Care*, Wheatsheaf, Brighton.

Mooney, G and Henderson, J. (1986) Option appraisal in the UK National Health Service, *Financial Accountability and Management*, **2**(3), 187–202.

Mooney, G and Olsen, J.A. (1991) QALYs: where next?, in McGruire *et al.*, *Providing Health Care*, Oxford.

Noyce, J., Naismith, A.H. and Trickey, A.J. (1974) regional variations in the allocation of financial resources to the Community Health Services, *Lancet*, 30 March.

Perrin, *et al.* (1978) *Management of Financial Resources in the National Health Service*, Research Paper No.2, Royal Commission on the NHS, HMSO.

Piliavin, S and Briar, S. (1964) Police encounters with juveniles, *American Journal of Sociology*, **52**, 206–14.

Pollitt, C. (1986) Beyond the managerial model: the case for broadening performance assessment in government and the public services, *Financial Accountability and Management*, **2**(3), 155–70.

Rosser, R.M. and Watts, V.C. (1978) The measurement of illness, *International Journal of Epidemiology*, **1**(4), 1972.

Scott, R.A. (1969) *The Making of Blind Men*, Russell Sage, London.

SHHD (1980) *Scottish Health Authorities: Priorities for the Eighties*, HMSO, Edinburgh.

SHHD (1986) *Health Building Procurement – Appraisal in Principle, Conduct of Options Appraisal*, DGM (86), SHHD.

Thomas, A.L. (1969) The allocation problem, *Studies in Accounting Research*, No. 3, AAA.

Thomas, A.L. (1974) The allocation problem: Part Two, *Studies in Accounting Research*, No. 9, AAA.

Torrance, G.W., Boyle, M.H. and Horwood, S. (1982) Application of multi-attribute utility theory to measure social preference, for health states, *Operations Research*, Nov.–Dec., **30**(6), 1043–69.

Wickings, I, Cole J., Flux, R. and Howard, L. (1983) Review of clinical budgeting and costing experiments, *British Medical Journal*, Vol. 286.

Willcocks L, and Mark, A. (1988) Information technology in the NHS: from strategy to implementation, *Public Money and Management*, **8**(3), 41–4.

Young J. (1975) Working class criminology in I. Taylor *et al.*, *Critical Criminology*, Routledge, Kegan and Paul, London.

Zeckhauser, R.J. (1974) Commentary in *Ethics of Health Care*, (ed. L.R. Tancredi), National Academy of Sciences, Washington.

Is the NHS a 'deviant' organization?: Discussant's comments

MICHAEL BOURN

IRVINE LAPSLEY'S QUESTION

Irvine Lapsley raises, but cannot yet really answer, an interesting question. It is the extent to which government-inspired recommendations and pressures, to promote accounting and managerial systems based on perceived practices of private sector organizations, 'translate effectively to the NHS or . . . merely demonstrate the distinctive nature (or, alternatively, "deviance") of the NHS'.

This calm formulation makes a pleasing contrast to the frantic furore aroused by the question of whether the changes referred to by Lapsley are part of a not very deep-laid plot by a government intent on 'back-door privatization of the NHS', or some such conception.

The paper is not always clearly written. The early presentation of 'labelling theory' shrouds the thrust of the whole piece in something of a mist, which the short discussion of the role of the Treasurer does not entirely blow away. What is being raised is the question of whether the NHS body accepts or rejects the introduction to its system of a range of managerial and accounting practices intended to promote efficiency (and no doubt effectiveness and economy). Whether their rejection is called 'deviance' or 'distinctiveness' does not really matter very much.

Evidence of the failure, or relatively slight success, of several such grafts (e.g. clinical budgeting, specialty costing, Körner minimum data sets, management budgeting and the resource management initiative) is referred to, if not fully addressed. Both technical incompetence, and cultural mismatch, are indicated in varying degrees. Not all of these ideas were government-inspired, and indeed by no means all of them post-date the 1979 General Election result in their conception. A government dedicated to rolling back the frontiers of government and reducing levels of taxation and public expenditure may nevertheless continue to seek further grafts, and Lapsley discusses two of these: new methods of capital accounting and the purchaser-provider split. The capital accounting methods are intended 'to make managers sensitive to capital costs, which, at present, may be regarded as a free good in their decisions'. The purchaser–provider split is intended to generate an internal market, which will mimic 'the private sector norm of the market place'. It is concluded that 'time will tell' if these newer grafts are accepted, since they are only newly introduced.

It is, of course, possible to engage in a good deal of activity in re-organizing structures, tasks, and processes, giving a pleasurable sense of achievement, without advancing the ultimate purpose of the organization – in this case, a healthier population. As Petronius remarked nearly 2000 years ago: 'We trained hard – but every time we were beginning to form into teams we would be re-organized. I was to learn later in life that we tend to meet any situation by re-organizing . . . and a wonderful method it can be for creating an illusion of progress while producing inefficiency and demoralization.'

There is, indeed, a respectable enough view, to be found in the literature of economics, that the whole notion of organization and management can be dispensed with, because the economic imperatives of working with scarce resources dominate them. If such an heroic assumption (as Lipsey calls it) can indeed be made, it has an immense potential to simplify the analysis of economic behaviour. On the other hand, interrogations of managers by researchers such as Steiner seem to show a keenly-felt belief that 'good management' is the key to economic success. Of course, one might remark with Mandy Rice-Davies that 'They would say that, wouldn't they!'. Lipsey's approach would render Irvine Lapsley's question redundant; Steiner's would place it in a central position.

The thrust towards simplification is clearly significant for some purposes; and effective simplifications may tell far more of a story than many much fussier and busier a tale. Yet, in the organizational context, those large-scale simplifications must ultimately accord with, and account for, the great complexity which characterizes so much of the activity patterns in the day-to-day and month-to-month life of so many organizations – especially, perhaps, those like the NHS which have fuzzy, ambiguous, and/or multiple objective functions.

The issue of complexity is a problem well-known to anyone who has tried to design an information system of any consequence. Writing ten years ago about some changes to the relatively routine accounting systems of two American hospitals, Marina Malvey called her book *Simple Systems, Complex Environments*. Her theme was that no formal system can fully replace the complex web of formal and informal negotiations by which the work of the members of an organization is actually carried out coherently and effectively. Her title is itself a masterly simplification, but one which has to be continually refined and finessed if it is to be operationalized in any particular setting. For these reasons, Irvine Lapsley's question does seem to me to be of interest. There is substance in such managerial questions.

What is the answer to his question? Do practices derived from private sector organizations translate effectively to the NHS, if competently designed and introduced? The paper does not give us much of a lead on this. However, it does suggest that, incompetence aside, there are reasons to anticipate that translation will not be effective.

One of these is the rather startling suggestion that, 'in the implementation of management control systems in the NHS, . . . "rational, logical" systems do not fit into the realities of organisational life'. Although described as 'an area worthy of further research' it is difficult to imagine which realities require that life in the NHS should be any more irrational and illogical than in any other large organization. This does, of course, beg the question of the extent to which the systems proposed for grafting on to the NHS are rational and logical, but that is part of the 'competence' issue.

Two other reasons are advanced. One is the centrality of equity as a criterion in resource allocation in the NHS, a criterion which is said to be difficult to operationalize 'in part (because) there is an absence of pricing systems to ration activities in the face of . . . increasing demand'. This does seem to imply, even to state, that the kind of private sector practice being transferred across actually supports, rather than prohibits, the achievement of equity. The underlying question is whether equity is necessarily inimical to efficiency (and effectiveness and economy), and vice-versa. The paper offers no evidence to support its implicit view that there is likely to be mutual exclusivity.

The other reason offered for anticipating that the translation to the NHS of variants of private sector practices will not be effective is the clan control exerted by clinicians over the NHS. This is a difficult issue. If it is accepted that, as seems inevitable, resource rationing is unavoidable in the NHS, then the question is how that should be done. The traditional attitude of 'clinical freedom' is that the needs of each successive individual patient should be dealt with by the individual doctor who is diagnosing or treating his/her condition. To pretend that this does not involve rationing is nothing short of fatuous. In practice, it becomes a system of first come first served, with some additional recognition of the position of actually or potentially influential patients. This may be inefficient, ineffective, uneconomic, and inequitable, especially if, for example, it leads to the closure of wards and theatres towards the end of a financial year. But rationing it most certainly is.

The issue then is whether it can be done better. The laudable intent behind schemes such as management budgeting and the resource management initiative was to focus the issue of resourcing limitations more clearly. This need not be inconsistent with clinical freedom, any more than, in a University, devolved budgeting need be inconsistent with academic freedom and control. Indeed, there is every reason to think that such freedom might be enhanced, because it can be exercised against a fuller information set. It is then difficult to see why, in principle, the clan control of clinicians should inevitably be inconsistent with the effective translation to the NHS of practices derived from private sector organizations. That such inconsistency has been evident in the past does not make change impossible, even though there is little or nothing in most medical education to indicate recognition of the issue.

This does not address the closely-related, but separable, issue of whether the NHS is underfunded. The government claims that resource inputs have gone up in real terms over a sustained period, while many in the NHS consider that funding is increasingly tight. What seems to have happened in the hospital service in the UK over the last twenty years or so, is that:

(a) the supply of hospital beds in most specialties has fallen by 20% or more;
(b) the rate of throughput of patients treated has increased by 25% or more, largely through a much reduced average length of stay in hospital;
(c) these combine to show an increase of 50% or more in the patient through-put per bed; and
(d) the number of doctors has increased by 60% and of nurses by 50%, leading to a reduction in the number of patients treated of about 20% per doctor and about 15% per nurse.

Is this efficient or inefficient? Does it demonstrate underfunding or improved funding? The answers are not clear-cut. If the reduced length of stay results often in patients returning for further treatment, or dying sooner, it is less efficient than if it does not. If the reduced length of stay imposes heavy additional burdens on relatives and friends it is less efficient than if it does not. It is also less effective and less equitable. Conversely, if it places more weight on general practitioners, with commensurate funding, it may be more efficient, more effective, and more equitable than if it does not. There is not much information available about such matters.

In summary, Lapsley's paper raises an interesting question, but is not able to answer it. The paper does not rest on ill-defined 'labelling theory', and is not much shaped by the discussion of the role of the Treasurer. The longer discussion of the financial management initiatives is neither extensive enough nor deep enough to answer the key question. The conclusion that 'the various attempts to reform (the NHS's) financial controls by government . . . serve to underline the distinctive nature of this organisation' is, perhaps, thus as yet 'Not proven'.

11
Financial control and devolved management in central government

CYRIL TOMKINS and IAN COLVILLE*

INTRODUCTION

Financial control has a variety of meanings when related to central government. To some, like Mrs Thatcher, at least initially during her time as Prime Minister, it seemed to mean making a considerable effort to reduce public expenditure as a proportion of Gross Domestic Product. Indeed, mainly through a combination of privatizations, sale of assets (e.g. council houses), reductions in contributions to nationalized industries and lower interest payments through reduction of the National Debt, her successive administrations have reduced public spending (before deducting receipts from privatizations) from about 43% of GDP in 1979 to about 39% in 1990 with every prospect of the percentage remaining at about that level for a while. Moreover, the said percentage never fell below the one inherited (43%) until late 1986 and went as high as 47% in the interim. One may debate the extent to which the prime objective was achieved and whether it was likely to have been achieved without a much more rigorous consideration of spending options, but constraining or reducing public expenditure, as a percentage of GDP, has been an

* The authors are grateful to HM Customs and Excise for permission to describe aspects of their research in that Department in the latter part of this paper.

Perspectives on Financial Control: Essays in memory of Kenneth Hilton.
Edited by Mahmoud Ezzamel and David Heathfield.
Published in 1992 by Chapman & Hall, London. ISBN 0 412 40980 1.

often declared interpretation of financial control during the last eleven years. A widespread interpretation which, it will be shown later in this paper, also created problems in achieving success with alternative interpretations of the term.

A quite different interpretation of the term central government financial control seems to emanate from HM Treasury. There it will be second nature to interpret the term as the maintenance of control over expenditure in order to serve macro-economic policy. Traditionally, this viewpoint tended to over-ride considerations of benefits which might accrue from a more decentralized form of operation, although changes of emphasis have been seen in recent years as will be described later in this paper. Traditionally too, financial control was seen as ensuring that expenditure was on the purposes for which it was approved with minimum virement allowed. Control was exercised through the process of expenditure votes.

Yet another view of financial control has strong political connotations. Successive restrictions placed upon local government spending by the Conservative Government have been motivated largely by the perceived need to rein back spending by left wing councils who were often seen as incurring expenditure on frivolous concerns. If all electors were compelled to pay a local standard community charge to contribute to this expenditure, it was thought that they would be concerned at the levels that they had to pay and force local politicians to operate with more responsibility. The electors certainly became more concerned, but the impact of the new charge was often quite severe upon electors in both Labour and Conservative Councils and the electors turned their wrath upon the Conservative Government for introducing the change, irrespective of its motives.

All these interpretations are different from that which would naturally be assumed in the private sector. A private sector financial controller is seen much more as reporting upon and providing support for improving 'the bottom line', i.e. the net profit figure. While even in the private sector excessive focus on short-term profits can be harmful, financial control is seen there to be part of the process by which the enterprise survives and grows as a prosperous entity. Financial controllers certainly still monitor expenditure and deviations from plans, but they also have a more pro-active role to play in supporting their local general managers to evaluate different options as the basis for making decisions to improve profitability. Also this is a continuous process. Virement is practised widely (although the term is rarely used in private sector financial language) as resources are shuffled to meet unexpected events and beat the competition. Financial controllers in most large corporate groups have merely a 'dotted line' responsibility to the Group Controller for the operation of standard accounting procedures, but primarily serve their local general managers.

Our reference above to the Conservative administrations from 1979 to 1990 was critical on the assumption that the intention was really to cut public expenditure as a percentage of GDP, rather than use it merely as a political slogan. Over an eleven-year period one might have expected a government really determined to cut public expenditure to have achieved a level of spending below that inherited in more than four years out of the eleven and done better than achieve an average annual reduction over the whole period of only about 0.4%. This is not meant to imply that the authors think that this would have been desirable; this is not a party political statement.[1] But it does seem a pretty poor managerial performance if the objective was to be taken seriously and literally. In marked contrast, Mrs Thatcher has had a significant effect on the move towards introducing a notion of financial control into the Civil Service which is akin to private sector practices and that may yet prove to be one of her most important achievements. In the long run, this may well be seen as more important and less easily reversible than even a substantial cut in the proportion of GDP devoted to public expenditure would have been. If a lasting change of this nature is achieved, it amounts to a substantial shift in long-standing cultural norms of the Civil Service and it is this notion of financial control that this paper will address. It will be seen, however, that with no clear 'bottom line' in the public sector, financial control is very much enmeshed into the total management control process. In fact this paper will argue that the most important matter for senior government officials to grasp at the current time, in moving to better financial and managerial control, is a better understanding of the complex processes involved in managing large scale change. New technical systems may be needed to support decision making, new organization structures may need to be designed and organizational rules re-written, but the really difficult task is to manage changes in attitudes and behaviour of both staff and clients of the system.

EARLIER EXAMPLES OF MISMANAGEMENT IN IMPROVING PUBLIC SECTOR CONTROL

Over the last twenty-five years or so, there has been much debate about how to get better managerial control over public expenditure and there have been one or two significant attempts to introduce new systems to achieve that. From the mid-1960s, developments began in the USA which tried to introduce a more rational planning and control process into central government affairs. There was a thrust to:

(a) set clear objectives;
(b) improve the evaluation of delivering value for money; and

257

(c) measure and monitor what was happening.

This resulted in two main developments in the USA:

(a) PPBS (Planning-Programming-Budgeting-Systems; and
(b) zero-based budgets.

PPBS (Planning-Programming-Budgeting-Systems)

This was to be President Johnson's bequest to public sector management: the application of the type of rational planning procedures perceived at that time to be in vogue in large private sector corporations. The approach was conceptually simple: set objectives clearly, break them down into subsidiary goals, develop plans to achieve those goals cutting right across government department lines if necessary, allocate resources to facilitate achievement of the goals through a priority orientated budgeting process and the provision of adequate systems to support the work. There was little wrong with the proposal as a piece of deductive logic; all purposive action must have elements of such a logic underlying it or it is likely to lose direction and impetus. The defect was in the structure into which these elements were placed. The whole architecture of PPBS implied a top-down perspective of total rational planning which was quite simply impractical. Many countries also followed the USA lead, but virtually all of these initiatives failed (Wildavsky, 1975; Tomkins and Colville, 1980). They failed because the 'comprehensive', top-down, 'scientific' model ignored the following:

1. *Cognitive realities* – the sheer scale involved in creating an ordered set of social goals.
2. *Organizational realities* – the government departments were not structured according to programmes adopted hence departmental rivalries tended to inhibit the establishment of well co-ordinated action across departmental lines. Also the realities of organizational communication and influence were ignored.
3. *Political realities* – the need for detailed budget line accountability by elected representatives and the inconsistency of the political negotiating process with comprehensive rational planning.

Anthony *et al.* (1989) say that the term PPBS is no longer used in Washington, but its essential concepts continue. Certainly PPBS made the public sector more aware of the need to consider objectives and long term planning and the need for better co-ordination across different departments, but it would be a mistake, in our view, to imply that the full notion of PPBS was adopted in all but name. The essence of PPBS was a total, rational planning system. Unless one radically changes the structure of democratic government, an attempt at a full implementation of PPBS ignores the political realities and organizational realities listed above and, therefore, simply cannot work, unless, perhaps, the country or government unit to which it is applied is very small. Hence, a move to take a longer run, more strategic view and develop some major social programmes is not really the same as implementing a complete PPB system. Moreover, even in a tightly centrally planned economy, the cognitive difficulties encountered are likely to be insurmountable. While one might argue that such deficiencies can be 'papered over', perhaps for a long time, recent experience has shown that such dirigiste regimes eventually fail.

Zero-based budgets

With the demise of PPBS, President Carter, on becoming President of the USA, declared that his own State of Georgia had developed the secret of good public sector management: zero-based budgeting. He was going to apply it at Federal level. The essence of this approach was to start right at the bottom of the organization and divide all activities into 'decision packages'. These packages were to be costed and ranked in order of priority and passed up to the next level of management. That level of management cannot possibly review all packages and so it was expected to accept those specified as most important from each organizational unit and rank, across such units, the lower choices of each unit. Then the combined list for several units was passed up to the next level of management. This continued through all levels of management to the top of the organization.

ZBB clearly offered advantages in being 'bottom-up' and commencing from what is and yet avoiding the process of annual incremental budgeting. The idea was to challenge what was in budgets and had been there for some time and not simply to evaluate requests for increases. Also the process involved more staff, at many different levels, in resource allocation procedures. Nevertheless, as a systematic approach, ZBB also failed. There was doubt about the necessity for such extensive analysis; at least in every year and across all activities. There was criticism that most managers did something like this anyway on an informal basis. Possibilities for game playing were pointed out as organization units could put low priorities at the top of their list and high priorities at the bottom knowing that when examined senior management must include them in the total budget. There was also often difficulty in constructing discrete packages. In general, once more, the system attempted to be too rational and too comprehensive. It ignored political and organizational realities, just as PPBS did and suffered the same fate. This does not mean that the attempt to apply ZBB achieved nothing. Like the attempt to introduce PPBS, it focused attention on deficiencies in traditional methods. Also many organizations now take parts of their budgets in different years and analyse them down to zero or near zero base in order to identify expenditure on items or activities no longer required. But, again, this is not the same as adopting the comprehensive system.

The fate of PPBS and ZBB are now well known and debates about them rather old, but they are introduced here because they demonstrate very clearly the dangers of trying to shift well-established practices on the basis of centralized deductive logic alone. Especially when that logic is based on very general arguments divorced from specific contexts.

This view supports Greenwood (1984) who, in discussing the failure of PPBS and ZBB to displace the logic of incrementalism, concludes that there are three antecedent conditions for bringing about change:

(1) an *opportunity*, created by an external crisis which impairs organizational performance;
(2) *authoritative* commitment; and
(3) an alternative *ideology*.

He places great stress on antecedent (3) arguing that public servants have a strong sense of what they are and how they operate (see also Tomkins, 1991 for a discussion of both individual and organizational schemas) and that proposals for change which contradict those values are likely to be ineffective unless antecedents (1) and (2) are present and a strong alternative ideology is offered. Only by having the three antecedents in combination, Greenwood argues, will there be both necessary and sufficient conditions for real change. At a broad level we have no wish to quarrel with Greenwood or others who have written similarly within the organizational theory literature, but it must be recognized that these are only 'Level One antecedents'. They may be sufficient basic concepts, but knowledge of them is in no way sufficient actually to bring about change, in practice, in a large organization: the world of organizations is more complex as is quite apparent in Greenwood's more recent work (Hinings and Greenwood, 1988).

Tomkins (1991) argues that it is very important to recognize the ongoing nature of trying to bring about fundamental change. Would-be change managers must keep in touch with organization actors' perceptions and actions throughout the change process. There will be a stream of actions required which, though informed by the basic tenets of the new ideology to be implanted, will themselves lead to reinterpretations and negotiations which come to constitute the new ideology itself. This is inevitable in a large organization where different forms of power over operations, processes and decisions reside at different levels and locations in the organization and as different sets of actors come to realize more fully what proposed changes actually mean for them. These implications are not all easily forecastable. Also, such forms of power do not necessarily find expression in open conflicts, but simply the adoption of the way things will be done. This, coupled with limited cognitive capacity of top managers, often ensures continuity according to an established

260

ideology as Greenwood suggests, but may also lead to a variety of responses, both positive and negative, to attempts to bring about change.

This is the very stuff of political, organizational and cognitive reality in large organizations. In addition, while it may be usual for significant change, particularly in the private sector, to be preceded by a crisis, that is not an inevitable antecedent. Indeed, in the organization to be discussed later in this paper (HM Customs and Excise), there is no sense of crisis over performance and yet significant change is being attempted. Of course, that makes it much more difficult to achieve, but not necessarily impossible if the majority of organizational participants can be persuaded that they will be better off after the change. The Japanese notion of continual improvement and learning can also be cited in support of this argument. Indeed, an externally generated crisis could provide the conditions for establishing a new ideology which accepts change in future without the need for a crisis to initiate it. The basic motivation for change then becomes the prevention of crisis. Such an organization would not take the way things are done for granted and always be contemplating change, while, at the same time, getting on and doing the main thrust of the business according to tried and trusted methods until some new form of experience or knowledge shows specific change to be desirable. In other words, achieving real change involves a lot more than just recognizing 'Level One antecedents'. The central problem is how to manage the process of creating a new ideology and helping it to develop. Nevertheless, a lack of apparent serious intent to address these basic antecedents did make it difficult for PPBS and ZBB to be used to replace incrementalism as Greenwood says.

The failure of these 'rational systems' to replace incrementalism should not, however, have been taken as a signal to give up the search for improvement on the assumption that traditional approaches could not be bettered. While PPBS and ZBB seemed to ask too much in terms of changing institutional realities, it should not be assumed that no institutional realities could be changed at all. In Greenwood's terms, it would still seem to be possible to find a new ideology which introduced more 'rationality' into traditional methods, but a way had to be found which blended that with pragmatism. With these thoughts in mind, attention will be shifted to the UK at the time that Mrs Thatcher became Prime Minister.

DEVELOPMENTS IN FINANCIAL AND MANAGERIAL CONTROL IN THE UK CENTRAL GOVERNMENT SINCE 1979

The Financial Management Initiative

The UK government, either Labour or Conservative, never adopted PPBS or ZBB. Nevertheless through the 1970s, it became increasingly necessary to exercise tighter control over public expenditure. This was emphasized particularly by the oil crisis of 1974 which gave rise to thinking about allocating government budgets on the basis of cash sums rather than the convention of issuing them in real terms and allowing departments to expect supplementation to their budgets to cover any subsequent inflation. With inflation around 25%, automatic supplementation became infeasible and departments were expected to arrange their affairs such that they could keep within the total cash sum.

The Conservatives then came to power in 1979, led by Mrs Thatcher. As explained earlier, they saw themselves as having a mandate to develop a more market driven economy and remove considerable elements of public expenditure to the private sector. Once again, irrespective of personal views, much was achieved by that process and is still continuing. It is also probable that any Labour Government in the foreseeable future would not dismantle the 'privatizations' which have taken place, perhaps with just one or two exceptions. The focus of this article is, however, on the management of the activities left within the public sector and under Civil Service control.

Mrs Thatcher's first step was to take advice from Lord Rayner and what became known as the Rayner Scrutinies were introduced. He, wisely after earlier experiences in the USA with the more comprehensive systems, wanted to avoid the use of bureaucratic processes to improve bureaucracy. Bright persons were to be identified in each government department and given a period of about three months to study some feature of that department and make a proposal for improving efficiency. These scrutinies were given the personal backing of the Prime Minister and proved quite successful. They did not, however, lead to large proportionate cuts in public expenditure – they were not the correct vehicle for doing so. It then became clear, that something more comprehensive and systematic was going to be needed to make a significant impact. The danger was, of course, that this would lead back to the errors of PPBS and ZBB. In fact these errors were avoided.

The solution to this dilemma was offered in the Financial Management Initiative, announced by Mrs Thatcher in 1982. The FMI had some broad similarities with PPBS in so far as it called for government departments to clarify their objectives and measure performance, but the essential idea was quite different from PPBS. Under the FMI, responsibility was to be delegated to the level most able to influence the quality of service and control costs. That was to be the level at which budget responsibility was to reside and that meant giving budget responsibility somewhat lower down than had been given before. Devolved management and budgeting were now to be the secret to success. Control was to be maintained through a system of output measures. Budgets were to be based more upon outputs delivered and not control over inputs.

By 1987, five years after the launch of FMI, what had been achieved? The situation was summed up by Richards (1987) when she said that the FMI had failed to bring about widespread change. She blamed top civil servants for the lack of ability at managing change and argued that the government's basic idea to cut the size of the public sector was more of a motivating force behind the FMI than improving effectiveness. It was not, therefore, very surprising, in her view, if the FMI had not galvanized enthusiasm for change among departments. There is, however, reason to examine this view more closely. Mrs Thatcher certainly exhibited a determination to cut back the size of the public sector on coming to power in 1979 and, no doubt, still had that desire right up to 1990, but the figures quoted at the beginning of this paper seem to indicate that, perhaps through the need for political pragmatism rather than adoption of new principles, this had ceased to be the immediate and overriding concern by 1987. The emphasis seemed to have changed to one of privatization in order to move activities into the market place coupled with a search for increased efficiency, rather than just cutting expenditure, with regard to activities which were to remain in the public sector. Of course, what determined attitudes to FMI was the perceived underlying motivation of the government rather than one inferred from latest statistics on expenditure levels and, given the force with which the initial ideology of reduced public spending was set in 1979, perhaps that tended to dominate thinking in government departments. The FMI was not couched in terms of cutting back the Civil Service, but if it was interpreted as a vehicle for so doing then that would have influenced behaviour and Richards' argument has validity. At least, if the initial stance on the level of public spending was being modified, either it had not been effectively communicated to the mass of civil servants, or, if it had been communicated, it had not been widely believed. Nevertheless, whatever the reason, it does seem clear that Richards was correct in saying that little fundamental change had occured.

The House of Commons Public Accounts Committee Report (1987) supported this view:

Scepticism and mistrust of the FMI seem to be widespread amongst middle and lower management grades. This is all the more worrying given that the Initiative is concerned with a fundamental cultural change in ways that managers discharge departments' business.

Also, Collins (1987) said:

Very few of internal or external observers of FMI would say that the FMI has yet brought about the real management revolution signalled when it was heralded in 1982.

A picture was therefore building up, once again, that efforts to bring about significant change in the way government expenditure was managed and controlled were failing – albeit on the eastern side of the Atlantic this time. Once again, too, fundamental organizational and cultural factors were being identified as the reason for this failure. Essentially doubts were being raised as to whether the cultural values of central government operations, established over many centuries, could be changed. Values which reflected the avoidance of risk, 'keeping to the rules' and a governing set of 'fast streamers' who focused on policy rather than management. There seemed to be no explicit place for management in such a process. Indeed, the very term 'management' seemed to be considered beneath the concerns of many at the top reaches of the Civil Service.

Referring to Greenwood (1984) again, the authority (antecedent 2) was there at the very top in the form of prime ministerial directive, but it did not appear that the commitment had been spread down through the government departments. Also a sense of crisis did exist about the level of public expenditure and, indeed, the future status of many public sector bodies, but this did not seem to be a crisis which organizational participants thought could be dealt with by becoming more efficient. It would seem that it is not just the existence of a crisis, but the interpretation of its nature which is critical in determining behaviour. Also, in this case, a clear alternative ideology of decentralized operation was being offered in the form of the FMI, but that does not mean that it had to be accepted passively. Greenwood's antecedents suggest the importance of power in stating the need for authoritative commitment, but this tends to reduce the complexity of organizational power to a possession of power at the top of the organization with only a one-way downward exercise of it. The experience of FMI suggests this is a gross simplification. Moreover, the experience shows that the exercise of organizational power against the proposed change does not have to be in the form of open and direct opposition. Lack of enthusiasm, coupled with some cynicism and a tendency of many simply to carry on as before appear to be effective resistors. The achievement of change through the exercise of top level power alone is severely circumscribed by the ability to get right down into the organization to make life uncomfortable for those who simply carry on as before. Given that limitation, the approach which relies on top level power to specify the alternative ideology may not be the best way to achieve change.

The Next Steps Initiative

Partly because of the growing criticism of the lack of progress under the FMI and, no doubt, also because of the advance in thinking about how to develop better financial control over central government expenditure, a major new initiative was launched called *The Next Steps.* This was based on a report from the Prime Minister's Efficiency Unit led at that time by Sir Robin Ibbs who felt that the Civil Service still had not established a system for continuing improvement in performance. This initiative is still very much alive and still developing. While the FMI tried to be more business-like in moving towards a model of control more like that used in the private sector, The Next Steps went somewhat further in principle and, in effect, took the model of a divisionalized company as its template. The main proposal was that the government departments should, where possible, remain responsible for policy, setting targets and performance standards and monitoring results, but the provision of services was to be delegated to *agencies* led by a chief executive who would have the clear responsibility to manage. Agency chief executives would write contracts with their parent ministries. Ministers would cease to be responsible for detailed operational matters (as distinct from policy) although it has yet to become completely clear how this will work. Until recently the Conservative Government has been very conservative over the size of The Next Steps to be taken. Initially, the Treasury expressed much anxiety about the loss of possible control over the aggregate level of expenditure. A full implementation of The Next Steps would imply a cash budget and set of targets would be given to each chief executive who would then manage the activity as he or she saw fit; switching funds between headings, paying non- standard salaries and rewards, etc. All that would matter would be the delivery of the required results within the agreed budget, subject to observance of the law and basic principles of justice. In fact, this is not just a divisionalized company model, but more like a specific type of corporate model – that of a widely diversified conglomerate, such as Hanson or GEC, where the Head Office keeps very much at arms length from the divisions provided that the required returns on capital are delivered. With the prospect of such agency independence, the Treasury, so it is believed, fought long and hard to retain central control.

In view of this, the government initially, and probably wisely, chose relatively easy parts of the central government to convert into agencies. The programme is, however, gaining momentum and a wider set of agencies has been announced recently. Kemp (1990), the Project Manager for The Next Steps, says that he had been set the target of applying Next Steps principles to half of the Civil Service by the end of 1991 and he expects that his earlier estimate of the need for ten years to reach 75% coverage can probably be bettered. Also, Sir Robin Butler, Head of the Home Civil Service, used the 1990 RIPA Redcliffe-Maud Memorial Lecture to emphasize that the work being put into The Next Steps Initiative was to serve all future governments and not just Conservative ones. There is, therefore, a growing sense of acceptance of the direction of change in central government. Sir Robin also expressed, nevertheless, some factors which might yet cause the initiative to founder. Among these he included (a) an excessive focus upon the measurement of performance without achieving real change, (b) applying a standard model of operation to all departments with little regard for the nature of the activity and what arrangements best suited it and (c) a failure of agencies to exercise responsible financial discipline which would legitimize a re-imposition of direct control by the Treasury. Also a senior member of a major government department said recently in an address to civil servants that, while progress was being made, 30% of his senior staff still remained to be convinced that The Next Steps Initiative was anything more than a temporary phase. Meanwhile, the Prime Minister's Efficiency Unit has launched an enquiry into the impact that executive agencies will have on the structure of government, its aim being to indicate how central departments can avoid 'double guessing' their agencies and setting up competing support systems. Also, in view of Members of Parliament raising concerns about the new practice of referring parliamentary questions to agency chief executives whose replies to Members do not appear in the public domain, the government has stated that these replies will be placed in the House of Commons Library and public information office. The Next Steps Initiative really does seem to be gaining momentum.

At the time of writing, the government has just issued its reply to the Treasury and Civil Service Committee Eighth Report: *Progress in the Next Steps Initiative* (1990). In that response the government strongly asserts its intention to take the Initiative further and lists sixty-two governmental activities as either already possessing Agency status or under active consideration for it. In addition, the two major revenue departments, HM Customs and Excise and HM Inland Revenue, are earmarked for 'moving towards operating fully on Next Steps lines'. Moreover, the government stresses 'there is no question of going for merely superficial change . . . the preparation should not be rushed' and:

> while agencies need to be set up on a sound basis, they continue to develop once established . . . indeed modification and development in the light of experience is an essential part of the Next Steps concept.

Furthermore:

> The Government agrees that the Next Steps has a role as a catalyst in releasing energy, enthusiasm and commitment of civil servants. Staff are most likely to give of their best when they are enabled to do so rather than when they are told to do so. The objective is to move away from 'management by command' to 'management by contract' and to greater delegation.

> *Progress in the Next Steps Initiative*, 1990, p. 15

The government also recognizes that there must be arrangements to provide a continuing pressure for improvement and to ensure that the changes are consolidated and durable. At the end of 1990 the government, therefore, seems to recognize the need for careful preparation for change on a continuing basis and that genuine and widespread staff commitment, not just top level authoritative commitment, is vital if success is to be achieved–merely changing the organization structure and responsibilities, though necessary, will not be sufficient to bring about lasting change. On the other hand, the Next Steps Initiative can also be seen as an exercise of top level power to create an organizational shift aimed to overcome some of the resistances felt to have inhibited the FMI. The creation of separate accountable units was clearly seen as a mechanism for putting pressure on those reluctant to change. The need to manage the process of organizational change and integrate the viewpoints of different groups of organizational participants seems to be increasingly recognized, but there is still a recognition that a strong political will is needed to see the change through and that some aspects of power to resist may be neutralized by changes in organizational structure. In that sense the stick has not been replaced by the carrot. There is a new form of stick in the form of the creation of an internal market between the provider and acquirer of services which may be used from time to time to create a crisis for a inefficient organization, but it is now coupled with the carrot that there may actually be advantages for staff in subjecting themselves to that stick.

THE EXPERIENCE OF ONE DEPARTMENT: HM CUSTOMS AND EXCISE

All the statements made so far in this paper about changes taking place in central government have related to information in the public domain. Now attention will be turned to the developments which have been taking place in one of the two main revenue collection departments, namely HM Customs and Excise.

The authors are now in their fourth year undertaking research as a support activity to that Department's efforts to bring about changes in management control and culture. As developments in that Department are discussed below, they need to be considered against the general pressures for change in central government already described. It will then be seen that the Department was developing a grasp of some of the key issues associated with change somewhat before they began to appear in the recent published government statements referred to above. The following description of the story in one department will also help to identify more precisely the sort of path these changes will take and the key factors which will determine whether the change is successfully managed.

267

Before beginning the description of our work in Customs and Excise, two points need to be considered by readers. First, our work has been used as a direct input to decision making in the Department. We are, therefore, directly participating in the changes and having some influence upon them. As a consequence of this, it has been put to us by some academics in response to a previous paper, that our analysis cannot be an objective academic statement. Our response to this can be both philosophical and practical (and we will resist the strong inclination to be dismissive). It is debatable whether any form of organizational enquiry can be completely objective. Apart from subjectivity of interpretation, there is always some obligation for trust and confidentiality in order to gain access. So, philosophically we are just a little further along a continuum. There is no absolute dividing line with us on one side and the rest of academia on the other. Certainly, we are closely involved with HM Customs and Excise; more closely than the researcher conducting interviews would be. However, our value to that Department is based upon our independent analysis and interpretation of a wide series of views given to us and we have our own personal academic values and futures to consider which we would not be prepared to prejudice. Of course, the reader can only take this on trust, but we would point out that we are not the originators of action-research!

The editors also responded to our first draft by asking whether we could not substantiate some of the claims that we make in the paper by providing quotations of views made to us. We managed to persuade them that, in this instance, this was not really appropriate. Over four years of considerable involvement with the Department, we certainly have a very large number of taped conversations and notes of many other meetings and discussions. We also have a considerable array of Departmental reports and written comments. To select just, say, half a dozen quotations in a paper of this size might illustrate a point, but in no sense could such a few comments be taken as representative of the huge amount of material we have. However, our comments in the rest of the paper represent our summaries of the wide discussions we have had. They are extracts from a number of feedbacks we have provided to the Department which has taken them seriously as a basis for debating the management of change. Moreover, a range of other enquiries, by both external consultants and internal reviews, have exhibited similarities in response. We also have regular and frequent contact with many people in the Department and so have developed a strong feel for the balance of views. So, we admit that these are our summaries of data not available to the reader. All we can say is that we are confident that the general thrust of what we are saying has been accepted in the Department in which these views have been widely debated.

In general, in response to both these possible concerns, we would also point out that hardly any academics have been given the almost total freedom that we have been given to move around a major government department asking questions coupled with an agreement to let us publish our findings subject to prior clearance of a reasonable nature by the Department. We have not found this at all constraining to date and the Department is aware that we intend to produce at least one book, but probably more than one, to give a much fuller picture. It is quite unrealistic to expect such help without giving something in return and, in any case, one might argue that one test of an academic's contribution to knowledge in such an area is whether he or she can offer insights to practitioners. However, we simply believe that the so-called loss of independence, which we consider marginal, is far outweighed by the deeper insights that we have been able to obtain which are just summarized in this paper. We are confirmed in our view that one only starts to appreciate the complexity of bringing about a change in culture and norms of a major civil service department by actually being a part of it. This obviously does not apply to all areas of management research, but we think it applies to this one. We are, therefore, prepared to argue that this is a better way to research such issues and not some second-best to 'pure research' which has difficulty in penetrating the veil.

HM Customs and Excise, 1987: was the FMI working?

The authors became involved with the Customs and Excise following an address at the CIPFA Public Sector Management Awards, 1987. The first named author then raised exactly the same notions as were raised at the beginning of this paper; namely, that if the government had really wanted to cut public expenditure as a proportion of GDP, it was not succeeding in doing so and, consequently, the question arose as to whether the appropriate approach was being adopted. An invitation followed to come for preliminary discussions at the Customs and Excise Department, not to discuss how to cut total expenditure, but how to assess the current state of the FMI Initiative in that Department. Extensive training efforts had been made and new operating systems were being developed to facilitate more delegation in accordance with the declared FMI philosophy, but there was reason for various persons occupying very senior positions in that Department to require an independent assessment of the position and particularly of the views of staff in the Outfield. HM Customs and Excise has about 26 000 staff of which about 5000 are located in either Headquarters functions or policy divisions. The remainder are employed in twenty-one Collections, each covering a different region of the country. The collective name for these Collections is The Outfield. The Director of the Organization Directorate and the Director of The Outfield jointly asked the authors if they would be interested in conducting research to ascertain Outfield views on the actions taken to date and concerns about future

269

moves. Incidentally, the Department currently collects about £50 billion revenue each year (equivalent to just less than half of total government expenditure) and comprises three separate functions: Value Added Tax, Customs activities and Excise. The Customs activities include protection against drug and other forms of smuggling. The Excise responsibilities include levying duties and taxes on betting and gaming, hydrocarbon oils, wines and spirits, etc.

During 1987–8, the authors' first task was to interview a wide set of people in three Collections. Interviews were held at all levels from Collector down to executive officer grade. In the Spring of 1988, the authors reported back informally that there was a need to take further steps if the attempt to implement the FMI philosophy was to be successful. This feedback was given just at the time that more general comments, quoted above, were being published about the lack of real change yet under the FMI. The findings in Customs and Excise were quite consistent with those comments. There was, however, a major difference in emphasis between the interpretation placed upon this situation in Customs and Excise in comparison with the general implications underlying most of the more generally published statements. In the authors' view, other critics of progress under the FMI had significantly underestimated the complexity and extent of the challenge of the task of changing the methods and culture of the Civil Service, many aspects of which had been developed over 100 years or more (the Customs and Excise Department has a history which can be traced back to Aethelbald, King of Mercia in AD 743 – see Smith, 1980). These critics expressed views about the inability of civil servants to manage change, but, perhaps through not having adequately studied processes of change themselves, and this includes the PAC, they did not adequately take into account how long the change process would take. The FMI had commenced in 1982 and it might be thought that significant change in work practices should have been achieved after five years. Indeed, if change is going to take so long, there is always the chance that other events will occur which lead to the effort being diverted. In this case, however, the view was taken that five years was not an unreasonable time to take to lay the foundations of such a radical change.

The need for a considerable time to bring about such a change was evident from very early on in the research within Customs and Excise. Extensive new operating systems were needed to facilitate a move to a more delegated form of managing the Department. These new systems needed to be computerized and by 1987, five years after the first announcement of the FMI, were only just coming on stream – and then on an experimental basis. Critics of the pace of change did not seem to appreciate the lead time needed for such developments in very large Civil Service departments. The new systems also called for more paperwork by middle managers and this was certainly leading to many complaints. Given the suspicions about the fundamental motivation for the change and the political declarations to cut the size of the civil service, these moves were often seen as steps to make everyone work harder and increase, rather than decrease, central control. Many did not see the new systems as a means of delegation, but as more control information for Head Office to enable it to exert tighter pressure on staff. Such declarations as there were about decentralization were thought by some to be mere rhetoric, yet it was difficult to see how this stage could have been completely avoided. The Department was traditionally governed by very detailed rules and procedures. There was a strong culture of working 'according to the book'. Computerized systems told each local VAT office which traders to visit and how much time to spend on each one. Detailed rules for checking freight at ports determined the allocation of time spent at Customs locations. Moreover, these rules were based on extensive statistical analysis and had proved their value in improving the performance of the Department in detecting underdeclarations of tax and attempts at smuggling. The idea of gaining more local autonomy appealed to many staff, many of whom thought that a blend of local knowledge with centralized guidance based on statistical evidence (rather than mandates about procedures) would lead to even better performance, but many could also not see it as really going to happen. It seemed too radical a change to be believable. As a consequence there was no widespread, positive commitment 'to make it all happen'. Many were waiting to see what would happen when, to galvanize significant change, a positive stance would be required from those same people.

HM Customs and Excise: trying to develop commitment in the Outfield

After discussion of the authors' views on reactions to the FMI in the Outfield, the Board decided to do three things. First, a series of experiments in autonomous operation was to be launched as soon as possible in two major Collections. Each Collection was invited to put forward a number of experiments for ways of operating free from adherence to Head Office rules and regulations, subject, of course, to basic requirements such as observing the law. There were several objectives behind the launch of these experiments. They were to be a clear signal to the Outfield that the Board was serious about delegation. They were also to be a chance for Outfield staff to demonstrate that they really could be trusted and capable of operating their systems responsibly and just as effectively without close central control – this was particularly required to give comfort to some in Headquarters with more aggregate responsibility for performance of the individual functions and the Outfield as a whole. The need for such comfort was not unreasonable given the very large sums of money at stake and the growing social and political significance over the control of drugs. Mrs Thatcher might be urging more delegated forms of operation and accountability, but she would probably not have been so pleased if that had led to difficulties in balancing the public sector budget.

In addition, the experiments were to be proposed 'bottom-up' so that specific, real proposals had to be considered by relevant Head Office functions affected. There was to be a presumption that delegated responsibility would be allowed unless specific objections could be raised by Head Office to the particular initiatives suggested. Hence, extensive, action-delaying debates about the dangers of delegation in general were to be avoided.

The second step taken by the Board was to issue a set of messages specifying key aspects about how it saw the Department being managed in future. This served to enhance communication to the Outfield that the Board, as a corporate body, meant what it was saying. The Chairman played an assertive and important part in this process. In accordance with Greenwood, this was an important but, as will be seen, only one small part of gaining widespread organizational commitment.

Finally, a new grouping was established whereby a few Collectors would meet regularly with key Board members to exchange views about impending changes, the management of the Department and likely responses from the Outfield. The authors were invited to join this group and are still part of it.

Following these three actions taken by the Board, the authors were asked to work for another year with the Department and during 1988–9 their work involved keeping in close contact with the experimental groups to discuss with them the nature of their proposals and how to monitor and evaluate them. Clearly, therefore, well before the recent general declarations by the government about the need to understand the process of managing change. The Department was becoming aware of the need to build up change from the bottom as well as applying top down pressure, to attempt to create belief in the ability to operate freely after decades of detailed central control and instruction and to develop enthusiasm for the changes envisaged. This interaction between the Department and the authors in thinking about gaining momentum for change led, in fact, to the latter submitting a paper to the Treasury and House of Commons Select Committee (1989) pointing out that the discussion of The Next Steps had not adequately recognized the need to focus on the *process* of bringing about change within Departments nor the necessity of embarking upon change as a learning process over a number of years, altering emphasis as lessons were observed in the continual search for improvement. If local responsibility and accountability were to be the means of improved effectiveness under The Next Steps, there was not much fundamental difference from the factors supposedly underlying success in the FMI. Under Next Steps there was to be a more clear distinction between service procurers (the government departments) and the service deliverers (the agencies), but merely constructing contracts between these separate entities would not amount to much more than changing labels. Agencies might well contract to deliver services, but the underlying objective was surely to change the culture of the Civil Service such that continual improvement would be sought through local initiative. The fundamental requirement for success was therefore to change attitudes and work behaviour of Civil Servants. Without that, contracting would contribute little that was new. The real problem was not to identify the new ideology, but how to get it established and internalized into the daily thinking within all levels of the organization.

HM Customs and Excise: the Headquarters perspective

While the 'Bath experiments', as they came to be called, were being developed, they were being monitored by a research officer. Meanwhile the two authors were asked to research Headquarters' views on the experimentation and decentralization in general. It needs to be remembered that Headquarters consists of three sets of functional activities (VAT, Customs and Excise) as well the policy arm of the Department. Consequently, a movement towards more delegated forms of operation could have had a considerable impact upon the power and responsibilities of some areas of Head Office. Also the authors took steps to keep in touch with the development of views in the Outfield, although on a more selective basis.

The process of monitoring the experiments and assessing Head Office views led to a report to the Department in the Summer, 1990, although emerging findings had been fed back to Board and other members during the year via the meetings of the new grouping of Collectors and Head Office personnel described earlier. In general it appeared as though there was not much opposition at HQ to the principle of a more devolved form of operation *per se* – in the words of some: 'If the Board says it is for delegation, I am for delegation'. But there was a repetition in Headquarters of many of the doubts and concerns expressed in the Outfield (and still being expressed in 1990). The Outfield often saw the relationship between itself and the Head Office as one of 'Them and Us', but there was a common, well-implanted notion of the long-standing culture of the Department and many common attitudes about changing it. It was as though it was easy to agree to more delegation in the abstract, but what really counted was what did it actually mean for each person in his specific task.

These concerns may, nevertheless, be summarized as follows. The taxation and Customs regimes are built on the notion of equity, that is people in similar positions should be treated similarly. How was that to be ensured if different local practices were to be allowed and how was equity to be interpreted with regard to the task with which the respondent at hand was concerned? If delegation meant taking local decisions on resource allocation how was risk management to be interpreted in different functions and settings? Who would bear the consequences if risks taken in managing resources led to significant errors or politically sensitive events? Exactly what did delegation mean? What responsibilities were to be delegated and which retained? How was performance to be measured? There was scepticism about measures developed to date if they were to be used to appraise individual performance. What transitional arrangements were to be made and what support offered to help staff cope with a radically different way of operating? Did the skills for greater independence exist in the Outfield? How could one be sure that the statistical experience acquired over many years was still used to guide decision making in an effective way? These were just illustrative of many of the issues raised. The clear implication was that it was easy to set an ideology at 'Level One', but until one had examined all the detailed ambiguities in interpreting its practical application, the ideology itself was of very limited meaning to people throughout the Department.

As regards the 'Bath experiments' themselves, nearly all of them proved to be successes from a technical perspective. Indeed, one in Customs relating to air passenger searches, led to immediate testing elsewhere and then adoption nationally in airports and seaports with the prospect of significant savings in costs. Also this particular experiment was, initially, strongly resisted by Head Office which admitted afterwards, openly and honestly, that it only agreed to the experiment because the Board intervened and 'ordered' it to do so. The very success of this experiment, however, suggests a paradox. If a local experiment offers national gains, is it against the spirit of the delegated form of operation to impose this new practice on all Collections? Clearly it is. Presumably, if the case is strong enough and well publicized, each Collection will choose to adopt the improvement, but there is still the problem of what to do about it if some Collections do not change and cannot do equally well by alternative means. There may well be an answer to this through the system of contracting for delivery of service at a prescribed cost if the Centre sets the cost level with the results of improvements elsewhere in mind, but will that be seen as pseudo-delegation? Obviously, delegation cannot be allowed to mean a complete absence of central control, no more than it does in the corporate sector, but there are still issues to be faced about the way in which control is exercised. Is it simply on some equivalent of the 'bottom line' or can one have true delegation while still being able to specify some types of practices?

In fact before the authors could report back on the way the projects were or were not serving as a vehicle of change, each experimental group had fed back information about the technical outcomes of their work. The general reaction was so favourable that the Board decided to implement a programme of up to

100 experiments across all Collections. Each Collection was invited to submit, for central approval, up to five experiments in operating outside of Head Office rules, but some Collections have had up to 100 proposals from their staff, i.e. just in one Collection. Many of these do not require Head Office approval and are changes in practices not governed by rules. It is possible that benefits from such 'non-experiments' could be just as important as those submitted to the centre for approval; much depends upon how each Collector follows up all proposals made. It will be interesting at a later stage to research what has happened. Furthermore, it was very interesting and reflective of the existing organizational culture to note that development of the experiments revealed a number of requests for Head Office approval where none was needed. Certain parts of the Outfield had assumed that their well-established local practices had been established to be in compliance with central rules when this was not the case. Even the search for experimental proposals, therefore, played a significant part in setting the climate for change with regard to a wider set of practices than just those affected by central rules. Perceptions of existing freedoms to act were clarified as well as widening those freedoms. By late 1990/early 1991 the second tranche of up to 100 centrally approved experiments is just getting under way.

Our research findings on the value of the experiments as a vehicle for major change in the Department, could not be as enthusiastic as most of the technical feedback. Most, but not all, of the experiments did not attempt a radical shift in management between levels. Also, unfortunately, what was the most radical proposal looks likely at present to be the least successful. There is a similar experiment in a different area, however, which aimed to reach a similar end point, but in a more cautious, incremental fashion, which is showing signs of being very successful. On closer examination this may reveal lessons about the way to build up radical experiments gradually, rather than try to be too radical too soon.

Extensive discussions with staff at experiment locations also revealed the continuance of the sorts of concerns discovered nearly two years earlier and also reflected in the Head Office interviews. Moreover, the accuracy of these views has recently been corroborated from several different sources (i.e. by both internal and external consultants) as they have been monitoring staff attitudes in work they have been contributing to the total change process.

HM Customs and Excise: the current position (end 1990)

As a result of the findings in our Head Office research, it was decided that it was now time to attempt to clarify some of the concepts associated with the expressed concerns about change. Three study groups have been established. One will look at policy issues like the interpretation of equity, another will

275

examine the various organizational factors which will prescribe the nature of delegation to be implemented and a third will consider the question of rewards, performance measurement and motivation. Moreover, the Department has already moved ahead during 1990 to implement the recommendations of a series of strategic reviews (one for each main function) and supporting strategies (e.g. there is a 'People Initiative' emanating from the Personnel Directorate which is looking for ways to improve trust relationships between the centre and the Outfield, improve communications and training, etc.). This movement was, no doubt, partly spurred on by The Next Steps initiative, but was also encouraged by the perceived need for change with the Single European Market. It might be said, also, that the growth in scale of business generally would probably have led to pressure, in due course, to delegate more and undertake more selective testing, but this was not used throughout the Department as a major reason for the change. In other words, moves in this direction were begun under the FMI and would probably have been needed eventually without these initiatives, either the FMI or The Next Steps, but these central government initiatives have considerably strengthened the pressure for change.

The current position, in the authors' perception, is that there is now a widespread recognition that more devolved management will happen and that the Board is seen to be wholly committed to a more decentralized form of operation. This means that at a broad level Greenwood's antecedents (2) and (3) have been established, but there is much work yet to do before one can say that the change has been achieved. On the other hand, this achievement should not be underestimated – the ways of many years are being changed. Creating the right climate for change takes a long time in such a strong organization culture when there is no felt need for change due to an obvious crisis through failing performance [Greenwood's antecedent (1)]. One senior member of the Department has stated that the cynicism about the intention to grant more local autonomy has been replaced with 'suspended cynicism', but that, in itself, he said was a big achievement. While disbeliefs are suspended, the change process is now moving to a stage of widespread implementation rather than just experimentation, although there is still a role for the '100 experiments' referred to earlier.

A better way of putting it would be that there is a need to institutionalize experimentation. Nevertheless, as stated already, there is still a long way to go. The three antecedents are not sufficient conditions for change and change is being attempted without antecedent (1). One could argue that there is some sense of crisis for the Civil Service generally which is being felt in the Customs and Excise, but there is no crisis of performance within the Department; in fact its performance continues to improve and its critical importance as a main government revenue provider makes it less vulnerable to general ideological threats. Nevertheless, core concepts still have to be clarified so that everyone has a better idea of what the change might mean for them. Key success factors underlying each functional strategy are being identified, but they have yet to be given the support needed. The change process is now reaching a very critical stage. Widespread expectations have, at last, been created. The next few years must satisfy those expectations in a practical way. The Department recognizes this and considerable effort is now being expended to prepare the way for more decentralization. Training in team building and professional management development has commenced on a large scale. Detailed manpower controls are being scrapped in favour of overall control by budgets with greater freedom to vire between heads of expenditure. If the Department wishes to decentralize its operations, all these actions are moves in the right direction. But, if a really significant shift in the organizational culture is required, there must be a determination to persist with such measures over an extended period. The Board says that there can be no going back, but major change processes like this, which cannot be enforced by changes of ownership of the organization or large scale replacement of staff, need continuing management through multiple stages as opinions are formed and reformed and experience is acquired of what the change means and re-negotiations are attempted. Without continual and co-ordinated attention to the management of change, the threat of enforced recantation is always present (one is reminded of the situtation faced by President Gorbachev with the hard-liners hovering to re-enter centre stage before the change is complete and irrevocable.)

SUMMARY

Financial control in central government makes little sense looked at in isolation, unless one takes a very narrow view of financial control being concerned only with the economy of inputs. A number of attempts have been made to cope with the control over government expenditure in the wider sense of delivering efficiency and effectiveness. Methods like PPBS and ZBB have not, on the whole, proved successful, although they did stimulate much thinking about the problem and offered some marginal improvements if used with considerable discretion.

The current thrust in the UK is to deal with the problem by delegating decision making within a structure of accountabilities. This has some similarities with ZBB and PPBS, in very general terms, but take better account of political, organizational and cognitive realities. The chances of success of this approach seem better, but politicians and civil servants must be patient. Major changes in culture will not be achieved by just recognizing a few basic antecedents, although their recognition is important for commencing the debate about change. Even with a more pragmatic approach than that employed with PBBS and ZBB, significant changes are required in terms of introducing more on-line management into a process traditionally dominated by personal risk avoidance and administration of rules. New relationships have to be established between different levels and some organizational restructurings must occur as parts of organizations become agencies or, in Customs and Excise from 1 April, 1991, Executive Units operating 'like' agencies. New ideologies cannot be just offered, they must be nurtured and grown. Even those willing to accept the new culture early in its development will need to gain confidence that they can operate successfully within it. New skills will need to be developed and a willingness to try to develop new skills. Confidence will need to be built through giving experience through limited change to begin with. Time must be given for those initially less enthusiatic about change to learn from the experience of those willing to experiment. Some political adjustments will also be required through the need to accommodate reporting differences and yet still retain accountability to the public on detailed issues. The scope and extent of the changes must not be underestimated. Pressure for change needs to be maintained from above, but it needs to be reasonable pressure recognizing the scale of effort required. Otherwise, Next Steps frameworks will be put in place which reflect delegation and contracting, but the likelihood will be that they will be superficial: the fundamental move to the innovative Civil Service will not have been managed – just changes in labels will have been dictated. It might also help to overcome the pockets of suspended cynicism, if both main political parties clearly specified that there will be no going back whichever of them is in power – but perhaps that is also not recognizing political reality.

There also needs to be a better recognition by academics and journalists of the scale of change needed and the extensive process involved. Articles specifying a few basic requirements for change do say something important, but also hardly get the change manager beyond first base in solving his or her specific change problem. The big problems only begin when trying to translate the general ideology into meaningful language for a variety of organization participants. Also, articles saying baldly, and sometimes disparagingly, that little change has occurred can serve to fuel resistances to those striving to bring about change. All change managers need to be told occasionally of the state of the organization they are trying to change because they may often not be in a position to see that state clearly themselves. Pressure may, therefore, be needed from various sources to keep the change managers on their toes, but this needs to be balanced with understanding. The view of the authors is that no really fundamental shift in the way the Civil Service operates has yet been achieved, but the building blocks have been put in place, at least in the Department we know – HM Customs and Excise.

Momentum is building up for change. Mrs Thatcher may not have reduced public expenditure much in aggregate as a percentage of GDP, but she may well be in a position in five or six years' time to look back and see what an impact she had on introducing new management practices into the Civil Service. Until then the authors as academics, like some of their 'risk averting' civil servant friends, suspend judgement . . . but not cynically! And if they were really forced to bet on the issue, they would now say that, given a reasonably stable environment, the odds are now in favour of achieving real change. But even if the change is properly managed, it is still possible that all the good work will 'be blown away' by some large macro-effect. If, for example, a major economic crisis were to occur (no pun intended), would the Treasury feel compelled to restore tight central controls? It is hoped that it will not be necessary to find out.

NOTE

[1] See also Tomkins (1987) Chapter 1 for the views of one of the authors on the available evidence of benefits received from shifting resources into the private sector.

REFERENCES

Anthony, R., J. Dearden and N. Bedford (1989) *Management Control Systems*, 6th edn.

Anthony, R. (1977) ZBB is a fraud, *Wall Street Journal*, 27 April 1977.

Collins, B. (1987) Update on central government, *Public Finance and Accountancy*, 13 November 1987.

Colville, I. and Tomkins, C. Changing attitudes to innovation in the civil service, *The Treasury and Civil Service Committee 5th Report, Developments in the Next Steps Programme*, House of Commons.

Greenwood, R. (1984) Incremental budgeting: antecedents of change, *Journal of Public Policy*, No. 4.

Hinings, C. and Greenwood, R. (1988) *The Dynamics of Strategic Change*, Blackwell.

Kemp, P. (1990) Can the Civil Service adapt to managing by contract? *Public Money and Management*, Autumn.

Progress in the Next Steps Initiative (1990) HMSO, Cm. 1263.

Public Accounts Committee (1987) *House of Commons Public Accounts Committee Report*.

Richards, S. (1987) the financial management initiative, in *Reshaping Central Government* (eds A. Harrison and J. Gretton), Policy Journals.

Smith, G. (1980) *Something to Declare: 1000 Years of Customs and Excise*, Harrap.

Tomkins, C. (1987) *Achieving Economy, Efficiency and Effectiveness in the Public Sector*, The Institute of Chartered Accountants of Scotland, Kogan Page.

Tomkins, C.R. (1991) *Corporate Resource Allocation – Financial, Strategic and Organisational Perspectives*, Blackwell.

Tomkins, C. and Colville, I. (1980) Value for money in the public sector, *Local Finance, International Journal for Local Credit*, June.

The Treasury and Civil Service Committee Eighth Report (1990) *Progress in the Next Steps Initiative*, July, HC481.

Wildavsky, A. (1975) *Budgeting: A Comparative Theory of Budgeting Processes*, Little Brown.

Financial control and devolved management in central government: Discussant's comments

ROBERT W. SCAPENS

Tomkins and Colville provide us with an interesting insight into the process of change in the public sector. Using a case study they examine the introduction of decentralized decision making and the setting up of financial control systems in HM Customs and Excise. Their analysis brings out the complexity of the change process and illustrates the social processes which are necessary for 'successful' change. In particular, they argue that it is essential to change the attitudes and work behaviour of Civil Servants. This suggests a need to change the way in which the organizational participants make sense of their day-to-day work experiences.

It would have been helpful to have had more detailed descriptions of the processes by which such changes come about, including both the historical and organizational contexts in which the change process is set. However, a single paper cannot achieve everything, and we are promised at least one book from this research project. I look forward with anticipation to its publication.

In this discussion I would like to take up three issues: first, the methodology used; second, the relationship between decentralization and control; and third, the concern for rationality in the public sector.

281

METHODOLOGY

I have considerable sympathy for case study research (see Scapens, 1990) and in general I support the position taken by Tomkins and Colville. Any research, which analyses social processes and particularly where the researchers have direct contact with the social actors, is likely to have an impact on the processes being studied. There can be no meaningful concept of a neutral and objective observer. Researchers have to acknowledge the subjectivity of social research in terms of both their impact on the social actors and the social construction of their interpretations. As is pointed out in the paper, action research is 'just a little further along a continuum'.

One particular danger of action research, however, is that the researchers might become 'overly' committed to a particular position in relation to the social process being studied. For instance, they may come to 'support' one group of social actors, or promote one component of the social action. Action researchers must guard against uncritical or unconscious support of particular positions. It is all too easy for such researchers to take on the values and understandings of the actors who have given them access to the organization and who expect to receive some return. Obtaining clearance for publication itself implies that, to some extent at least, a certain sympathy must be shown for the position of the actors whose permission is needed. The authors are quite open about these problems of action research and we are asked to take on trust their attempts to provide an 'independent analysis'. But as is implied above (and accepted by the authors) this may be impossible to achieve.

The use of quotations and detailed illustrations to support particular arguments adds interest to a paper, but they cannot by themselves substantiate individual claims. It is only in the wider context in which particular statements are made that arguments can be developed. Thus, I agree with Tomkins and Colville that to select just a few quotations for this paper would have made little sense. But I hope quotations, etc., will be a feature of future more detailed publications. However, the limitation of this paper is that we have neither quotations nor an extended analysis of the historical and organizational contexts.

While I do not believe that a case study has to be written from the standpoint of a single theoretical perspective, as there is no possibility of a neutral and objective case study it is always helpful for a reader to have a clear understanding of the theoretical framework(s) used by the researchers in making sense of the case material. Although some theoretical issues permeate the case, we do not know a great deal about the authors' own theoretical positions. Perhaps this will also be clarified in their subsequent publications.

DECENTRALIZATION AND CONTROL

The paper describes a process of organizational change in which the introduction of greater decentralization initially gives rise to a variety of concerns, both at the Head Office and in the Collections. But gradually these concerns seemed to be overcome and now there appears to be some enthusiasm for decentralization, or at least 'a widespread recognition that more devolved management will happen'. The initial concerns seemed to reflect a perception that the process of decentralization would lead to reduced, rather than increased autonomy for local managers. In other words, decentralization was seen as a mechanism for increasing central control rather than relaxing it. In an environment in which cost cutting in the public sector had become a general expectation decentralization of decision making responsibility with limited (and possibly contracting) budgets could easily be seen as a mechanism for the greater control of individual managers.

The paper describes how FMI led to devolved management and budgeting with control monitored through a system of output measures. Although FMI was not couched in terms of cutting back the Civil Service, there were certainly those who believed that it was. Tomkins and Colville describe how the suspicions of FMI gave rise to a lack of enthusiasm, coupled with cynicism leading to effective resistance. Their analysis demonstrates the limitations of conceptualizing power as a possession of senior managers which they use to impose their objectives and values on the lower levels of the hierarchy. Although it is not necessarily exercised overtly, subordinates are frequently able to exercise power in various forms to resist change. As the case demonstrates it is not the exercise of power which is crucial in implementing change, but the ability to change the ideology, i.e. the ways of thinking, of the social actors. In studying change it is important to recognize that the ways in which social actors make sense of their day-to-day activities are inextricably linked with their relations of power (see Giddens, 1984).

The Next Steps Initiative extended the ideas of delegation by establishing agencies with chief executives given clear responsibility to manage. Tomkins and Colville explain that this development has a particular advantage for the instigators of change as the agencies must subject themselves to a financial discipline in order to maintain their viability and to avoid organizational crises. Accordingly, members of the agencies are likely to begin to make sense of their activities in financial terms. Thus, although the process of delegation appears to give greater freedom to individual managers, it has the effect of imposing far greater financial control.

There are considerable parallels between this case of HM Customs and Excise and a case study of a private sector organization with which I have been involved (see Scapens and Roberts, 1991). In the private sector organization the introduction of a new management information system, which was ostensibly designed to improve the information available to local managers, was perceived as a means of achieving greater central control. Initially, there was resistance to the new system, but as it became clear that the new system would go ahead the local managers attempted to subvert the system to ensure that local concerns took precedence over the central controls. It would be interesting to explore whether the actions of local managers in HM Customs and Excise are now designed to enhance their own autonomy and to limit the impact of central controls.

Informing the case study in the private sector organization were two conceptions of power (Giddens, 1984). In a broad sense power can be viewed as the ability 'to do' – to achieve some productive transformation. But in a narrow sense power can be conceptualized as domination, whereby one social actor is held accountable by another. Power in both senses is implicated in management information systems. The management information can be used to enable local managers 'to do' their day-to-day activity, but at the same time it is also the mechanism by which local managers are called to account by their superiors. It is impossible to separate these dual roles of management information, they are both inextricably part of the process of financial control. However, an excessive reliance on a functional view of control (such as the view that management information is concerned with 'controlling' the behaviour of managers in a way which denies their autonomy) is likely to lead to resistance to the process of change. What is interesting about Tomkins and Colville's case study is that the initial resistance appears to be overcome, although we are not shown in detail the process by which this has been achieved. Nevertheless, the insights gained from this study are likely to extend beyond the public sector.

This brings me to my final issue. Why are the methods of the private sector apparently so attractive for the public sector.

CONCERN FOR RATIONALITY

In the early sections of the paper Tomkins and Colville describe the search for rational planning and control procedures in the public sector, e.g. PPBS and ZBB in the United States and FMI and Next Steps in the United Kingdom. They provide an analysis of the various reasons given for the failures of the past. In their analysis they place quotation marks around such words as 'rational systems' and 'rationality', but they do not enter into a discussion of the concept of rationality in the public sector. To some extent the need for rational planning and control systems in the public sector is taken for granted in the paper.

It would be interesting to explore the reasons why on both sides of the Atlantic there has emerged a desire to introduce private sector methods of planning and control into the public sector. This is despite continuing criticism in recent years of the achievements of the private sector. It is only ten to fifteen years ago that British Industry was considered to be the sick man of Europe and currently there is considerable concern that Western businesses are not able to compete with the Japanese. It has been suggested by writers such as Johnson and Kaplan (1987) that American (and British) industry are continuing to use methods of management accounting that were developed fifty, sixty and a hundred years ago. Are private sector methods really so suitable for the public sector?

Academics such as Wildavsky have been very critical over the years of attempts to introduce so-called 'rational' management techniques into public sector organizations. Yet new proposals continue to be put forward. Furthermore, it has been observed that when such 'rational' methods of management control are introduced, managers who are critical when they are the subject of the control can be seen to use the same methods to control their subordinates (see Humphry and Scapens, 1991). There seems to be a desire for 'rationality' of some kind. But from where does this emanate? Is it the result of our socio-economic system or is it due to some psychological desire for order? Such issues remain to be explored.

Tomkins and Colville's paper, however, gives us valuable insights into the difficulties of employing 'rational' financial control techniques in complex organizations. Their focus was in the public sector, but the difficulties they identify and the process they describe also exist in the private sector.

REFERENCES

Giddens, A. (1984) *The Constitution of Society*, Polity Press.

Humphry, C and R. Scapens (1991) Whatever happened to the lion-tamers? An examination of accounting change in the public sector, *Working Paper*, University of Manchester.

Johnson H.T. and R.S. Kaplan (1987) *Relevance Lost – The rise and fall of management accounting*, Harvard Business School Press.

Scapens, R. (1990) Researching management accounting practice: The role of case study methods, *British Accounting Review*, Autumn, 259–81.

Scapens, R. and J. Roberts, (1991) Accounting control: A case study of resistance to accounting change, *Working Paper*, University of Manchester.

12

Accounting and the uncongenial twins: Viewing financial standards from the perspectives of critical theories and market-based research

TREVOR HOPPER, LINDA KIRKHAM and
LEN SKERRATT

INTRODUCTION

This paper is concerned with critical theory and market based approaches to the brands debate. So what has this to do with a volume on financial control in memory of Ken Hilton? We think that it has everything to with *financial* control. A number of papers in this book are evaluations of how financial control is being exercised in organizations, such as the NHS, in which previously other criteria have tended to operate.

Financial criteria are becoming more and more prevalent in our society. We would argue that this is no accident; but a systematic attempt by accountants

Perspectives on Financial Control: Essays in memory of Kenneth Hilton.
Edited by Mohmoud Ezzamel and David Heathfield.
Published in 1992 by Chapman & Hall, London. ISBN 0 412 409801.

to expand their industry and power base. Interestingly, the brands debate is a situation in which accountants themselves are under attack from other measurement professionals. The brands debate is not simply about the valuation of brands; it is a frontal attack on the expertise of the accountancy profession. For the accounting profession, there is much at stake; that is why the debate has consumed so much energy and time. Indirectly, there is also much at stake for society in general. It is not at all clear why the criteria used to evaluate such operations as the NHS, should be in the hands of a single group of individuals, even if they are called the accountancy profession. In this paper we analyse the accounting profession's control of the way in which companies are held accountable to stakeholders and society. The brands debate is used to illustrate how this control is exercised and retained.

This paper rests on two basic beliefs. First, accounting standard setting is beset with a series of significant problems, and current practices attempting to alleviate them leave much to be desired. Second, academic thought and research can help illuminate current problems, identify new ways of looking at them and provide fresh alternatives for policy makers to consider, though at times this may be discomforting.

Two important schools of research that have emerged over the past two decades are critical theory (CT) and market-based research (MBAR). Critical theory is an umbrella rubric for the work of a divergent group of scholars, including ecologists, neo-marxists and post-modernists to name a few. What unites critical accounting theorists is a strong commitment to recent developments in philosophy, political economy, history and qualitative research. Above all, and probably transcending any internal divisions within the school, many are united through a disdain for markets-based research, viewed as emanating from Friedmanite Chicago-style economics and the academic accounting establishment which it has spawned. In North America especially, this has led, at worst, to MBAR becoming elevated to religious orthodoxy when academic employment and publication decisions are made.

Markets-based research has a strong commitment to empirical research conducted in the manner of conventional science, namely rigorous mathematical modelling and statistical analyses of hypotheses. It is primarily rooted in market economics derived from neo-classical economic theory. Accounting is seen as a good called information: the objective of regulation is seen as ensuring that users (typically investors) have sufficient information for economically rational decisions. A typical example of such research is 'events' studies, which seek to establish whether financial disclosures generated in the context of companies' financial reporting practices impact upon share valuations. Such research is criticized by CT, not least for its claim that such studies are 'value-free' 'objective' observations of 'reality' (e.g. Arrington and Francis, 1989; Cooper and Sherer, 1984; Tinker *et al.*, 1982).

288

OBJECTIVES

The aim of this paper is not to adjudicate between the two camps' theoretical differences and to try and resolve their mutual uncongeniality. Important though these differences are, this paper has a broader objective, namely to consider and evaluate the policy recommendations of the two approaches in the context of the brands debate in particular, and the battle for measurement in general. A major conclusion of the paper is that, despite their differences in theory and approach, the outputs of each set of scholars have a degree of overlap in terms of practical policy implications for standard setting, and that such a 'twinning' of views is often at odds with current professional and regulatory practices and policies. Both schools of thought are committed to academic discourse and standards of analysis concerning accounting problems rather than opportunistic pragmatism. Both have a theoretical rigour and consciousness still unfortunately rare in accounting practice and policy circles. Both tend to raise questions and issues potentially discomforting to the accounting profession, especially with regard to the value and range of services it offers and their role within regulation. Both tend to be ignored in arenas of policy formulation. Given such mutuality, often at odds with professional wisdom, the ultimate uncongeniality of MBAR and CT may be less important than their commonality, in relation to the accounting profession in practice.

An important purpose of this paper, therefore, is to compare the policy recommendations of CT and MBAR. Apart from the obvious practical relevance of such a goal, it has the added advantage of requiring us to specify what the policy implications of CT actually are; despite the volume of literature, such implications are still not well documented. By contrast, although MBAR can be criticized for having too narrow a focus, in relation to policy matters at least it has delivered substantially on recommendations for evaluation by policymakers. Unfortunately, the more eclectic framework of CT research has tended to be devoid of much in the way of practical suggestions.

In defence of this assessment, many proponents of CT would argue that such policy recommendations are conditional upon fundamental changes in corporate and national governance. The present authors see such views as valid, but tending to provide a recipe for inaction. As we seek to illustrate here, CT can contribute to medium-term policy goals, and this may indeed provide a motor towards addressing more fundamental concerns of the role of information within society.

The remainder of this paper is devoted to comparing and contrasting the two sets of researches on accounting regulation and exploring their consequences for future policy. The third and fourth sections outline the main features of MBAR and CT, respectively. The fifth and sixth sections try to tease out the policy implications of both schools, in relation to the brands debate. This particular issue is chosen for two reasons. First, it is a topical debate which can be understood without much recourse to technical accounting; other subjects, such as off balance sheet finance, would require a layer of accounting knowledge which may sidetrack our attention from the concerns of this paper. Second, and more important, it is an area in which the concerns of CT are most easily grasped; specifically, that accounting numbers not only report on, but also help to define, the dimensions of corporate accountability. The final section provides a short summary.

MARKETS BASED ACCOUNTING RESEARCH AND BRANDS

MBAR is an umbrella title for a variety of experimental designs and opinions about financial reporting practice. There is no attempt, here, to represent fully the spectrum of opinions within the school. The purpose of this paper is to compare and contrast MBAR with the CT school. Consequently, the MBAR views presented here are personal, but are hopefully representative of the views of others as well.

One of the main working assumptions of MBAR is that information is a good and, despite its special characteristics, can be analysed much like any other. A major market in which this good is used is the stock market, for the valuation of securities. Typically, MBAR argues that the information market should be a competitive one. The reason for this is that competitive markets are able to provide goods (including information) at minimum cost. Consequently, MBAR believes that accountants should provide information for a market only when they are in a position to do this more cheaply and/or more efficiently than other groups.

One consequence of this minimum cost framework is that the accounting function is normally limited to reporting and validating transactions, in contrast to valuing them (Peasnell, 1977). It is argued that accountants are not in a particularly special position to value corporate assets, since the valuation process includes not only the forecasting of future cash flows, but also the assessment of risk and preferences over time. MBAR suggests that the unique role of accountants is to verify and give credence to information from corporate management; this is achieved through the application of assumed accountants' professional integrity and expertise in both financial reporting and auditing.

So, how do brands fit into this way of thinking? From an economic perspective, brands are seen as ways in which companies attempt to differentiate their products in the market place. Any achieved differentiation affects both price and income elasticities; the demand curve in elementary economics is shifted to the right, and demand is less sensitive to downward shifts in income. The basic objective of branding (and advertising for that matter) is to affect profits by increasing the mean and decreasing the variance of earnings. Brands are a standard weapon in the armoury for participating in the competitive market.

From a reporting perspective, the main question in the brands debate is whether companies should report the values of brands in the Annual Report and Accounts. While there is little doubt that brand information is useful to investors, from a MBAR viewpoint it is not at all clear that accountants have any special advantage in structuring and verifying the disclosure.

Although brands may appear as an asset in the balance sheet, their valuation is a matter of assessing the income stream which can be attributed to them. Typically, the prediction of earnings (and indirectly, therefore, the valuation of assets) is a task undertaken for investors by firms of analysts. Their prediction of future earnings is based not only on the company's earnings history, but also on industry-specific and economy-wide factors. Given this, analysts would seem to be a natural and obvious group to provide brand information to investors; the object of branding is to affect the future earnings number, and the effect will depend on both the response of competitors (who may have their own brands) and the state of the economy. Indeed, given the function of analysts as described above, it is likely that the brand factor is, in fact, already incorporated into their earnings forecasts; it is just one factor, among many, which are included in the assessment of the future cash flow to shareholders.

However, this analysis does not really get to the heart of the fundamental issue in the brands debate in the UK, even judged from a straightforward MBAR perspective. The central controversy in brands is one of regulation; and yet the above model of financial reporting could appear to function quite well without regulation. Nevertheless, accounting and auditing standards exist; why so? The main rationale for regulation in an MBAR framework is market failure, that the market is not able to provide the desired solution. For example, it may well be that market pressures will eventually force recalcitrant companies to disclose particular items to shareholders, but this process may take too long. Along the way to equilibrium, there may be substantial welfare losses by investors. In such a situation, the role of regulation would be to speed up the process by which market equilibrium is achieved.

It is in this light that a case can be made for brand disclosure in the Annual Report and Accounts. If analysts as a whole are unable to incorporate the full impact of the company's brands in their predictions of earnings, then there might be a case for the disclosure. However, there would need to be some convincing evidence that management (or some valuer, external to the organization) could improve on the achievement of analysts. Certainly, from the many studies which compare analysts' forecast accuracy with that of management, it seems clear that where industry-specific and economy-wide factors are important, analysts have a distinct advantage.

Another case for brand disclosure is on equity grounds (Lev, 1988). If only a few analysts have access to brand information to construct their forecasts of earnings, then the resultant information asymmetry may lead to the withdrawal of uninformed parties from the market place. Disclosure, by reducing information asymmetry, may help to keep markets functioning.

However, even if a market demand for brand information can be established, it does not necessarily follow that the disclosure of brand *values* are the answer. For example, a more effective remedy is likely to be an increase in segmental reporting. Indeed, such a solution would be in keeping with the notion, referred to earlier, that value is an outcome of a market process rather than the prerogative of any specific individual market agent.

But this analysis of brands still fails to capture the essence of the debate, which is the reverse of typical financial reporting controversies. These are normally concerned with regulators forcing companies to disclose items. With brands, regulators are trying to prevent disclosure! How might this be explained within a markets framework? One explanation probably lies in a different market to that normally associated with MBAR, namely the market for corporate debt. With costly contracting, debt covenants are expressed in terms of accounting numbers; in this context, one consequence of having brand values in the balance sheet is that some measures of gearing are reduced. The implied market failure in the brands debate is now clear. It is that companies may exploit the loopholes in debt covenants. The benefits of such manipulations are not likely to be permanent, since the lenders will wish to rewrite the contract to block the loophole; however, the blocking will still consume scarce resources. Consequently, the banning of brand disclosure would prevent such exploitation in the short run and save resources in the longer run.

From an MBAR perspective then, the concern of regulators about brand disclosure is attributable to the potential market failure in the writing of debt covenants. But it should be noted that empirical evidence to support this may be difficult to collect; for example, the evidence that brand values may reduce gearing ratios is not, in itself, sufficient. Lenders may be well aware that accounting numbers can be flexible and are largely in the hands of the management. Consequently, lenders may anticipate such manipulation when writing loan agreements; for example, they may lower the gearing ratio which will trigger action, or they may impound the losses, such as the expected contract rewriting costs, in the rate of interest. Consequently, in a well-functioning market for corporate debt, the disclosure of brand values may not in fact give rise to the welfare losses described above, namely the exploitation of short-run loopholes and the rewriting of contracts in the longer run.

In summary, then, this brief analysis of the brands issue incorporates the three main concerns which drive MBAR views:

- the demand for information by market agents;
- the relative advantage of accountants (and others) in supplying that information; and
- the market failures that may arise.

CRITICAL THEORY: ACCOUNTING AS POWER–KNOWLEDGE

This paper does not profess to resolve the internecine wrangles within critical theory. Rather, its concern is that excessive concern for theorization, important though theory is, can dissipate energy from policy formulation and practical action. The spirit of this paper is to argue that, given the problems of falsification in the social sciences, an important test of theory is its usefulness or otherwise in informing individuals about practical problems according to their own needs and desires (Caldwell, 1991).

The CT approach within the paper, although it draws from a diverse set of literatures, has its own roots within political economy approaches. Accounting research utilizing the works of Habermas has been particularly useful in this respect (Arrington and Puxty 1991; Laughlin 1987) insofar as they stress the importance of socially created and contestable interests, action governed by a notion of rationality that transcends reductionism to self-interest and given individual goals, and the ensuing importance of ethics, language and democracy. Habermas attempts to address such issues in his 'ideal speech communities' is particularly apt for this paper as it provides a model of a practical mechanism for creating inter-subjective consensus which is of relevance to accounting.

Perhaps the major contribution of critical theorists has lain in bringing to the fore the issue of whether accounting exists as a coherent body of knowledge and, relatedly, the powerful roles it and the accounting profession play in society. These issues are confronted as an integral part of any understanding of specific or general accounting policy issues. For example, critical theorists would argue that the focus of much of what has been written concerning the recent controversy over brands is too narrow, concentrating as it has upon issues of recognition criteria and valuation methodology (e.g. see Barwise *et al.*, 1989; Birkin, 1990; Egginton, 1990; Tweedie and Whittington, 1990). Such analyses are viewed as both potentially misleading and unfruitful in terms of identifying and understanding the significance and implications of the brands issue. Critical theory offers a more comprehensive understanding of the brands debate through its questioning and exploration of both the claims being made for the possibilities of accounting knowledge and the powerful role of the accounting profession in regulation.

Knowledge

The questioning of accounting knowledge has been built upon the importation and application of philosophical literatures to accounting problems. This has led to many researchers rejecting conventional research assumptions (held by MBAR researchers) that an objective reality exists external to the researcher which can be mirrored and built up with increasing accuracy through piecemeal studies of relationships between variables. By contrast, critical researchers would argue that reality exists only as a social creation (Lukka, 1990). What we understand about the world is a product of social negotiation and consensus and is not determined by deterministic rules of science. Thus a multitude of 'knowledges' may exist in a fleeting fragile form, none of which can be proved to be 'right', though each can be tested upon the canons of reasonable argument and yardsticks of ethics, values and beliefs (Cooper and Sherer, 1984). The notion of an independent detached researcher and the associated beliefs of being able to distinguish between prescription and description is debunked as impracticable and philosophically impossible. For example, the researcher's selective perceptions and prior socialization influence what is studied, what is seen and how it is interpreted; accounting knowledge is created rather than discovered. Detachment from the social processes creating knowledge debars the researcher from closer understanding: understanding requires involvement on the part of the researchers.

Critical researchers emphasize holism and qualitative research in the belief that parts can only be understood in relation to the whole, rather than static detailed studies of disaggregated or sub-divided phenomena conducted without reference to broader contexts. They reject the notion that there is, or ever could be, an objective solution to the brands controversy derived from existing or developing accounting knowledge. Rather, they would seek to explore the brands issue, not only in relation to microcosms of established accounting knowledge such as goodwill or group accounting, but also as part of a wider set of socio-economic relationships and structures.

Power

A recurring theme in critical work is the study of power. One strand, following the subjectivist approach, is interested in studying not only how accounting is socially created, but also how it shapes conceptions of reality, by prioritizing issues, approaches and languages (Hines, 1988). For example, the question of 'objectification', i.e. how socially created accounting knowledge comes to be promulgated and perceived as objective and scientifically derived, is typical. A second strand, emanating from political economy, focuses upon how accounting practices are related to a broader institutional context. The profession, its management of internal differences, its relationship to accounting firms, and the presentation of its own interests are of central concern. The regulatory process and self-regulation are viewed within a framework that incorporates interdependencies between the accounting profession, the state, corporate clients and the social processes of negotiation stemming from their differences and shared interests.

Similarly, the maintenance of professional policies and images, the expansion of the profession and accounting firms into new domains of proffered expertise, and the protection of their interests through professional monopoly are of central interest. The essential theme is that the accounting profession is seen as a complex body of disparate but self-interested sub-groups concerned with legitimating their powers, influences and expertises, not least in relation to regulation, while simultaneously needing to accommodate sectional interests emanating from business corporations and the state. By focusing upon power as a central theme, critical theorists would seek to explore and understand the network of power relations within which the brands debate has emerged and is being reformulated.

Conceptual frameworks for accounting standards

Whereas critical theorists use concepts such as power and knowledge to expose and understand the complexity and subjectivity of accounting policy choice, accounting regulators and some academics seek to establish the possibility of a neutral and objective set of rules within which such choices can and should be made (Solomons, 1989). Accounting knowledge is portrayed as requiring discovery rather than being created and the presence and influence of (unequal) power relations is either denied or assumed to be within the control of the regulators themselves. Thus a frequent plea by commentators concerned with theoretical inconsistencies between accounting standards has been to call for a single all-embracing theoretical framework through which all standards could be evolved and checked against.

Critical theory reveals the philosophical impossibility and naïvete of this approach to accounting standards (Hines, 1989). It would require elevating one set of beliefs and values above others and, given that the choice would have to be elaborated and made in social interaction, it would remain essentially subjective. The search for a single objective truth derived from scientific method is doomed from its inception. If the accounting standard setting process is imbued with lobbying, interests, opportunism, fog and uncertainty to name a few frequent criticisms (e.g. Hope and Gray, 1982), then it is not aberrant in these respects. Rather it is reflective of how knowledge is created more generally. The first step in reform is understanding this and, as is discussed later, formulating improvements in political processes so that interested parties can negotiate solutions in accordance with their values and beliefs, rather than a regulatory body, handing down a single set of rules or laws. To deny the inherent complexity and subjectivity of accounting policy choices, such as those bound up with the issue of brands, will not eliminate the conflicts and contradictions: rather it may serve to transform or compound them. This is emphasized by recent postmodernist work produced by deconstructionists and Foucauldians.

Deconstructionists argue, from philosophical debate, for a particular and rigorous method of examining documents or texts. They claim that nothing exists outside of the text and that ultimately the prescriptions of any text can be shown to reside ultimately on tautologies and contestable creeds or values. The aim of deconstructionist analysis is to show not only the ultimate theoretical incoherence of any text, but also, by examining poorly substantiated claims, to show how the text also denies space to alternative views. The aim of deconstructionists is to puncture the authority of pronouncements in texts and provide a method to create space for counter-views. Thus, they argue, any accounting pronouncement is capable of being stripped down to its essential contradictions and bare prejudices (Arrington and Francis, 1989). To deny otherwise is to promote error and privileging of viewpoints, be they radical, conservative or any other possible hue.

Whereas deconstructionists concentrate on the text, Foucauldians concentrate upon historical incidents that give rise to particular discourses about knowledge (Hoskin and Macve, 1986; Miller and O'Leary, 1987). They are sceptical of notions of continual progress in knowledge and the human condition. Instead they argue that since the Enlightenment, societal control has shifted from physical sanctions over the body to new technologies of control embedded in abstract codified calculative devices resting on scientific allusions. They point to how a series of pseudo-sciences in psychiatry, sexology and criminology for example, have waxed and waned. Relatedly, new methods of control, exemplified in the design of Panopticons, have provided for the powerful ways of making visible their subjects and thus providing a means of rendering them docile. Foucauldians have provided powerful challenges to the notion of a trajectory of progress often assumed by others, regarding accounting issues. They have revealed how issues such as value-added reporting, employee reporting and inflation accounting have been discussed intermittently since the inception of the subject. Their appearance in discourses and policy agendas tends to be a reflection of the relative importance of various social issues at a particular time, such as the need to pacify employees, or to accommodate state concerns over inflationary pressures, rather than a continuous pursuit of an intellectual agenda of improvement on the part of the accounting profession. Moreover, it is argued that the use of accounting in this way may serve, in part, to create social definitions and understandings of what is or isn't an issue or a concern.

One does not need the services of deconstructionist philosophers perhaps to illustrate the internal inconsistencies of accounting standards and their embed-dedness in, and reproduction of, certain values. For example, policy makers have proposed that the recognition of intangible assets, such as brands, on the balance sheet should rest upon their ability to satisfy particular conditions; the identification of their historical cost, their separability from other assets and their independent measurability (ASC, 1990). The latter condition is seen to be the most contentious and restrictive (Carey, 1990). Market criteria is seized upon to adjudicate:

> In order for this (the independent measurement of an asset's cost) to be possible when the historic cost of acquired assets is deemed to be their fair value, there will normally need to be an active market in intangible assets of the same kind independently of the purchase and sale of busi-nesses or business segments. (ASC, 1990)

It is envisaged that brands will fail to meet the test of an independent asset. However, to apply such an approach consistently should lead to the consider-ation of including other intangible assets such as human capital on the balance sheet. Indeed, on this criteria, certain 'human assets' can be seen to go a long way to satisfying the three conditions. For example, it could be argued that 'labour' is separable from other assets and there is an active labour market wherein costs can be identified and independently measured either directly (e.g. the transfer market for football players) or indirectly (e.g. through occu-pational wage rate indices). The failure to recognize the implications of their criteria for human assets leaves standard setters open to the charge of incon-sistency within their own terms. Moreover, this inconsistency is derived from an underlying set of assumptions and value judgements which not only privi-lege market criteria in the 'meaning' of an asset' but serve to elevate the 'value' of capital and denies the 'value' of labour.

Apart from revealing internal inconsistencies, post-modernist work raises fresh questions such as: why should accountants aspire to simple definitive pronouncements?; why is their work presented as objective, neutral when it is a reflection of social interaction and interests?; why does society turn to accounting for 'solutions' at certain junctures and how and why does the profession promote this?; and what is the basis of accounting knowledge?

Much of the discussion on brands has located the 'problem' as emanating from a changing environment wherein capital markets have been slow to respond to the changing nature of business and thereby have failed to recog-nize the 'true' worth of companies whose major assets are intangible. Account-ing systems and reports are viewed as compounding these market shortcomings through their own inadequacies in reflecting new business structures and assets. It is claimed that financial reports, in part through their exclusion of brands, currently fail to meet the information needs of management and other users. The controversy over brand accounting and its eventual resolution is represented as a natural step in the development of accounting in a changing environment (Tweedie and Whittington, 1990).

Such explanations are questioned by critical theorists who challenge the notion of a natural, positive progression in accounting knowledge. They seek to understand how the brands debate might reflect and constitute wider developments in society. The focus of enquiry extends beyond questions of the efficiency of capital markets to incorporate such issues and developments as: corporate and state concerns over the lack of confidence in capital markets following the stock market crash of 1987; political and economic concerns over the level and nature of investment in British industry, not least its preoccupation with the service sector and its failure to invest in productive capacity; competitive pressures from overseas economies such as Japan and Germany; concerns over the takeover activities of large unproductive conglomerates such as Hanson Trust; and the interrelations of these developments with the ongoing criticisms of the accounting regulatory process. The crucial point is that such developments and the accounting changes which accompany them are not assumed to be either progressive or natural developments in society.

The brands debate might thus be seen as emerging from a general concern over the activities and competitive position of British industry. Moreover, state policies over the last decade have promulgated and promoted market values and mechanisms for allocating capital and distributing wealth. The need to reassure investors and the public of the superiority of unfettered market forces and allay fears of the poverty of British industry may thus have contributed to the concern over accounting and market (under) valuations of companies and, relatedly, the emergence of the brands issue. Recognizing the value of brands in published accounts may also have implications for licensing such 'assets' and may create new possibilities for the conferment of property rights; developments which are consistent with the state's vision of a property-owning democracy. Thus from a CT perspective, the brands issue might be seen to be as much to do with legitimating and rationalizing state policies and market criteria, as any attempt to respond to a changing economic environment. Consequently, the accounting knowledge about brands which emerges from this context should be viewed as being created in relation to these wider economic, political and social processes.

The accounting profession and interests

Conventional explanations of professional monopolies tend to purport that a set of persons possess exceptional specialized expertise. Thus it is in societies' best interests to delegate certain powers to professional bodies comprising of such experts. The latter, it is assumed, will behave altruistically and in the public interest in return for professional privileges, powers and monopolies. Thus, in part, resides the accountant's claims for professional monopoly and self-regulation regarding accounting matters. It is a claim put under increasing scrutiny by critical researchers. It is normally argued that, in part, recognition of a profession rests upon it having a coherent bounded set of knowledge and expertises. However, as has been discussed above, the knowledge base of accounting has been increasingly questioned in this respect: its contradictions, inconsistencies, its malleability and its shifting boundaries to incorporate new areas of expertise, have led to a questioning of whether a coherent knowledge base exists over and above the needs to adjust to political and economic circumstances. Relatedly critical researchers (like their MBAR counterparts) question whether the accounting profession is, or can ever be, altruistic, independent and capable of acting in the public interest. This, and the associated question of accounting regulation has been increasingly addressed in critical accounting research.

In the first instance, they argue, it is erroneous to talk of the accounting profession as a unitary construct. The profession consists of accountants working in private sector organizations, those in practice, be it small or large firms and those working for professional or regulatory bodies. Examination of standard setting processes reveals significant differences on occasions between fractions of the profession. It is suggested that the differing responses (including indifference) of professional accountants on issues such as deferred taxation and the treatment of research and development costs are better understood in terms of their allegiances and relationships to groups who are perceived to be affected by proposed changes to accounting policy, rather than in terms of differing interpretations of technical arguments (Hope and Briggs, 1982; Hope and Gray, 1982).

Accountants have not adopted a united response to the brands issue and each sector has brought specific interests and concerns to bear on the topic (Power, 1990). Critical theorists seek to understand if and how these interests and concerns are bound up with economic relationships and issues of power and influence, not least in relation to control over accounting regulation and practice. The varying reactions of accountants and the alternative solutions they have offered to the brands controversy, can be categorized, in part, by their location and role within society. Thus differing responses have emerged from accountants in industry, accountants as regulators or representatives of professional bodies, and accountants as practitioners.

Accountants in industry have invariably advanced the case for the inclusion and valuation of brands in financial statements (e.g. Moorhouse, 1990). They have generally argued along the dual themes of the inadequacies and failures of stock market valuations and the need to reflect the economic reality of brands in shareholder funds (e.g. Bains, 1990). Such opinions can be seen to represent the views of companies such as Rank Hovis McDougall (RHM) and Cadbury Schweppes, whose activities in including brands on the balance sheet have contributed to the emergence of the debate into the public domain. Such companies, it is suggested, have most to lose (and gain) from the outcome of the debate. Thus, the reactions of accountants in industry may be influenced, not only by the persuasiveness of the technical and economic arguments taking place, but by the perceived impact of any outcome on their company's, and thereby their own, interests.

In contrast to the above, professional and regulatory bodies have, so far, argued against the wholesale inclusion of brands in the financial statements and outlined proposals which, if implemented, would require brands to be treated as part of goodwill (ASC, 1990). Their views have been represented essentially as deriving from the inseparability of brands from other assets and the subjectivity inherent in their valuation (Carey, 1990). Implicit in such views is a rejection of the proposal that the balance sheet should be read as a statement of value. While not denying the difficulties that may arise from incorrect valuations of companies by capital markets, such 'problems' have been deemed to be the responsibility of markets themselves, rather than of professional accountants. Thus, markets are assigned the responsibility of valuing companies and are imputed with the accountability for any company failures resulting from 'incorrect valuations'. Accounting regulators and professional bodies might thus be seen to attribute the responsibility for failing to account for brands to markets themselves, not least in terms of the absence of an active market in such assets.

To move towards a position where accounting might be held 'accountable' for the activities of capital markets is seen by critical theorists as exposing the profession to a renewed scrutiny as to its independent status, its altruistic motives for action and its legitimacy and effectiveness as upholder of the public interest through control of the regulation process. In this way, its power and influence may be further questioned and challenged. Thus, it is argued, the profession's role and interests in regulation must be understood as a central issue in understanding their response to the brands controversy (Hopwood, 1990).

Whereas accountants in industry and accountants as representatives of professional or regulatory bodies have responded to the brands debate, for the most part, as unified groups in opposition, accountants in public practice have adopted differing and changing stances on the issue. It is possible to identify practitioners who have argued in support of the position taken by firms such as RHM or Cadbury Schweppes (see Bains, 1990), others who have cautioned against the recognition of brands without a complete overhaul of accounting

300

statements (Rutteman, 1990) and some who have remained silent on the issue. To understand the differing positions taken by practising accountants, critical theorists argue, it is insufficient to explore their commitment to alternative technical approaches to the problem. Rather their arguments should be understood, in part, in relation to how their interests might be related to, and affected by, the alternative policy outcomes. For example, those who have argued most vehemently in support of the accounting treatments adopted by companies such as RHM and Cadbury Schweppes appear to have close involvements with such firms through the supply of services such as auditing or consultancy, or even through the provision of brand valuation services. For example, in order to gain support and legitimacy for brand accounting, Nigel Bains, the 'architect of Cadbury Schweppes brands strategy' points out that:

> Our auditors, Arthur Anderson and Coopers & Lybrand Deloitte are fully in agreement with our approach. John Andrews, a partner of Coopers, has publicly said 'we fully support Cadbury Schweppes' approach which is in accordance with our stated position'. (Bains, 1990, p. 22)

Thus, critical theorists would not view the diverse responses of accountants to the brands issue, as simply a reflection of the variety of approaches available for the resolution of accounting problems. Rather they would seek to understand them, in part, in terms of the interrelationships of accountants' interests with those of other groups in society such as industry and the state, not least in terms of the possible implications for the demand for accountants' services and the profession's role in regulation.

The economic structure of the accounting profession has changed markedly over its development, as has the range of services offered. The growing concentration of professional firms has coincided with the audit function becoming less significant as a proportion of firms' earnings. Accounting firms today represent large 'corporate-like' institutions operating in diverse areas such as taxation and management consulting as well as auditing. It has been argued that the strategic growth of accounting firms' services and proffered domain of expertise has depended upon the exploitation of their reputation for financial expertise and independence secured from their role in auditing. Yet in the new areas, such as consulting, accounting firms compete with other private sector organizations in normal market exchanges. Given the diversification strategies of large firms, their adoption of market criteria in formulating strategic growth and their engagement in markets not circumscribed by exclusive professional regulation, it is increasingly difficult to assume an altruistic, public-interest mode of professionalization dominating over profit-driven market behaviour on the part of firms, though, of course, the arguments for 'Chinese walls' in professional defence must be noted.

Professional monopoly and self-regulation is achieved by reference to professions adjudicating according to a coherent body of knowledge and an ethos of public service rather than private interest. However, when comparing the accounting profession with other older, more established, professions such as law and medicine, substantial differences emerge. First, as noted previously, as a body of knowledge, accounting has proven to be remarkably elastic, inconsistent and 'unscientific' in its creation, say when compared to medicine. While the Law may have similar problems (which are being addressed by its own band of critical theorists) it can claim, in part, that its principles are statutorily based and their role is primarily interpretation rather than creation of legal principles. With respect to grey areas, it has an established branch of jurisprudence to enlighten it. In contrast, accounting is remarkable in the degree to which it has become both judge and jury; it plays a major role in determining both the rules and regulations, and their interpretation. Second, as noted previously, professional firms have expanded remarkably into areas not normally expected to be covered by professional jurisdiction thereby becoming a curious jumble of professional and business concerns. One of the most remarkable features of the last decade has been the expansion of the accounting firms into adjudication of other areas of professional activity, not least through their espousal of the three 'Es' – Economy, Efficiency and Effectiveness – despite their lack of any obvious training or expertise in adjudicating effectiveness. Third, in contrast to law and medicine, the accounting profession is remarkably dependent upon a narrow range of clients within society, namely private corporations. This is reinforced in social relationships by the substantial proportion of qualified accountants expected to enter such corporations. The argument is, that the profession may have been unduly captured by sectional interests in society.

A major theme of critical research on accounting and power has lain in the realm of the subjective, especially how accounting despite its subjectivity, malleability, and its roots in sectional interests, is able to present itself as neutral, objective and scientific. It is argued that, under the guise of ideology dressed as science, accounting creates a vocabulary of motives and language which privileges a particular conception of events. For example, reality is defined as a cash nexus: market-based measures and criteria are defined as objective imperatives whereas counter-conceptions, by their exclusion, denial or devaluation, are rendered subsidiary (Hopper *et al.*, 1987; Lehman and Tinker, 1987)

To return to the brands debate. An aspect of the brands debate, in market terms, has been how the market value of a brand might be measured. From a CT perspective the question is not what is its correct worth but rather why such a measure is of concern. It can be argued, from economics, that branding is a consequence of market imperfections stemming from product differentiation. If the products vary only according to irrational (but created) preferences for brands then public policy should be directed at removing such market imperfections. One possible consequence of valuing such market imperfections is that accountants may not only legitimize a market imperfection but also confer property rights to it by providing the abstract concept with a formal status and an asset value. Thus a socially undesirable artefact, created by advertising and market dominance, becomes legitimized as a business asset.

Professional management

The above has sought to establish how the accounting profession is an amalgam of interests interdependent with the state and corporate clients especially, whose own interests may be disparate. Nevertheless, in totality, the interests represented are drawn from a relatively narrow, if powerful sector of society. A feature of accounting knowledge is its subjectivity, malleability and inconsistency, yet the power of the profession in part, derives from its ability to present itself and its knowledge as objective and independent.

From a CT perspective, the apparent professional panic over the brands issue can be seen to be as much a response to the threats and challenges it poses for professional closure and the meaning of accounting, as any attempt to improve financial reporting. In particular, the intervention in the accounting information market by 'outsiders' such as Interbrand potentially threatens the accounting profession's monopoly in, and claims to, expertise in financial reporting matters. These 'non-accountants', through their activities in placing values on brand names have implicitly and explicitly brought into question the profession's expertise and its legitimacy to monopolize financial measurement. For example, the managing director of Interbrand, writing in *Accountancy* in October 1989, claimed:

> Brands are as identifiable and readily transferable as companies' plant and machinery or freehold buildings. . . . It is the inability hitherto to come up with a viable method of valuing a brand (together, we submit, with a fundamental misunderstanding of the marketing, financial and legal characteristics of a brand) that has led accountants to conclude that intangibles must somehow be part of purchased goodwill.
>
> (Stobart, 1989, p. 27)

In making their case, Interbrand have employed similar language and rhetoric to that identified with the claims of accountants. Rationalizing the subjectivity of their valuation methods in terms of expertise, they claim that brand values will 'provide shareholders with *hard* information about some of a company's most important assets' (ibid, p. 27, our emphasis). Such claims can be seen to constitute a challenge to accountants on two levels. First, they question the scope of accounting expertise and its ability to respond to a changing environment. Second, they challenge the judgment of accountants in defining and controlling the financial reporting measurement system, both present and future. This system is represented as objective, rational and 'hard' by both groups but its underlying subjectivity and malleability is both a source of power and a threat to the success of the group who control it. Thus attempts to gain access to even parts of it by 'outsiders' may result in accountants' losing control over other parts, for example by further challenges from competing bodies of 'experts'.

There are a number of responses available to a professional group whose expertise is challenged or questioned by 'outsiders', including the following strategies. First, it can attempt to deny the legitimacy of those advancing the new expertise and thereby attempt to discredit and exclude their 'knowledge' claims. Second, a profession may attempt to usurp elements of this new expertise and claim it for its own, as part of its own body of knowledge. Lastly, it can differentiate its own sphere of expertise from that being claimed by its challengers, thereby acknowledging the legitimacy of the latter while denying any implications for its own body of expertise. The initial response of the accounting profession exhibits evidence of all three strategies taking place. Thus, while some firms of accountants have begun to get involved in developing and offering their own brand valuation services to clients as a means of claiming the expertise as their own, the professional and regulatory bodies have sought to challenge and cast doubt upon the legitimacy and credibility of such claimed expertise in financial reporting matters. Others have accepted the expertise involved in brand valuations but have likened it to that of any other specialist valuer, such as property valuers (Sherwood, 1990). These divergent responses of accountants are seen by critical theorists as in conflict with the notion of a unitary profession with a unique, defined body of knowledge. They must be reconciled in order to preserve the professional image of accountants which lays at the heart of its ability to monopolize crucial elements of information provision in society.

From a CT perspective, the outcome of the struggle to establish the scope and nature of accounting expertise in relation to brands is unlikely to be resolved on technical grounds alone. Rather, it will depend on the wider pressures and concerns which infuse the debate and the power relations of those involved. Given the growing involvement of accountants in the measurement process of brands and the threat of non-compliance by some large companies, it may seem that the credibility of accountants as regulators may best be retrieved or enhanced by assimilating the new 'expertise' within the profession itself, either as valuers or as auditors of expert valuations. Indeed, already the signs are that the professional and regulatory bodies may be losing the battle to exclude brand valuations from the balance sheet. Influential bodies of opinion such as the state and the financial press have at best, declined to intervene and at worst they have signalled the unacceptability of existing accounting practices which fail to accommodate the changing nature of businesses. However, those accountants claiming the new 'expertise' for their own have been supported by their powerful clients. The balance of power would seem to be in favour of the brands lobby. It is in this light, critical theorists would argue, that the new regulatory body, the Accounting Standards Board (ASB) has decided to 'shelve' the unpopular proposals advanced by its predecessor and has signalled its intent to rethink the issue of brand accounting.

The increasing demands made upon accountants to 'account for themselves', emanating in part from their increasing involvement in commercial business beyond their traditional role of auditing means that they must explain and rationalize their policies and prescriptions to a greater extent than ever before (Hopwood, 1990). This may serve to further expose the ambiguities, conflicts and contradictions inherent in their knowledge bases. To adopt a strategy which is widely acceptable and thereby unlikely to be challenged, may seem to minimize the growing pressures on the accounting profession to rationalize the bases on which it claims its professional powers and privileges and the underlying knowledge structures of its practices. The recognition of these factors and pressures is advanced by critical theorists as a means by which the issue of accounting for brands and the (changing) response of the profession to it, might be better understood.

Managing the threats and challenges which the issue of brands poses to the profession's expertise while maintaining good relations with corporate clients, satisfying state preferences, and accommodating external commentators' varied concerns, requires skilled negotiation. In order to maintain the confidence and trust of the general public, this negotiation must be portrayed in terms of rational, disinterested arguments, employed by objective, independent professionals. It is the ability of the profession to manage such contradictions which is its strength and not a weakness.

MBAR, CRITICAL THEORY AND ACCOUNTING REGULATION POLICY

MBAR argues that the justifications for regulation include (a) the speeding up of market processes and thereby reducing the costs of reaching market equilibrium and (b) the maintenance of the market itself by reducing information asymmetry, that is, by protecting those investors who otherwise would be relatively uninformed. While CT is appreciative of the need for equal protection to all parties, it would question whether stable economic equilibria are often achieved and, if so, whether this would equate with an acceptable social equilibrium. CT would argue that market studies often ignore important externalities and ecological effects. Further complex modelling is not in itself considered to be adequate since it can obscure or misrepresent relationships which cannot be satisfactorily measured in economic terms. Also MBAR analysis tends to work within the economic status quo by taking current distributions of power and wealth as given. In contrast, CT argues that recognition of inequalities of power and economic resources of the various parties within economic processes must be integral to any analysis. However, the seemingly narrow focus of MBAR has allowed it to make clear policy guidelines, whereas the wider framework of CT has meant that such guidelines have been very thin on the ground.

CT argues that the relevant parties to financial disclosure are too narrowly defined by MBAR as mainly investors and creditors and that they need extending to employees, communities and consumer groups for example. It rejects arguments based on the assumption that other users' interests can be subsumed within a capital market focus and argues for explicit recognition, and thereby legitimacy, of these other users' rights to information. Lastly, they would argue that MBAR is not merely reflective of an economic and social reality but it also helps create the reality. For example, MBAR research by emphasizing the relationship between share prices and financial information and ignoring alternative roles of accounting helps shape a popular conception of the primacy of the functioning of financial markets in policy matters and accounting's obligation to investors rather than other stakeholders. Although MBAR researchers are typically aware of the narrow focus of their analysis, this aspect of the approach tends to take a back seat to the claim to being scientific, neutral and objective. Thus the differences between the two schools are substantial. Nevertheless, the remainder of the article seeks to argue that the policy conclusions of both schools have similarities and, to a degree, they may be complementary.

Some, though not all, MBAR tends to be sceptical of the economic worth of accounting regulation and statutory requirements for audit. It argues that investors' demand for information will be heterogeneous. Consequently, although accounting standards may be a suitable mechanism for achieving economies of scale in information transmission, standards alone are unlikely to provide information which is appropriate for all decision situations. Therefore, the emphasis is on market agents having additional access to more specialized, and sometimes raw disaggregated, data and letting market forces calculate their economic significance. Similarly, it argues that if an audit is effective for stockholders, then economic pressures will force firms to employ one, thus rendering a statutory obligation redundant. Consequently, the emphasis of MBAR is upon full disclosure, leaving the interpretations to market processes. Accounting transformations of underlying transactions may be unnecessary, and auditing for stewardship is likely to be enforced by market pressures if it is effective and desirable. Moreover, the introduction of detailed accounting regulation may have dysfunctional effects whereby market equilibria are delayed or transformed and allocations are distorted (Watts and Zimmerman, 1990).

As has been noted earlier, CT is equally sceptical of accounting standards and services but for different, though related, reasons. Like MBAR, it notes the philosophical impossibility of constructing single conceptual framework whereby objective neutral standards can be derived, given a society of conflicting interests and values. This arises not because different investors may have different demands for information (as in the MBAR argument), but because of the inherent conflict between different classes of user. A single conceptual framework would merely privilege a particular set of interests, values and beliefs. Qualitative research of practice has shown that accounting standards and data are shaped socially in processes of negotiation. This is not regarded as a weakness by critical theorists, rendered, say, in a belief that si h issues can be abstracted from a political arena to one of detached scholarsl ip. Rather it is seen as recognition of the inevitability of accounting questions being rooted in political processes.

Access to information and the ability to refine it in a manner consistent with constituencies 'values and beliefs is taken as integral to political processes. The involvement and control of the user over what information is derived and how it is refined is of central import. This does not preclude the use of established accounting methods or professional accountants, but the central issue is that the choice should be the users', rather than being confined to professional expertise or monopoly. It could be argued that under current arrangements in financial reporting, some users (notably corporations and the state) already enjoy the benefits of being able to influence what constitutes financial information while others are denied the choice and even the knowledge that such choice exists. The contention is that users should choose between alternatives based on an appreciation of the subjective nature of all accounting information; accounting information needs to be demystified.

Thus both research schools share a commitment to open access to financial information of an untransformed nature. However, the criteria for such advocacy is very different between the two schools. For MBAR the argument is that to do so may be more efficient in economic cost-benefit terms. CT might not wish to deny some of the possible benefits of market exchanges; however, the criteria would not be market equilibrium, but rather social consensus in a genuinely pluralistic society. For CT, the primary issue is pluralistic democracy and negotiated consensus even, if necessary, at the expense of economic efficiency. Thus CT would argue for a wider range of individuals and groups, including consumer groups, employees and community organizations, to be given access to corporate information according to their needs, and CT would encourage the identification of these needs free from preconceived notions of accounting objectivity.

Furthermore, for conditions and structures that provide for a more equitable debate, less privileged groups require not only information, but also access to expertise to transform it in a manner consistent with their own aims, values and beliefs. This requires additional resources and development of expertises not copiously available to them at present. The impact of recent critical theory is an admission of the impossibility of the modernist belief in 'ideal' solutions administered by experts. However it does not espouse relativism or intellectual anarchy, rather it points to the importance of core values in political processes, the need to tolerate and encourage diversity and the need to examine facts according to each parties values and beliefs, and equitable, free and unconstrained debate within negotiation. Thus the emphasis is upon opening up and facilitating pluralistic processes rather than closing them by single solutions proffered by experts. The argument of CT is that one must take a value position regarding democratic interchanges which entails positive discrimination with respect to providing information, expertise and access to political processes to groups currently inadequately resourced. While this might not be inconsistent with liberal economics, it tends not to be addressed by the latter work, thus opening them up to the allegation that they are defenders of the status quo by default. However, both CT and MBAR lay a heavy emphasis on decentralized and individualized processes in contrast to centrally imposed solutions, be they from the state or the profession.

As is indicated, both MBAR and CT share a scepticism towards professional monopoly and jurisdiction and similarly regarding the state as adjudicator. MBAR research tends to portray the accounting professional, accounting firms and the profession itself as self-interested economic wealth maximizers. CT makes similar observations with respect to professional closure, interprofessional rivalries, the expression of accounting services etc. However, neither school argues for abolition of accounting firms, rather they draw attention to the need for changes in accountability of the accounting profession itself. MBAR would tend to favour the abolition of statutory monopolies and leave it to market forces to decide; critical theory would argue for accounting services to be more widely defined and accessible (and resourced) to other sectors of society. Current necessary expertise is not confined to the accounting profession, nor need it be. The issue is to permit a wide range of clients to choose from accounting firms or other providers if they so wish. Accounting knowledge and services, in the first instance require demystification, and should ultimately be determined by the clientele exercising choice.

For MBAR, the role of the state is essentially the maintenance of competitive market structures. For CT it is the maintenance of pluralistic processes with an explicit recognition of the advantages of resourcing disadvantaged groups, since efficiency considerations are secondary to notions of pluralistic democracy. Ultimately, the ideal is that everyone should be their own accountant.

MBAR, CRITICAL THEORY AND THE BRANDS DEBATE

Such generalizations are fine, but what do they mean in practice? One of the objectives of this paper is to translate such broad generalizations into policy recommendations with respect to brands, so that the contribution of MBAR and (particularly) CT can be more easily understood.

The MBAR policy recommendations are relatively straightforward, and are the product of the discussion in the third section. Although unlikely, it is possible that brand disclosure may have some beneficial effects, by impounding information which is not available to investors via analysts. The increased disclosure of such information would ensure that prices reflect a wider information set, and would reduce the benefits from insider trading.

However, there are two reservations concerning the implementation of this through disclosure of brand *values* on the balance sheet. First, the valuation instrument might be used for other purposes, namely to evade the covenants imposed by debt contracts. However, such evasion will only be a significant matter for the debt market if the action is unanticipated by lenders when they set the level of the constraints in the covenant. The second and more serious concern is that valuation of part of the company's earnings stream would have been passed from a market process to a group of market agents. The problem would *not* be that some market agents would be offering investors valuation advice, but that the opinions of a particular group may have undue influence by being associated with audited information. Consequently, MBAR would suggest that brand information from management, although unlikely to add significantly to the information set already available to investors, should be in the form of segmental reports.

The CT view on brands is, in fact, only slightly more complex. Branding is seen as a mechanism whereby companies legitimize their considerable activity (and expenditure) in the consumer market place, by way of advertising and other promotional devices. Managers want or need to legitimize their actions to society in general and to shareholders in particular. Branding is a mechanism by which this can take place. The corporate management, spending millions of pounds on advertising, want to do more than take it to the P&L account, written off as of no future value. However, the reporting of brand *values* rather than expenditures, is not, and is not intended to be, neutral; market value is also seen as a measure of societal worth.

There are two consequences of this. First, the legitimators of corporate activity (traditionally accountants) find themselves in competition with outsiders. While the accounting profession has subcontracted some of its activity to specialist groups, such as the valuation of land and buildings, it has been able to do so without compromising its integrity. This has been possible because the subcontracting is seen as being related to a peripheral activity, the valuation of productive assets which have alternative uses. However, brands are different. The brands issue strikes at the very heart of the role of accountancy; this is probably because it is so closely related to major components of business activity, namely marketing and the earnings stream.

The second consequence is that advertising and promotional activity is now legitimized. In effect, corporate management, by their close ties with the financial community have been able to have their activity socially validated. But other groups need to be a part of such a process. Groups with other interests should be able to assess corporate activity with respect to the dimensions which *they* think are important. For example, in the context of branding in the tobacco industry, some groups may wish to know what proportion of tobacco advertising is aimed at third world countries, upon what age group the advertising is effective and whether advertising enlarges the market as a whole (or simply redivides the existing cake).

There are many ways to look at advertising; corporate managers should not have the monopoly. The long term aim of CT researchers is for all groups to be able to obtain the information they wish, depending on their particular concern for societal welfare. The medium term objective of CT is to demystify the current reporting environment so that no one group has the monopoly of the dimension along which events are reported. In terms of brands, this medium-term objective is for the public to understand that attaching a value to a corporation's advertising expenditure and quality controls is only one facet of the activity. This might be achieved in part, if advertising expenditures were disclosed segmentally rather than placing subjective values on such activities and representing them as objective assets, namely brands.

SUMMARY

Clearly, in pursuing the objectives of this paper, much (if not all) of the richness of both CT and MBAR models has been lost. For example, views of MBAR proponents range from (a) the provision of all disaggregated accounting data (leaving the market to assess the economic implications) to (b) the strict enforcement of detailed regulation to avoid the substantial consequences of market failure and adverse selection. Similarly, many critical theorists would argue that it is naïve to examine accounting regulation and reform without deeper consideration of other more fundamental economic and political arrangements.

In addition, it may be that the values and assumptions of CT and MBAR are so fundamentally different that areas of convergence are not much more than chance and meaningless when taken individually out of context of their own theoretical position.

While these reservations are obvious and well understood, we have sought to argue here that there are also advantages to standing back and identifying the themes which run through each school of thought. In this way, the relative strengths and weaknesses of CT and MBAR can be used, and even perhaps combined, to provide advice to policy makers. A by-product of this analysis has been the surprising commonality in outlook which CT and MBAR seem to share. These commonalities include the following:

1. Both schools question the theoretical basis and consistency of accounting standards. For only slightly different reasons both CT and MBAR argue that a single conceptual framework is both impossible and undesirable.
2. Both schools argue that protection is best provided by ensuring access to detailed, even raw, information. MBAR would argue that sufficient protection for the naïve investor is given if the major players in the market are well-informed, and if this gives rise to a competitive equilibrium. CT would argue that disadvantaged groups need to be empowered through not only provision of alternative forms of information, but also resources and positions within decision-making structures to act upon such information.
3. Both schools emphasize facilitating processes, rather than solutions by professions or regulatory bodies. MBAR stresses market processes whereas CT emphasizes political processes.
4. Both schools seriously question the notion of a profession (accounting, finance or otherwise) as an independent altruistic body. MBAR emphasizes the economic self-interest and profit driven behaviour of such organizations. CT points out the interdependence of accounting firms with corporate interests and the state and their neglect of other interest groups within society.
5. Both schools are sceptical of state regulation as the all providing mechanism for information dissemination; MBAR on the grounds of efficiency, CT on the grounds of representativeness. Both emphasize the need for a decentralized approach to accounting information, with users ultimately determining the choice of methods and the provision of relevant expertise.
6. Both schools are essentially libertarian and emphasize decentralized pluralism. In the case of MBAR the role of the state is to maintain competitive structures and the free flow of information. Critical theory would argue that additionally the state needs to make value judgements about existing mal-

distribution of powers and to provide resources and representation for groups deemed as disadvantaged.

7. MBAR argues that market transactions which reflect individual preferences and beliefs are fundamental to attainment of social equilibrium. Critical theory appeals to wider concerns and would argue that the use of language in the definition and analysis of accounting issues is central and that, consequently, negotiating processes need to reflect different parties' views about what is conceived as reality.

REFERENCES

Arrington, C.E. and Francis J.R. (1989) Letting the chat out of the bag: Deconstruction, privilege and accounting research, *Accounting Organizations and Society*, 1–28.

Arrington, C.E. and Puxty A.G. (1991) Accounting, interests and rationality: a communicative relation, *Critical Perspectives on Accounting*, 21–58.

ASC (1990) *Exposure Draft 52, Accounting for Intangible Fixed Assets*, Accounting Standards Committee.

Bains, N. (1990) Brands debate: Cadburys makes its views clear, *Accountancy Age*, 15 March, 22.

Barwise, P., Higson, C., Likierman, A., Marsh, P. (1989) *Accounting for Brands*, London Business School/ICAEW.

Birkin, M. (1990) A methodology for valuing brands, in *Brand and Goodwill Accounting Strategies* (ed. M. Power), Woodhead-Faulkner, Cambridge, pp. 108–14.

Caldwell, B.J. (1991) Clarifying Popper, *Journal of Accounting Literature*, 1–33.

Carey, A. (1990) Coming to grips with intangibles, *Accountancy Age*, 6 September, 19.

Cooper, D.J. and Sherer, M.J. (1984) The value of accounting reports: arguments for a political economy of accounting, *Accounting, Organizations and Society*, 202–32.

Egginton, D.A. (1990) Towards some principles for intangible asset accounting, *Accounting and Business Research*, 193–205.

Hines, R.D. (1988) Financial accounting: in communicating reality, we construct reality, *Accounting Organizations and Society*, 251–61.

Hines, R.D. (1989) Financial accounting knowledge, conceptual framework projects and the social construction of the accounting profession, *Accounting, Auditing and Accountability*, 72–92.

Hope, A. and Briggs, J. (1982) Accounting policy-making – some lessons from the deferred taxation debate, *Accounting and Business Research*, 83–96

Hope, A.J. and Gray, R.H. (1982) Power and policy-making – the development of an R&D standard, *Journal of Business Finance and Accounting*, 531–58

Hopper, T.M., Storey, J. and Willmott, H. (1987) Accounting for accounting: towards the developments of a dialectical view, *Accounting, Organizations and Society*, 437–56.

Hopwood, A.G. (1990) Ambiguity, knowledge and territorial claims: some observations on the doctrine of substance over form: a review essay, *British Accounting Review*, 79–88.

Hoskin, K.W. and Macve, R.H. (1986) Accounting and the examination: a genealogy of disciplinary power, *Accounting, Organizations and Society*, 105–36.

Laughlin, R. (1987) Accounting systems in organisational contexts, *Accounting Organisations and Society*, 479–502.

Lehman, C. and Tinker, T. (1987) The 'real' cultural significance of accounts, *Accounting, Organizations and Society*, 503–22.

Lev, B. (1988) Toward a theory of equitable and efficient accounting policy, *Accounting Review*, January, 1–22.

Loft, A. (1986) Toward a critical understanding of accounting: the case of cost accounting in the UK, 1914–1925, *Accounting, Organizations and Society*, 137–69.

Lukka, K. (1990) Ontology and accounting: the concept of profit, *Critical Perspectives on Accounting*, 239–62.

Miller, P. and O'Leary, T. (1987) Accounting and the construction of the governable person, *Accounting, Organizations and Society*, 235–65.

Moorhouse, M. (1990) Brands debate: wake up to the real world, *Accountancy*, July, 30.

Peasnell, K.V. (1977) A note on the discounted present value concept, *Accounting Review*, January 186–9.

Power, M. (ed.) (1990) *Brand and Goodwill Accounting Strategies*, Woodhead-Faulkner, Cambridge.

Rutteman, P. (1990) Boosting the profits of the brands industry, *Accountancy*, January, 26–7.

Sherwood, K. (1990) An auditor's approach to brands, in *Brand and Goodwill Accounting Strategies* (ed. M. Power), Cambridge, Woodhead-Faulkner, 78–86.

Solomons, D. (1989) *Guidelines for Financial Reporting Standards*, Institute of Chartered Accountants in England and Wales.

Stobart, P (1989) Brand valuation: a true and fair view, *Accountancy*, October, 27–8

Tinker, A.M., Merino, B.D. and Neimark, M.D. (1982) The normative origins of positive theories: ideology and accounting thought, *Accounting, Organizations and Society*, 167–200.

Tweedie, D. and Whittington, G. (1990) Financial reporting: current problems and their implications for systematic reform, *Accounting and Business Research*, 87–102

Watts, R.L. and Zimmerman J.L. (1990) Positive accounting theory: a ten year perspective, *Accounting Review*, January, 131–56.

Disconnected, overlapping or negotiable circles? A comment on accounting and the uncongenial twins: Discussant's comments

RICHARD C. LAUGHLIN

INTRODUCTION

The desire to highlight the commonalities in knowledge generated from disparate philosophical schools of thought is always to be commended. To extend this analysis to include, and even give greater emphasis to, common prescriptive policy outcomes is worthy of greater adulation. The paper by Trevor Hopper, Linda Kirkham and Len Skerratt (Chapter 12, pp. 287–313) attempts such an ambitious agenda and, clearly, they are to be commended for attempting what many would maintain is an unfruitful, even impossible, task. I am sure that Ken Hilton would have respected such an ambitious endeavour. He would also have found the focus for tracing these commonalities – the regulation of accounting standards with a particular emphasis on brands – worthy in terms of interest and significance. However, he, like this reviewer, would no doubt be aware of the tremendous challenge of such an endeavour and would approach the resulting analysis with an open mind but also mindful of how others, over many centuries, have faltered and failed on similar agendas.

Perhaps it is with these failures or, more positively, with the philosophical, historical and epistemological roots of market-based accounting research (MBAR) and critical theory (CT) that this comment should start. This will provide an important context as well as some of the difficulties that the authors face in realizing their goals. MBAR is traceable to a form of positivism coming from the philosophy of its so called 'father': Auguste Comte. CT, as used by the authors, on the other hand, finds its roots in an amalgam of the thinking of Immanuel Kant, Georg Hegel, Karl Marx and aspects of the philosophy of Jürgen Habermas. Both Comte and Kant have generated a range of alternative schools of thought yet what is clear is that the commonalities in the Comtean line are very great indeed whereas those derived from Kantian thought are notable by their diversity. It is for this reason that the authors rightly make little play of the diversity in MBAR whereas they highlight the immense differences in what they initially loosely describe as 'critical theory' before settling on a particular interpretation of Habermasian critical theory as their primary perspective.

While the differences between Kantian derivatives are immense the difference between Kantian and Comtean thinking is even greater. Both, interestingly enough, were trying to amalgamate what was a disagreement of some substance between the European 'rationalists' (e.g. Descartes, Spinoza, Leibniz) and the English 'empiricists' (e.g. Locke, Berkeley, Hulme). The rationalists believed that through rational processes, unpolluted by experience or empirical insights, absolute truths about the world could be discovered. The empiricists, on the other hand, maintained that it was only through experiential involvement with the world that truths about its reality could be discovered. Kant amalgamated these traditions but in the process gave a highly subjective twist to understanding by highlighting the importance and diversity of the observer in the process of discovery. Comte, on the other hand, amalgamated these traditions but in a way which preserved the essence of both and continued the belief in the possibility of discovering absolute truth, unpolluted by any bias of the observer, through defined logical reasoning *and* controlled experiential behaviour.

This contextualization of MBAR and CT highlights two important points in relation to the authors' agenda. First, that diversity and disagreement and an indifference to the need for seeking commonalities have been the nature of the process of discovery. Second, that the differences between MBAR and CT are immense due to their historical roots (Comtean and Kantian respectively). Given this situation it has to be said that lesser and greater scholars than Hopper *et al.* have purposefully abandoned any attempt at seeking commonalities both in levels of understanding and any resulting policy prescriptions.

This is not to say that some have attempted to explore the potential commonalities in this divided picture in the hope of bringing greater coherence into epistemological thought. Max Weber certainly attempted this reconciliation. The 'pragmatists' (as they have been called), particularly Herbert Mead and Charles Pierce, can be seen as trying to achieve this reconciliation process. More recently Anthony Giddens' theory of structuration purposefully sets out to combine the great divide in epistemology. However, all these notable scholars have not simply traced commonalities in processes of understanding they have actually created new systems of knowing which, in effect, require some abandoning of previously held beliefs. None have addressed what Hopper *et al.* are trying to do, which is *not* to build new epistemological processes, *not* even to give great emphasis to common knowledge but to go a stage further to trace common policy prescriptions.

Given this context we are dealing with a brave and adventurous agenda of concern upon which few, if any, have attempted before. It is important, therefore, to explore the standing of the authors' conclusions and see whether they have achieved where others have clearly failed. The following, therefore, looks critically at the heart of the paper's contribution – the policy prescriptions contained in the sixth and seventh sections – to discover whether the claimed commonalities actually stand up to investigation. The conclusion is not very encouraging and, as a result, the final section explores some possible pathways the authors, along with others, might like to follow.

COMMON POLICY PRESCRIPTIONS: FACT OR FALLACY?

Perhaps we could start this critical review of the policy prescriptions by looking at the seven points of convergence presented at the end of the paper (in the seventh section). This discussion will end with some brief comments on the contents of the sixth section with regard to the brands debate in the light of this critique.

The first summary point of convergence suggests that both MBAR and CT question the theoretical basis and consistency of accounting standards and maintain that a single conceptual framework is philosophically impossible and politically undesirable. There is some truth to this from the perspective of both MBAR and CT yet there are marked differences which raises serious questions as to the degree, if any, of convergence. While MBAR may well question the value freedom of the standard setting process they (assuming MBAR can be personalized as a set of believers in this philosophy) would be quite happy to live within this biased world where it suited their purpose. Put simply if investment analysts needed certain types of information and could not get the information any other way than through the standard setting machinery they would happily agree to the activities of the standard setting body despite its apparent theoretical lacunae. On the other hand CT would never be happy with this pragmatic solution. Their belief in the ideal speech situation would always hold out the hope of achieving a set of standards and a conceptual framework which comes out of a justified and grounded concensus between all parties although recognizing the value laden nature of this solution. In sum, based on this amplification, any commonality on this first summary point is difficult to see.

The second summary point of convergence suggests that both MBAR and CT 'argue that regulatory protection is best provided by providing greater access to raw more detailed information'. Again on the surface this seems valid but closer investigation and amplification reduces the reality of this convergence. MBAR would not necessarily always support this view. In some cases it is clearly better to have disaggregated information to allow the analysts to produce the information they require. In other cases either such information is redundant, and, therefore, irrelevant, or, alternatively, being deemed to be 'efficiency experts', they would be happy to live with the aggregation of accountants if their information provision could be proved to be reliable. CT, on the other hand, does not always maintain that more information in a raw form is necessarily to be welcomed. All information, raw or not, is a particular 'reality creator' (see Hines, 1989; Morgan, 1988). It constructs one aspects of reality and downplays another. The dangers of this creative act are great and are well recognized in CT suggesting that more information is not necessarily always to be welcomed – a point recently highlighted with regard to the 'green' accounting debate (see Gray and Laughlin, 1991, and the articles by Power, Hines and Maunders and Buritt in this special issue). In sum neither MBAR and CT can be seem to share this claimed commonality.

The third summary point of convergence suggests that 'both schools emphasize facilitative processes rather than solutions by professions or regulatory bodies'. Again while there may be some surface validity in this, closer investigation suggests enough hesitations on this claimed common view to make it questionable at best. MBAR may well be happy to live with solutions from regulatory bodies where it allows the information needs of analysts to be realized and consequent efficient market behaviour to ensure. CT, on the other hand, would also, in different circumstances, be happy to work within a regulatory framework if it facilitated an ideal speech situation between all participants.

The fourth summary point of convergence suggests that 'both schools question the notion of the profession as independent altruistic bodies'. This fourth commonality is closely connected with the first and the points raised there are relevant here. Indeed MBAR and CT both share this view but the former is happy to live with this situation and encourage its continuance in certain circumstances where it suits the analysts' purposes. CT would always want to do something about this situation and would not accept such a pragmatic

318

compromise. However, apart from seriously doubting the common nature of this insight there is the added problem with wondering what this conclusion has to do with policy prescriptions. A policy prescription based on this insight should tell us what we should do about the value bias and it is here where the commonalities between MBAR and CT are conspicuous by their absence.

The fifth area of claimed convergence suggests that 'both schools are sceptical of state regulation'. Again this is not a policy prescription and apart from that is a questionable commonality anyway. It is possible to envisage the situation where MBAR would encourage the use of state regulation (presumably through law) with regard to the provision of certain information where first, the information cannot be supplied through alternative means and second, where the self-regulatory profession cannot ensure information provision. CT, on the other hand, may look to particular forms of law to provide legal backing for conducting an ideal speech situation where no other means are available to ensure this happening. This would undoubtedly not be any 'normal' law but would be nearer to the concept of what radical lawyers call 'reflexive law' (see Teubner, 1983; Laughlin and Broadbent, 1991). In sum while they may be sceptical concerning state regulation neither are averse to it in particular circumstances. However, these differing circumstances are such that they obliterate any commonality in terms of policy suggestions.

The sixth area of claimed convergence suggests that 'both schools are essentially liberatrian and emphasize decentralized pluralism'. While again there is some intuitive commonality in this conclusion closer investigation suggests how spurious this commonality really is. MBAR is very biased in its libertarianism and decentralization. It privileges the role of the investment analyst as an expert supposedly working in the interests of all. CT, on the other hand, is sceptical, at best, about the role of experts and more generally about the privileges of expertise. CT is concerned with liberty for all and active participation by all in the discovery of alternative futures. It is difficult to see how these are in any way commonalities.

Finally, the seventh area of potential convergence does not seem to exist even in the authors' view. What this seventh point does is highlight the *diversity* of MBAR and CT rather than their convergence.

In sum this critical review seems to suggest that the commonality in policy prescriptions as suggested by the authors is very tenuous. This is also reinforced when looking at the specific policy suggestions concerning the brands debate. In sum, according to the authors, under MBAR the need for reporting information on brands may be important where the information cannot be discovered through other means. On the other hand the authors see CT suggesting that all relevant events around the branding issue should be reported to *all* users in *all* circumstances. Again one might question this conclusion in terms of dangers of reality construction through information (see above).

However, what is more important is that this detailed analysis of the brands debate highlights major policy differences rather than commonalities.

In sum, based on this analysis, the prescriptive policy commonalities are weak at best and non-existent at worst. The suspicion aired in the first section sadly seems to be the case. If this is true what can be done to salvage something from what is still an important agenda of concern? It is to this the following section addresses.

COPING WITH DISCONNECTED CIRCLES – A WAY FORWARD?

The sad but not altogether unanticipated conclusion from the above analysis is that MBAR and CT live in disconnected circles. The overlap is marginal at best and when probed is largely non-existent. Given the fundamentally antagonistic and very different historical roots of these diverse approaches this, sadly, is inevitable.

The difficulty is that despite the rhetoric the authors are not really wanting reconciliation between these diverse schools of thought. If there is some commonality then that is fine but neither the proponents of MBAR nor those of CT in the authorship are willing to shift ground in terms of their values and beliefs. But if the above analysis is correct and they have discovered a largely empty set where do they go from there? Either they could abandon any chance of reconciliation and encourage the continued generation of multiple diverse theories concerning standard setting. Alternatively they could pursue their desire for commonality although this time recognizing the need for possibly abandoning cherished epistemological beliefs.

It is the latter approach which has been dominant in all reconciliation attempts which have occurred over the years.

Thus, as indicated, in the introduction, the philosophies of people like Weber, Mead, Pierce and Giddens have all taken what is perceived to be best from diverse schools of thought and designed a new epistemological approach. How successful these scholars have been is uncertain. However, the very fact that there is still a proliferation of alternative approaches suggests that the resulting model(s) for understanding has (have) failed to be that convincing.

Perhaps, however, there is an alternative way forward not only for accounting but for other social science disciplines. This would involve a two-stage process. The first would involve not closing down alternative epistemological approaches in some abstract way but rather actively encouraging 'many flowers to bloom' through operationalizing these differing approaches with multiple empirical foci. This, in many ways, is not dissimilar to current research practice in accounting and other social science areas. The second stage, which is rather different, is to design some process whereby the resulting insights and the consequent epistemological approaches can be evaluated. It would be surprising if this could be conducted without some form of discourse analysis which suggests the likely relevance of something similar to Habermas' ideal speech situation to provide the vehicle for this endeavour. It may be that we will never get to the second stage but it is important to keep a hope alive that there is some consensus out there yet to be discovered. Maybe this is the real commonality, which certainly does not exist to date, which the authors of this paper should be encouraging to emerge.

REFERENCES

Gray, R. and Laughlin, R., (1991) Editorial: the coming of the green and the challenge of environmentalism, *Accounting, Auditing and Accountability Journal* **4** (3), 5–8.

Hines, R. (1988) Financial Accounting: in communicating reality, we construct reality, *Accounting, Organizations and Society* **13** (3), 251–62

Laughlin, R. and Broadbent, J (1991) Accounting and juridification: an exploration with specific reference to the public sector in the United Kingdom, *Proceedings from the Third Interdisciplinary Perspectives on Accounting Conference*, University of Manchester, pp. 1.01.1–1.10.16.

Morgan, G. (1988) Accounting as reality constructor: towards a new epistemology for accounting practice, *Accounting, Organizations and Society* **13** (5), 477 – 85.

Teubner, G. (1983) Substantive and reflexive elements in modern law, *Law and Society Review* **17** (2), 239–85 .

Author index

All entries in **bold** type represent tables, those in *italics* are figures.

Subject index

All entries in **bold** type represent tables, those in *italics* are figures.